How to Self-Publish Your Book
&
Have the Fun & Excitement
of
Being a Best-Selling Author

An expert's step-by-step guide to marketing your book successfully

by
Melvin Powers

Melvin Powers
Wilshire Book Company

12015 Sherman Road, No. Hollywood, CA 91605

Printed in the United States of America
Library of Congress Catalog Card Number: 83-51140
ISBN 0-87980-406-8

Dedication

To my daughter, Joy Melody

To my son, Daniel

Table of Contents

Chapter One

Who is Melvin Powers? How is He Uniquely Qualified to Write This Book?
How Can He Guide You to Fame and Fortune?

To enable you to assess the qualifications I bring to this book, let me tell you something about my professional background. With this knowledge, I think you will develop an understanding as to why I confidently believe that I can guide you to a new, exciting, highly effective and affordable way to have your material published and help you to achieve the goals you have set for yourself.

I have spent a lifetime working with books. From that work and my allegiance to readers and potential writers by the thousands, there has evolved from a dream, a realization—the Wilshire Book Company, one of the nation's prestigious publishers of self-improvement literature.

As a self-publisher, I have personally brought nine books to completion—one, *Dynamic Thinking*, has sold upwards of a million copies. In addition, I have published hundreds of books by other authors, as evidenced by the current list of my company's books on pages 236 to 240.

As a ghost-writer or in collaboration with other writers, I have participated in the authorship of numerous best sellers, and just to exercise my creative abilities and give release to a long-submerged aspiration, I turned briefly to song-writing. To my gratification, the effort turned out to be a rewarding one, and, in addition to my business interests, I became a successful songwriter and record producer.

Many of the books I have published and promoted have sold in the millions. Among them are such well-known works as *Psycho-Cybernetics* by Maxwell Maltz, M.D.,

The Magic of Thinking Big by David J. Schwartz, Ph.D., *Think and Grow Rich* by Napoleon Hill and *New Guide to Rational Living* by Albert Ellis, Ph.D.

My books are sold throughout the English-speaking countries and many of them have been published in foreign languages. Among my largest outlets are such important bookstores as B. Dalton, Walden and Crown. Added to these are numerous independent bookstores and libraries throughout the nation.

Depending upon the subject matter, you'll find my books in such outlets as health food stores, riding goods stores, sports stores, tennis shops, golf shops, bridge instruction academies, numerous religious gift stores, hobby shops and pet stores.

I launched my career as a self-publisher selling books by mail order, a method which has proven enormously profitable. Using this marketing device, I experienced the excitement of opening countless envelopes that arrived in the mail containing checks, cash and money orders amounting to millions of dollars.

Such success generates incentive and motivation, which inevitably conditions one to meet with confidence virtually every conceivable creative challenge.

Why do I tell you these things? Because I believe that by following the techniques explained to you in subsequent pages of this book, you, too, will experience the thrill of achievement you have envisioned for yourself. When that time arrives, share with me the exhilaration that will surely be yours.

However, if all of this sounds too simple, let me post some warnings. Whether you are an author of books, a writer of songs, or someone involved in other aspects of creative art, the rewards inherent in these endeavors don't happen just by chance. *You have to make them happen.* You must plan for them with as much care and deliberation as you would to structure a building.

I've seen happy, prosperous authors, and, equally, those who are unhappy and disillusioned. I've seen the same in songwriters. And the bottom line never varies—those who become successful had planned for it. They had done their homework thoroughly, with care and a high degree of motivation. Their books and songs were topical. They had been written and rewritten, polished and repolished until they attained the inevitable sheen of perfection that comes with a job well done. In short, success in the arts as in anything else is achieved through deliberation and planning. And for those of you who are aware of these facts and are willing to adhere to the rules, my plan for selling your book is practically infallible. It is not a plan predicated on an esoteric theory. Rather, it is based on realistic, tried-and-tested techniques that are working for me and have with consistency worked for others. Applying the techniques I advocate and personally subscribe to, I have written many books, among them such titles as *Hypnotism Revealed, Advanced Techniques of Hypnosis, Self-Hypnosis, Practical Guide to Self-Hypnosis, Mental Power Through Sleep Suggestion, Practical Guide to Better Concentration, Dynamic Thinking, How to Get Rich in Mail Order* and, in collaboration with Tommy Boyce, *How to Write a Hit Song and Sell It. How to Get Rich in Mail Order* is a book to which I will make considerable reference. In compiling it, I developed a marketing technique so effectively simple and so financially rewarding that I suggest you use my strategy in the marketing of your own books.

Every week, with rare exception, I see someone in my office who has self-published a book but is unaware of how to sell it. Why devote the time and hard work it takes to write a book (potentially a ticket to fame and fortune), only to discover that you've wound up with the best-kept secret in town? Just knowing this problem exists is largely responsible for my decision to write this book— to give marketing guidance to self-publishers. Writing is only half the story. Of equal importance is the other half—how to go about marketing what you've written.

Discussing marketing is, of course, predicated on the fact that you can and will write a book. Or that, at the very least, you will seek help in writing and editing it. Finding help is not a serious problem. There are numerous books on writing available in your local library and I urge you to read some of them. Furthermore, there are many writing courses available to you, daytime or evening, at your local high school, college or university. Take advantage of this convenient opportunity to get into the book-writing community. It will inspire you to achieve what once you might have thought to be beyond your capability.

Don't be reluctant to seek editorial assistance. We all need it. An honest critique of your book before it is published possesses an importance that cannot be overestimated. So emphatically do I subscribe to this principle that I'll have this book professionally edited by two editors before it goes into print. Why? Simply because my *modus operandi* is to refine my copy until I am convinced that the final draft represents the best that I can do. Before I go to press, I want to know the weak as well as the strong points of the manuscript, what sections require rewriting, where (if at all) ambiguities and inaccuracies exist, and I am open to constructive suggestions.

I follow what, for me, has become standard procedure with every book I write and publish. Having completed the book, I photo-copy one copy of the manuscript and give it to a freelance editor. He goes over every page, making what he considers appropriate revisions, deletions, editorial notes and comments. Equipped with the benefit of his thinking, I go over the manuscript again and make the changes I feel are appropriate and necessary. I then give the revised manuscript to a second editor and, again, incorporate any of his editorial changes I consider valid. Upon completion, I have the final copy, ready for the printer.

Even though I am an editor and a publishing consultant, I follow this procedure without exception, as it is difficult to be objective about one's own work. I found this method to be particularly workable during the time I was writing songs. While attending song-writing classes, I either recorded my songs on cassette tape or played and sang them in person. Invariably, I received excellent suggestions from the other students and from the instructor which enabled me to improve both lyrics and melody to the degree that eventually I "made it" with chart songs, became a member of ASCAP (American Society of Composers, Authors, and Publishers), and won an ASCAP award for writing one of the outstanding country-western songs in 1976. *Who Wants a Slightly Used Woman?* was recorded by Connie Cato on Capitol Records. See page 16.

You should not be reluctant to make changes in your

manuscript. It is a natural, normal inclination on the part of writers in general to fall in love with their own words, but this is a love affair which, unfortunately, must face the hard realities of commercialism in the world of literature. Changes are inevitable. The most important and prestigious of writers make them, and they are the first to acknowledge the wisdom of the practice. Should you have the opportunity to speak with an accomplished writer—particularly a novelist—ask what percentage of his final draft is the result of rewriting. You'll be surprised by the answer. A close friend of mine is a reasonably successful screen and television writer. Some time ago, he wrote a play and it was produced on Broadway. Whenever anyone asks to read his play, his stock reply is, "Which of the eight 'final' drafts would you like to see?"

I have had the experience of refusing to accept manuscripts which have made the rounds and have met with rejection by other publishers. The writer will defend his work adamantly, condemning the editors as frustrated writers so lacking in knowledge as to be unable to distinguish between a good and a bad book. This is an erroneous judgment. Editors can make mistakes, of course. They are as human as you and I and are not impervious to error. But when a dozen editors and publishers reject a manuscript, there is usually a well-founded reason. Disparity of thought and opinion between writer and editor can exist outside the printed page. The book might be beautifully written, but, for a number of reasons, not salable.

In evaluating songs for amateur songwriters outside the context of the classroom, I have encountered this same reluctance on the part of writers to change a word or a note, in spite of the fact that they sought my advice as a professional songwriter. On the other hand, when I was in the recording studios making demos of my songs, professional musicians were invariably interested in my comments. They incorporated my suggestions into their own songs and thanked me profusely. Interesting, isn't it? With success comes the ability to accept constructive criticism.

I have often been asked how long, when listening to a song for the first time, it takes me to determine whether or not the song has what it takes to make the commercial grade; does the song have that certain "star quality?" I can tell in a matter of seconds, and it has nothing to do with magic or supernatural powers. It's purely a question of instinct. Creative people develop a certain indefinable "sixth sense" which reacts with immediacy to that which is good or right. The terms are not interchangeable, because "good" is not always "right," just as "well written" is

not always "commercial." But the closer the writer comes to that plateau of professionalism in the development of his career, the more precisely attuned become his instincts for what is commercially "right."

There is nothing more frustrating than the experience of trying to sell a song or a book that "doesn't make it." I want you to avoid that frustration. And the way to do it is to develop a solid book that has good sales potential—a book of which you may be justifiably proud and one that will make a great deal of money for you.

Easier said than done? Of course. If it were easy, everyone would be doing it. But you are not just "everyone." You're a creative individual and you're motivated, which has already been indicated by your interest in what this book can do to direct your manuscript to the marketplace. Those are two important plus marks in the three steps to success. Trust me to supply the third.

I want to touch briefly on the publisher's point of view, his attitude toward literary submissions by writers not known to him. There is a prevailing sentiment among writers that the publisher automatically rejects any manuscript that reaches his desk not sent by someone who has been previously published, or someone well known to him as a salable and acceptable writer with a list of previous credits. Nothing could be further from the truth! It is of great importance to you to know this. Books in print are the publisher's lifeline. Without them, he will perish. Publishing new books is vital to the growth of his company and the black ink in his ledger book. Publishers devote time, energy and talent looking for material to publish. When a publisher rejects a manuscript, there is a reason for it—usually that it is not something he can profitably use.

This is not to say that there are not classic examples of wrong judgment—honest and sincere differences of opinion. Some of them can be disastrous. One need go no further than the motion picture, *Raiders of the Lost Ark*. The film was turned down by every studio in town except Paramount, and it turned out to be the fifth most profitable film in the history of the motion picture industry. Universal, a giant among giants in the movie industry, turned down *Star Wars*. It has been estimated that when the theatrical take on the picture is added to all the residual and fringe returns from sequels, spin-offs, toys, books and video games, the Universal mistake in judgment will come to over a *billion* dollars. However, that mistake will be largely rectified by the studio's sound judgment with regard to the film, *E.T.* (All of this, incidentally, is documented in William Goldman's book, *Adventures in the Screen Trade.*)

So mistakes do happen, but nobody purposely sets out to make them. The doors are always open for creative endeavors that are right. The book, movie, music and television industries spend tremendous sums of money every year ferreting out talent. Don't be trapped by negative thinking. Don't buy the loser's cliché which would have you believe that "it's who you know that counts." Knowing people might get you to the starting gate, but it's going to take talent and hard work to get you off and running.

I receive close to 500 manuscripts and/or submissions for books every month. Of these, only a small percentage is worthy of consideration. Why? Principally because the material is lacking in professionalism. The author has not given enough thought to the material to enable him to have a fresh and viable approach to the subject matter—something to make the book a winner. And spending a fortune on advertising, promotion and publicity isn't going to make it a best seller. It's like hyping a bad movie. You can do it for only so long before you run out of money.

When you decide to publish your own book, I want you to be just as critical as any of the other publishers. Ask yourself, "Does this manuscript have the elements to make it a best seller, to accomplish what I want it to accomplish, and, or course, to make money?" If you have answered those questions in the affirmative, ask yourself the most important question of all: "Am I sincerely confident that I've done the best I can?" It's the affirmative answer to *this* question that will set you apart as a real pro.

If you have already published your book, use the promotional and merchandising techniques suggested in this book to sell out your first printing. Depending upon various factors related to that sellout, such as length of time required, extent of consumer resistance and critical reaction, you might want to consider some revisions in the next edition to enhance its sales.

If you have not yet published, but are thinking of writing a book, do not begin the writing until you have determined its salability by subjecting the book's premise to the test embodied in the techniques in Chapter Four, *How to Test If You Have a Salable Book Before You Write One Word,* and Chapter Eleven, *How to Write a Winning Advertisement—Your Strategy for Success.*

In an effort to establish a sound and workable rapport between author and reader, I have avoided writing in the third person. Instead, I have attempted to color the book with much of my own personality. In it, you will learn a great deal about my philosophy, my various interests and my business thinking. By creating this relationship at the outset, I confidently assume that we are conferring on a personal level. Mindful of this, I want you to feel free to communicate with me whenever you wish, always with the assurance that you will be heard and answered. You may write, phone or visit me at my office. I'll be pleased to give you a guided tour of the offices and warehouse and give you a first-hand account of how we operate. You'll see one of the most efficiently run book-publishing companies in America.

In the next chapter, we'll deal with your reasons for wanting to publish your book and how to ensure its success.

Chapter Two

What Is the Motivation Behind Your Decision to Publish Your Book? What Would It Mean to You If Your book Were on the *New York Times Best-Seller List?* How Would You Then Maximize Your Success Using Your Creative Talent?

Before you write even a single word of your book, the first question you should ask yourself is, "What is the real purpose in publishing my book?"

Assuming your book is highly successful, what are the secondary gains you believe will accrue to you?

All answers are valid and could include some of the following:

1. seeing your name in print
2. writing the book as a hobby
3. sharing your book with family and friends
4. getting newspaper and magazine articles about you and your book
5. enjoying the fun of being on radio and television
6. becoming a celebrity
7. making a little or a great deal of money
8. challenging your creativity
9. using your accomplishment as a means to job advancement, as a stepping-stone to becoming a teacher or lecturer, or as a forerunner to giving seminars
10. establishing yourself as an expert with professional credibility
11. obtaining high-paying consultation work
12. starting a new career
13. promoting your business or personal self

Can you think of anything more satisfying than the sheer joy of contemplating a successful book and all that it can lead to? The consequences are innumerable and part of a very special dream—seeing your words in print for countless readers to consume and enjoy. It's a dream I'm determined to help you transform into a wonderful reality, just as I've helped many others achieve goals they set for themselves. Let me refer you to pages 236 to 240. Each of my current books listed there represents an author and his dream.

Not the least of the many residual benefits associated with the writing of a book is the opportunity to divert the expertise employed in the book into other lucrative and generally rewarding channels. For example, I have used any number of my books as a basis for a variety of extremely entertaining and financially rewarding avocations. Predicated on the content of books I have either written, published, or both written and published, I have been a professional hypnotist, an entertainer, a motivational speaker, a psycho-cybernetics group leader, a songwriter and record producer, a mail-order seminar teacher and consultant, and currently a self-publishing seminar teacher and consultant.

One of the more persuasive elements in the Melvin Powers success pattern is my being able to use my books as an introduction to my readers. You can employ the same technique. Through your book, you will establish contact with a person or persons with whom you share a common interest. You will have your reader's undivided attention. Now, can you whet his appetite for further correspondence, which might include selling an additional book, a cassette tape, a video tape, a seminar, or newsletter?

As an example of how a book can double as a good-will

ambassador, one of my authors and a close personal friend, Albert Winnikoff, wrote a book, *How to Make a Fortune in Real Estate*. I put Al's picture on the cover of his book. See page 14. Al very cleverly and most effectively uses the book as his calling card. It is a real conversation piece in that it invariably starts up a friendly conversation. The recipient finds the device a unique one and is very apt to realize that he is dealing with someone who has intelligence and imagination. Anyone who ever received Al Winnikoff's calling card in the form of a book remembers the incident and remembers Al. When his name comes up in conversation, someone will invariably say, "Oh yes, he's the real estate agent who hands out books for business cards." As you might already have surmised, the gimmick has contributed notably toward making its innovator the successful realtor he has become. It has enabled him to crack the exclusive Hollywood celebrity circles. And all from writing a book. Who says the pen isn't mightier than the sword?

To demonstrate the importance of a "trade mark" as opposed to anonymity, my wife and I are looking for a house at the very time this book is being written. Within the last six months we have encountered perhaps two dozen realtors. They all performed professionally and diligently, showed us what they had to offer, and used virtually the same dialogue in making the conventional pitch that goes with the sale of a house. However, there was about them such a uniformity of sales presentation and personality that they seemed to be clones of each other. At this point, it is difficult to remember any of them or differentiate one from the other. Now, what if one of them had had the ingenuity to write a small book, possibly titled, *What to Look For and How to Save Money in Buying a House?* If one had handed me such a book, with possibly his photograph and phone number included, I would not only have admired the agent's business acumen and remembered his name, but I would have given serious consideration to the selling points made about the property. I certainly would have saved the book with its guidelines for the prospective home buyer for future use. Moreover, it is very possible that this man or woman might have sold me a home.

So, you see, there is considerable impact connected with unique marketing devices, and your book could certainly serve you in that respect, representing you with people you never expected to encounter.

The realtors I referred to could have run small display ads in their community newspapers, offering their books for sale at a nominal fee, or extending them gratis. Think of all the good leads they would have received for both listing and selling houses. That's what I mean by putting your book to work for you, letting it open doors that might otherwise have remained closed to you. That in itself should at least partially give you the incentive to write a book.

Once you have written a book incorporating the techniques and principles which I have found to be infallible, there is no limit to the opportunities that will be open to you. Assume, for example, that you want to become an inspirational speaker. You would allude to that fact in your book, making it known that you are available for business and organizational engagements. You are planting seeds for future exposure.

When, some 25 years ago, I first published my book, *Dynamic Thinking*, it sold for only one dollar. But as a direct result of that dollar book, I wound up with speaking engagements that netted me as much as one thousand dollars. I've made tens of thousands of dollars as a motivational speaker. And what do you think made it all possible? My book! The leads that stemmed directly from my book. It was my calling card.

That calling card has never stopped working for me. Just recently, I was offered the opportunity to travel around the country appearing as a motivational speaker. It was a generous offer, and I was pleased. However, I had to reject it because of lack of time. The responsibilities of my book publishing business and mail-order seminars left no time for a new undertaking. I am, at this time, booked at certain colleges for almost a year in advance.

If you are planning a book in the inspirational genre, I can tell you that the field is wide open—not only for the book, but for the services of the writer. All types of businesses are looking for new speakers. Some of my authors make thousands of dollars for a single one- or two-hour lecture. In other situations, multi-level marketing companies sell tickets to their lectures and divide the profits. The sale of books autographed by the author after a lecture is big business. You just have to be willing to reach for it. All it takes is incentive—don't let anyone tell you otherwise.

Quite recently, one of my authors, Dr. David J. Schwartz, who wrote the multi-million best seller, *The Magic of Thinking Big*, was invited to be a guest speaker on Dr. Robert Schuller's television program which emanates from the Crystal Cathedral in Garden Grove, California. See page 15. Millions of viewers around the world saw the program and millions will see it at a later date as the program was taped for a repeat telecast. This is the kind of publicity money can't buy. And think of the sales potential. After the service, Dr. Schwartz autographed copies of his book for more than an hour.

If you want the rare and inspirational experience of listening to a dynamic speaker, attend one of Dr. Schuller's Sunday-morning services. He is a thoroughly gracious host, and his entire staff reflects his engaging personality. His magnetism and positive attitude helped to raise the money to build as awe-inspiring an edifice as I ever expect to see.

When I was introduced to Dr. Schuller, he said to me, "Are you *the* Melvin Powers?" He went on to explain that he had read many of the books I had published and was pleased to meet me. It was, for me, a delightful moment, just as many previously have been when I discovered that truly accomplished and important persons invariably have the time to be gracious and hospitable toward others and, when the occasion justifies, are willing to share the limelight of professional accomplishment.

Let us, for the moment, indulge in the fun of some positive brainstorming. Assume that your book is on *The New York Times Best Seller List*. What would it mean to you? Obviously, a great deal. Do your feelings have to do with personal satisfaction, pride, fame, money? Probably a combination of all of these, and other factors as well.

All right. You have reached the zenith in publishing. Where do you go from there? Write out a description of your feelings and objectives, because doing so will help clarify the direction of your manuscript and your marketing strategy. Would you like to share your fantasies with me? Perhaps if I knew your goals, I could suggest a viable way of achieving them.

To my way of thinking, reaching the pinnacle of the bestseller list constitutes the rarest of rare opportunities to maximize your success. There can be no greater creative opportunity. In order to do it, you need to brainstorm as to what your next logical step would be. Look at your success as a beginning for a new creative challenge—a new adventure.

It is not possible for me to stress too greatly the importance of maintaining a positive mental attitude. Do not allow yourself to be swayed by persons with negative attitudes. They're probably envious of you for accomplishing that which they themselves could never hope to achieve—the belief that success is at hand and a willingness to reach for it. Always bear in mind that your chance for success is as good as that of anyone else. You have already given positive evidence of that by deciding to read this book.

I do not hesitate to tell you that in deciding to explore the principles advocated in this book you have evidenced good judgment. I say that not because I wrote the book, but because it issues directly from a success pattern covering years of research, hard work and careful planning and includes the enormous advantages associated with trial and error. Following the course of one who deals entirely in theory is quite different from relying on, and attaching credibility to, the representations of someone who has confronted the realities of the commercial world through years of research and practical experience.

If I seem to be repetitive in the references I make to the sound practicality I am prepared to place at your disposal, please understand that the practice is not without design. There is a very definite purpose to it—to drive home to you the importance of using the expertise of others as a means to achieve your own goals. Success in any field is difficult and elusive. Few attain it without the help of others. Oh, there is talk now and then about the so-called self-made man, but, take my word for it— no matter how much a man has contributed to his own success, a careful assessment of the situation will inevitably reveal that somewhere, somehow, directly or indirectly, there was help along the way from the expertise of another. Our entire system of education is predicated upon the principle of cumulative knowledge.

And so I urge you to read this book with care and understanding, for the knowledge it expounds is the end result of a long and difficult search for the methods that work. Take advantage of my expertise so that you may avoid the pitfalls that could easily retard your advancement to ultimate success.

The next chapter is designed to save you a great deal of time and money as well as to help you plan your sales strategy.

"A place where people care about people"

CRYSTAL CATHEDRAL CONGREGATION NEWS

A weekly publication from the Crystal Cathedral

Vol. 13, No. 23   June 5, 1983

Special Communion Service in the Cathedral Sunday, June 12

Holy Communion will be administered next Sunday, June 12 at the 9:30 and 11:15 am services in the Cathedral. This aspect celebration of the Lord's Supper will include a challenging Communion message by Dr. Schuller and the offering of our tithe pledges. Plan to take part as this church family joins together for worship and giving honor and thanks to God.

Welcome, Visitors!

Guided tours are available on Sundays by meeting at the altar steps inside the Cathedral after the 11:15 am service.

On weekdays, tours originate at the Visitors Center across from the Tower of Hope lobby, Monday through Saturday between 9 am and 4 pm.

Membership Seminar *Next Week!*

Plan to deepen your faith and strengthen your understanding of this church by taking part in the Membership Class Seminar, next Sunday, June 12 from 10:45 am to 4:30 pm in the Chapel-in-the-Sky.

Dr. Herman J. Ridder, President of the Cathedral Congregation, will preside over this New Members Class Seminar. Prepare a brown-bag lunch; beverages are provided. For registration information, call 971-4059.

Today at the Cathedral

8 am—Dr. Henry Beltman will deliver his communion message, *The Church of the Living God,* in the Chapel-in-the-Sky.

9:30 and 11:15 am—Dr. Schuller welcomes motivational speaker and writer, **Dr. David Schwartz.** Author of *The Magic of Thinking Big,* which has sold several million copies, Dr. Schwartz will share his faith and how he overcame great physical and mental obstacles from his youth as a diabetic.

7:30 pm—Festival of Choirs! This annual event featuring the combined children's, youth and adult choirs will add inspiration and worship to this evenings **Celebration of Praise.** Plan to participate in this hour of insight as Dr. Schuller delivers a challenging message.

Autograph Party Today!

Dr. Schuller will autograph copies of his latest book, *Tough Times Never Last, But Tough People Do,* today in the Book Center after the 9:30 and 11:15 services.

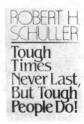

ROBERT H. SCHULLER

Tough Times Never Last, But Tough People Do!

Chapter Three

Why You Should Read This Chapter Even If You Already Have an Idea For a Book.
Where Do Ideas Come From? How to Use the Technique of Brainstorming
to Generate Ideas. The Three Major Categories of Book Topics.
How to Determine the Basic Soundness of Your Idea.

Do you like riddles? Well, here's a good one to tease your brain: how is having an idea for a book like being in love? Give up? The answer is this: once an idea has generated in your mind, it can easily begin to absorb all your attention, inspiring greater enthusiasm with every passing day until you're so "hooked" on it you can think of little else. We can fall in love with our ideas even to the point of obsession. That's one of the reasons I'm going to ask you to read this chapter carefully, *even if you think you already possess the perfect idea for your own book*. In publishing, as in every other endeavor, your initial enthusiasm for an idea can only be enhanced by gaining the confidence that comes from knowing you've made a wise choice. And confidence in the selection of book ideas is precisely what this chapter is about.

Now, the case may be that you're uncertain as to the validity of your idea or possibly even discouraged about finding a good topic at all. Take heart! In the next few pages, you'll learn not only how to take advantage of the infinite variety of idea sources all around you but also to test—before writing a single word of your book—the viability of the idea you've selected.

My many years of experience in the publishing business have revealed to me an interesting fact: there's a potential author in every one of us. That's right. For every reader of this book who believes he has an idea that will make enlightening or entertaining reading, there are thousands of people with equally fascinating material that could be transformed into salable books. Everywhere I go, I meet people who could easily fill the pages of a book with the knowledge they already possess, with their humorous observations, or even with the basic drama of human existence from which works of fiction largely derive. Sometimes I'm asked outright, "Melvin, do you think I could write a book on such-and-such a topic?" Most often, however, people remain unaware of the treasure within themselves, that vast storehouse of material lying dormant in their minds and which I, as a successful publisher, am convinced would make a very readable, perhaps even best-selling, book.

You'll note, however, that I said we were all *potential* authors. That does not mean we are born with an inherent ability to write, anymore than it means we all have received the education and training usually associated with being able to write clearly. Nor am I suggesting that everyone with an idea will automatically see it through to publication. What I'm trying to get across to you is simply this: *ideas abound*. Good subjects for a book are all around you and within you. Ideas, rather than talent, are really our natural birthright. They are fostered by experience, developed as we mature, and come to fruition when we choose to communicate them to others. It is virtually impossible not to have any ideas! To the person who knows how to observe selectively, even the most uneventful life can offer material for a very moving, meaningful book. So never fall into the trap of thinking you'd like to publish—if only you had an idea! The secret of self-publishing lies in carefully choosing the best among the many ideas you already possess.

And now, to help you do so, let's examine in greater detail the broad array of subjects that are at your disposal. We are going to lay to rest any qualms you may have had concerning lack of confidence in a topic for your book.

Brainstorming

Before turning to specifics, I'd like to impart to you a very useful piece of information—a technique for generating ideas that I hope you'll always rely on whenever you're involved in a creative venture, whatever its nature. The technique is called brainstorming, and I'm sure you've not only heard of it but have used it, perhaps without having been totally aware that that's what you were doing. Brainstorming is a marvelous way to get those creative juices flowing. All it takes is concentration on your objective and the determination to allow total freedom to your thoughts. The best way to achieve this is to set aside a chunk of time, the more generous the better, to devote solely to the activity of dreaming up ideas. You should permit no external interference during this time since, as all creative thinkers know, it is essential that a single-minded focus on your goal—the best idea for your book—be maintained.

Let your mind wander where it will, making all sorts of free associations around the subject. You'll be amazed, I'm sure, at the sheer abundance of ideas that can be generated, often in a short period of time once you free yourself of the critical restraints we usually place upon our brain's activity. Brainstorming can help you discover one or several book topics to which you might want to commit yourself. Moreover, it is of great assistance in *refining* your idea. Let's say you've decided you want to write and publish a book on hamburger recipes. But, you think, how can I fill a whole book with this material? A brainstorming session can quickly provide you with a solution. You write down, as it comes into your mind, every idea that occurs to you when you think of hamburgers. "Buns," "ketchup," and "relish" may be among the first associations you make. Why not expand your book with an additional section on "Dressing Up the Hamburgers," in which you could include delectable relishes and buns for which you've devised the recipes? There's really no limit to the creative ways you can refine your original idea, shaping it exactly to your requirements, when you put into practice the art of brainstorming.

The Three Categories

To simplify matters as we now consider the specific sources for ideas, I intend to discuss with you three broad categories of books: instructional, inspirational and humorous. Frequently, these categories tend to blur, as when a how-to book also manages to inspire or motivate people, or when a book whose main purpose is to entertain also teaches its readers a few things along the way. The best books defy categorization, but, for our present purposes, I am going to treat these three broad areas as distinct and separate.

Instructional

Instruction, in the form of how-to books, is one of my favorite areas of publishing. I derive enormous satisfaction whenever I bring out a book I am sure will be of use to the reader, educating and informing him. Personally, I have always turned first to books when I needed to learn more about a subject. Hasn't that been your experience too? A book possesses a certain authority and it is always there to refer to, time and again. So it makes wonderful sense to consider writing a book based on a particular area of expertise, a book to which the reader, hungry for information, can turn in order to share the knowledge you've accumulated. Remember, you are a virtual mine of information! Think carefully about every aspect of your life, from your daily chores to your line of work, to your special talents, to your hobbies or avocations. Haven't you perhaps developed a new or better way of doing things? Aren't there a couple of secrets you'd like to share with others eager to get started in, or to familiarize themselves with, that subject?

When I first began writing books, I chose hypnosis as an area of expertise I felt I could profitably share with a wide audience of readers. Mind you, I was not then a famous hypnotist. But I was confident that I knew enough about the subject—and was fascinated by what it could accomplish—to communicate my enthusiasm for it to readers. In the years since then, I've followed an identical pattern of writing books on topics on which, *through my own experience,* I've become an expert; namely, songwriting, positive thinking, mail order and self-publishing. My advice to you, therefore, is this: when seeking the right idea for a book, stick with what you know best. All it takes is some serious reflection and an open mind to discover the subject you can write about with the maximum confidence and authority.

While we're on the subject of expertise, let me suggest a fresh perspective to you. Suppose for a moment that the idea of writing a novel based on your life story appealed to you. We can safely assume that you and you alone know intimately the ups and downs you've been through, the funny and sad moments you've experienced, and the agony and ecstasy of your life. No one is more familiar than you with *your* experiences. Wouldn't it be fair to call you an expert in this domain? By the same token, life has undoubtedly provided you with other areas of expertise that would be perfectly appropriate subjects for a book. Stop and think. Expertise doesn't have to mean knowing all there is to know about a given topic. It can mean knowing a lot about a relatively narrow field, or knowing something others don't yet know, or simply having a new perception of the field or a proven method of success.

With these definitions of expertise in mind, can you think of some area in which you possess the knowledge to deem yourself an expert of sorts? I'd advise you to start with what you like to do—a hobby, for example, or a talent you've developed. If you've been playing the guitar for many years and are able to teach it to novices, you've probably discovered a few shortcuts to learning the technique, shortcuts you wish you'd known when you yourself first started learning. It is these methods of instruction you might want to communicate in a book. Never forget that simplicity is a highly valued commodity, especially among beginners in any endeavor. If you are capable of breaking down complex notions or actions into their component parts, clearly and succinctly, your book could be a gold mine for anyone starting out in the particular field you're writing about.

People's hobbies, talents and particular affections, such as a love for animals, have yielded countless books, year after year. Take a look at some of the titles I publish on bridge, tennis, poker, and calligraphy. All of these were written by authors like you who set down on paper what they already knew, and knew well.

Less obviously, another area of expertise is an activity you've been pursuing for some time, perhaps without giving it much thought. Traveling, raising children, repairing your car, cooking—these are all activities that concern a potentially vast number of readers who are only too eager to learn easier or better methods of accomplishing them. The activity you choose to write about need not be one for which you have a unique talent or even one you especially enjoy. As long as you've developed a new or more efficient technique or a particular slant (a humorous attitude, for instance), you can consider it a possible topic for a book.

Remember Peg Bracken's *I Hate To Cook Book*? It's a perfect example of a distasteful chore that became the lighthearted subject of a best-selling instructional book. If you give it some thought, you can probably discover several activities in which you have invested time and energy. Isn't there a way at least one of them could inspire a book? With the proper motivation, you can make even routine chores pay off for you—in the form of a best-selling book.

To sum up, how-to or instructional books always have a potentially large readership because they appeal to people of all ages who desire to learn something new or deepen their knowledge of a subject. If you can provide these readers with the information they crave, you'll be doing them a favor and you will derive much personal satisfaction from it.

Inspirational

Books that come under the heading of inspirational also educate people, but their aim is specifically to guide the reader in bettering his or her life. To this end, one of innumerable methods for attaining success, power, serenity and happiness may be the book's subject: biofeedback, religious faith, positive thinking. At the end of the book you are reading at the moment, you'll find The Midas Touch Library, a list of titles I publish that focus on motivating the reader through positive thinking. I have long found such books to be of tremendous assistance in stimulating creativity and ultimately enhancing people's lives.

If you've experienced new enthusiasm, joy and wisdom in your life by means of some psychological strategy, why not describe it in a book? Just think of the millions of books sold annually that deal with various facets of our psychological make-up, such as guilt, anger, fear, happiness in personal relationships or overcoming loneliness. It's wise to remember that there are countless ways of setting forth advice you wish to share with your reader. You can talk "straight from the hip," use dialogue, or even get your message across in a fable. *Jonathan Livingston Seagull*, the best-selling inspirational book, conveyed its spiritual theme in story form. The point is, don't overlook your personal experiences in life. More than anything else, they can inspire people and motivate them— through your example—to change in a dramatically positive fashion.

Humorous

The last broad category of book topics from which you may want to draw your own ideas is that of humor. As with those that instruct and inspire, humorous books can cover an almost infinite range of subjects. Furthermore, they can come in an extremely large variety of forms. In this category, you have not only the cartoon books, such as those irrepressible, best-selling *Garfield* volumes devoted solely to the antics of a cat, but also the spoof books, such as *The Dieter's Guide to Weight Loss During Sex* by Richard Smith which was on the *New York Times Best-Seller List* for many months. Also in this category must be considered books that poke fun at a trend or a particular group of people. Alfred Gingold's *Items From Our Catalogue*, for example, parodies the famous L. L. Bean mail-order catalogue with humorous photos and equally witty accompanying text—a very successful take-off, in my opinion.

In 1983, we were treated to *The Preppy Handbook*, to cite a popular example of a funny book that made us laugh at a national phenomenon. I'm sure that "right off the top of your head" you could list several other humorous books that have made it big over the past few years. There's no doubt that humor is greatly in demand, and if you're inclined to be witty or can devise a funny way of looking at an otherwise serious phenomenon, you could have a best seller in relatively little time. Again, I urge you to turn first to your own personal experience, for that's what you know best and can, therefore, view with humor that others may appreciate. If you are an inveterate observer of the human scene, the possibilities for writing a humorous book are endless. Someone like Irma Bombeck, who depicts in a hilarious manner the underside of daily life, can be virtually assured of a continuous variety of topics from which to choose. One note of caution may be in order, however, for you aspiring writers of humor books: take care not to offend anyone in the process, for that could spell disaster for your book.

Determining the Basic Soundness of Your Idea
At this point, those of you who have settled upon an idea for a book are probably very eager to "run with it," to set in motion the whole exciting process of writing, publishing and marketing your book. Nevertheless, I hope, in your eagerness, you will not skip the next part of this chapter, because it contains some of the most important information I can give you. So please be patient and carefully consider what I'm going to tell you now.

Unfortunately, it just does not make good business sense to decide on a book topic and immediately commit your thoughts to paper. What if your idea is not basically sound? What if it needs to be recast in a slightly different mold or totally revamped? You must honestly and as objectively as possible evaluate your knowledge of the subject. There is no point in writing a book if your readers already know more than you do about the material at hand, or if you unwittingly mislead them. Furthermore, do you have something different to say about the subject than what has been said over and over again? Have you provided an update on the topic or viewed it from an unusual angle? Now, I'm not saying your book has to be the epitome of originality, only that both you and your readers will surely derive greater satisfaction from a book that has been honestly researched and written.

What do I mean by research? To begin with, the basic knowledge that is conveyed by the printed page must be correct, and I assume you know at all times what you're talking about. That's how you instill confidence in the reader, a major element in continuing and word-of-mouth sales. But the kind of research I'm referring to here also involves comparing your work to that of other authors, making sure you've absorbed what's gone before by reading similar books on the topic. The best advice I can give you is to go to your public library and check out all the books on your chosen subject. Read them and feel confident that *your* book will be as good as, or, hopefully, even better than, the majority of them.

Next, your research must be directed at the potential audience for your book topic. How can you know in advance what people like to read? One sure way is to examine what they buy in the bookstores. At the library you can ask to see the *New York Times Best-Seller Lists,* published in every Sunday's Book Review section, and inspect them for recurring book topics. I'm a firm believer in copycatting successful books. By this I mean producing a book that matches in theme or subject matter an already-published book that has achieved healthy sales. I can tell you now that real estate and financial matters have furnished the subjects of many best-selling books; there's always a new angle to be written about when it comes to accumulating wealth. Psychology and humor have remarkable tenacity on the best-seller lists. More recently, health, beauty and exercise regimens have begun to appear with astonishing regularity. If your book topic falls under any of these headings, it's clear you're being sensitive to the market and can expect potentially large sales.

Incidentally, some books are easier than others to copycat in a relatively short period of time. I copycatted Coach Jim Everroad's two-million-copy seller, *How To Flatten Your Stomach,* with a spoof entitled *How To Flatten Your Tush* by Coach Marge Reardon, an entirely imaginary author. The book was written and photographs taken for it in 24 hours, and we had a marvelous time producing it. It went on to become a winner, selling 100,000 copies. See page 22.

What if your idea for a book doesn't seem to correspond to any of the more popular categories? Should you simply abandon it? I can't give you a definite yes or no answer without being familiar with the exact subject you have in mind, but I will suggest this much: above all, use common sense in determining your book idea's viability. If you've chosen an esoteric subject, something you are one of the few people in the world to know anything about, you must realize that your book is not going to sell many copies, no matter how brilliantly you plan to market it. Even if you are the number one expert on the topic, chances are that only libraries and a handful of other readers will purchase your book. This is, of course, an extreme example, but you'd be surprised at how many calls I receive from potential authors who, because they've become enamored of some highly specialized area of expertise, are unable to see it objectively. They simply can't understand why their books wouldn't sell like hot cakes.

Conducting research into the potential readership of your book can be accomplished in a couple of other effective ways as well. For one thing, you can ask other people's opinions. Don't overlook those around you—family, friends, and co-workers—when you seek advice in this matter. Ask them if they would consider buying a book on your subject and if they think it would appeal to many others. This may not measure up to the statistical accuracy of a legitimate opinion poll, but I assure you it helps to get an *initial* sense of your book's marketability.

Another simple method of determining what's topical and relevant (and, therefore, a guide to the popularity of a given book topic) is to keep up with the major magazines and newspapers. Certain subjects appear again and again in these periodicals; they seem to have lasting appeal. If the topic you've chosen for your book happens to be one of these ubiquitous ones, you can feel confident that your book has the potential to do well. On the other hand, new topics invariably pop up every year, retain people's attention for a while, then fade away. These subjects represent *trends*, and if your book deals with any one of these fashionable topics, you would be well advised to focus on the issue of timing, which is essential. For if you publish a book on an extremely popular subject just as the public's interest in it wanes, you'll come to regret your decision. Trendy subjects, such as medical topics and diets in particular, often come and go with astonishing rapidity. Hypoglycemia, toxic shock syndrome, herpes, liquid protein and countless other faddish diets are before the public's eyes for months; then they disappear to make way for the next "in" topic. However tempting it may be to add your book to the roster of those dealing with such "hot" topics, you must exercise great judgment as regards the timing of publication.

Frankly, I would much rather see you *predict* a trend

than get on the bandwagon once it has arrived. If you can sense what the next trend in any area of book publication will be, all the more power to you! You'll be that much closer to achieving best-sellerdom yourself. Now here's a hint for you would-be prophets. Sometimes you can spot next year's trend in something your children are doing *right now*. Kids' manias control a large segment of the marketplace. Don't you wish you'd been the first to write a book on, say, Rubik's Cube or Pac Man?

Clearly, there exists to date no scientifically proven method of predicting book trends, anymore than the so-called experts on Wall Street can accurately predict the fortunes of the stock market. If, however, you have analyzed all the data to the best of your ability and feel reasonably confident that your chosen topic is going to be the next "hot" subject, you must, of course, get your book into print and sell it vigorously so as to profit from the novelty of heralding a trend. By the way, the Olympics represent a wonderful opportunity for anyone interested in writing and publishing a book on a timely subject. Once the games are over, though, there will be nothing more difficult to sell than a book about the Olympics!

As you have realized by now, there are no shortcuts to determining the salability of a given idea. You have to study what others have written and be aware at all times of the trends in the marketplace. Subscribing to such magazines as *Publishers Weekly*, which deals with the business aspects of the book trade, and *Writer's Digest*, which views the book world from the perspective of the writer eager to cash in on it, can only put you ahead of the game. Remember, even seasoned publishers, who develop a sort of "sixth sense" where salable book ideas are concerned, are rarely right all the time. It just isn't possible to know with 100% accuracy what will catch on with readers and what won't. But that also happens to be the beauty of this business: where would the excitement and challenge of hoping to publish a best-selling book come from if it were all totally predictable?

Let me conclude this chapter by reminding you that, after all is said and done, only *you* are the final arbiter. Only you, the potential or actual author, can evaluate the extent of your commitment to a given idea and the depth of your belief in its salability. In the next chapter, I am going to show you a way to test your book's strength in the market before you write it. Market testing of your idea will often clarify the issue dramatically for you, dispelling any doubts you may still harbor as to the soundness and profitability of your idea.

Chapter Four

How to Test the Salability of Your Book Before You Write One Word

The prime challenge confronting the writer who decides to self-publish his book is to produce a creative idea so persuasively provocative that it will immediately "hook" the reader. This is absolutely essential if you hope to fulfill the goal you have set. The reader must be interested in what you have to say from the very first word. To hold your reader's attention, you must start piqueing his interest right on page one. Your reader is not captive; as with a television program, start him yawning and he'll turn you off.

So, how do you know if the idea for your book can accomplish this; hook a reader and hold his interest throughout the book? There is a way, and it is very effective. You test the subject for your book in the market place *before you write it*. Why spend the money to print a book if you don't know whether the book and the advertising campaign can succeed in making a profit?

Having now posed that threat to your peace of mind and your financial security, let me now show you a way to counteract it. Here is the Melvin Powers formula for coming up with a winner without enduring any of the slings and arrows of commercial crap-shooting. Simply stated, we test the advertising copy before you even write the book. It is an almost infallible way of taking the gamble out of your project. You know the results of the roll before you even toss the dice. I have designed this technique as an insurance device for the many persons who spend their time and money producing a book only to discover later that their marketing strategy isn't working. And, unfortunately, the marketing strategy was the last thing they had considered. Make it the *first* thing you have in mind. Give it the top priority it deserves.

Regrettably, as I have mentioned before, there is hardly a week in which some self-published author doesn't come to me with the lament that he's stuck with his book. After a brief conversation, it becomes readily apparent that he doesn't have the slightest idea of how to go about marketing it. This same story often applies to authors who have been published by *bona fide* publishing companies. The misfortune is that the initial announcements and publicity did not produce the desired returns, with the result that the company then refused to spend any more promotional dollars. When that happens, and you're able to confer with someone in authority, the most you can hope for are excuses. Your book is headed for the remainder house.

I'm going to cite the case of my book, *How to Get Rich in Mail Order*, and explain how I made this technique of advance testing work. All I had was a title. Instinctively, I knew it was a good title, but the big challenge was to design a good display advertisement or mail-order circular that would sell the as-yet-unborn book.

I've had the good fortune to have an outstanding freelance copywriter and talented mail order advertising expert working for me on assignment. The man to whom I refer, has written a guest chapter for this book on advertising copy. See Chapter Ten—How to Write a Winning Advertisement—Your Strategy for Success.

The assignment I gave him was to write a classified ad and a circular to be sent in response to inquiries received about how to sell a book on mail order. The requirement I specified was that he not mention anything directly about my book, which, of course, had not as yet been written.

I tested his ad with someone else's mail order book, referring to the book's title only in the coupon. Once the ad was successful, it was a simple matter merely to change the name of the book in the coupon and make some minor descriptive changes in the last column of the ad. It's a clever device that works like a charm and saves the author money which might otherwise have gone down the drain.

See page 28 for the ad. Study it carefully so you will get a feel for the clever technique employed and be able to copy it for yourself.

Don't be reluctant to sell someone else's book. It's a skillful way of testing advertising copy and strategy. Had I wanted to do so, I could have sold a dozen different books on mail order by using the ad. Notice that the ad does not zero in on the book itself, but, rather, concerns itself with the general subject of mail order. As a result, any book on mail order would fit the generalities expressed in the ad copy.

I ran the following classified ad in numerous publications:

Learn how to get rich in mail order. Expert's secrets revealed. Write for free, fascinating details that could change your life: Melvin Powers, Dept. 5, 12015 Sherman Road, North Hollywood, California 91605.

In response to this, I sent out the ad on page 28. The department number refers to the particular publication in which the ad was run.

When the ads paid off, and when I had sold out the inventory of books I had purchased, I stopped running my ads. I resumed after I had published my book.

Bear in mind that I wasn't particularly interested in selling the other author's book; I was trying to determine the selling power of my ad and find out whether my ads were capable of selling several thousand copies of his book. When that became evident, I knew I was home free because the mail order buyers were making their purchases without knowing anything at all about the contents of the book. I now knew that I could write and publish my own book *with the absolute assurance that there would be thousands of guaranteed sales*. And that's exactly what I want you to do. Think how much

safer it is from the standpoint of dollars and cents than writing and publishing a book and then being faced with the prospect of not selling a single copy.

Note that I offer the book on a 365-day, money-back guarantee basis. Not a single buyer returned the book for refund, a fact which emphatically gives credibility to the ad. Isn't it better than a 14-day, or even a 30-day, guarantee? Perhaps you might want to offer the same guarantee in your ads.

Now, how do you find a given non-fiction book to be used in your experiment? Go to your library and ask for the reference book, *Subject Guide to Books in Print*. It's a volume that contains 425,000 entries, 62,000 subject categories, and 53,000 cross references. Without exception, every library has the set. It's a basic reference book that is a standard and essential library source. It lists the title of each book, the author, and the price. Volume II contains the names and addresses of the publishers. Write to the publishers for their catalogs and discount schedules, and then request an application for credit. Or, if you prefer, pay for the books as you order them.

If you are not familiar with the book listed, order a sample copy, mention that you would like to mail order the book, and ask what the minimum purchase and discount schedule is for mail-order dealers.

Most publishers will give you a 40% discount plus an additional 10% as an advertising allowance. This adds up to a 46% discount. But don't stop there. Ask for 50%.

To illustrate, let's assume the book sells for $10.00. 40% off $10.00 is $4.00, making the cost of the book to you, at this point, $6.00. The additional 10% discount is on the $6.00 figure and amounts to 60 cents. The book now costs you $5.40 plus postage charges. I have found that in most cases if you ask for the 50% discount you'll get it. The standard store discount is 40% off the list price of the book, plus postage. The discount to wholesalers is 50% off the list price, plus postage.

I must caution you never to tell anyone the real reason you are purchasing the books. Suppose you were to start selling hundreds or thousands of copies. If you are purchasing from a major publisher, it is doubtful that anyone would inquire about how you are selling the books. If you are dealing with a small publisher the chances are you still will not receive an inquiry. If, by chance, you do happen to get a call or a letter of inquiry, do not disclose to them how you are selling the book. I know you will be tempted to do otherwise. When you're selling a great many books, you are rightfully proud of yourself and experience a euphoric sense of achievement with the discovery that you've written and published an ad that's a winner. Don't make a mistake. Do not send your prize-winning ad to anyone, and give the publisher as little information as possible. Having spent time and money on an ad that pays off big, you and you alone are entitled to reap the profits.

Assume, on the other hand, that you do not like the idea of selling someone else's book as a means of testing the salability of your own idea. Assume further that you are eager to put your thoughts on paper; that you favor the creative challenge of writing your book. Fine. I still want you to wait before you typeset and publish your book.

Let me suggest the following plan to test your book: Double-space your manuscript on one side of 8½" × 11" sheets of paper. Type it letter-perfect so that it can be photo-copied. Condense your first draft to about 96 pages for test purposes. Photo-copy 12 copies of your book and put each copy into a plastic or paper binder. The photo-copying will cost three cents for each page, making a total of $2.88. The cover will cost about 12 cents, making a total of $3.00 for your book. Do not put a price on the cover of the book.

You are now ready to test your advertising copy. Hopefully, you'll write an excellent ad. When you start receiving hundreds or thousands of orders, you'll be ready to set type for your book in its final form and publish it. If you find there is reason to expand the book, you can, of course, do so. You'll be able to determine that from the feedback you get from your readers.

I suggested photo-copying only 12 copies, but it can be 25, 50, 100 or more copies. Photo-copy your book as you get sales. Small runs will also give you a chance to test reader response; then you're equipped to make necessary changes and improvements as suggested by the reactions of the readers. It's a practice founded on the same idea as, for example, an out-of-town tryout of a play in Boston or New Haven before bringing it into New York, or a variety of preview showings of a movie before the official opening. As with the book, these advance showings give you the opportunity to determine by the reactions of the consumer what your soft spots are and where to make changes and improvements before sending your brainchild out into the commercial world to shift for itself. Please refer to page 28 again and copy my format designed to enable you to achieve maximum success.

It is also possible for you to test the prospective ceiling price for your book. In your literature, offer the book at various prices. To make the price determination, for example, list the book in 100 pieces of literature or order forms at $5.00, in another 100 pieces at $10.00, then $15.00, and upwards as far as you wish. Tabulate the results, and you'll wind up with a reasonably accurate gauge as to the best price.

When it comes to pricing, disregard the myth that off prices, such as $4.95, $9.95 or $14.95, are psychologically more persuasive to the buyer than rounded-out numbers like $5.00, $10.00 or $15.00. It is a totally fallacious concept that contributes nothing to your sales, but does contribute to the complications of your bookkeeping. I've sold millions of books at rounded-out figures and doubt that I could have sold more at odd prices. Rounded numbers also make your invoicing easier.

I recently paid $50.00 for a book in response to a six-page advertising piece received in the mail. In the same way, I recently purchased another six books, each priced at approximately $25.00. These direct mail sales make it convenient for me to keep up with the latest books in advertising, promotion and marketing, a policy which I consider extremely important in my business, not only as a publisher, but as a teacher who, through an unending series of meetings and seminars, is striving to point the way for aspiring writers, publishers and businessmen. It's very much like the case of a doctor. If he wants to keep his patients alive, healthy and competitive, it behooves him to keep up with the latest information and documented discoveries in the field of medicine. That, in a commercial way, is what I'm trying to do for you and others who solicit my help. But to do it properly, I must be well-informed. And to be well-informed and stay well-informed, I turn to books.

Most technical books are sold through direct mail. If the prospective customer feels the material is worthwhile, he'll usually buy it, regardless of cost. The element of risk is minimal because these books are always sold on a money-back basis. I find myself eagerly awaiting every book I order and read it as soon as it arrives. It's somewhat like taking a seminar, seeking information to apply to my own needs and to my various business enterprises.

The publisher's cost on the above-mentioned books could not have exceeded three dollars at the outside. Each of the books carried a money-back guarantee. I kept all I had bought, so obviously I was pleased with the purchase. When it comes to selling information in any form, if the presentation meets the requirements of clarity, authenticity and organization, price is no object, regardless of the form of presentation—book, manual, newsletter, cassette tape or video tape. I'm always pleased with whatever investment I make even if it gives me just one idea with which to enhance my business. And I know I'm not alone in that kind of thinking. It's a truism in the trade that when it comes to selling technical or business books, price is a secondary consideration.

For years, people who are familiar with my library of self-improvement literature, the quality of the book bindings and of the art work—the sleek feel of the book—have asked me why I don't sell my books at higher prices. This is a clear indication that whatever I undertake to sell, I invest with quality. In books, as in anything else, I am a firm believer there is no substitute for quality. And since you are starting out in a business and profession which can open wonderfully broad parameters of success and personal gratification to you, I urge you to think the same way. Think quality hard enough and long enough, and soon it will become second nature with you.

Let me introduce another workable technique. Forget about the initial charges that go into the first edition of your book when you price it. Why? Because those are one-time charges and, in my opinion, should be written off on the first printing. Find out what the price of the book is for the second printing. Bear in mind that for the second printing you are no longer paying for the editing, typesetting, art work and negatives. You'll pay about $1.00 a book for a 96-page, 5½″ × 8½″ paperback.

Generally, I put a four- or five-to-one mark-up on my books. If a book costs me $2.00 or $2.50, I'll mark it up to $10.00. That allows me to sell it to the bookstores at $6.00 (40% discount) and to wholesalers at $5.00 (50% discount). In mail order, I sell the book at $11.00 or $12.00. The extra dollar or two covers postage. I charge full price for books at my seminars.

I recommend that you follow the same pricing guidelines. Assume your book costs you $1.00. You can sell it for $4.00 or $5.00. Possibly more. Joe Karbo, who wrote *The Lazy Man's Way to Riches,* came right out in one of his ads and told readers that the book he was advertising cost him less than fifty cents, but the cost to them would be $10.00. In spite of this startling disclosure, he still sold well over a million copies. Don't forget, what you are selling is valuable information. But "valuable," like anything else, is a relative term. What might prove valu-

able to one person might be worthless to another. So there is no way that you can be sure you are setting a "correct" price. The only way to determine the best price is by merchandising your book at various prices.

A well-known facial cream has been marketed by mail order for many years. The principals of the company decided to use their marketing skills to test the market value. Their objective was to find the best-selling price for the product. Price had nothing to do with the actual cost of the product.

They ran split-run advertisements in the same publication. This means that half of the publication's circulation carried the ad with one selling price while the other half carried it at another selling price. The price was the only difference between the two ads, except for the key number. The $40.00 price tag had a draw that exceeded that of the $10.00, $20.00 and $30.00 tags. Psychologically, these findings might be likened to the price tags on expensive perfumes. Buying expensive perfume is probably one of the world's most luxurious forms of self-indulgence. The price tag is not material.

Therefore, I repeat, when it comes to pricing your book, it is incumbent upon you to experiment in the same way. In no other way will you be able to accurately determine your best price. However, it has always been my belief—and one which has been proven to be sound—that the best practice is big volume, small profit. At the end of each year, I can look back to great volume in sales, and those small profits have added up to great financial satisfaction. I'm confident that in time your philosophy on the subject will coincide with mine.

My theory is supported by the sale experienced with the book *Psycho-Cybernetics* by Maxwell Maltz, M.D. I sold over three million copies at a retail price of only $2.00 a book. I could have charged more, but I was delighted with the sale. From a business standpoint, the result turned out to be one of remarkably good judgment. My net profit on that one book was over $1,000,000.

Another effective way to test the viability of the idea you have in mind for your book is to write an article on it and have it published in a magazine or newspaper. If composing the article presents a problem, I suggest that you peruse some library books on the subject of writing magazine articles. I would also highly recommend that you read some issues of *Writer's Digest.* It is a very informative magazine for writers and could be of considerable help to you. There are probably copies in your local library. If not, I'm sure you'll find it at the main library. Failing that, it can be purchased at any bookstore and you will find it's well worth the investment.

Try to get an assignment from a magazine or newspaper to do an article about the main subject matter of the book. Simply write a letter of inquiry to the publication's editor, offering to write such an article, tailored to the format of his publication and the character of his readership, and complying with any limitations on length prescribed by him or the policy of the paper or magazine.

At the end of your article, appeal to the reader for feedback, listing your name and address, or ask that mailings be sent to you in care of the publication carrying the article. Make notes on the kind of information that is supplied in the letters received and incorporate any well-received ideas into your book material.

When your testing processes have proven successful and indicate you should proceed, you are, of course, ready to publish your book. Initially, you would be well-advised to start with a first-run of about 3,000 copies, perhaps 5,000. When attempting to arrive at the appropriate retail price of the book, the determination should depend on the results of your experimentation with the mailings. Did you pull twice as many orders at $5.00 as you did at $10.00? Did you pull more orders at $10.00 than you did at $15.00? Is your interest primarily in catering to volume at high profits, or in a selective readership at a lesser profit? Are you looking for leads to whom you will be able to sell additional products? Only *you* can decide the direction you want to go. Only *you* know the answer. If you were to ask my opinion, I would say go for the largest volume of sales.

My next chapter will explore the intricacies of mail order and will detail the methods employed so that sales of my book, *How to Get Rich in Mail Order*, amounted to over $2,000,000.

I give these examples to show you where dedication, discipline and proficiency can lead in this fascinating field of endeavor. These attributes can be your key to success, independence and the attainment of your goals.

WOULD YOU LIKE TO MAKE $1,000 A MONTH IN YOUR SPARE TIME?

For the past 25 years, I've sold millions of dollars worth of books and merchandise all over the world through mail order. What is my secret? Experience-tested and proven mail order techniques! The results? Checks, cash and money orders—a continuous flow of money coming into my office every day. And I still get a thrill shaking all this money from the stacks of envelopes on my desk each morning! Such glowing evidence confirms the fact that these techniques are virtually infallible.

In addition to enjoying financial success, I have the satisfaction of knowing that the remarkable books I publish enrich people's lives and bring them genuine fulfillment. You have no doubt read or heard of some of the many books I publish that have achieved international acclaim: *Psycho-Cybernetics, Think and Grow Rich, Magic of Thinking Big, I Will, New Guide to Rational Living, Three Magic Words, Ability to Love,* and *You Are Not the Target.*

Direct mail and/or space ads produce so much volume at times that it becomes necessary to stop the ads so I can catch up with the heavy mail flow. For example, a few years ago, during the Fisher/Spasky chess tournament, my chess books sold as fast as they could be printed. This went on for three months. I doubled my office staff, but still could not handle all the orders!

I want you to have this delightful experience in your own mail order business. Here is some insight into the field of mail order in general. What can you sell through radio, TV, direct mail, and classified and display ads? Everything and anything, from needle threaders to airplanes. The first step is to zero in on something that interests and excites you. Choose a product or a service that you want to sell. If you need some ideas, check the ads in magazines and newspapers at your library or newsstand. Which ones attract you? Do they contain services or products you'd like to sell? Research them carefully—you'll find the mail order possibilities unlimited.

Selling through mail order is comparable to selling in any other business. Research the field. Start small. Avoid "pie-in-the-sky" schemes. If you progress slowly, you're less likely to have a financial disaster. I've had my share of mailings and ads that have failed, but these failures have been part of a creating-and-experimenting experience. Once you understand and implement the formula for successful mail order merchandising, you'll earn plenty of money. You can turn your talents into a second income that will surpass your present one.

To illustrate this, look at McDonald's restaurants. No matter where they open, they're a hit. Management has found the success formula and simply repeats it in each new location. The same is true for many multi-outlet businesses, such as pizza parlors, fast food chains, and department stores. Running a profitable mail order operation is no different from operating these businesses. The principles are the same.

The more you read about and study successful mail order businesses, the more information you'll acquire. Send for mail order catalogues. Order one of the advertised products or services to get on the mailing lists. To see how these companies follow up after the initial sale, key your address with an extra letter in your name (i.e., Melvin A. Powers or Melvin B. Powers), or add a suite number to your mailing address. This will help you to check

how often they sell their mailing list and to identify which list is being used.

If a particular product or service interests you, send for it. See if you can improve on it. This is called the "copycat" technique. It's legitimate and is one of the easiest ways to begin your mail order business.

Here's an important mail order secret. If you can collect thousands of names for a list of your own, it doesn't matter whether or not you make one penny from your product or service. Mailing lists rent from $30 to $50 per thousand. Therefore, if you have a hot list, you can make a fortune selling these names. Many businesses are willing and eager to pay for the names of good mail order prospects. Renting your list is known as the "back end" of the business. That's where dollars add up. It's also the easy part.

While studying classified and display ads in various publications, be sure to note whether they repeat over a period of time. If they do, you'll know they're paying off and are successful. Keep track of these ads. Start your own file.

The next step for a successful operation is to write sound advertising copy. Convincing ads will persuade the reader to take action—to place an order for your product or service. Notice the toll-free telephone numbers on many TV and display ads. The aim is to generate spur-of-the-moment, impulsive buying. You might want to use this technique.

To write good mail order advertising copy, follow this formula:

1) Capture the reader's attention with an eye-catching headline.
2) Arouse interest by describing the benefits of your product or service.
3) Stimulate desire with proof, testimonials, or further explanation of the benefits.
4) Solicit orders.

I'm using this copywriting technique here. At the end of this advertisement, I'll ask you to order an outstanding book on mail order. If my presentation has been logical and clear, you'll order it. If not, you'll pass. If enough readers respond, I will have made my point.

If this ad doesn't pull well enough to pay for itself, I won't be discouraged. I'll know the missing ingredient can be found and included in new advertising copy. I'll rewrite the ad from a different angle or enlist the help of a professional copywriter. I'll run the ad again and check the results. A successful ad requires persuasive copy. You don't learn these techniques overnight—it's a matter of trial and error.

If your ads don't pull, you can do the same thing. Use a fresh approach. Study successful ads and borrow some of the techniques used. Read books about advertising. Enroll in an evening class in advertising. By taking advantage of educational opportunities, you'll improve quickly.

Even after 25 years in the business, I find that self-education pays off. For example, I participate annually in a seminar for mail order experts. The most successful persons in the mail order business come from all over the country to meet in Los Angeles and share their expertise. They are inquiring, resourceful individuals, open to new ideas. Informal round-table discussions stimulate creative thinking. One idea often translates into thousands of dollars. As knowledge and techniques are shared, new ideas are born.

These mail order giants, entrepreneurs of the highest caliber, continue to seek information to enhance their businesses.

Do I learn my "mail order secrets" at these seminars? Absolutely. The most important one is to be aware of new trends and current interest. Another, learn to watch for a unique product or service. And, very important, strive to acquire a good sense of business.

Are you motivated for success? If your answer is "yes," you are going to appreciate the special offer I have for you. I have written a book filled with practical, concrete information on how you can succeed in the fascinating world of mail order. The specific instruction and information I've talked about for starting and maintaining a money-making mail order operation is detailed in this book. Whether you are a beginner or an established professional, I guarantee that my book will increase your effectiveness in developing and expanding your current mail order operation.

Not only is the book packed with down-to-earth ideas, useful how-to's and nitty-gritty facts, it contains over 200 illustrations as well, making it a virtual encyclopedia of mail order information. It even shows you how to run a mail order business in your spare time. What's more, you get an extraordinary, 365-day, money-back guarantee when you purchase this book. If, by the end of one year, you are not making thousands of dollars in your mail order operation, simply return the book for a full refund. Fair enough?

Mail order is my business and my hobby. It's fun, it's creative, it's fascinating—and it means big money, too! Your secret dreams can come true because there are millions of customers out there just waiting to send *you* their dollars for your product or service. I am continually amazed at the incredible money-making opportunities in this field.

To experience the joy of shaking thousands of dollars from stacks of envelopes addressed to *you,* send for *How to Get Rich in Mail Order* by Melvin Powers. 336 pages, over 200 pages of illustrations, 8½" × 11" size. Allowable as a tax deduction.

Copyright 1980 by Melvin Powers

Chapter Five

How I Achieved Sales Totaling $2,000,000 on My Book *How To Get Rich in Mail Order*

Of the various ways to sell books, the method I prefer is mail order. Mail order permits you to retain control of all phases of the selling campaign: The idea of the subject for the book is yours; the writing or the approval of the advertising copy is solely at your discretion; the selection of the media in which to run your ads—magazines, newspapers, tabloids—is your decision; and the choice of the rental lists of names is your preference. You can, of course, get useful input from many directions for any or all of the areas of your sales promotion, but there is nothing to compare to the fun and excitement of making your own decisions on how to turn your book into a best seller. Make it your own show. Think of yourself as a movie producer charged with the responsibility of turning an idea into a hot script, and the script into a movie that's a smash hit. His challenge is basically the same as yours. It's an assignment filled with excitement and rewards.

I'm going to share with you a trade secret that should prove invaluable to you when it comes to selling your own book. Use it as a guide. And I hope it will bring to you the same results it brought to me—it skyrocketed sales of my book, *How to Get Rich in Mail Order,* to a stupendous $2,000,000. I cannot estimate what percentage of this was due to the fact that I am continually changing my ads. But I am confident that the practice does produce good results. It is a procedure I definitely recommend, at least until you become a publisher with the rare good fortune to wind up with a pre-sold best seller of such magnitude that advertising of any nature becomes a matter of minimal importance.

As previously mentioned in Chapter Four, I had an ad

that was a winner. All that was required was to continue sending out the circular with some minor changes in the copy, and, of course, put the title of the book in the order coupon. But at no time did I discontinue the practice of experimenting with the ad copy.

When do you stop experimenting with the advertising copy? You never stop. It happens to be a large part of the fun and excitement of selling books by mail. It is fascinating to structure advertising copy in such a way that it is destined to bring maximum results. Just how you make your statement, juggle and juxtapose the lines is all part of the challenge, all part of the fun. Get everything in just the right position, properly organized, effectively stated, and CLICK!, it works.

Your experimentation with ad copy is an ongoing process. You are constantly polishing, improving and refining to a point that projects you far beyond mediocrity and into the realm of high effectiveness. It is here that your sales strategy becomes unassailable and will produce a handsome financial return. Bear in mind that at all times your job is to strive for better sales. It is that motivation which will stimulate your creative talent, driving it to further heights.

Make a conscious effort to develop an awareness of advertising copy in newspapers and magazines promoting the sale of books. Let some of the good copy rub off on you. Be equally attentive to the direct mail you receive extolling the virtues of the book being offered for sale. Save these ads and study them; then decide how you would rate them. In your opinion, are they winners or losers? Why? Observe whether or not the ads have been repeated over a period of time. If they have with any reasonable degree of regularity, you can safely assume they are winners. Were you able to correctly tab some of the losers? When you see an ad repeated with regularity, save it and put yourself to the test of trying to determine what in the ad makes it a winner. If you do this often enough, before long you will have become sufficiently astute to separate the winners from the also-rans with unerring accuracy. Imagine what that could be worth to you when it comes to preparing your own ads.

The first edition of my mail-order book carried a $15.00 price tag. I had certain misgivings about the price and tested the book at $10.00. It might sell more at that figure. It was worth the try, and to my outgoing mail advertising which listed the book at $15.00, I appended an announcement in red stating the reduced price. See page 35. As it turned out, the change was justified. Sales increased substantially, and I changed the price in the next printing.

I had arrived at the $15.00 price for the book by way of compromise between the prices of two other books sold by mail order. Joe Karbo's book, *The Lazy Man's Way to Riches*, was ticketed at $10.00, while Ben Swarez's book, *Seven Steps to Financial Freedom*, was sold for $20.00. Originally, I had even considered charging $25.00 for the book, after selling myself on the psychological persuasion that because it was the highest-priced popular book on mail order, the public would decide that it had to be good. However, common sense prevailed and I yielded to the evidence in Joe Karbo's case. With a price tag of only $10.00, he was selling 250,000 copies of his book annually. So convincingly did this state a point that I wisely dropped the high price I had originally planned.

My monthly assignment is to improve the pulling power of my ads. I accomplish this by employing a combination of devices which might include writing a new ad, changing a headline, changing some of the body copy, changing graphics, using color and experimenting with price. It is not an easy assignment, but, more often than not, I'll come up with a modification that will translate into thousands of dollars. You can achieve the results you want only by constantly thinking of ways to improve your ad copy. However, changes don't always work in your favor. Some will improve the results while others may actually diminish your returns! With careful attention to your strategy, you will eventually arrive at the right formula and success will quickly follow.

As an indication of my penchant for constant change and innovation, I recently handed several copywriters the assignment of selling my mail-order book on television, using two-minute spots. The challenge to the copywriter is to write a one-minute-forty-second television commercial that will persuade the viewer to go to the phone, dial an 800 number, and order a copy of my book. A 20-second tag is required to instruct the viewer how to order.

We aspire to make our commercials as successful as that of the Ginsu knife. Our effort to emulate its success has involved making a video tape and studying it word for word, picture for picture. Would you believe it possible that someone could write a television commercial that would sell hundreds of thousands of sets of knives at $20.00 a set? However, it begins to make sense when you consider the extent to which this prize-winning commercial promoted superior performance and a 50-year guarantee. Who could resist that kind of reassurance? This ad has been repeated with consistency over a period of many years. Incidentally, the knives originally sold for $10.00 a set.

The first direct-mailing piece for my mail-order book was a self-mailer as shown on pages 37, 38, 39 and 40. Observe that the address panel contains the words: OR CURRENT OCCUPANT. This insures that even if the original addressee has moved, the mailing piece will be left with the new occupant. You can use the bulk rate, which is approximately half the cost of first-class mail. This will save you approximately $100.00 for every thousand pieces of mail.

Let us analyze some of the basic features of the circular. The first mailing, comprised of 20 different lists, totalled 100,000 names. Pages 37 and 40 could actually constitute a mailing piece. Page 37 consists of the sales-promotional copy, photos of some of the best-selling books I have published, an order form, and a 365-day money-back guarantee. Also featured is the cover of our book. Page 40 contains unsolicited testimonials from those who have read the book and chose to express their enthusiastic approval of its contents.

Subscribing to the theory that advertising copy sells books, I packed the inside pages with my story and a good overview of the book. It is my belief that if anyone were slightly interested in mail order and took the time to read those two inside pages, I'd have a sure sale. Consider the prize-winning headline to caption the center two pages:

WOULD YOU LIKE THE THRILL OF SHAKING THOU-SANDS OF $$$ FROM STACKS OF MAIL SENT TO YOU? (See pages 38 and 39.) Notice the use of the capital letters for appropriate impact. There can be no question that a headline of this nature will immediately "hook" the reader. Think of the succession of images it immediately calls to mind.

Consider the sub-headline: 25 YEARS OF SUCCESS-FUL, MONEY-MAKING SECRETS REVEALED BY MAIL-ORDER EXPERT! Can't you immediately sense the degree of credibility it lends to the main headline? Note the word SECRETS, purposely employed in the headline. Experience has established that whenever the word SECRETS can be appropriately tied into the title or headline, it will materially enhance the sale of the book. An example that at once comes to mind is a meta-physical book I have been publishing for many years *The Secret of Secrets* by U. S. Andersen. It's a big seller, and I have been told by many of its readers that they bought the book because of the title. This, again, is evi-dence of the importance of a catchy title, something we'll discuss at length later in the book.

While we're on the subject of secrets, you might glance at page 38 where I make public disclosure of what was once the best-kept secret in town. I tell my secret success story, revealing how, starting with a "kitchen-table" opera-tion, I became one of the nation's most successful mail order entrepreneurs. I mention this to instill in you the kind of incentive that will point the way to goals you've set for yourself. And remember that I attained this status not through luck nor magic but through the use of the same methods I'm prescribing for you. By the time you finish reading this book, I will have told you of every method of operation I use to help point you in the direction of success.

We spoke of the selling value of words with impact. How do you feel about the sub-heading, MAKE MORE MONEY THAN YOU CAN SPEND? Perhaps it leans a bit towards exaggeration, but it titillates the imagination of the reader. Column two has the motivational force of compelling the reader to ask specific mail-order ques-tions he would like answered.

The entire advertising copy is orchestrated with skill and precision. To me, it is suggestive of a beautiful mu-sical score. In reading, it is literate as it describes the book in a serious and logical manner, direct without ambiguity or evasiveness. Superlative advertising copy has a profound effect on me. Let me illustrate a passage that I think is truly outstanding. On page 39,

column one, I make the following statement for the serious reader: "I am not advocating a 'get-rich-over-night' scheme; there's really no such thing in legitimate business. I am talking about building up a respectable, enduring mail order business based on sound and imaginative business practices." To my way of thinking, that is terrific copy.

On page 39, column two, I again make reference to my success as an entrepreneur in mail order and employs a direct quote which I believe to be enormously effective. "For the first time I reveal the mail order secrets that have helped me generate millions of dollars worth of business!" Can you doubt that anyone even slightly interested in mail order would not be eager to hear those secrets?

On the same page, instead of supplying the book with the conventional table of contents, I use what I consider to be a very original and creative idea. In bold letters, I employ the caption: HERE IS YOUR GUIDE TO SUCCESS. This is followed by copy similar to the table of contents. All in all, it's a very effective and intelligently conceived mailing piece. One would be hard-pressed to improve on it and to match it for clarity. I urge you to use it as one of your guides. After all I've said about it, you're probably interested in knowing how well it pulled. Three of the ten lists paid off, and I continued mailing it to those lists.

In picking 10 lists, I chose five that I thought would pay off, and five that were totally unrelated to one's interest in making money through mail order. The latter five were long shots—and they didn't pay off. I knew the chances were slim, but I still wanted to use the 50,000 names they listed for experimental reasons.

Let's experiment as to how well you're doing so far. Here's your first test. I want you to make a judgment on a piece of mail-order copy. Read pages 41, 42, 43 and 44. This four-page circular has the questions in red ink. Your assignment is to decide which four-page circular—the first one I referred to, or this one—pulled better, and con-tinues to pull better. I'd also like you to decide why you selected one in preference to the other. Or might it be your opinion that they both pulled equally well? Please read the question-and-answer circular and make your evaluation before reading further.

After I had used the original circular for about two years, I tried an entirely different style of circular, one which ws totally uncomplicated and of the question-and-answer variety. It was so simple in make-up that it could easily be read in a matter of minutes. We originally printed the entire circular in black. When, at a later time, we changed the printing color of the questions to red, the results were significantly better. Accordingly, I am continuing to use the question-and-answer circular exclusively and have dropped what I term "a prize-winning circular." The decision has increased the sales of my books appreciably, despite the fact that this circular has none of the literary style of the first. Surely there is a reason for it. Can you guess what it is? In any case, you might want to adopt this form of circular for your own book. Why not go with a proven winner.?

See page 44 for another illustration of how books are sold in a way that is advantageous to both seller and buyer, but particularly to the seller. Observe that in response to the question as to what the first step is in getting started profitably in mail order, the reader is directed to visit his local bookstore and/or library. As a result, we have received countless orders from book dealers who normally would not have ordered my book. The orders are frequently accompanied by letters which, in effect, say that they have had several requests for the book, *How to Get Rich in Mail Order*. I fill the orders immediately with the usual trade discount, and, together with an explanatory letter, enclose a current catalog of my books which contains around 400 titles. This practice has opened up many new accounts, resulting in the sale of a great many books—something which might otherwise not have occurred.

Because of my policy of referring readers to their local libraries, I have sold thousands of copies of my mail-order book. Here, too, I follow the procedure of thanking the librarian and sending a copy of my catalog. It's the opportunity to familiarize the librarian with my complete catalog that makes the pay-off so profitable. As an example, I publish five books on the subject of calligraphy. I have sold thousands of copies as a result of the initial contact I made with the librarians. In fact, I've sold them more books on calligraphy than on the subject of mail order, a perfect example of follow-up sales not even related to the initial offer. Incidentally, the usual discount to libraries is 20% off the list price.

It's a marketing plan that works well. If you were to check your local library, the chances are you would find a copy of my mail-order book, just as you would in every B. Dalton bookstore and all the Waldens, both firms among the leaders in the country. The technique which has made this so workable and has pyramided sales on a continuing basis throughout the years will be comprehensively discussed in the next chapter. You should have no difficulty putting it to work in your own hometown.

To supplement the direct-mail sales of my book, I used display ads in magazines, tabloids and newspapers. The continuing challenge for you and me should always be the ability to produce an ad that will either generate a sale or invite inquiries to which you can reply with sales literature. This, in turn, will result in sales.

Once you've achieved the ability to create display ads that will promote sales, not only will you receive a great deal of personal satisfaction, but your career as a publisher and book seller will start to prosper. It is, therefore, enormously important for you to judge the pulling power of ads.

You may sometimes wonder whether it is possible to teach someone to become an excellent ad writer. Whether it's possible to teach someone to become any kind of writer—for ads, novels, screenplays, newspapers—is a moot question. We don't know the answer. But what we do know is that through education it is very possible to sharpen one's innate abilities and significantly increase one's potential. So don't ever excuse yourself from participation on the theory that you don't have the talent to write. Allow books and skilled people to help you and you'll be surprised how well you'll do. I'm sure that many of our top display ads were written by people who once really believed they didn't have writing skills.

Now, just for practice, and in an effort to start sharpening your skills, I'm going to ask you again to act as a judge and try to determine which of several are the best-pulling ads. Assume you, not I, had written the mail-order book. Three ads are submitted to you, of which you are to choose one to run in print. Which one would you select? See pages 45, 46 and 47.

I actually ran all three ads. Which, in your opinion, came in first, second, and last? Note your answer and reasons, and then explain the points you took into account in arriving at your decision. As you can readily understand, this exercise is a highly important one as it confronts you with the kind of decisions you're going to have to make in the marketing of your own book. I happen to know the answers, but only because I spent thousands of dollars testing the ads.

AN IMPULSE MADE ME BOSS OF MY OWN $1,000,000-A-YEAR MAIL-ORDER BUSINESS. I hope that's the ad you picked, because that one, on page 45, is the winner. Second best, on page 46, was MONEY-

MAKING $ECRET$ REVEALED BY SELF-MADE MIL-LIONAIRE! Finishing last was SELF-MADE MIL-LIONARE REVEALS HIS $ECRET$. RESULTS GUAR-ANTEED!

In retrospect, I've come to the conclusion that the third ad was hurt by the use of the phrase, RESULTS GUAR-ANTEED. Somehow this seems to deprive the ad of credibility. Do you agree?

I think the ad that ran second (page 46) is an excellent ad. What is there about the ad on page 45 that makes it a winner? The answer is to be found in column two of the ad—*solid copy*. The ad deals in specifics rather than in "dream copy." Do you agree with that assessment? Al-though in this instance I am faulting the ad for its "dream copy," all such copy is not to be denounced as ineffec-tive. Some of my most successful ads have been com-posed entirely of "dream copy." There is no general rule. The character of each ad must depend upon the particu-lar circumstances of the case in point.

What you actually have been doing is making a study of the evolution of my ads. This sampling is just a small portion of the many ads I have run in marketing my book on mail order. I've spent thousands of dollars testing var-ious elements in the ad. We can all be experts after the fact. What's not so easy is deciding in advance just what the right ingredients are to make the ad a winner. Your chances to come up with the right answer will be materi-ally enhanced if you will make a careful, conscientious and inquisitive probe of each of the ads. Study them as you would a textbook, for contained within them might lie the key to your future success.

And now the final test for this chapter. Study the ad on page 48. Is it your opinion that this ad did or did not pull better than the one on page 45—AN IMPULSE MADE ME BOSS OF MY OWN $1,000,000-A-YEAR MAIL-OR-DER BUSINESS? If you believe that it did, what is the basis for your answer? Compare your answer with mine.

In our first ads we printed only testimonials of people who had read the book and commented favorably on it. There were no success stories. Now, for the first time, we are printing testimonials of people who have been profit-ably using the techniques explained in my mail-order book. Let's take a look at those figures which are in-cluded here. They made great advertising copy, particu-larly in the headline and in bold type. They made it the best-pulling ad of its time.

I am currently running a series of "blind ads." This, in effect, means that the reader is unaware of the fact that

what he is ordering is a book on mail order. I am also testing a package of two books on the subject of mail order for $20.00.

It would be natural for you to ask, "When do the copy changes stop?" The answer is that if you're astute, com-mitted and progressive, the changes never stop. Your advertisements are the lifeline to your sales and ultimate success. It behooves you to become as proficient and professional as you can possibly become, both in writing and in recognizing good copy. Start paying close atten-tion to the commercials on television. These are the work of high-salaried experts. Try to decide whether you could do just as well, or, perhaps, better. There is every likelihood that you could. You might even write a couple of two-minute commercials for your book.

Once you've become knowledgeable and proficient in the techniques of mail-order advertising, your chances for success will increase. You'll have the facility for trans-lating what you know into good, solid advertising copy, and that, in turn, will sell your book.

Even after 25 years of successfully mail-ordering books, I still look forward with anticipation to the results of new ads. I'm particularly eager to see how our ads will do on television. And I'm always looking for ways to improve my efforts. Would you like a chance to write for me? All right, here's a writing assignment for you. Write a two-minute television commercial for my book, *How to Get Rich in Mail Order.* That's about 250 words or one 8½" x 11" sheet of copy double-spaced. If your creation turns out to be a winner, I'll pay you handsomely for your effort, and I'll give you further assignments.

As I have previously mentioned, I am a songwriter and one who is fortunate enough to live near Hollywood, the music center of the West. I sold some of my songs be-cause I had the inner strength to refute discouragement when I was turned down by record company personnel. An example of my perseverance is connected with an album, *The Willie Burgundy Five on the Midnight Train from Boston.* I spent months producing the album. I hired the very best musical arranger in Hollywood, and when I recorded the music I hired the very best studio musicians that money could buy. I even paid double-time. I finally had my "masterpiece." I was confident it would be an easy sale. How wrong I was. It was a Hercu-lean task just to get someone in authority to listen to it. The turndowns were issued with courtesy, but with total indifference to the record. Occasionally, a record execu-tive would listen to a song for 30 seconds, and then ren-der an automatic rejection with "It's just not for us." I can't tell you how many doors I knocked on before I finally got a breakthrough and sold the album to MGM Records, Inc. in Hollywood. See page 36.

Trying to get people to listen to your material, only to meet with rejection, is certainly not the most pleasant part of the business. But I can assure you, it's just as important as the creative part. I certainly don't consider myself the world's greatest songwriter, but I know that what I might lack in talent I more than compensate for in conviction, perseverance and discipline. My reservoir of strength stems from a belief in myself. Once I believed with all my heart that I had a song with the potential of becoming a hit, I was prepared to run with it until I got it recorded.

And therein lies my message to you. When it comes to success, there are no half-measures. Become involved not only in the writing, but with the mechanics of constructing a productive program for your book. To become a success doesn't happen by luck or by chance. It happens by design, the only indestructible formula that true success has ever known.

I think you're really going to like the next chapter because it spells out one of the most enjoyable rewards of developing an expertise in your chosen line of work. Money can't buy the degree of personal satisfaction you'll find in conducting and teaching seminars in your particular field of expertise. I'll discuss with you some of the important guidelines in conducting seminars to ensure that they will be as pleasurable for you as for your students.

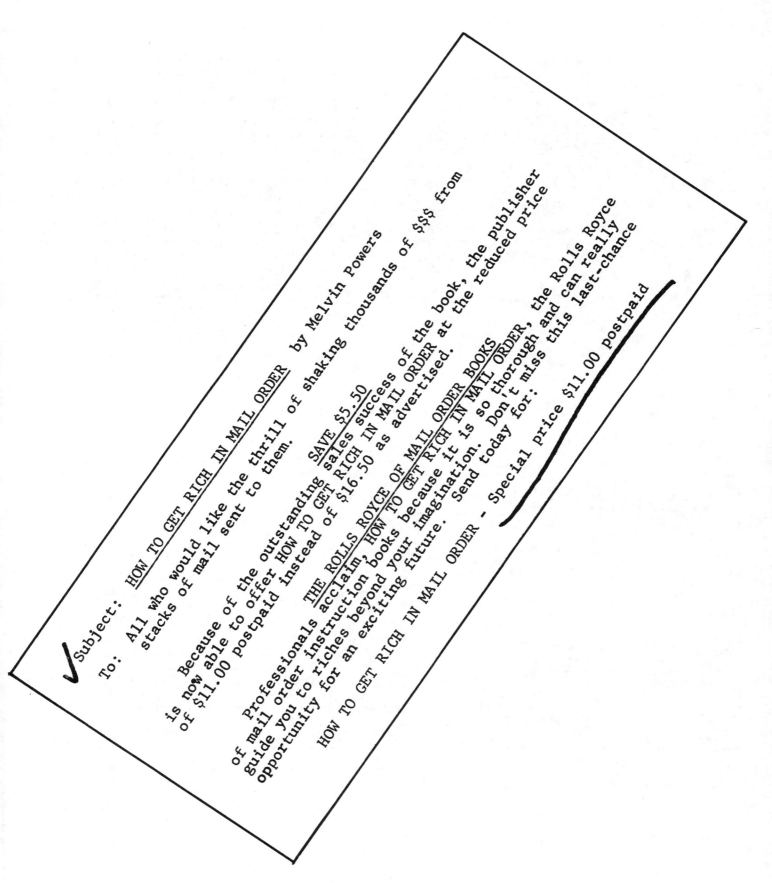

Subject: HOW TO GET RICH IN MAIL ORDER by Melvin Powers

To: All who would like the thrill of shaking thousands of $$$ from stacks of mail sent to them.

SAVE $5.50

Because of the outstanding sales success of the book, the publisher is now able to offer HOW TO GET RICH IN MAIL ORDER at the reduced price of $11.00 postpaid instead of $16.50 as advertised.

THE ROLLS ROYCE OF MAIL ORDER BOOKS

Professionals acclaim HOW TO GET RICH IN MAIL ORDER, the Rolls Royce of mail order instruction books because it is so thorough and can really guide you to riches beyond your imagination. Don't miss this last-chance opportunity for an exciting future. Send today for:

HOW TO GET RICH IN MAIL ORDER - Special price $11.00 postpaid

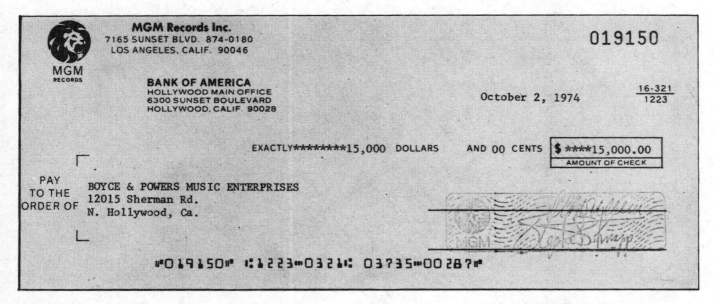

Here's a $15,000 check from MGM Records to Tommy Boyce & Melvin Powers Music Enterprises representing an advance against royalties for the album WILLIE BURGUNDY FIVE—ON THE MIDNIGHT TRAIN FROM BOSTON

AN EXPERT'S GUIDE TO GETTING RICH IN THE FASCINATING WORLD OF MAIL ORDER

Have you purchased any of the best sellers illustrated on this page?

Every one of the best sellers illustrated on this page is mine. That's right, I published them all, and their total sales run into the millions. How did I do it? My new book, *How to Get Rich in Mail Order*, reveals in detail how I hit the jackpot again and again—and how *you* can, too! I give you a precise plan that will help you create your own best sellers while you realize the same financial success I have enjoyed.

You see, although my book encompasses every aspect of the vast field of mail order, the emphasis is on making money by selling special interest and "how to" books. Is it easy? Yes, once you are armed with the knowledge that I will give you.

I outline clearly and concisely the creative processes involved.

I tell you how to sell books by mail order and how to merchandise them with proven, sure-fire techniques.

I explain how to deal expertly with bookstores, special interest retail outlets, and wholesalers.

And, because advertising is the key to it all, I reproduce my prize-winning ads and money-making direct mail literature, explain how the ads were created, why they produced gigantic sales, and how you can duplicate these techniques for your own mail order success.

WOULD YOU LIKE THE THRILL OF SHAKING THOUS.

25 YEARS OF SUCCESSFUL, MONEY-MAKING SECRETS REVEALED

Dear Friend:

I'm Melvin Powers, founder and president of the Wilshire Book Company, specializing in selling books by mail. For the past 25 years, I've sold millions of dollars worth of books and products all over the world through mail order, and I'm proud to be known as the "dean of mail order publishing." I can show you how you, too, can attain great financial success by using the proven techniques revealed in my new book, which details the secrets of the lucrative world of mail order.

The multiple opportunities in mail order are overwhelming. Consider this: mail order businesses do $77 billion a year in sales, and many individual entrepreneurs, such as myself, account for millions of that $77 billion every year. It's a booming field and there's lots of room and profit in it for you, too. All you need is the will to take steps to begin—in your spare time.

In typical Horatio Alger fashion, I started out slowly in Hollywood with a "kitchen table" operation. As a young man from Boston new to the area, my initial efforts were filled with trial and error. But soon I could afford a small office, so I rented a room from an advertising agency located on the famous Sunset Strip. This proved to be the biggest bargain of my life. My proximity to sophisticated copywriters, art directors, type experts, marketing men, and media buyers enabled me to converse with them daily. This first-hand exposure gave me a free education—and I gathered a mother lode of information that led me straight to gold. I have been living and practicing their philosophies every day of my mail order career.

I learned everything I could about classified and display ads, direct mail, letters, brochures, catalogs, take-ones, freebies, and radio and television advertising. I learned about lead costs, conversion costs, and costs per thousand—in short, I accumulated a wealth of data that eliminated many trial-and-error failures and paved the way to success. I learned valuable shortcuts—what to do and what not to do—and all the fundamentals necessary to make an advertisement succeed. Above all, I learned that advertising is the key to any successful mail order operation. Today, I have a building of 15,000 square feet plus additional storage space, 21 employees, and an inventory of over 400 book titles ready for immediate shipment. I work only three days a week to keep it running smoothly and profitably.

MAKE MORE MONEY THAN YOU CAN SPEND

In a comprehensive, concise, detailed manner, I elaborate on the proven practices that will soon have you shaking checks, cash, and money orders from their envelopes after the mail arrives each morning. It's a demonstrable fact that copying success brings success. My book not only tells you how it's done, but shows you how you can achieve your own success and financial independence. In addition to the more than 200 pages of illustrations it contains, my book gives numerous case histories and many examples of winning mail order advertisements that hit the sales jackpot over and over again. You will learn why certain ads worked, why certain headlines pulled, and why some copy may have been effective in one case but not in another.

Everything is explained in clear, simple language free of technical jargon so that you can use each example as a format for your own fast profit, no matter what you are selling. These techniques are the very same ones I've used profitably. As a mail order consultant, I have been paid handsomely by clients for just this kind of information.

The book focuses on how the beginner can make money in the mail order business. If you come to it prepared, it is easier than you think. The principles, practices, theories, and pitfalls have all been charted to help you escape failure and organized to insure your success.

Specific questions have been dealt with in detail:

- How do you know if you're the successful mail order type, and how do you get started?

- How much cash do you need up front?

- How, when, and where do you tell people about your product? How do you do it without paying a penny?

- How do you write blockbuster, sales-generating ads, and what are the most important selling words in the ad?

- How do you analyze responses, pyramid sales, and maximize profit margins?

- How do you start a catalog, and which are the best months of the year to mail it?

Answers to these and many more questions are examples of some of the crucial insights I have gained and now offer to you. The important thing to remember is the money-making formula is there. The next step is up to you. How many times have you thought about having your own business and being your own boss? There is no more satisfying and fulfilling way to live. This is your opportunity to make your secret dreams come true.

Start to read the book and you'll soon realize that the facts, principles, and examples revealed can change your life, as they have changed the lives of many others. This virtual encyclopedia of mail order knowledge is written in an easygoing style that makes it simple to understand. And the illustrations can't be beat. Winning advertisements, for example, are reproduced on full 8½" × 11" pages.

Most important, though, is the way the "Melvin Powers techniques of mail order," diligently applied, will work for you as they have for others. I'll show you how to develop expertise in—

- finding unique, profitable products

- making money with creative classified and display ads

- writing headlines that translate into dollars

- using trigger words that build visual images in your reader's mind

- determining when to use short or long copy

- selling virtually any product or service by direct mail

- copycatting successful mail order operations

- creating a fortune quickly from very little investment

You may wonder why I am trying to sell you a book about mail order if my own business is so successful. To make more money, of course! That's part of my business—another facet of the back end of the mail order business, such as selling additional books and products, renting names, and conducting seminars.

Here is my promise: if you are ambitious and willing to work with diligence and dedication, I can help you become financially independent. I can help you pyramid your initial mail order profits into an amount of money that will spell

IDS OF $$$ FROM STACKS OF MAIL SENT TO YOU?
Y MAIL ORDER EXPERT!

wealth and financial security for you. All you need do is conscientiously use the plan I have devised for you.

How can I make such a promise like this that sounds too good to be true? Because I have devoted years of hard work and intensive research to the development of a technique that has consistently worked for me and, through the changing years, has successfully withstood every kind of economic challenge.

The technique is a factual, realistic blueprint for the accumulation of big money. It gives specific guidance on how to start and build from scratch. I provide you with innumerable sources for new products to sell. I reveal the secrets that have helped many individuals to become millionaires in a relatively short time.

My book is filled with success stories to inspire, to encourage, to follow. I use the actual names of persons, reproduce their prize-winning ads, and clarify the rationale governing their operations. Then I clearly explain how you can duplicate their success by creating your own money-making ideas and transforming them into personal wealth. I'll show you how you can take a good idea and make a fortune from it, even in your spare time.

I advise my readers to invest as little as possible while testing methods leading to the probability of success. Mail order is a unique business because it does not demand that you start with a large investment. You can start with an idea, invest a small amount of money, pyramid your profits, and become extremely wealthy.

I share with you the secrets of experts on how to get free display ads that can quickly put you on the road to riches. Yes, thousands of dollars worth of free ads will help you test the probability of your product's success while you put dollars in your pocket. This information alone is worth the price of the book.

In fact, the same could be said for each of the chapters in the book. My favorite chapter is, "How to Make Your Advertising Copy Sizzle to Make You Wealthy." Good advertising copy is the thrust that sets the wheels of mail order in motion. On that subject, I reveal how you can write prize-winning ads. To emphasize the book's enormous practicality, all the highly informative aspects of this how-to-do-it text are enhanced with numerous illustrations.

In this same chapter I share with you the details of how I, a complete novice in the field of music, wrote a song that not only became a hit but, sung by Connie Cato on Capitol Records, won an ASCAP award! Remarkably, the song, *Who Wants a Slightly Used Woman?*, was the subject of two phone calls in one week from major record companies in Nashville, each wanting to record it.

Writing and selling this song was accomplished by using the very same mail order principles and techniques discussed in my book.

The book points out the wide variety of opportunities that await you in the mail order business, each one offering you the prospect of becoming a winner on your own terms. If read with proper motivation, the book will give you your chance now for an exciting, new career as your own boss. Best of all, you can operate your mail order business in your spare time and still realize financial success.

Virtually no overhead is needed to begin your operation. Using the Melvin Powers special mail order techniques, your investment is minimal. I am not advocating a "get-rich-overnight" scheme; there's really no such thing in legitimate business. I am talking about building up a respectable, enduring mail order business, based on sound and imaginative business practices.

Mail order represents a special way of doing business that requires creativity. As I demonstrate and explain numerous examples of my creative thinking (and that of others) which have resulted in ever-increasing stacks of mail and profits, you will inevitably be helped to develop your own creative potential. For the very first time, I reveal the mail order secrets that have helped me generate millions of dollars worth of business.

Mine is a unique mail order book, predicated on my 25 years of success as an entrepreneur in the mail order field. It is based on fact and practical experience —success and not theory. I give you professional techniques for building a profitable business, starting with classified and one-inch display ads. Even if you are currently in the mail order business, I can guarantee you greater sales as a direct result of using my special mail order techniques.

There's a gold mine waiting to be discovered! Follow my course of proven instruction, and the opportunity to become rich is yours!

Now here is my unique guarantee. I'm so confident you will begin to reap riches within one year that the book is sold with a 365-day guarantee. If, for any reason, the book does not live up to your expectations or you are not making the money you anticipate, return the book and I will immediately refund your money. What other publisher offers a one-year guarantee?

HERE IS YOUR GUIDE TO SUCCESS

Examine the table of contents:

1. How to Develop Your Mail Order Expertise
2. How to Find a Unique Product or Service to Sell
3. How to Make Money with Classified Ads
4. How to Make Money with Display Ads
5. The Unlimited Potential for Making Money with Direct Mail
6. How to Copycat Successful Mail Order Operations
7. How I Created A Best Seller Using the Copycat Technique
8. How to Start and Run a Profitable Mail Order, Special Interest Book or Record Business
9. I Enjoy Selling Books by Mail—Some of My Successful and Not-So-Successful Ads and Direct Mail Circulars
10. Five of My Most Successful Direct Mail Pieces That Sold and Are Still Selling Millions of Dollars Worth of Books
11. Melvin Powers' Mail Order Success Strategy—Follow It and You'll Become a Millionaire
12. How to Sell Your Products to Mail Order Companies, Retail Outlets, Jobbers, and Fund Raisers for Maximum Distribution and Profits
13. How to Get Free Display Ads and Publicity That Can Put You on the Road to Riches
14. How to Make Your Advertising Copy Sizzle to Make You Wealthy
15. Questions and Answers to Help You Get Started Making Money in Your Own Mail Order Business
16. A Personal Word from Melvin Powers

Send your check or money order for
How to Get Rich in Mail Order by Melvin Powers.

Invest today for tomorrow's riches.

Price $10.00 plus $1.00 postage.

Copyright 1980 by Melvin Powers

HOW TO GET RICH IN MAIL ORDER
by Melvin Powers

Comments from readers. All letters are on file as required by the United States Federal Trade Commission. Initials are used to preserve the privacy of the individual.

How to Get Rich in Mail Order is, without a doubt, the finest book ever written on the subject I have spent several hundred dollars on mail order books and none can compare with yours. I now have a picture of what mail order is all about. Thanks again for your informative book. It will have the place of honor in my mail order library.　　　　G. W., Laguna Hills, California

How to Get Rich in Mail Order is worth much more than you charge for it! It is a combination training manual, directory, practice workbook and personal motivator! It deserves to be read, re-read, studied, and applied.　　　　S. S., Pomona, California

Just finished reading your book, *How to Get Rich in Mail Order*, and, of all the books I have read on mail order, yours is tops. Thanks for writing such a beautiful and informative book. I've gained more knowledge from it than from the others put together.
　　　　B. G., Tampa, Florida

I've just read your very interesting and informative book, *How to Get Rich in Mail Order*. It has really motivated me to succeed in the mail order business.
　　　　J. S., Warren, Ohio

I have just completed your book *How to Get Rich in Mail Order*. It is fantastic. Do you ever rest? Your mind must be working full speed 24 hours a day to have accomplished what you have. I have also read and studied other courses, but your book, in my opinion tops them all by a wide margin.　　T. E., Boca Raton, Florida

Am sending this letter to thank you for writing *How to Get Rich in Mail Order*. It is one of the most helpful, enjoyable, readable, and well written "how to" books I've ever read. Your method of getting the reader involved, of asking questions, and of providing mental exercises worked wonders for me. It kept my mind receptive and alert to whatever you were presenting. Thank you again for your tremendously helpful book and for your assistance in getting me started. E. S., San Rafael, California

After reading your wonderful book, *How to Get Rich in Mail Order*, I feel that I know you as a personal friend. I have read many books on mail order and self-publishing, but yours is in a class by itself—head and shoulders above the rest.　　　　E. K., Great Falls, Montana

Never have I read such a book as *How to Get Rich in Mail Order*. It has to be the book of the year. Thank you for what is going to change my entire life.
　　　　W. J., Houston, Texas

Looking forward to the day when I, as a thriving mail order entrepreneur, can meet you personally and thank you for helping me get started.　K. V., Manfield, Ohio

I know you have another winner in your book, *How to Get Rich in Mail Order*. The book was fantastic in its coverage and examples. Believe me, I have read them all and your book is on the top of the list!
　　　　D. K., Western Springs, Illinois

How to Get Rich in Mail Order really has me talking to myself. The wealth of information it contains makes it more like a reference book than anything I have seen relating to the field.　R. K., Landover Hills, Maryland

Have just received your new book, *How to Get Rich in Mail Order*. It is quite a compendium on mail order and one of the most exhaustive, complete treatises on the subject that I have ever read.
　　　　L. O., Prospect Heights, Illinois

Want you to know your book, *How to Get Rich in Mail Order*, is fantastic. I have never tried mail order before and am excited about getting into it.
　　　　S. K., Bakersfield, California

Am impressed with your mail order book. It is thorough, covers solid information for the person about to invest in the mail order business, and points up many worthwhile suggestions for established mail order people.　　　　G. P., Chicago, Illinois

I received your excellent book, *How to Get Rich in Mail Order*, and am enjoying page after fascinating page. One of the elements greatly appreciated is your openness and freeness to share your knowledge with others.　　　　E. G., Huntington Beach, California

This letter is to acknowledge receipt of *How to Get Rich in Mail Order* and to congratulate you on putting together such a fine informative book.
　　　　F. S., Bergton, Virginia

I have just finished reading your book, *How to Get Rich in Mail Order*. You give authoritative and unhedged advice to both the mail order beginner and to the "old pro." You're definitely an inspiration.
　　　　M. W., Encino, California

Late last night I spent a most enjoyable hour reading your new book. It was a lot of fun. I'd like to sell your new book to my friends. I had in mind keeping a stack of 10 copies or more in my office so that when friends stop by here I'll encourage them to take a copy with them. Have you determined your wholesale price yet? Let me know and I'll send you a check for 10 copies.
　　　　J. F., Torrance, California

Your mail order book is fantastic and fun to read. It is the most complete and thorough book I've ever read on the subject. Congratulations.
　　　　J. S., Montecito, California

FREQUENTLY ASKED QUESTIONS AND THE ANSWERS THAT WILL HELP YOU START TO MAKE MONEY IN YOUR OWN PROFITABLE MAIL ORDER BUSINESS

Question: Can the average person make money in mail order?

Answer: Yes. There is nothing unique about the thousands of individuals who are successfully making extra money in mail order. They are following sound mail-order techniques--techniques you can learn from my book *How to Get Rich in Mail Order* or audio cassette program *Mail Order Millionaire*, which includes a copy of my book. If you are willing to invest the time necessary to attain your financial goals, I'm willing to help you.

Question: Do I need an office?

Answer: No. Conduct business from your home until your volume necessitates moving into business quarters. Keep overhead to a minimum.

Question: How can I find products to sell?

Answer: My book contains numerous sources for suitable mail order products. Simply zero in on something you would like to sell.

Question: How do I know how much inventory to order?

Answer: Initially, whenever possible, make arrangements to have merchandise drop-shipped until you can estimate how much inventory to carry. Drop-shipping means that orders are shipped to your customer by your supplier upon receipt of your instructions and payment. This is done only after you receive payment from your customer. Thus, you avoid spending money on inventory and can concentrate on sales.

Question: Can you recommend a supplier of gift items who will drop-ship merchandise?

Answer: I enthusiastically recommend Specialty Merchandise Corporation. This company was founded in 1946 and has supplied mail order dealers with a reliable source of products from all over the world. You can select from over 3,000 items. Write to: Specialty Merchandise Corporation, Mail Order Dept. 322, 6061 De Soto Avenue, Woodland Hills, California 91365. If you are in the Los Angeles area, you can visit the showroom and see merchandise on display. The showroom is open Monday through Saturday.

Question: In which magazines should I advertise?

Answer: The same ones that other mail order companies use to sell products similar to yours. These magazines, which consistently run the same ads, are the survivors of the trial-and-error method of choosing media employed by successful advertisers. That doesn't mean you can't experiment. Hunches sometimes pay off. But customers, by habit, have become programmed to look in particular publications for specific types of merchandise. I advise you to take advantage of the publication's ability to attract a large audience that is interested in the type of merchandise you have to sell. Then your challenge will be to attract the attention of potential customers and sell them your product or service from the ad, or motivate them to send for further information.

Question: I have heard that some magazines will run a free advertisement on a product. Is this true?

Answer: Yes. In my book, I devote a chapter on how you can get free ads to put you on the road to riches. You should also try to get free publicity in your local newspapers. An excellent book on the subject is *Publicity: How to Get It* by Richard O'Brien. If your local library or bookstore doesn't have it, you can get a copy from my office for $12.00 postpaid.

Question: Should I run a classified, or display ad?

Answer: My advice is to begin with a classified ad.

Question: Should I sell directly from the ad, or offer free literature?

Answer: I suggest you offer free literature. It takes too many expensive words to write a classified ad that will convince people to send money. Once you draw the inquiries, send advertising literature to do the selling.

Question: What should I include in the advertising literature?

Answer: As much concise information as possible about your product or service. Stress the benefits to be derived and support them with testimonials from authorities in the field or from satisfied customers. Include illustrations and specifications, if the items call for it. State price, postage, and guarantee. Don't forget to ask for the order!

Question: I'm using the two-step approach to sell my product. What is the optimum sales literature package?

Answer: The literature that comprises the classic response to an inquiry is a sales letter, advertising literature that includes photographs or art work of the product, testimonials, guarantee, credit card option, toll-free 800 telephone number, postage paid reply envelope, and an incentive (such as a gift) for prompt response.

However, it may not be necessary to use the optimum literature. This is something you need to find out because of the expense involved in printing, envelopes, and postage. Your objective is to develop a mailing package that will generate maximum response at the lowest cost. Keep testing until you are satisfied that you have achieved this. For example, you might not need four-color circulars to sell your product or expensive coated stock for your mailing pieces.

Question: Can you recommend a source that has non-fiction books and will drop-ship single orders?

Answer: My own Wilshire Book Company drop-ships and can supply beautifully illustrated brochures like the ones enclosed, advertising 300 books on a wide range of subjects, such as astrology, chess, cooking, gambling,health, hobbies, humor, hypnotism, marriage, sex, parenthood, metaphysics and occult, self-help and inspirational, sports, pets and horses.

In my book, I tell in detail how I created a bestseller that took exactly one day to write and 50¢ to produce. Following my instructions, you could do the same. I also give you sources for out-of-print books, records, and tapes in perfect condition at a fraction of their original cost. These items are excellent for mail order as they are highly profitable.

Question: What is the best way to get started selling books?

Answer: Choose a category and contact publishers selling that particular type of book. You'll find them in *Subject Guide to Books in Print*, a reference guide found at all public libraries. Inquire whether the publishers will drop-ship books for you. If not, order the books as you receive the orders. When you determine which books are selling well, order small quantities and gradually build your inventory. Advertise the same way you would for a product.

Question: I think I have a good mail order idea and want to run a display ad. How many ads should I run to begin with?

Answer: Run one advertisement in the best of the publications that you think would logically produce orders for your type of product. Although you would get a better advertising rate by committing to running three times in succession, I advise against it. If your first ad doesn't pay off, you'll be wasting money by running the next two. Generally, ads do not pull better with repetition. Running one time gives you the opportunity to revise and strengthen your ad as soon as you have determined that it needs to be improved. The rule in mail order is to keep testing to minimize your losses and maximize your earnings. If you have written an ad that pulls well, your potential customers will still be there when you run your ad again.

Question: What are the best months to advertise?

Answer: The best mail order months are September, October, November, January, February and March. The first three months of the year are great because people are home much more during the winter than at other times of the year. That means more time for reading and activating New Year's resolutions for self-improvement. Many companies do the greatest percentage of their business during the months of September, October, and November. These months produce a great volume of orders, as people buy gifts for the holidays. Some products have a well-established seasonal period. If yours is one that does, accept it, and advertise accordingly.

Question: I have found a product and have written an ad. How do I know I've written a good one that will pull?

Answer: Do market research on it by asking friends and family what they think of the ad. In time, you'll develop a sixth sense about what works. Keep in mind that your success depends not only upon finding a product, but in developing and recognizing copy that will sell it. Advertising copy is the catalyst that makes your operation go. Spending small amounts of money on good ads will lead to success. Spending a fortune on ads that don't have a chance will spell disaster. Don't fall in love with your advertising copy. Be willing to change it to make it better. My favorite book on advertising is *How to Write a Good Advertisement* by Victor O. Schwab. If your local library or bookstore doesn't have it, you can obtain a copy from my office for $22.00 postpaid.

Question: How can I further develop a sense of what might be a good mail order product?

Answer: By studying the repeat advertisements in publications, analyzing the direct mail that you receive, reading success stories in publications, and reading books dealing with all phases of mail order. Eventually, you'll develop that indefinable sixth sense for knowing what is right.

Question: What are some of the reasons people are not successful in mail order?

Answer: I have found the common denominators to be a lack of information and conviction as to what makes a good mail order product. People often have perfectly good products, but lack persuasive advertising copy. Poor returns cause them to doubt their products and give up before they find out they have winners.

Question: I have an uneasy feeling that I will not be successful even though I understand the principles and procedures to follow. Do you have any comments about this?

Answer: Fear of failure is a common apprehension among beginners in any field of endeavor. Success seems so far down the road. It may be difficult to imagine yourself as being successful, but your potential for success is as great as anyone else's. Don't worry about it. Proceed one step at a time, initially setting only small goals. You'll be exhilarated when the first order puts you into the mail order business. Belief will come with experience.

Question: What's the first step to start making money in mail order?

Answer: Read my book *How to Get Rich in Mail Order* published by Wilshire Book Company. It is carried by B. Dalton, Walden, Crown, and most independent bookstores. It's 8½" x 11" and contains 352 pages and 200 illustrations. The book is jam-packed with details and examples of my own successful and not so successful media advertising and direct mail campaigns--all used as teaching aids that give you the benefit of my 40 years of mail order experience.

Mail 30-Day No-Risk Coupon Today

YES, I want to invest in my future.

( ) Please send me *How to Get Rich in Mail Order*. $20.00 plus $2.00 S&H. (CA res. $23.65)

( ) Please send me the *Melvin Powers Mail Order Millionaire Course*, which includes the book *How to Get Rich in Mail Order*, 11 cassette tapes of practical instruction and the special bonus tape, *50 Proven Mail Order Products*. $100.00 plus $7.00 S&H. (CA res. $115.25)

Enclosed is my ( ) check ( ) money order for $_____ payable to Melvin Powers.
Charge to my ( ) Visa ( ) MasterCard. Or call (818) 765-8579.

Number_____ Expiration Date_____

Name_____ Date_____
                        (Please print)

Address_____
                (Give street address for UPS delivery)

City_____State_____Zip_____

Mail to: Melvin Powers, 12015 Sherman Road, North Hollywood, California 91605

Whatever you do, don't miss this last-chance opportunity...
MONEY-MAKING $ECRET$ REVEALED BY SELF-MADE MILLIONAIRE!

Would you like to experience the thrill of shaking thousands of dollars from stacks of mail sent to you? If your answer is "yes," I can positively make this scene become a reality for you. How can I make such a statement? Easily—because I'm shaking those thousands of dollars out of envelopes myself every single business day of the year and I'm willing to share my money-making secrets with you. Does it sound too good to be true? Take a few minutes to read on, because an exciting future filled with riches is yours for the asking. That's my promise, and this is your lucky day!

In addition to enjoying financial success, I have the satisfaction of knowing that the remarkable books I publish enrich people's lives and bring them genuine fulfillment. You have no doubt read or heard of some of the many books I publish that have achieved international acclaim: *Psycho-Cybernetics, Think and Grow Rich, Magic of Thinking Big, I Will, New Guide to Rational Living, Three Magic Words, Ability to Love,* and *You Are Not the Target.*

SECRETS REVEALED FOR FIRST TIME

The field of mail order is filled with success stories in which people start with an idea and little money and pyramid their earnings into fortunes. There is no end to the variety of ways to make money in mail order.

I personally love selling how-to and special interest books by mail. I have published over 500 different books covering a wide variety of subjects. My book *How to Get Rich in Mail Order* concentrates on instruction in selling your own or other publishers' books. I tell you how to come up with book ideas, how to get them written, and how you can successfully publish them *only after you know you have a winner!*

In fact, I'll show you exactly how I sold millions of copies of the book, *Psycho-Cybernetics,* by Maxwell Maltz, M.D., as well as other million sellers. I reveal to you how I recently created a 48-page best seller, *How to Flatten Your Tush* by Coach Marge Reardon, based on the idea of spoofing exercise and diet books. The book took exactly one day to write, 20¢ to produce, and made a small fortune for me. Besides selling it by mail order, I sold it to every bookstore in America using mail order techniques. And to top it all off, I had the book prominently displayed on check-out counters next to the cash register. I tell exactly how I did it by showing you mail order ads, actual copies of orders for thousands of books, book reviews, and publicity releases. I even got the fictional author on TV and radio. It was easy to do, and you could do the same thing following my step-by-step instruction.

YOU CAN TRUST ME TO HELP MAKE YOUR SECRET DREAMS COME TRUE!

The chances are you have some of the books I publish in your home. I've taken my share of the vast amount of wealth from mail order buyers around the world and, because the mail order business has been so good to me, I want to share my success with you. That success formula reveals in detail how I keep hitting the jackpot again and again, making millions of dollars. You can, too! In fact, I give you a detailed plan that will help you create your own best sellers while you realize the same financial success I have enjoyed. Is it easy? Yes, once you have the information I give you in my enlightening book on how to achieve mail order riches.

And because advertising is the key to it all, I have reproduced my prize-winning ads, explaining why they generate gigantic sales and how you can duplicate the techniques for your own mail order success.

You may wonder why I am selling you a book about mail order if my business is so successful. To make more money, of course! That's part of my business—sharing knowledge that will make money for you and at the same time make money for me.

COPY MY SUCCESS FOR FINANCIAL INDEPENDENCE

One very important part of my book is worth the price of the entire book. For the first time, I reveal the inner secrets of mail order experts on how to get free magazine and newspaper ads that can quickly put you on the road to riches. Yes, thousands of dollars worth of free ads that will help you test the probability of your product's success while you put dollars in your pocket.

PROVEN FACTS — NOT THEORIES

I offer practical, tested, how-to information on successfully selling books or products. Furthermore, I say there's plenty of room for anyone who is ambitious and willing to follow my blueprint for success. You see, regardless of the product being sold, the basic mail order technique is virtually the same for all.

FREE PERSONAL HELP FROM MELVIN POWERS

All you need to do is zero in on something that interests you. My book gives you an endless supply of sources for mail order products and book ideas. I'll show you how to pick mail order winners. Your only decision is to choose a product or book idea and then follow my step-by-step, money-making guide. It's that simple. And if that isn't enough, you are free to call or visit me for further help. I'm as close to you as your telephone. I can be reached in Hollywood at (213) 875-1711. This is your golden opportunity to invest in success.

WHY BUY MY BOOK?

I know you have seen ads on other mail order books, and you may be wondering if you can really believe this ad. My answer is, "Absolutely yes!" If it isn't all I say it is, your money will be refunded immediately, leaving you nothing to lose. *How to Get Rich in Mail Order* is written by one whose 25-year old business operation is a shining example of the success to be obtained by following the instructions contained in the book.

THE ROLLS ROYCE OF MAIL ORDER BOOKS

Professionals acclaim my book as the Rolls Royce of mail order books because it is thorough and a guide to riches beyond your imagination.

Here are comments from readers of *HOW TO GET RICH IN MAIL ORDER* by Melvin Powers. All letters are on file as required by the United States Federal Trade Commission. Initials are used to preserve the privacy of the individuals.

I recently purchased your book, HOW TO GET RICH IN MAIL ORDER. I feel that this is one of the finest books I have read for either pro or beginner. It is worth more than I paid for it, and it is refreshing to deal with a person of your honesty and integrity. Z. W. Memphis, Tennessee

I have finished reading your book, HOW TO GET RICH IN MAIL ORDER, and want to congratulate you on a job well done. You have an excellent writing style, and the reference material and illustrations alone are worth the price of your book. That you present your own personal success stories, as well as those of others in mail order, adds tremendous credibility to the advice you pass along to your readers. Your book was an enjoyable experience. *R. J. Boston, Massachusetts*

Have just received your new book, HOW TO GET RICH IN MAIL ORDER, and must say it is a compendium on mail order. You have presented one of the most exhaustive, complete treatises on the subject that I have ever seen. L. S. O. Prospect Heights, Illinois

I just finished reading your book, HOW TO GET RICH IN MAIL ORDER, and I think it's terrific. You give authoritative advice to both the mail order beginner and to the old pro. You're definitely an inspiration. M. W. Encino, California

Your mail order book is fantastic and fun to read. It is the most complete and thorough book I've ever read on the subject. Congratulations. J. S. Montecito, California

DO YOU WANT TO BE RICH? THE MOMENT OF TRUTH!

Not only is the book packed with down-to-earth ideas, useful how-to's and nitty-gritty facts, it contains over 200 illustrations as well, making it a virtual encyclopedia of mail order information. It even shows you how to run a mail order business in your spare time. What's more, you get an extraordinary, 365-day, money-back guarantee when you purchase this book. If, by the end of one year, you are not making thousands of dollars in your mail order operation, simply return the book for a full refund. Fair enough?

Mail order is my business and my hobby. It's fun, it's creative, it's fascinating—and it means big money, too! Your secret dreams can come true because there are millions of customers out there just waiting to send *you* their dollars for your product or service. I am continually amazed at the incredible money-making opportunities in this field.

To experience the joy of shaking thousands of dollars from stacks of envelopes addressed to *you,* send for *How to Get Rich in Mail Order* by Melvin Powers. 336 pages, over 200 pages of illustrations, 8½″ × 11″ size. Allowable as a tax deduction.

Copyright 1984 by Melvin Powers

Whatever you do, don't miss this last-chance opportunity to get rid of money worries ...

SELF-MADE MILLIONAIRE REVEALS HIS $ECRET$. RESULTS GUARANTEED!

When a long-time friend comes to you visibly depressed, you have to listen.

"I'm having a rough time making it with the job I have," Bob complained. "Everything keeps going up but my wages."

Bob swallowed hard. I waited.

"If I had a college degree, I guess it would help, but I don't have any special education."

As he talked, my mind traveled back to the day I came West from Boston, without connections and with very little money. I couldn't help comparing my early struggles with the comfort and security I now enjoy as president of the Wilshire Book Company. I founded this company 25 years ago, in my spare time, and with an investment of only a few hundred dollars.

"Bob," I interrupted, "I know what you should do. Get into the mail order business!

"You don't need a lot of money to get started. You don't need any special education. The money-making opportunities are unlimited, and you can start in your spare time. Keep your job until you get going. You'll discover your untapped potential."

PROVEN FACTS – NOT THEORIES

As I spoke, I determined to put my words down on paper – to outline a detailed, risk-free program that Bob and others could follow to start making big money in mail order.

Mail order has given me all the material things one could wish for – time to travel, ownership of property, good investments, and even Arabian horses as a hobby. Above all, I enjoy my work and have peace of mind. Perhaps you have read some of my best sellers such as: *Psycho-Cybernetics, Magic of Thinking Big, Think & Grow Rich, New Guide to Rational Living, Three Magic Words, Ability to Love,* and *You Are Not the Target.*

So why would I invite competition? The truth is, I don't look at it as competition. The mail order field is so huge – $77 billion a year, there's plenty of room for all.

Selling by mail is my business. My book, *How to Get Rich in Mail Order*, lives up to its name and will show you exactly "how to get rich in mail order."

Guaranteed!

WHY BUY MY BOOK?

What to sell? My book gives you *unlimited sources* for finding unusual and profitable products. I have specialized in books because they are an important part of my life. But you can bring whatever you like most from your life into your business ... items for the home, food products, crafts, hobbies, clothing, books or anything else that is of interest to you.

After you have picked a product you like, I will teach you how to test it to see if it's a winner with *free ads*. Meanwhile, the free testing puts money in your pocket.

The real secret of mail order success lies in advertising. By investing your profits in more and more advertising, you pyramid your earnings into really big money.

There are many ways to advertise and my book shows you all of them. You will learn how to write powerful ads. Over 200 illustrations show block-busting mail order techniques that are working for others and that will be profitable for you, too.

There are 336 pages of detailed information in this big 8½" x 11" book and it's all up-to-date. Names and addresses of sources and suppliers are from my own files.

COPY MY SUCCESS FOR FINANCIAL INDEPENDENCE

You don't have to go it alone, dreaming up unusual and novel ways of doing business. *How to Get Rich in Mail Order* describes a proven system that works time after time.

Can you imagine anything more exciting than shaking cash, checks, and money orders out of stacks of envelopes? I never tire of having the mail come across my desk every day.

And to think you can begin with very little money. Some of the millionaires you read about were able to actually start their businesses in their kitchens and garages as customers never see one's place of business. Remember, the whole country is your market place and you can expand as fast as you desire.

Why not cash in on my know-how and experience? Start now and get set for tremendous earnings.

Send today for *How to Get Rich in Mail Order.* A fantastic future is within your reach in this rapidly growing field.

YOUR SECRET DREAMS COME TRUE!

If you will guarantee that you'll let this book be your guide, I will guarantee your success. Furthermore, if you're not making thousands of dollars within one year, I'll return your money.

Now is the time to do something about your future. Everyone has secret dreams – and yours are about to come true.

Act now.

THE ROLLS ROYCE OF MAIL ORDER BOOKS

Here are comments from readers of *How to Get Rich in Mail Order* by Melvin Powers. All letters are on file as required by the United States Federal Trade Commission. Initials are used to preserve the privacy of the individual.

I recently purchased your book. How to Get Rich in Mail Order. I feel that this is one of the finest books I have read for either pro or beginner. It is worth more than I paid for it, and it is refreshing to deal with a person of your honesty and integrity. Z. W., Memphis, Tennessee

I have finished reading your book. How to Get Rich in Mail Order, and want to congratulate you on a job well done. You have an excellent writing style, and the reference material and illustrations alone are worth the price of your book. That you present your own personal success stories, as well as those of others in mail order, adds tremendous credibility to the advice you pass along to your readers. Your book was an enjoyable experience.
R. J., Boston, Massachusetts
Your mail order book is fantastic and fun to read. It is the most complete and thorough book I've ever read on the subject. Congratulations.
J. S., Montecito, California

MELVIN POWERS PERSONAL HELP

All you need to do is zero in on something that interests you. My book gives you an endless supply of sources for mail order products and book ideas. I'll show you how to pick mail order winners. Your only decision is to choose a product or book idea and then follow my step-by-step, money-making guide. It's that simple. And if that isn't enough, you are free to call or visit me for further help. I'm as close to you as your telephone. I can be reached in Hollywood at (213) 875-1711. This is your golden opportunity to invest in success.

DO YOU WANT TO BE RICH? THE MOMENT OF TRUTH!

To experience the joy of shaking thousands of dollars from stacks of envelopes addressed to you, send for *How to Get Rich in Mail Order* by Melvin Powers. 336 pages, over 200 pages of illustrations, 8½" x 11" size. Allowable as a tax deduction. *Copyright 1984 by Melvin Powers*

This could be you in a short time—here's proof:

$30,000 in 1 month
W. White, Los Angeles, Ca.

$100,000 in 4 months
Barrie K., Grand Rapids, MI.

$40,000 in 1 month
George Bowman, Canton, Mi.

$1,000,000 in 5 months
George Campion, Los Angeles, Ca.

DOLLARS EVERY DAY

I sell hundreds of thousands of books by mail ranging in price from $2 to $10. Every day I shake out checks, money orders, and cash from stacks of envelopes. You can do the same thing.

There will always be books. $1 billion worth is sold through mail order every year. You don't have to be a genius to get your share of that market. You can get it a lot easier and faster than I did. I show you how in my new book, *How to Get Rich in Mail Order*—the same book that made the above men and women successful.

MAIL ORDER BEGINNING

Years ago, I wrote a self-help book that no publisher would accept. After 17 rejection slips, my wife said, "Forget it or sell it yourself."

I agreed and placed an ad in *Popular Science*. After five days, only seven orders had come in. I thought, "That's that! $500 of our life savings down the drain." But on Monday, the twelfth day, my wife called me at my job, hysterical with joy. She said the mailman had to come to the door because the letters wouldn't fit in the mail slot. There were 201 orders!

CASH PROFIT $3,781

That night we mailed out 201 books at $5 each. More money than I made in a month. Day after day, for 48 days after the ad appeared, the money kept rolling in. We sold the complete supply of 1,000 books. Total sales $5,000. Total profit $3,781.

THE ROAD TO RICHES

I was excited! Now I was sure I was on the way to riches. The direction was clear. Over a period of 25 years, I've sold millions of books of all varieties using mail order techniques.

UNLIMITED BOOK SUPPLY

I'll tell you how to get all the books you want at wholesale and will provide sources for surplus books at a fraction of the original cost. I'll show you successful ads for books that are still pulling in dollars.

PROVEN FACTS—NOT THEORIES

I offer practical, tested, how-to-information on successfully selling books or products. Furthermore, I guarantee there's plenty of room for anyone who is seriously willing to follow my blueprint for success.

MILLIONS IN MAIL ORDER

Selling books by mail is what I know best. You will be shown how I sold over 3,000,000 copies of *Psycho-Cybernetics*. Here are more books still bringing in mail order dollars year after year:

The Lazy Man's Way to Riches—1,200,-000 at $10—$12,000,000
Wake Up the Financial Genius Inside You—850,000 at $10—$8,500,000
Winning Through Intimidation—1,000,000 at $10—$10,000,000
How to Prosper During the Coming Bad Years—1,000,000 at $9—$9,000,000
Think & Grow Rich—7,000,000 at $3—$21,000,000
Dollars in Your Mail Box—200,000 at $13—$2,600,000

INCOME 24 HOURS A DAY

Believe me, you can build a fortune quickly. Check any newspaper or magazine and you'll see ad after ad for books because there's always a market—people love to buy books. Day and night, these ads keep working. Your ad will work for you the same way, even while you sleep.

COPY MY SUCCESS

How to Get Rich in Mail Order explains my money-making technique with easy-to-follow, step-by-step directions. It tells you the important things you must do and the mistakes you must avoid.

I'll show you
- how to get free ads
- how to write ads that are winners
- where to advertise for the best results
- how to reach 5,000,000 potential customers for only $50

You've seen other ads on mail order and didn't respond. You perhaps were a "doubting Thomas." So here's what I suggest. Send for your copy of my book—right now—to start you making big money fast, just as the people documented below did. You have everything to gain and nothing to lose. To convince you, you get a one-year, 100%-money-back guarantee.

CERTIFIED SUCCESS STORIES

Here is authenticated proof. You can duplicate the success of these persons who got started with *How to Get Rich in Mail Order*. Testimonials are on file as required by the United States Federal Trade Commission.

$30,000 IN BUSINESS IN ONE MONTH

You have written the best book on mail order. After reading your book and following your advice, I did $30,000 worth of business in one month. Many thanks.

W. White
Los Angeles, California

$40,000 THE FIRST MONTH

Your book on mail order is, without reservation, the finest and most complete book I've ever read. The tips and instructions showed me how to write a winning ad that grossed me $40,000 the first month, and the money is still rolling in. I ran the ad in Popular Science.

George Bowman
43726 Simsbury
Canton, Michigan 48187

$100,000 IN FOUR MONTHS

Your mail order book is great! Using your techniques and expertise, I made over $100,000 in four months. Keep up the good work.

Barrie K.
Grand Rapids, Mich.

$1,000,000 IN 5 MONTHS

"I was completely broke and in the depths of depression when I read your material. Believe it or not, in five months I did $1,000,000 worth of business and I am now in the process of purchasing a building worth close to $500,000.

My whole life has been changed due to you. How can I ever thank you?

George Campion
6314 Santa Monica Blvd.
Los Angeles, California 90038

TAKE THE FIRST STEP

To experience the joy of shaking thousands of dollars from stacks of envelopes addressed to *you*, send for *How to Get Rich in Mail Order* by Melvin Powers. 336 pages, over 200 pages of illustrations, 8½" x 11" size.
Copyright 1984 by Melvin Powers

---ORDER FORM---

365-DAY, MONEY-BACK GUARANTEE

Enclosed is my ☐ check or ☐ money order for $12.00. Please rush me *How to Get Rich in Mail Order.*

Name _____
(Please print)

Address _____

City _____

State _____ Zip _____

Please send your order to:

**Melvin Powers
Dept. 17
12015 Sherman Road
North Hollywood,
California 91605**

California residents please add 65¢ sales tax.

Chapter Six

How to Develop a Second Career by Using Your Expertise As a Basis for Conducting Seminars. How to Record Your Seminars and Sell Them in the Form of Cassette and Video Tapes. How to Use Your Book and Seminars As a Basis for a Highly Informative and Profitable Newsletter.

I love seminars! And I've been conducting them for as long as I can remember. I want to interest you in the practice because it is a natural follow-up step in the progression of marketing your book. There is no better way to capitalize on the advantages of a one-to-one confrontation with potential buyers than through the medium of a seminar. It allows you to employ the persuasive force of your own personality. It allows you *the chance to sell yourself.* Once you've established your credentials through the force of your own personal magnetism, everything else will follow. And not the least of it is the pleasure you will derive from the undertaking, as well as the money and the opportunity to meet interesting and career-minded people. Each one, beyond the prospect of becoming a client or buyer, projects the possibility of a future relationship which could be stimulating and financially rewarding. Seminars can become a dynamic marketing tool for you.

Whenever I speak of the opportunities inherent in every seminar, I immediately think of two or three real estate men and some investment counselors who have made fair game of the seminar bonanza.

Mark O. Haroldsen, who wrote *How to Wake Up the Financial Genius Inside You,* is making a fortune giving seminars all over the country advancing his theories. The book deals with making money in real estate and has sold up to 250,000 copies in one year using the same mail-order techniques I will have explained to you in detail by the time you have finished reading this book. Haroldsen also has a newsletter working for him at $39.00 a copy.

Following the same pattern with equally remarkable success are two other real estate authors: William Nickerson, who wrote *How I Turned $1,000 into $3,000,000 in Real Estate,* and Albert J. Lowry, author of *How You Can Become Financially Independent by Investing in Real Estate.*

Howard Ruff, famed for his flamboyant investment scenarios and author of *How to Prosper During the Coming Bad Years,* has turned his seminars into extravaganzas of national dimensions. He conducts them at major convention centers and his enrollment runs into the thousands. He also published a very successful newsletter at a subscription charge of $95.00 annually. Not a bad take when you figure that he has 200,000 subscribers. This is in addition to his 58-station, nationally syndicated TV and cable show. And he still manages to make time to be a guest speaker for a large number of deserving organizations. He's doing everything just right.

E. Joseph Cossman is author of the book, *How I Made $1,000,000 in Mail Order.* Although he is retired from active business, he never misses an opportunity to promote his mail-order seminars.

After I had published *How to Get Rich in Mail Order,* I instituted a one-day seminar which I called "How to Start and Operate a Successful Mail Order Business in Your Spare Time." My mailing list of prospective students was made up of individuals who had either purchased my book directly from me, or, having purchased it elsewhere, had written to me about it. The names are kept on a computer. See pages 55, 56, 57 and 58 for a sample of the mailing piece I use. Feel free to use the layout, or copy the style for your own seminar requirements.

Community colleges, universities, high schools covering adult courses, public-park departments, and private schools are eager to offer new courses. It is to their advantage to change the curriculum every so often. New teachers and new courses attract new students and more profits to their facilities. See pages 59, 60, 61 and 62.

This need provides you with an opportunity to teach and to test the popularity of your class. It is not necessary for you to be a college graduate or have teaching credentials to conduct a seminar. As long as the feedback is good and the course is making money, your seminar will be considered a welcome addition to the curriculum.

To propose a new course is a very simple matter. Call any school and ask who is in charge of community courses, which means the courses are not for credit. Explain who you are, what you have to offer, and the class you would like to teach. You'll be asked to submit a one-page synopsis, outline, or list of topics you propose to discuss in your class. If there is interest in what you have to offer, you'll be asked to appear for an interview. These interviews are invariably friendly because they are prompted by a genuine desire on the part of the school personnel to hire you. Once you have reached this stage, you are as good as in. Be relaxed and talk about your projected plans simply, articulately and with enthusiasm. Invariably, you'll find it to be true that your enthusiasm will spread to them.

Let me refer to pages 63 and 64 for an example of a new class proposal I sent to various colleges and schools where I teach. The new class I proposed was eagerly accepted by everyone connected with coordinating extension courses. My only problem has been that there are not enough Saturdays in the year to accommodate the demand for both my mail-order classes and my book-publishing classes. I even received an unsolicited call from the administrator of a college to which I had not sent my résumé. Good word-of-mouth has a way of working to one's advantage.

Your fees will vary from school to school, ranging from payment on an hourly basis to a per-student basis or to a percentage of the gross receipts. But at this point, that should be your secondary interest. If you have never taught, it will be a good practical experience for you. And if you have taught in the past, repeating the experience will keep your teaching skills at the peak of proficiency.

One of the prime advantages to evolve from your experience as a teacher is that it will help crystallize your thinking about your subject. This, in turn, will be of help to you in improving your book. Then there is the pleasure, as well as the inherent prestige, of being an educator and meeting with people who share a common interest. Surely your students will derive a great deal of benefit and pleasure from the class, and the amount of personal satisfaction that will come to you is immeasurable.

From the standpoint of the writer as well as the publisher, there is an advantage of such significance that it cannot be overlooked—the opportunity to use his textbook for the class as required reading. That can mean considerable income, depending on the size of the enrollment. I have had enrollments as high as 100 students.

To give you an idea of potential attendance at seminars, Joe Karbo and I conducted a joint seminar in 1980 sponsored by the Orange Coast College in Costa Mesa, California. Five hundred people showed up at the auditorium, which could accommodate only 300. The turnout was so unexpected that I couldn't believe my eyes. We knew that a mail-order seminar would be effective, but this exceeded our wildest expectations. To handle the overflow, we were compelled to conduct another meeting at a future date. I had never underestimated the potential draw of Joe Karbo's name as a star attraction, but I could not have expected anything like this.

Joe and I gave an inspiring seminar filled with the techniques of running a successful mail-order business. It was an exhilarating experience for both audience and speakers. Needless to say, at the end of the seminar our books were completely sold out.

I employ what I consider to be an unbeatable technique for selling books in huge quantities to prospective students, bookstores and libraries. Announcements of my mail-order seminars are listed in over a million catalogs sent out every semester by the colleges and schools where I will be teaching. In the class description contained in the catalog, I recommend that potential enrollees for my course read my book, *How to Get Rich in Mail Order*, suggesting that it be purchased at any bookstore in Los Angeles or obtained free at public libraries. The result was phenomenal from a standpoint of sales. I will do the same thing with my book on self-publishing once I have it in print, and I know that the results will be equally gratifying. This is precisely the procedure I want you to follow when you become affiliated with a school. It is impossible to beat the continuous flow of free publicity associated with this practice.

In some schools, the cost of the book is included in the tuition. In the beginning, my books were, of course, not stocked by libraries. However, in compliance with the constant requests for the books, they are now to be found in almost every library in the Los Angeles area. In fact, I have been told that *How to Get Rich in Mail Order* is one of the most-often-requested books in libraries.

Ever mindful that you should glean the very most from your teaching experiences, let me suggest that after you have taught a few classes, record your lecture on cassette tape. To do this properly, you will need a lapel microphone to effectively record your own voice and an additional microphone pointed in the direction of the class to pick up questions and comments. You can edit the tape until you are entirely pleased with it and then offer it for sale to readers of your book. It is another excellent source of revenue.

My plans for the future call for video-taping my book-publishing and mail-order seminars. Besides selling the tapes, I'll offer them for rent. This will give the viewers, both those who did and those who did not attend the courses, an opportunity to avail themselves of the class instruction.

From the standpoint of a personal livelihood, you should be able to make an excellent living from teaching classes and selling your book, cassette tapes, newsletters and additionally related material. There is no better showcase for your talent, and the classes could lead to consultation work, which is both satisfying and financially rewarding.

Once your name becomes known through the classes you teach, there is always the chance of ancillary benefits accruing to you. A local college where I had taught was interested in expanding its enrollment for its community courses. This would involve hiring new instructors to bring fresh ideas to the school through their courses. And to obtain this new range of courses, they planned to seek the thinking of persons other than those on their staff.

Because of my former association with the college, the job was offered to me at a substantial monthly salary plus a percentage of all enrollment fees for the new classes I brought in. Nothing would have pleased me more than to have been able to accept the offer, but, unfortunately, I just did not have the time.

Whenever I teach, the pride of authorship is present. I want my endeavor to be the very best I can give it.

Money, of course, is a consideration, but of far more importance to me—and I hope to you—is the quality of performance. My reputation for being responsible, conscientious and creatively cooperative is extremely important to me. To that end, I take a deep personal interest in the operation of each of the schools I work with. I make suggestions, offer ideas and am critical when it is warranted. As a result, administrators are genuinely trusting and cordial. They welcome my interest and my creative feedback. Because of my contact with the public, I am able to refer people with special talent, or a special fund of information, for teaching positions. In fact, I make announcements in all my classes informing interested enrollees that I would be very happy to help them secure teaching assignments. I ask them to remain after class, and I confer with them at length on the subject. If you live in the Los Angeles area and would like to contact me, I'll do whatever I can to assist you. I'll need a synopsis of the course you propose to teach and an outline, such as shown on pages 63 and 64.

If you live outside of Los Angeles, drop me a line and include a brief synopsis and outline of the class you plan to teach. I'll suggest how you can get started in your area. The plan is to start with one school and then keep adding schools as your time permits.

The advice I've given to both authors and others regarding the teaching of seminars has met with excellent results. Those who have books to offer find that they have a steady flow of books going to students, bookstores and libraries. Even those who are not writers, or have no books to offer, find the experience a thoroughly rewarding one. There is a certain indefinable sense of well-being that goes with teaching and being a part of a college or university. Consultation work that normally follows is a bonus.

I encourage those who are not authors but who already have successful classes to put their material in manual form. Again, it's an additional source of revenue and eventually leads to self-publication. Moreover, it tends to put those persons in a writing mood and helps to clarify their thinking. Understandably, the natural result of this is to give substance and better organization to the material used in their teaching curriculum.

Several years ago, I had occasion to encourage one of my friends, a professional writer, to start teaching classes. He's now teaching at a dozen colleges and receiving more offers all the time. He has also started private classes. He loves the role of teacher and is ideally suited to the profession. He's making money and has never been happier, because he carries into his classes the conviction that what he is doing is, in its way, just as creative as his work at the typewriter. As a result, he has added a new facet to his career. The only thing he hasn't done as yet is write a manual or a book based on one or more of the courses he is teaching. When he does, I'm sure it will be a winner.

I encouraged another friend of mine, a book publisher, to start teaching a course on how to be a best-selling author. I also persuaded him to write a book about the subject which would tell the story from his perspective. Here's the good news: He now enjoys teaching classes, and a major publisher will soon be publishing his book. Can you keep a secret? We have each agreed to recommend the other's book at our seminars!

When you start teaching seminars, I urge you to keep me informed of your progress. Depending on the nature of your seminars, I'll have suggestions that will further enhance your career. Perhaps you could conduct a seminar as part of a cruise ship's daily activities in exchange for free passage for you and a guest. I've been on cruises where instructors in pastimes ranging from bridge to dancing have contracted for this kind of arrangement. In fact, one of my authors, Edwin B. Kantar, a leading bridge authority, travels around the world with his companion as guests of people who want the privilege of playing bridge with him in tournaments. Additionally, he is paid an honorarium. And as an avid tennis player, he has the best of both worlds—tennis by day, bridge by night. Not the least of his accomplishments is his authorship of a series of eleven bridge books, all published by me.

Now, let me call your attention to page 57. Notice the offer to sell *Melvin Powers' Eight-Hour Mail Order Seminar on Cassette Tapes,* priced at $87.00. The number of tapes I sell at times exceeds the number of students attending the seminar. My total cost for the twelve cassette tapes comprising the eight hours of lecture-material is $12.00, and the cost of mailing is $5.00—a net profit of $70.00. I prominently advertise the availability of these tapes in my mail order book. As a result, readers of my book all over the world have bought these tapes by the thousands.

The cost of duplicating a one-hour tape of your subject matter should come to about $1.00. The going retail price for a one-hour tape is $10.00, leaving you with a very substantial profit of $9.00. I do very well selling inspirational tapes at that price.

Also capable of producing big profits is the newsletter, an instrument of communication which has enjoyed tremendous popularity in recent years. Its popularity stems largely from the fact that the subscriber is able to consume a vast amount of pertinent information in capsulated form and on a highly selective basis. In short, for a given fee the subscriber has a direct pipeline to information that might not otherwise be available to him and that might lead to important decisions materially affecting his financial posture. So cost is not usually too great a consideration. The price of important information comes high, and the subscriber is prepared to pay it.

It becomes significant that the newsletter can command a good price when you figure the cost to you, the writer of the newsletter. Printing cost of the usual four-page instrument is minimal. Your main cost is postage. Assuming the newsletter will be sent out between 10 and 12 times a year, the overall cost to you would not exceed $5.00. The decision as to its actual worth is up to you—$25.00, $39.00, $??? That's the price you place on it.

A big plus with regard to the newsletter is the opportunity it will give you to keep in touch with your readers. It is a highly effective device for getting feedback and for enhancing your chances to sell more books, tapes and curricular courses.

I was part of a speaker's panel at a recent meeting of the Southern California Publicists' Association. The topic dealt with selling books by mail order. I was the main speaker. I came up with the idea of video taping the program and selling it by mail. As a result, I have sold about 500 of the video tapes at $25.00 each. My cost, including mailing, is $15.00. The idea has already paid off to the tune of $5,000 in net profits.

In the next chapter, I'll discuss the importance of a good-selling title. You have often heard, What's in a name? My answer is, "Plenty—especially when it relates to a book." I want you to know why a title is important and how you can apply the reasons outlined to your own book.

I'd like to close this chapter on a personal note which I feel could be of enormous importance to you. I, therefore, urge you to give it thoughtful consideration. As a public service, I, motivated by my interest in the business community and deep-seated desire to serve it as best I can, have arranged to conduct, without charge, a business and entrepreneurs' seminar every two months. It is held at a school that has agreed to extend its facilities to me at no cost and to appropriately publicize the seminars as well as the speakers who donate their services.

The purpose of this endeavor is to bring together in a bond of communal interest those people, of whatever pursuits, who look forward to owning their own business. Throughout the session we exchange ideas, discuss problems, and provide speakers equipped to offer supplemental information about critical facets of business.

In conducting the seminars, it is my sincere hope that I will in some measure give direction and fulfillment to those with the American dream of owning a successful business. In helping to make this a reality, I, at the same time, help individuals establish good business contacts.

I am often asked why I don't charge for this service. My answer is that the opportunity to share my expertise without charge enhances my own sense of well-being. In short, it makes me feel good.

Teaching seminars has become an integral part of my life. It's fun, and the feedback it generates is good for one's ego. I hope that you'll become excited about the idea of teaching seminars and learn to experience the pleasure connected with it. It's like the performer waiting in the wings for applause—it's music to his ears.

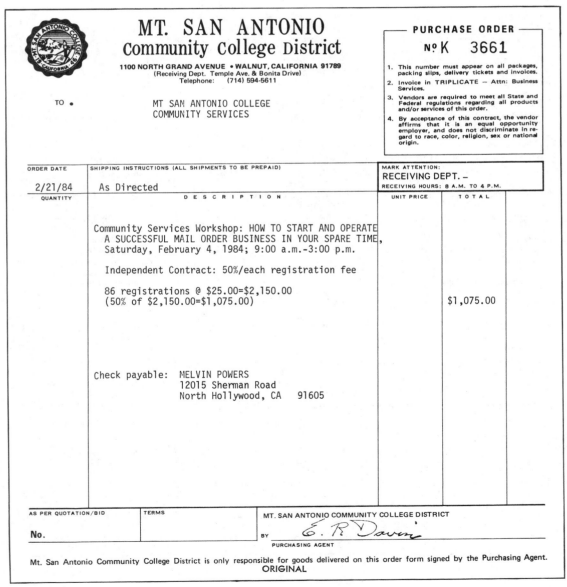

Laurie Edmonds

101 reasons for not buying a book

Laurie Edmonds has retired after 16 years with Michael Joseph. Before he went 'inside'—he left the road and became sales manager—he compiled this list of reasons for a bookseller not to buy a book. It was published in THE BOOKSELLER *about a decade ago.*

At his retirement party recently he told me that things hadn't changed much, except, of course, 'for 30,000 titles each year now read 40,000'. And there is less prejudice against women writers, and prize-winners actually sell books. But a number of new reasons have been invented. The two most popular current put-offs are 'It's not on TV', or, worse still, 'It IS on Channel 4'.

1 You're the 14th rep I've seen this morning.
2 Three of the others were carrying books on the same subject.
3 Don't you know that over 30,000 titles are published each year?
4 This is a scissors-and-paste job.
5 You're flogging a dead horse.
6 You should have saved this one for the Christmas market.
7 Why do you all wait for Christmas to produce your big books?
8 Nobody reads this kind of story these days.
9 What we really need is a good, old-fashioned yarn.
10 I could read this in half an hour.
11 Who's got time to plough through 900 pages?
12 Nobody's interested in books in January.
13 There's so little about in January, why don't you publish a big one?
14 This sold last year, it can't happen two years running.
15 This didn't sell last year, I'll have to cut my order.
16 It's not technical enough.
17 The layman couldn't possibly understand this.
18 It's got no index.
19 Who writes your blurbs?
20 Oh, economising on paper?
21 I see you've padded it out with wide margins.
22 The jacket's too arty-crafty.
23 The jacket's too commercial.
24 This chap writes for every publisher in the country.
25 This type of spine gets lost on the shelves.
26 The only way to sell this is to display a large pile.
27 I haven't got room for a large pile.
28 My assistants are morons.
29 My customers are morons.
30 This volume will be thumbed through and not bought.
31 The coffee-table book is finished.
32 It's all so sordid; what we need is a good laugh.
33 You just can't sell funny books outside Christmas.

34 Christmas is late this year.
35 The author repeats himself with every book.
36 Why doesn't the author stick to what he knows?
37 It's just a gimmick.
38 What it needs is a gimmick.
39 It hasn't had any publicity.
40 It's been over-publicised.
41 Book clubs are killing the book trade.
42 Paperbacks are killing the book trade.
43 Mail order is killing the book trade.
44 The public libraries are killing the book trade.
45 I suppose the paperback's coming next month?
46 Everybody's waiting for the paperback.
47 Isn't there a pre-publication price?
48 This pre-publication lark loses you customers.
49 Can't go mad; got to give everyone a fair share.
50 Can't spend any money; I've just gone mad on X's book.
51 This isn't publishing: it's book-making.
52 Fancy your firm stooping to this!
53 Why doesn't your firm get with it?
54 It's ghost-written!
55 They'll be getting the linesman to write his memoirs next.
56 You chaps think sex is the sole recipe for success.
57 All people want nowadays is sex.
58 There's an obstruction in the road outside.
59 They've introduced meters.
60 They haven't introduced meters.
61 Everybody's on holiday.
62 There are no visitors this year.
63 The sun's shining.
64 It's raining.
65 It's too cold to come out.
66 The news is depressing.
67 The Budget is coming.
68 The Budget came.
69 The more books we have, the more pilfering there is.
70 If I order it, it'll never arrive.
71 If I order it, your warehouse'll treble the order.
72 It's by a woman.
73 It's by an American.
74 It's a translation.
75 The Bank Rate's up.
76 The Bank Rate's down, and people will spend their money on cars, houses and holidays.
77 It's all blank spaces and chapter headings.
78 It's cramped and unreadable.
79 It's the silly season.
80 It's the textbook season.
81 It looks like a remainder.
82 I'll wait for the National Book Sale.
83 It's just a picture-book.
84 There aren't any illustrations.
85 It's ten years since this chap wrote his last book.
86 This chap churns them out three times a year.
87 Not another cookery book!
88 Not another gardening book!
89 Please, not another soccer book!
90 A few excerpts in one of the Sundays would have helped this one.
91 The Sunday excerpts have killed interest in this one.
92 It's only a reviewer's book.
93 I'll wait for the reviews.
94 I leave merchandising to my grocer, ha-ha!
95 It's nearly lunchtime.
96 It's too soon after lunch.
97 I'll wait till I get asked for it.
98 You're jumping on the bandwagon.
99 How about my overstocks?
100 No buying on early-closing day.
101 It won't fit my shelves. All right then, if you must have a 102nd reason. I don't like you!

Melvin Powers Mail Order Seminar
California State University Northridge
Saturday, October 23, 1982
9:00 A. M. to 3:30 P. M.

I am pleased to announce that my next one-day mail order seminar will be held in the Santa Clarita Room of the University Student Union at California State University Northridge. See page four for map to find location of University Student Center and free parking.

Come spend a day with me and other mail order enthusiasts--a day that could change your entire life. You'll learn to make money in the fascinating field of mail order and to take charge of your life. You'll be inspired with the know-how material that you'll get first hand.

Specifically, you'll learn how to make money with small classified and display ads, as well as with the use of direct mail. The goal of the seminar is to help you build your own successful mail order business. Even if you are just starting, I can analyze your present mail order operation and suggest ways to increase your sales. You are welcome to bring your products, ads, literature and whatever other material is pertinent to your business for a complete analysis. I'll show you how to improve your advertising copy to put dollars in your pocket.

Do you have a hobby or a particular skill? I'll suggest how to utilize it to create a profitable mail order business.

Would you like to sell products? You'll be given information on innumerable sources of supply for unique items from all over the world. Searching for winning products is like an exciting treasure hunt. I'll give you a success formula for how and where to sell your products, how to get free editorial ads, how to get free publicity for your product and for yourself, and how to build a substantial business.

Are you interested in selling information or how-to books, or possibly publishing your own books? Since publishing is my specialty, I'll give you ideas for manuals and books and how to find authors to write for you. I'll share techniques that can make you wealthy in less time than you think. I'll explain how you can become part of the prestigious and money-making book business. I'll detail my methods of operation so you may duplicate them. I have a unique direct mailing piece that has sold and continues to sell millions of dollars worth of books. I'll tell you about this technique which can be used to sell any book.

After I analyze numerous types of mail order operations, you will be motivated to develop similar businesses. We'll do some creative brainstorming that will have unexpected money-making results. I'll cover all the aspects of successful mail order operations and answer your questions to your complete satisfaction. You'll have an opportunity to spend a delightful, relaxing day, learning mail order techniques that will be personally and financially rewarding.

Here's good news! The cost of the course is fully tax deductible. An income tax deduction is allowed for expenses incurred for education (including registration fees, travel, meals and lodging) undertaken to maintain or improve professional skills--Treasury Regulation No. 1.162.5

The cost of this one-day course is $100. Payment and reservations must be made prior to the starting date. Registration form is enclosed. The class runs from 9:00 A.M. to 3:30 P.M.

We will have an hour lunch break. There are many restaurants close by, including the restaurant at the University Student Union Center.

Should you have any questions, please feel free to call me.

I hope to hear from you and to meet you personally at my mail order seminar for mail order success.

Sincerely yours,

Melvin Powers

Melvin Powers

Registration Form

Mail to: Date_____
Melvin Powers
12015 Sherman Road
No. Hollywood, California 91605

Dear Melvin:

Enclosed is my _____check _____money order for $100.

Please enroll me in your mail order class for
Saturday, October 23, 1982.

Name_____
                    (Please print)

Address_____

City_____State_____Zip_____

Telephone_____
            (area code)

I am particularly interested in learning more about:

(1)_____

(2)_____

(3)_____

Melvin Powers' Mail Order Library

HOW TO WRITE A GOOD ADVERTISEMENT
by Victor O. Schwab

Contents:

Chapter 1: GET ATTENTION—How Important Is the Headline? What Kinds of Rewards Do Good Headlines Promise? 100 Good Headlines and Why They Were So Profitable. The Attraction of the Specific. How Many Words Should a Headline Contain? The Primary Viewpoint—the "Point of You." Don't Worry about a "Negative" Approach. Neophobia?—Americans Don't Suffer from This Ailment! Stale News to the Advertiser May Be Fresh News to the Reader. MAKING YOUR LAYOUT GET ATTENTION Two Ways to Do It. The Use of Pictures. Show Product in Use. What the Illustrations Should (and Should Not) Do. QUIZ ON CHAPTER 1. **Chapter 2:** SHOW PEOPLE AN ADVANTAGE—You're on Both Sides of the Counter. What Do People Want? Psychological Background Behind These Desires. New Trends for Old. HOW SHALL WE SELECT OUR COPY APPEAL?— Judy O'Grady and the Colonel's Lady. Eliminating the "Testing of the Obvious." IMPORTANCE OF YOUR FIRST PARA-GRAPH—Two Examples—One Bad. QUIZ ON CHAPTER 2. "TELL ME QUICK AND TELL ME TRUE." **Chapter 3:** PROVE IT—Why You Need Facts—and Where. Two Forces Are Needed to Pull a Sale. Never Forget This Psychological Truth. The Heart Dictates to the Head. The Kind of Facts to Get. The Missing Ingredient in Many an Otherwise Good Advertisement. How to Present Your Facts. QUIZ ON CHAPTER 3. **Chapter 4:** PERSUADE PEOPLE TO GRASP THIS ADVANTAGE—A $600,000,000 Example. A Simple Illustration of It in Action. How a Salesman Uses This Factor. It May Be Negative or Positive. The Sixth Prune. Aim at the Hardest Target. QUIZ ON CHAPTER 4. THIRTEEN AGAINST THE GODS. **Chapter 5:** ASK FOR ACTION —The Gap Between Reading and Acting. What Kind of Action Shall We Ask For? Guarantees Get Action. "Delay Is the Enemy of a Sale." The Fallacy of "Sometime." Not What People Say—but What They Do. The Battle for the Bucks. QUIZ ON CHAPTER 5. **Chapter 6:** HOW LONG SHOULD THE COPY BE?—Platitudes Won't Answer This Question. Eight Milestones to a Sale. The Qualities of Quantity. How Far Will You Carry the Majority? The Vital Key Word. The Quantity of Quality. 22 Ways to Hold Interest Longer. How To Make It *Look* More Inviting. The Form vs. Substance Mistake. A Condensed Recapitulation. HOW TO DECIDE THE BEST COPY LENGTH —It's Easier to Get Attention and Interest than to Hold It. The Everlasting Yea and Nay. If It Isn't There It Can't Do Any Work. When Shorter? When Longer? And Now You're Going to Cut—or to Expand. You Need This Additional Guidance. THE LOWLY SUBHEAD—How to Make Them Do More Work. Use Questions—Sequence. Let Them Speak Out Strongly. QUIZ ON CHAPTER 6. **Chapter 7:** HOW TO GET MORE INQUIRIES—Inquiries—the Cornerstone of Many Businesses. Ten Ways to Increase Them. HOW TO REDUCE THE NUMBER OF INQUIRIES—A Delicate Balance. What to Decide First. How to Decide Whether to Reduce Them. Ten Ways to Reduce Them. HOW TO MAKE THE INQUIRY COUPON ITSELF DO A BETTER JOB—Three Kinds of Prospects. Ten Ways to Improve Your Coupon. COUPON RIDERS—WORTH MUCH, COST LITTLE OR NOTHING—Allow People to Trade Up if They Want to. SEVEN OTHER FACTORS WHICH INFLUENCE THE EFFECTIVENESS OF AN ADVERTISEMENT—Size of Advertisement. The Use of Color. When It Appears. Position. The Effect of Big News Events. The Effect of Weather. And the Most Important Factor of All. QUIZ ON CHAPTER 7. **Chapter 8:** HOW TO SIZE AN ADVERTISEMENT—Your Vision May Be Too Narrow. Look Beyond the "Nuts and Bolts." If You Are Testing a New Product. QUIZ ON CHAPTER 8. **Chapter 9:** DO COPY APPEALS HAVE A SEX?— "Longer-Haul" Thinking. "Shorter-Haul" Thinking. Do Your Observations Check with This One? Why It Has Bearing on Your Copy. QUIZ ON CHAPTER 9. **Chapter 10:** FACTS OR FANCIES—WHICH SHALL YOU FEATURE? "The Most Wanted Product in the World." Some Ads Don't Need Much Factual Underpinning. QUIZ ON CHAPTER 10. **Chapter 11:** FOURTEEN INTERESTING AND INSTRUCTIVE SPLIT-RUN TESTS—Sufficiently Conclusive—if Properly Handled. Differences Should "Scream"—not "Whisper." The General Application of Split-Run Experience. QUIZ ON CHAPTER 11. **Chapter 12:** "CUMULATIVE EFFECT"—A COMMON ALIBI FOR POOR ADVERTISING—Why Multiply Zero? False Reliance upon the "Series" Idea. What's Profitable about Procrastination? You're Not in an Endurance Contest. QUIZ ON CHAPTER 12. **Chapter 13:** THE HARD-BOILED ATTITUDE—AND HOW TO ACQUIRE IT— What's Behind This Attitude? But There Are Two Compensations. When Is an Ad "Good"? Knowing and Avoiding That Which Is Most Likely to Fail. More Nays than Yeas. The Tougher the Job, the Better the Copy. Doubt Makes Demands. A Hair Shirt Worth Wearing. Not What They Think, but What They Do. QUIZ ON CHAPTER 13. **Chapter 14:** RANDOM OBSERVATIONS— INDEX

256 Pages...$22.00 postpaid

MELVIN POWERS' TEN-HOUR MAIL ORDER SEMINAR ON CASSETTE TAPES

Here is an opportunity for those of you unable to attend my mail order seminar to hear me discuss many aspects of running a successful part-time or full-time business. In the privacy of your home, office, or car, you'll hear the same seminar that thousands of entrepreneurs all over the country have attended. The ten hours of audio tape instruction will answer many of the questions you have wanted to ask. It will teach you how to successfully become your own boss.

After listening to the tape program, you will better understand mail order fundamentals and procedures, and will have an overall plan that will help you start making money right away in your own mail order business. The tape program is sold on a one-year, money-back guarantee. It must be of tangible help in teaching you how to make money in mail order, or I'll refund your money—no questions asked.

Here's how to gain maximum benefit from the tapes: (1) Listen to the material several times to fully comprehend the practical suggestions and information; (2) Put into practice the specific elements to be incorporated in your mail order plan; (3) Run your first classified or display ad; (4) Do a test mailng to one thousand or as many as three thousand people who would logically be interested in your product; (5) Evaluate the results; (6) Call or write to me to discuss your mail order plan and receive my suggestions for increasing your chances to attain success.

Send for: Melvin Powers' Ten-Hour Mail Order Seminar on Cassette Tapes. $87.00 postpaid

Send your order to:
Melvin Powers
12015 Sherman Road
No. Hollywood, California 91605

The Fellowship of The Golden Rule, Inc.

NON-PROFIT

418 SOUTH WESTERN AVENUE
LOS ANGELES, CALIF. 90020
March 9, 1981

Melvin Powers
Wilshire Book Company
12015 Sherman Way
North Hollywood, CA 91605

Dear Mel:

In the past year or so I have attended three seminars on mail order and book publishing. I received more information, more guidance, more help, and more inspiration from your seminar than all the others combined.

I felt that I had received my money's worth before we stopped for the mid-morning break.

You not only gave of your priceless store of experience but you also gave of yourself. You were a heart warming example of living The Golden Rule. You have our admiration and thanks.

Love and blessings,

Dr. V. Fred Rayser
President

VFR:s

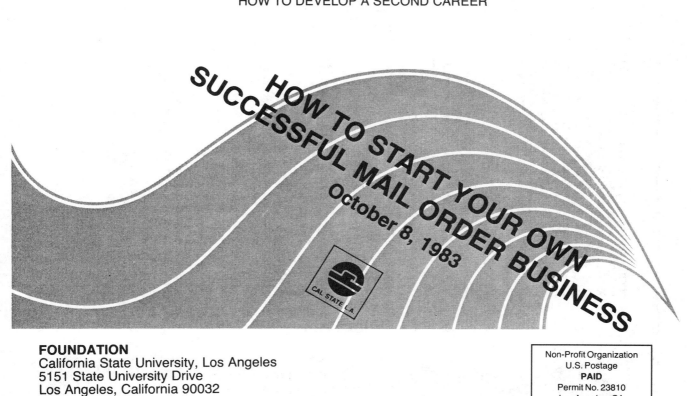

HOW TO START YOUR OWN SUCCESSFUL MAIL ORDER BUSINESS

October 8, 1983

FOUNDATION
California State University, Los Angeles
5151 State University Drive
Los Angeles, California 90032

**ATTN: PERSONNEL/HRD ADMINISTRATORS
MANAGEMENT SEMINARS**

Not Printed at State Expense

The California State University and Colleges

**HOW TO START YOUR OWN SUCCESSFUL MAIL ORDER BUSINESS
(C32917)**

Enrollment Form

FEE: $95.00

Name _____

Organization _____

City _____

State _____ Zip _____

Day Telephone No. _____

Call (213) 224-2871 if you want to enroll by credit card over the phone.

☐ VISA   ☐ MASTERCARD Accepted

Card No. _____

Signature _____

MAKE CHECKS PAYABLE TO:
FOUNDATION, CAL STATE L.A.

MAIL TO: FOUNDATION, California State University, Los Angeles, 5151 State University Drive, Los Angeles, CA 90032.

REFUNDS will be granted only if requested before the program begins. Ten percent of the enrollment fee will be withheld from all refunds requested within 5 working days of the seminar.

Thousands of entrepreneurs such as Joe Karbo, Joe Cossman, Brainerd Mellinger, Mark O. Haroldsen and others have made their fortunes in the fascinating field of mail order. In fact, the industry is growing at the rate of 16-18 percent every year and currently exceeds $80 billion in sales. This course focuses on the basics of the business and the proven techniques for success.

You will learn how to

- set up a mail order business
- make decisions on legal choices
- find mail order products
- do market research
- price products and services
- locate the largest U.S. & foreign manufacturers, distributors and importers
- advertise for best results
- unite classified ads and save money
- write copy
- prepare direct mail packages

Who Should Attend

Anyone who wants to start a mail order/direct mail business or who is now in business and wishes to expand rapidly.

Topics

- what's happening in mail order
- mail order for the entrepreneur
- why do people buy by mail
- what can you sell by mail
- rules of mail order product selection
- what products sell best
- how to control your product
- how to get your business started
- strategies of mail order selling
- mail order tactics
- cost calculations
- elements of the classified ad
- rules for display advertising
- direct mail
- how to use lists properly
- use of catalogues
- what and how to test

WILLIAM A. COHEN

Dr. Cohen is Director of the Bureau of Business and Economic Research, Director of the Small Business Institute, and Associate Professor of Marketing, California State University, Los Angeles. He has held senior marketing management positions with several companies and is a consultant in mail order/direct mail. He has had his own successful mail order business and has conducted nationwide seminars in direct mail/mail order marketing and other business topics. He started the first M.B.A. academic course in Direct Mail/Mail Order Marketing and the first undergraduate academic course in Southern California. He developed a system of executive self-marketing using direct mail techniques which the Chicago Tribune calls, "... a dedicated presentation of an organized campaign." He is on the Board of Governors and the Direct Mail Marketing Club of Southern California. He planned and initiated a successful mail campaign which sold research for a major university. He is the author of more than 100 articles and presentations and six books on business and management topics, including the best seller "Building a Mail Order Business" published by John Wiley & Son. He has a B.S. from the United States Military Academy, an M.B.A. from the University of Chicago and a M.A. and Ph.D. from Claremont Graduate School. Dr. Cohen's biography is listed in Who's Who in the West.

shire Book Company publishes more than 400 soft-cover non-fiction books, and is said to be the world's largest supplier of books sold by mail order. Mr. Powers is also in great demand at many colleges on the subject of mail order. He is a successful songwriter, a member of ASCAP, and recipient of an award for writing one of the outstanding country hit songs in 1976. He has sold millions of books using mail order techniques and even sold some of his chart songs using direct mail techniques.

PROGRAM LOCATION

This seminar will be held at Cal State L.A. Student Union Room 411. Cal State LA is located at the interchange of the Long Beach and San Bernardino Freeways. The campus may be reached by taking the Eastern Avenue off ramp from the San Bernardino Freeway or the Ramona Boulevard off ramp from the Long Beach Freeway and following the signs to the campus. A campus map will be sent on receipt of enrollment.

ENROLLMENT FEE

The fee for each seminar is $95.00 (A 115-page mail order/direct mail workbook will be provided to participants.)

PARKING

Information will be sent upon receipt of enrollment.

FOR ADDITIONAL INFORMATION ABOUT THESE PROGRAMS CALL (213) 224-3871.

IN-HOUSE PROGRAMS

Each of these seminars can be presented for your organization as an in-house program. These seminars may be presented in the same format as offered to the public or customized to meet the specific requirements of your organization. For details contact the Director of Professional Development Workshops at (213) 224-2871.

MELVIN POWERS

Mr. Powers is the Founder and President of the Wilshire Book Company and author of the best-selling book, *"How To Get Rich In Mail Order,"* which is now in its 4th edition. He is well-equipped to advise on the subject of mail order, as the Wil-

WHEN IT COMES TO MAIL ORDER...THEY WROTE THE BOOKS!

MELVIN POWERS, Founder and President of Wilshire Book Co., author of the best-selling book, "How to Get Rich in Mail Order" and popular college lecturer.

Powers is well-equipped to advise on the subject of mail order. Wilshire Book Co. publishes more than 400 soft-cover non-fiction books, and is said to be the world's largest supplier of books sold by mail order.

Several years ago, he authored the highly-successful book, "How to Get Rich in Mail Order." It became an immediate best-seller, and is now in its 4th edition. Powers is also in great demand at many colleges as a lecturer on the subject of mail order.

STUART WILLIAMS, Consultant, writer, teacher lecturer. Co-author of the new 117-page "Mail Order Handbook," published by Specialty Merchandising Corp. for its members. It has been hailed by many experts as the most definitive manual ever written on the subject. Easy, step-by-step instructions guide the novice or professional from start to success in the SMC mail order program.

Williams has been involved with mail order for more than a quarter-century. He has provided consultation, planning or creative work for nearly 100 mail order firms. It has been estimated that more than one out of ten Americans has responded to advertising he has created. He is currently a private consultant and instructor in mail order at

[Map of Orange Coast College showing Adams Ave., Fairview Rd., Arlington, Merrimac Way, Costa Mesa High School, Tennis Courts, Baseball Field, Gymnasium, Student Health Center, Library, Cafeteria, Administration, Auditorium, Forum, Parking areas, Fine Arts Lecture Hall, Merrimac Parking]

MAIL-ORDER SEMINAR ★8919

PLEASE PRINT

NAME _____

ADDRESS _____

CITY _____

ZIP _____   SS # _____

PHONE _____

MAIL TO: OCC Community Service Office
2701 Fairview Road, Costa Mesa, Ca. 92626

ORANGE COAST COLLEGE
COMMUNITY SERVICE OFFICE
2701 Fairview Road
Costa Mesa, Ca. 92626-0120
432-5880

Non-Profit Organization
U. S. POSTAGE PAID
Permit No. 28
Costa Mesa, California

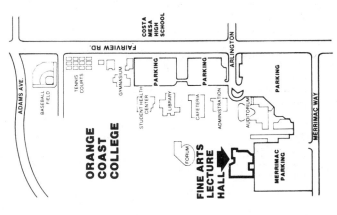

DON'T MISS IT...SATURDAY, SEPT. 24, 9 A.M.

ORANGE COAST COLLEGE

2701 FAIRVIEW ROAD
P.O. BOX 5005
COSTA MESA. CALIFORNIA 92626-0120
(714) 556-5651

Mail Order Seminars . . . a seven year tradition at Orange Coast College!

For years, "Mail Order" has been one of our most popular seminars. There have been times when we have had to turn away as many as two hundred persons, because there was no more room in the auditorium.

The up-coming seminar this September 24, promises to be another one of those jam-packed sessions, so we have arranged to use one of the largest auditoriums on the campus -- the main auditorium in the Fine Arts Building.

Stuart Williams, who has taught a popular evening course in mail order at Orange Coast College for more than a half a dozen years, will again be in charge of the seminar. As he so often does, Williams will be introducing a new innovation in the delivery of information. Together with Melvin Powers, a well-known author of books on mail order, Williams will present what he has termed a "conversational" seminar, in which both men will discuss a series of mail order topics.

"This format," Williams says, "eliminates the usual one-sided and unchallenged opinions presented by many seminar speakers. With two experienced mail order men discussing each subject, questioning the other where appropriate, and exploring every aspect in the light of their own understanding, the audience will get a more accurate and unbiased presentation of the facts."

The two-man conversational seminar will be followed after the "break" (about 10:45 a.m.) by questions from the audience, answered in the same conversational "give and take" that will characterize the first part of the seminar.

We would urge anyone involved with mail order -- or interested in this fascinating method of marketing, to attend. It is from 9 AM to 1 PM, and the fee is only $15 for the four-hour session. You can register in advance, or at the door if space is available. To register, simply fill out the form on the back of this folder and bring or mail to the Community Service Office.

Sincerely,

George Blanc

George Blanc
Associate Dean, Community Services

PS: Williams teaches a complete 18-week, 3-credit course in Mail Order Wednesday evenings from 7 to 10. There is still time to enroll!!

SERVING THE COMMUNITY SINCE 1947

Melvin Powers

Wilshire Book Company

12015 Sherman Road, No. Hollywood, California 91605-3781

HOW TO SELF-PUBLISH YOUR BOOK AND HAVE THE FUN AND EXCITEMENT
OF BECOMING A BEST-SELLING AUTHOR

YOUR SHORTCUT TO FAME AND FORTUNE

Self-publishing a book can establish its writer as an expert
in his field, a position that can lead to job advancement, high-
paying consultation work--or possibly a new career.

Given a good idea, anyone can become successful using the
tested techniques taught in this stimulating seminar.

Your instructor will be Melvin Powers, president of Wilshire
Book Company, who is one of the most creative and successful
publishers in the United States. Psycho-Cybernetics, The Magic
of Thinking Big and Think & Grow Rich are just a few of the titles
in his catalog of best-selling books.

You will be taught how to start your project with a minimum
amount of capital and then logically pyramid your profits. You'll
learn how to become a successful publishing entrepreneur in your
spare time, even if you have had little or no business experience.
This one-day seminar is designed to cover the basic points of book
publishing.

You'll be inspired when you learn how Melvin Powers' unique
methods produce his effective sales and promotional strategies.
And he will share his experiences and know-how in the building of
his multi-million-dollar publishing company--a company that enjoys
sales around the world.

Here is a partial list of subjects that will be discussed.

1. How to pick a winning subject and title.

2. How to perceive the beginning of a trend.

3. How to copycat successful themes.

4. How to test your book idea.

5. How to price your book.

6. How to copyright your book.

7. How to get on radio and TV shows as a guest to promote your book.

8. How to obtain free nationwide advertising and publicity.

9. How to obtain and use testimonials effectively.

10. How to make money in a short period of time using tested mail order techniques.

11. How to sell to bookstores, wholesalers, libraries, and non-traditional markets.

12. How to make extra money giving seminars and selling cassette and video tapes based on your book.

13. How to display your book at the American Booksellers Association Convention--your outlet for sales around the world.

14. Case histories of successful self-publishers.

> Saturday: 9:00 a.m. to 3:00 p.m.
>
> Date:
>
> Price:

Chapter Seven

Who Says You Can't Judge a Book by Its Cover?
How to Choose an Enticing Book Title to Attract Sales
How to Use Subtitles to Further Explain and Sell Your Book
How to Choose a Book Design That Will Promote Sales
How to Use Forewords and Testimonials to Your Advantage

Even before you start writing your book, you should give considerable thought to the selection of a catchy or factual title—one that will immediately captivate the reader and capture his attention. Particularly, the title should create anticipation in the reader.

Adding a subtitle to help clarify or define the title will create more interest.

Have you thought of a cover design or photograph for your book? Do you want graphics, a photograph, an illustration or a combination of these?

Do you want a foreword for your book? Do you know of an authority in the field who will lend his name to one? The prestige this gives to a book will significantly increase your sales.

What about testimonials? An effective device is to send galley proofs from your typesetter to those from whom you solicit testimonials. When you receive the testimonial, ask the person giving it to accompany it with a brief statement, such as, "You have my permission to use my testimonial in your book and/or advertising."

As a book publisher, I am a specialist in the practice of transforming losers or "also-rans" into winners. To accomplish this, I'll take a book that has made a poor showing in the market place, give it a new title and cover, perhaps write a foreword and then reintroduce it to the public with advertising or publicity. I've done it successfully many times.

As you know, there is a stable of accomplished men and women known as script doctors in movies, television and theater. They are called upon to ply their magic when the script is lacking in certain ingredients that would make it a hit. They carefully analyze the script, assess its potential, and then make the changes designed to give it the chemistry that will, so to speak, bring the manuscript to life. I do the same thing with books.

In this chapter, I propose to share with you my creative thinking on the subjects of titles, book covers, forewords and testimonials. Although details are not the most glamorous aspect of being a self-publisher, they are, nevertheless, extremely important. The more consideration you give to details, the better your chances for success. So, as you read on, read with care and a great deal of thought. Do you agree with my changes and titles? Do you disagree? How would you improve what I did?

Titles

Drs. Albert Ellis and Irving Becker recently wrote a new book based on a title I gave them—*A Guide to Personal Happiness*. I believed it would appeal to readers of Dr. Ellis' other book, *A New Guide to Rational Living*, and I was correct. We sold out the first edition of 5,000 copies immediately.

Incidentally, if you should have typographical errors in the first edition of your book, or if you want to change some of the material, corrections can be accomplished very easily. Be sure you save the original art and typesetting pages.

Ed Kantar writes a new book for me every year dealing with the subject of bridge. We have come up with a great series titled *Test Your Bridge Play*. It can go on forever using a series of titles, such as *Test Your Bridge Play–Volume 1*; *Test Your Bridge Play–Volume 2*; etc.

In using workable examples, I keep referring to songwriting because the creative process of writing a successful song is similar to writing a successful book. The Melvin Powers technique with each is to initially develop an interesting title. With this requirement satisfied, half the job is done because the title will invariably suggest the story line for the song or the subject of the book to be written.

During one of my brainstorming songwriting sessions, I came up with the title, *Who Wants a Slightly Used Woman?* I knew at once that I would have a hit song, even before I had written a single word of the lyrics. And as it turned out, the song, recorded by Connie Cato on Capitol Records, went to number 36 on the charts and won an ASCAP award for being one of the outstanding songs in 1976.

I encourage all writers to think about becoming songwriters. The lyricist has the responsibility of coming up with a good story line. The average song is a portrayal of a three-minute vignette delineating a slice of life. Something as restrictive in time as that clearly allows no time for a slow development of the theme. The listener's attention or curiosity must be sparked at once, either through an interesting, provocative statement at the outset or through a catchy melody, or both. In the parlance of song-writing, this is known as the "hook." Hook your listener before his attention is allowed to drift.

In principle, this idea of hooking your "audience" at the outset pertains to every form of creative involvement where the audience is *not captive*. For example, the television viewer or the radio listener is not captive. He has not paid one cent for his entertainment. If he doesn't like what he is viewing or listening to, he can turn the dial or walk out of the room. So, he must be hooked at once, or he is easily lost as a viewer. It is the same with the reader who glances at the first few pages of a book before he buys it, or the song-listener who lingers just long enough to hear the first few phrases of a song. This is contrary to the situation involving the moviegoer or the patron of the legitimate theater, who has paid a good price for his ticket. He's not about to walk out on his investment. As a result, he is considered a captive audience. It is advisable, but not imperative, that he be hooked at once. Hooked or not, he's not going anywhere, so the writer is permitted a more gradual development of plot and characterization.

Books with the words "How to" at the beginning of the title invariably enjoy good sales. With regard to the book you are now reading, you are probably wondering if the title, *How to Self-Publish Your Book & Have the Fun & Excitement of Being a Best-Selling Author,* might be too long. The answer is, Do not be afraid of long titles. They sell. Here is a list of some title ideas I have used which have proved extremely successful over the years. Try to incorporate some of these ideas into your own titles.

How to Improve Your Bridge
How to Develop a Better Speaking Voice
How to Make a Fortune in Real Estate
How to Win at Checkers
How Not to Lose at Poker
How to Win at Dice Games
How to Win at Poker
How to Improve Your Vision
How to Write a Hit Song and Sell It
How to Pick Winning Horses
How to Win at the Races
How to Be a Comedian for Fun and Profit
How to Stop Smoking with Self-Hypnosis
How to Write a Good Advertisement
How to Understand Your Dreams
How to Develop a Winning Personality

A variation on the "How to" titles is the "How You" titles I publish.

How You Can Stop Smoking Permanently
How You Can Have Confidence and Power

I'm partial to titles that contain the two words "made easy" and, whenever appropriate, I use them. They are particularly suitable for titles that suggest an invitation to learning and usually are good sellers.

Astrology Made Easy
Bridge Bidding Made Easy
Conversation Made Easy
Calligraphy Made Easy
Checkers Made Easy
Chess Made Easy
Vegetarian Cooking Made Easy and Delectable
Juggling Made Easy
Mail Order Made Easy
Handwriting Analysis Made Easy
Numerology Made Easy
Spelling Made Easy
Raquetball Made Easy

Table Tennis Made Easy
Tennis Made Easy
Horseback Riding Made Easy & Fun

A favorite word of mine to use, both in titles and in advertising copy, is the word "secret." Publications in which I have used this word are:

Exam Secret
Chess Secrets Revealed
Secrets of Winning Poker
Blackstone's Secrets of Magic
Secret of the Pyramids
Secret of Secrets
Secret of Bowling Strikes
Secret of Perfect Putting

The word "revealed" is very much to my liking, as evidenced by the following books I've published:

Hypnotism Revealed
Chess Secrets Revealed
Palmistry Secrets Revealed

I have often used the words "guide," "practical guide," and "expert's guide," as seen in the following publications:

Practical Guide to Concentration
Practical Guide to Public Speaking
Practical Guide to Self-Hypnosis
Practical Guide to Horseshoeing
Practical Guide to Owning Your Own Horse
Practical Guide to Being a Sexually Fulfilled Woman
Practical Guide to Being a Sexually Fulfilled Man
Guide to Developing Your Potential
Guide to Living in Balance
Guide to Personal Happiness
New Guide to Personal Happiness
New Guide to Rational Living
An Expert's Guide to Winning at 21
An Expert's Guide to Winning at Poker
An Expert's Guide to Winning at the Harness Races

The phrase "30 days" was used to give impact and definition to the following books, recently published:

30 Days to a Flatter Stomach
30 Days to a Beautiful Bottom
30 Days to a More Beautiful Bust

30 Days to More Beautiful Hair
Thin Thighs in 30 Days

There's a new book on the best-seller list called *How to Satisfy a Woman Every Time* by Naura Hayden. I'd rate that title A-1.

Dr. Albert Ellis wrote a book originally titled *How to Prevent Your Child from Becoming a Neurotic Adult*. The sales were minimal. I obtained the paperback rights and changed the title to *How to Raise an Emotionally Healthy, Happy Child*. The change in title resulted in robust sales. (See page 71.)

I followed the same procedure with equally gratifying results in the case of two paperbacks, previously called *1001 Ways to Checkmate* and *1001 Chess Sacrifices and Combinations*. I changed the titles to *1001 Brilliant Ways to Checkmate* and *1001 Winning Chess Sacrifices & Combinations*. Incorporating the words "brilliant" and "winning" into the titles turned both books into winners.

A singer-musician, Tommy Boyce, came to me with an idea for a book tentatively titled *How to Write a Hit Song*. I offered the simple addition of three words—"and Sell It." Three little words that spelled magic. What's the point of writing songs if you don't know how to sell them?

When I was actively involved in promoting and selling the book, *How to Write a Hit Song and Sell It,* I made an intensive search for a rhyming dictionary designed specifically for songwriters. To my utter amazement, I discovered there was no such thing, and I knew at once that I had stumbled onto something that had to become a best seller. I had hit upon a highly practical and essential tool that heretofore had been missing from the songwriter's do-it-yourself kit. I subsequently obtained the rights to a book called *The Improved Rhyming Dictionary* and changed the title to *The Songwriter's Rhyming Dictionary*. I've sold more rhyming dictionaries than songwriting books. Every songwriter needs one. Sammy Cahn, the famous songwriter, just wrote a rhyming dictionary with the same title.

On the subject of songwriting, my first chart song was called *Mr. Songwriter*. It was recorded by Sunday Sharpe on the United Artists Records, Inc. label, and went to #47 on the charts. To my recollection, no one, up until that time, had ever written a song about a songwriter, or a song in which the songwriter was the focal point of interest. The theme of the song had to do with asking a songwriter to come to the aid of the petitioner to help him avert impending disaster. The request was phrased with the following lyrics, which I wrote for the song:

Mr. Songwriter
　　Oh, Mr. Songwriter
Please teach me to write a love song
　　The way that you do
Two hearts have been broken
　　Unkind words were spoken
All because I was a fool to be untrue

Tommy liked the title, the melody, and the first two lines, but reacted unfavorably to the rest with the comment that they were "old hat." In their place, he substituted the following:

Mr. Songwriter
　　Oh, Mr. Songwriter
Please teach me to write a love song
　　The way that you do
One with a pretty melody
　　A lovely haunting melody
With words soft and sweet
　　And a phrase hidden deep saying
I love you

In retrospect, I would have preferred my original lyrics. Not merely because they suggested an interesting story, but because they were spiced with the essential ingredient known as conflict. Anyone listening to those lyrics could easily have identified with the trauma they posed.

Getting back to title changes, I made the following, all of them to the distinct advantage of the manuscripts as subsequently reflected in their sales:

Exercise for Figure Beauty to *Quick and Easy Exercises for Figure Beauty*
Exercises For Facial Beauty to *Quick and Easy Exercises for Facial Beauty*
How to Make Money with Junk to *How I Turn Junk into Fun and Profit*
How to Play the Harmonica to *How to Play the Harmonica for Fun and Profit*
Stamp Collecting to *Stamp Collecting for Fun and Profit*
How to Be a Comedian to *How to Be a Comedian for Fun and Profit*

How would you increase the effectiveness of the following title by making a slight addition? *How to Buy a Better Horse*. Answer: *How to Buy a Better Horse and Sell the Horse You Own*. Reason: When you buy a new horse, it is usually done with the idea of replacing another.

Subtitles

Consideration of subtitles is definitely warranted because subtitles serve a specific purpose; namely, to give the writer an opportunity to amplify a title. For example, my subtitle for this book is *An Expert's Step-by-Step Guide to Marketing Your Book Successfully*. This in effect gives definition to the title as well as direction to the book, *How to Self-Publish Your Book & Have the Fun & Excitement of Being a Best-Selling Author*. The title is the star, the subtitle the supporting actor giving meaning to the "star's" performance. The title, for commercial reasons, is designed for impact; it is the eye catcher, making attractive promises of things to come. The subtitle injects a note of reality, sharpens the focus on what the book is actually about. And that is what the reader really wants to know. But each title is important. One without the other lacks maximum effectiveness. In the subtitle, note that I have used two of my favorite title words: *An Expert's Step-by-Step Guide*.

In *Psycho-Cybernetics,* Dr. Maxwell Maltz used the subtitle, *A New Way to Get More Living Out of Life*. I changed it to *A New Technique for Using Your Subconscious Power*. That helped considerably to make the book the winner that it was. I had used a similar subtitle with equally good results in connection with an earlier publication, *Dynamic Thinking*.

Following is a list of books by title, and, below each title, the subtitle I gave it.

I Am a Complete Woman
An Adventure in Self-Discovery
Winning with Percentage Tennis
An Expert's Guide to Smart Court Strategy
Handwriting Analysis Made Easy
A Guide to Character & Human Behavior
Illustrated Yoga
Simple Yoga Postures for Good Health and Body Harmony
The Psychology of Handwriting
Secrets of Handwriting Analysis
Bee Pollen
Nature's Miracle Health Food

The Lame Horse
Causes, Symptoms, and Treatment
The Sexually Adequate Female
An eminent psychiatrist explains the physical and emotional causes of frigidity, how it can be cured, and how to achieve a satisfying sexual relationship.
The Sexually Adequate Male
An eminent psychiatrist explains the physical and emotional causes of impotence, how it can be cured, and how to achieve a satisfying sexual relationship.
Cosmopolitan's Love Book
A Guide to Ecstasy in Bed
New Approaches to Sex in Marriage
A sensitive guide to revitalizing sex and romance in marriage

In detailing the cover for the latter book, I took material directly from the content and incorporated it into the book's cover. See page 72.

Book Covers

Who said, You can't judge a book by its cover? It's a statement that is not irrefutably 100% true. If the book is going to be sold entirely by mail order, it is not essential that you devote too much attention to the cover. But in our marketing plan, we intend to sell your book in bookstores, special outlets (depending upon the nature of the book), and at seminars and lectures. In this case, the cover takes on special importance and deserves more than routine attention. An attractive and relevant cover will materially enhance your pride of authorship.

When you are ready to design your cover, select samples that appeal to you and convey your ideas to your artist. Give him as much input as you can with respect to the character of the book and the image you would like the cover to bring to prospective readers. If, after making a selection for your first edition, you change your mind or find you are not happy with the idea you have decided upon, don't hesitate to change it. You are never permanently locked into a given concept for a book cover.

A case in point is the book, *Guide to Rational Living.* I changed the cover three times (see page 73). The illustration, top left, was the first cover. It was a wash drawing of a famous couple. Do you recognize them? I later changed the cover to show a woman holding a cup. This produced a mild show of readership displeasure. "Why," asked the writers of letters we received, "do you have to use a sexy-looking woman to sell such a fine book?" It was at a time when the feminist movement was gaining momentum. I decided to change the cover to one that would be totally unobjectionable.

Once you have a successful book, you're going to experience a driving desire to follow that success with other books. And you should start to do so without delay, just as I did following my incredible success with *Psycho-Cybernetics*. I then published *Success-Cybernetics* by U. S. Andersen, *Cybernetics Within Us* by Y. Saparina, and *Dr. Psycho-Cybernetics* by Maxwell Maltz, M.D. (see page 75). Note the similarity of all four covers — a design which created immediate market identification. I added to the identification factor by personally writing a foreword for each of the books.

The spin-offs of the three books amounted to more than several million dollars in sales. Bear in mind that this was not accomplished by accident; it was achieved by design in thinking and design of the book covers.

I'm going to present some book covers that I particularly like. Most are in four colors as, obviously, it is not possible to create the same impression with black-and-white. I am extremely fond of the four horse-book covers on page 76. Four more of my favorites are on page 77. See page 78 and 79 for other good cover designs. All the books shown in the illustrations enjoy excellent sales.

Forewords and Testimonials

Both from a standpoint of sales and prestige, there is an enormous advantage in having an authority on the subject of your book write a foreword. This is accomplished by sending the authority in mind a copy of the manuscript, together with a letter soliciting his written foreword. Testimonials are acquired in the same way.

I write forewords for many of the self-help, inspirational books that I publish. I have often been told by purchasers that they bought the book on the strength of my foreword. I like a foreword with substance.

When I first published *Psycho-Cybernetics*, I wrote a foreword for the book. After the sale of a million copies, I wrote another foreword. (See pages 80, 81, 82 and 83.) This should give you some idea of the kind of forewords that will help sell your book. Read them, study and analyze them; then deposit them in your memory bank for future use.

New Approaches to Sex in Marriage

John E. Eichenlaub, M.D.

A sensitive guide to revitalizing sex and romance in marriage

Through no fault of your own or of your partner's, your sex life probably needs revitalizing. The basic problems with which this book deals affects a great many perfectly normal couples with perfectly normal sexual capabilities. In fact, those problems are so common that almost every couple faces them at one time or another.

Take the "seven-year itch," for instance—the boredom with each other, brought on at least partly by a sense of sameness in sex life, which leads so many husbands and wives to become sexually restless after a few years of loyal, satisfying marriage. Broadway viewed this situation as sufficiently universal to make it an apt subject for a comedy. Yet sex with one partner need never become "old hat" or tiresome if you use any substantial part of the wide array of varying approaches, caresses, positions, and special frictions available to you. Sex with the same partner can bring constantly enhanced response through emotional conditioning, and continual improvement in gratification through "zeroing in" on each other's sexual desires and needs, as this book discusses in complete detail. You can use *different techniques* to fulfill each other's need for variety, and promptly vanquish any yearning for an altered "team."

The feeling that sex has become mechanical, which so often plagues an otherwise satisfactory marriage, also can be attacked. Sex is the language of love, with each caress, posture, and maneuver a part of its vocabulary. You can express your feelings better, and appreciate your partner's love-making in much greater depth, if each of you knows more "gestures" and fully appreciates their significance. Sex reveals the man-woman relationship and always represents the state of your personal communion.

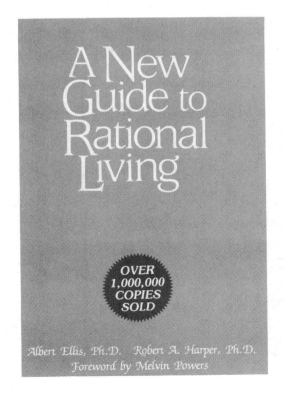

$7

SALES CYBERNETICS

New Scientific Techniques in
MOTIVATIONAL SELLING

BRIAN ADAMS

Foreword by
MELVIN POWERS

- **LEARN** the Secrets of the Top Sales Professionals
- **BECOME** a Dynamic Communicator and Motivator
- **APPLY** Cybernetic Principles and Increase Your Income

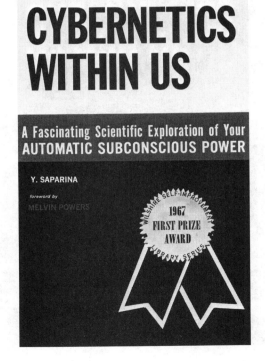

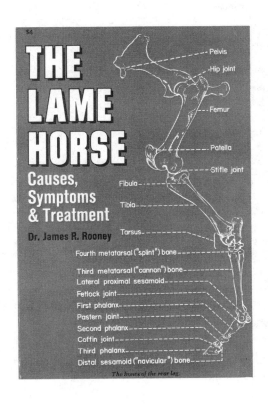

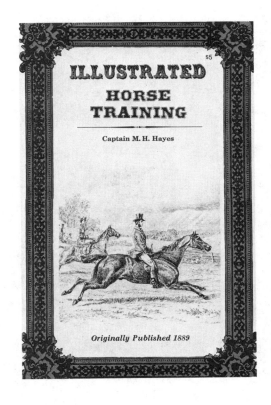

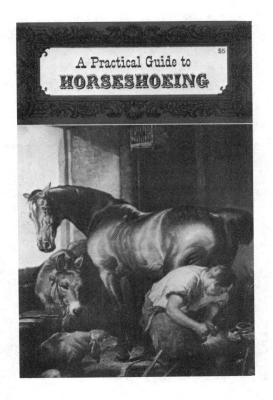

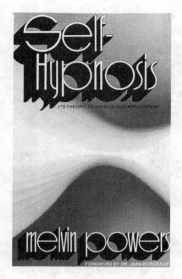

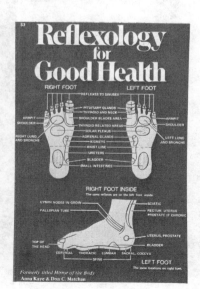

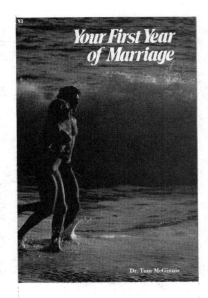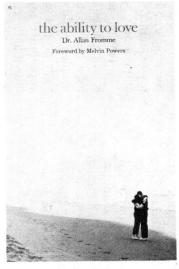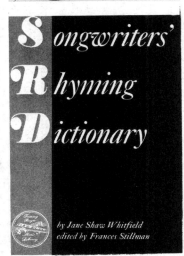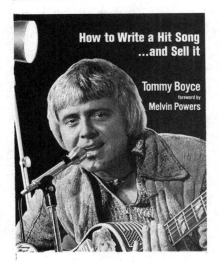

FOREWORD ON SELLING
ONE MILLION COPIES OF PSYCHO-CYBERNETICS

Not long ago, in looking over Wilshire Book Company's sales figures, I was delighted to discover that *Psycho-Cybernetics* had already sold well over one million copies—an event which always evokes a lyrical response from publishers. I am afraid I am no exception.

Psycho-Cybernetics, of course, has long since been hailed by its countless readers as a classic in its field, and is known to many, with no irreverence intended, as the "bible." Now, hopefully, it will join such giants as *How to Win Friends and Influence People, The Power of Positive Thinking* and Emile Coué's *Self Mastery Through Conscious Autosuggestion* ("Day by day, *in every way*, I am getting better and better").

Perhaps this may sound presumptuous, but every publisher is entitled to a dream and it is my dream that *Psycho-Cybernetics* will change the lives of many more millions of persons than have already found its philosophy meaningful and rewarding, capable of improving personalities and erasing negative habit patterns. In short, I hope many more individuals will find it a platform on which they can construct happy, useful, creative lives.

Gratifying as it might be to state unequivocably that I envisioned the astonishing success of this unique book, I cannot lay claim fairly to such omniscience. At the inception of cybernetics some years ago, I was enormously impressed by the application of cybernetic models of learning to human beings, but I am frank to confess I am constantly amazed by the vast number of persons who share my enthusiasm. After all, the advent of cybernetics was greeted with dismay by millions who thought it portended their doom in many fields it was invading.

III

I was, in fact, excited to find that eliminating negative personality patterns or establishing positive habit patterns using *Psycho-Cybernetics* principles produced results every bit as convincing as Pavlovian conditioning methods without evoking a mental picture of salivating dogs. It was, indeed, the most all-inclusive and effective methodology for changing an individual's total life style that I had ever encountered.

Quite naturally, with this sort of enthusiasm, I was desirous of finding some way through which readers of *Psycho-Cybernetics* could utilize its remarkable new concepts to the fullest extent, but the readers themselves supplied the answer. Thousands of letters poured in informing me that Psycho-Cybernetics study groups, hundreds of them, were being formed all over the country. Since then, I am happy to report that readers who have wished to share their experiences with others have written to ask me where meetings in their area are being held. This same service is available also to new readers.

One of the most surprising things to me about the many letters expressing the potent force for good that *Psycho-Cybernetics* has become in countless lives, is the multiplicity of purposes for which its philosophy is used. Conceived originally as a monograph on improving the self-image so that a more mature and adequate personality would evolve, the book is now being used to combat alcoholism, drug addiction, character defects and other problems of a serious nature. It must be added at this point that the book is in no way intended to replace psychiatric and medical consultation, nor is it meant to be a panacea for all human ills. Nevertheless, I am gratified that a number of physicians of my acquaintance consider the book of great therapeutic help, and not only because it was written by a fellow practitioner.

This has not been entirely unexpected because the book is built on sound and proven psychological practice. Written by a highly successful medical doctor, there is nothing in it which could conflict with personal professional advice. The basic proposition was based on the fact that changing one's appearance for the better did not necessarily increase the individual's self-esteem. The rest of the propositions followed in scholarly and orderly progression.

Properly, *Psycho-Cybernetics* is a masterful synthesis of several proven psychological and physiological processes. The

IV

V

first is the self-image concept as first postulated by Prescott Lecky, a Columbia University psychologist, who coined the now popular concept under the name of Self-Consistency. His theory, too, required a critical evaluation of one's assets and liabilities before an appropriate self-image could be perceived.

Some 12 years after Lecky did his original research on the incalculable benefits which accrued from an adequate self-image, Dr. Norbert Wiener, a brilliant mathematician, published *Cybernetics* in 1949. The original book, filled with abstruse mathematical equations, was fully understood only by a handful of scientists who had become interested in his work for the government during World War II when he developed an unerring method of keeping missiles on target.

In 1950, he wrote *The Human Use of Human Beings*, a book for laymen in which he demonstrated that the same method used to program computers to operate machines could be used to program the human mind so it could achieve desirable goals. It should not be difficult to see how the combination of the self-image concept and cybernetics became a potent factor in personality development. The two dissimilar theories, when united, became as homogenous as air and water.

However, there were still further refinements to come. Since the days of Dr. Ivan Pavlov (1849-1936), the great Russian physiologist, it had been established that bad habit patterns could be replaced by successful habit patterns by the application of conditioned reflexology, the so-called Pavlovian conditioning method which is still the basis of Russian psychiatry.

Individuals with an appropriate self-image could program supportive pictures into their minds consciously until it became a part of their subconscious, and constant repetition eventually made suitable actions and responses as Pavlovian as their old inappropriate images and responses had been.

Of course, many other ingredients enter into the total formula for success and happiness embodied in *Psycho-Cybernetics*. It is not the purpose of an introduction, however, to review the book it is introducing, but to clarify and reinforce it whenever possible. The writer thinks the story behind the story is of interest to all those who have taken this book to their heart.

VI

One more adjunctive aid, mentioned frequently in *Psycho-Cybernetics*, deserves elaboration here. Its most recent resurgence began in the early 40's and reached a peak when the A.M.A. accepted it as a valid modality in the practice of medicine and psychiatry. It must be added that it has languished in medicine for the past several years chiefly because many physicians have been too inept, too busy, or frightened by old wives' tales resurrected by some of their leaders. Psychologists, on the other hand, are using it frequently in the treatment of behavioral disorders.

In *Psycho-Cybernetics*, hypnosis is explained as part of the "normal operating processes of the human brain and nervous system." Nothing, it is added, of an "occult or supra-normal" nature is at work. Dr. Theodore Barber, a respected investigator of hypnotic phenomena, found that subjects were able to easily produce remarkable phenomena when they were *convinced* that the hypnotist's words were true statements. You can do the same thing for yourself with self-hypnosis.

An extremely important point in *Psycho-Cybernetics* is that one cannot convince oneself into developing new personality patterns until one becomes *dehypnotized*, which means all the old false beliefs must be methodically eliminated by hypnosis in "reverse." It is axiomatic that we are all hypnotized to some extent (TV commercials are a good example) whether or not we have undergone formal induction. It is no exaggeration to say that all of us are more or less hypnotized whenever we uncritically accept ideas from others.

Inasmuch as hypnosis, like psychiatry, is expensive, its use is limited by the economic factors involved. This is unfortunate, of course, but the fact remains that self-hypnosis can be every bit as effective and can be rather easily learned from a detailed book of instruction. Such a book is *A Practical Guide to Self-Hypnosis*, a book that has become a standard in the field. In simple, easily followed language it elucidates the most effective methods of inducing self-hypnosis, and the process of programming the subconscious mind so that appropriate actions become automatic, requiring no conscious, constant and tedious repetition once the rationale has been mastered.

I have seen so much accomplished by hypnosis that I feel quite strongly about psychiatrists and psychoanalysts

VII

who refuse to use this modality in psychological treatment. It is easy to say that the disorders are only symptomatic, that the real cause lies deeper, but the patient, under hypnosis, can lose his symptoms and deep sense of humiliation, thus facilitating treatment of the root cause, if only because communication is greatly increased.

In *A Practical Guide to Self-Hypnosis*, hypnosis is defined as a "state of heightened suggestibility in which the subject is able to accept uncritically ideas for self-improvement and act on them appropriately." When the suggestions come from the patient himself the process is known as self-hypnosis. When the suggestions are given by hypnotherapists it is known as hetero-hypnosis.

There are so many myths and fallacious beliefs about hypnosis it would be impossible to enumerate them all in this introduction. Suffice it to say that many of them revolve around the erroneous belief that a patient "surrenders his will to the hypnotist" and that he is "powerless to resist" inappropriate suggestions. Some individuals believe that they will become hypnotized and "never come out of it." Nonsense. All of it.

Some people ask how they can give themselves suggestions if they are under hypnosis. It must be remembered that the hypnotic subject is always aware of what is going on. He can think, reason, act, suggest or do whatever he desires. In self-hypnosis the subject can give himself audible or mental suggestions. The main thing to remember is that the pathway to the subconscious mind is unobstructed and deep thought must be devoted to the suggestions given.

Although self-hypnosis does not exhaust the self-improvement methods synthesized in *Psycho-Cybernetics*, it completes the major influences. Blending them all together is more art than science, and the results can be very gratifying, impressive and, indeed, at times, electrifying.

A truly extraordinary book which may be read to supplement *Psycho-Cybernetics* is *A Guide to Rational Living* by Drs. Albert Ellis and Robert A. Harper. Dr. Ellis is an internationally renowned sexologist and the book is the finest of its kind I have ever read. The authors list, along with suitable case histories, a multiplicity of methods to aid in achieving a happy, non-neurotic, eminently rewarding life style.

One of the most important points made in *A Guide to*

VIII

Rational Living occurs in the first chapter where Drs. Ellis and Harper ask, "How Far Can You Go With Self-Analysis?" An excellent question and one which I answered earlier in regard to *Psycho-Cybernetics*. Briefly, neither book is a substitute for intensive psychotherapy when such a probing analysis is desperately needed. Some people, deeply disturbed, simply cannot be objective about themselves, rationalizing all their faults and blaming them on others.

Whether such persons are overtly paranoid or just indulging in the inalienable American right to complain should be decided by trained psychotherapists. Nevertheless, Drs. Ellis and Harper have written a book in which the reader is shown how to help himself. It has helped and is helping countless thousands of individuals.

The authors suggest that many more could be helped if the readers did not distort principles of self-help, and "read into these principles what they *want* to read." Some, they say, "oversimplify, edit out most of the author's carefully stated *ifs*, *ands*, and *buts*, and use the most cautiously stated rules as if they were breezy slogans which can be cavalierly applied to any afflicted person in any situation."

Still, they report case after case in which confused and unhappy individuals have received insight into their own problems and empathy for the problems of those close to them through the medium of their books. This should be vastly encouraging to those who read *Psycho-Cybernetics, A Guide to Rational Living*, and other books recommended in these pages.

Those who are unable to afford individual therapy, but lack the confidence to embark on a program calculated by professional therapists to relieve their distressing personality and emotional traits should take their courage in hand and read the books we have commented on, beginning with *Psycho-Cybernetics*. Most of them will be delighted and astonished at the changes which will be wrought in their lives. The phrase, "The Good Life," becomes more than a chimerical bromide.

In the book, *The Human Use of Human Beings*, Dr. Wiener argued that man was not a closed or isolated system. He takes in food, which generates energy, from the outside, and becomes a part of that larger world which contains the sources of his vitality. More importantly, he takes in informa-

IX

tion through his sense organs and acts on the information received.

It should be apparent now that Dr. Wiener was in hot pursuit of a theory which had only a common equation between men and machines. He had used a feedback mechanism in guns and missiles to preclude error, and he reasoned man unerringly could thrust forward to his goal by the same mechanism, translated into human terms.

In *Psycho-Cybernetics* a constant flow of positive feedback, really a series of checks and balances by the subject, indicates the individual is "on course." Correction, when miscalculation occurs, is accomplished by negative feedback, utilizing just enough counter-action to correct one's course.

There are two dangers here the neophyte must learn to control. First is the impulse to overcompensate and apply too much negative feedback, thus deviating from your course in a different direction. A few experiences like this and you may have a tendency to undercompensate which leaves you basically on the same incorrect course.

If this inhibited reaction becomes an established pattern, the individual may become permanently fearful that he will be unable to make the proper response in the attainment of his goals and develop a permanent "block." Fortunately, trial and error usually indicate just how much negative feedback is necessary and inhibition is dissipated.

Letters to me indicate some readers were a little too gentle with their egos when they first evaluated their assets and liabilities prior to establishing a realistic self-image and attainable goals. Because this personal assessment is so vital at the start, it would be better to err in the direction of harshness than saving face. Be rigorously honest. It will pay priceless dividends later on in your self-improvement program.

Using the flashback method, I would like to return once more to *A Guide to Rational Living*, a complementary companion piece to *Psycho-Cybernetics*. In its pages is discussed one of the day's most pressing social problems: The apparent reversal of sex roles taking place all over America. Dr. Margaret Mead, the noted anthropologist, states that the discrepancy in sex roles, which leaves women in a "vacuum," is becoming so conspicuous that "both sexes are paying a heavy price."

X

What is causing this reversal of sex roles? It appears a moot question but in the meantime millions of males are becoming more passive-feminine and millions of females are becoming more aggressive-masculine. The high incidence of this neurotic striving is helping to make the identity crisis of our children more serious. Sons cannot identify with passive fathers nor girls with aggressive mothers without danger of, among other things, increasing homosexuality, something sexologists are noting far more frequently.

Drs. Ellis and Harper make some pertinent and perceptive statements about our new "girlish boys and boyish girls," and their remarks might fit in well in helping you to visualize a healthy, heterosexual self-image as suggested in *Psycho-Cybernetics*.

There is much more of interest that could be added to this new introduction to *Psycho-Cybernetics*, but the book contains aids to success of every description, including many fascinating case histories. Read it with care along with *A Guide to Rational Living*, follow its suggestions with exactitude and consciously do everything to improve your personality until your subconscious mind takes over and makes your task an easy one.

It is my earnest hope that you will have the same remarkable results from following the precepts laid down in *Psycho-Cybernetics* as the millions who have preceded you through its pages. Do not hesitate to write me if you encounter problems or if you wish to attend group discussions. These group discussions, incidentally, are an excellent medium for making friends who have a community of interests with you.

In conclusion, my congratulations in advance to the *new* you who will emerge from intensive study and much practice of the methods in this therapeutic and inspirational book.

Melvin Powers
Publisher

12015 Sherman Road
No. Hollywood, California 91605

```
                    INGRAM BOOK COMPANY
        347 REEDWOOD DRIVE        NASHVILLE, TENNESSEE 37217
                       615-361-5000


4177              PUBLISHER SALES BY STATE REPORT FOR WILSHIRE BOOK COMPANY
                          SALES FOR SEPTEMBER 1983
                                      UNITS          NET SALES


             TENNESSEE                145             256.28
             ALABAMA                   26              46.23
             ALASKA                     7              15.93
             ARIZONA                   54             114.33
             ARKANSAS                  20              35.19
             CALIFORNIA               666           1,610.44
             COLORADO                   3               5.76
             CONNECTICUT               23              42.03
             DELAWARE                   4               7.26
             DIS OF COLUMBIA            5              13.60
             FLORIDA                  184             361.39
             GEORGIA                   53             104.75
             HAWAII                    27              63.52
             IDAHO                     34              64.17
             ILLINOIS                  47              97.56
             INDIANA                   30              53.55
             IOWA                      23              44.92
             KANSAS                    30              53.19
             KENTUCKY                  44              80.97
             LOUISIANA                 26              55.46
             MAINE                      3               5.40
             MARYLAND                  25              44.97
             MASSACHUSETTS             27              50.88
             MICHIGAN                  86             172.59
             MINNESOTA                 40              72.92
             MISSISSIPPI               32              56.97
             MISSOURI                  22              46.44
             MONTANA                   17              29.94
             NEBRASKA                  26              48.36
             NEVADA                     9              18.38
             NEW HAMPSHIRE              5               8.85
             NEW JERSEY                22              47.02
             NEW MEXICO                17              30.39
             NEW YORK                  36              67.09
             NORTH CAROLINA            86             150.21
             OHIO                     178             322.23
             OKLAHOMA                  24              47.47
             OREGON                    48              84.27
             PENNSYLVANIA              52             106.60
             SOUTH CAROLINA            27              48.33
             SOUTH DAKOTA               7              12.36
             TEXAS                    219             455.17
             UTAH                      86             172.48
             VIRGINIA                  42              88.97
             WASHINGTON               126             236.18
             WEST VIRGINIA             18              36.20
             WISCONSIN                 31              59.70
             WYOMING                    7              12.57
             VERMONT                   13              22.98
                                       10              17.10

             GRAND TOTAL            2,792           5,699.55
```

Chapter Eight

Marketing Strategy Through Bookstores, Libraries, Colleges, Special Outlets and Wholesalers

Let us assume you have published your book and are now prepared to sell it to the book trade. As an initial suggestion, price your book sensibly at $5.00, $10.00, $15.00 or at whatever figure you have chosen. But I urge you to avoid the fragmented figures, such as $4.95, $9.95, $14.95. Contrary to practice and popular conception, there is no documented, irrefutable proof that this kind of pricing results in more sales than a system of rounded-out price tags. If the customer is willing to pay $4.95 for the book he wants, he's willing to pay $5.00. And by the same token, if he's unwilling to pay $5.00, he will not pay $4.95—a savings of five cents! In short, if the customer really wants the book, he will pay the asking price.

You would be well advised to start your sales campaign in your own hometown. Do whatever you can to coordinate some publicity about your book and yourself in your local newspaper, as well as on radio and television. A local person who has made good to the extent of getting his book on the bookstands is good copy, and newspapers are happy to print an article. It's a local achievement—a matter of local pride, and that's news. Avail yourself of such an opportunity.

You should make it a point to call on the booksellers in your area, introduce yourself, and carry copies of your book. Regardless of whether the book was self-published or company-published, the point is that it was published, and that makes you something of a celebrity. So the local treatment should be good, and it should be generous. Take advantage of the fact by asking for a counter and window display for the book. Chances are good that you'll get it, even if only on the strength of civic

pride. Every city loves to herald local achievement above and beyond the call of routine duty.

When I first published *How to Write a Hit Song and Sell It* by Tommy Boyce, I was able to get a large number of window displays. Tommy and I surrounded copies of the book with sheet music of his famous songs, such as *Last Train to Clarksville, Come a Little Bit Closer, Pretty Little Angel Eyes, I Wanna Be Free,* and *Valerie.* We even brought our guitars and walked into the bookstores playing and singing. Needless to say, it piqued the curiosity and attracted the attention of the persons we were hoping to see. We got a window display at the famous Pickwick Bookshop in Hollywood and had our pictures taken with Mr. and Mrs. Louis Epstein, the proprietors, and their store personnel (see page 89).

An idea that could pay big dividends is to arrange to have your picture taken with the bookstore owner, explaining that you would like the picture for a local newspaper story to feature yourself as a self-publisher calling on the book trade in anticipation of your book becoming a best seller. The dealer will be delighted with the idea because it means good publicity for his bookstore. Everyone in business is amenable to good publicity, especially when it's free.

Tommy and I also managed to call on the record shops, and we actually sold more books in these establishments than in the bookstores. Here, too, we got window and counter displays, and in some places the name Tommy Boyce even got marquee mention. (See page 89.)

Don't be defensive about your publicity-seeking endeavors. Adopt the attitude that calling on the book trade and special outlets is a pleasant, profitable and learning experience, and that what you're doing could be just as beneficial to the dealer as to yourself. Dealers need books that they can sell. This is the meat-and-potatoes of their business, their source of profit. As a rule, their doors will be open to you. But there are those who adhere to the theory that all salespeople are guilty until proven innocent, and from them you are apt to meet some resistance. Be ready for them by careful preparation. For this, you need a hook, a gimmick, a story or sales pitch to enlist their interest in what you have to sell. It's been my experience that most retailers are receptive and will give you at least five minutes to make your presentation.

Now let's assume that your book is already in the bookstore, and what is needed is some method to get it moving. What do you do? Well, you might find it advisable to run an ad in your local newspaper informing the reader that the long-awaited book is now available and directing him to procure it at his favorite bookstore.

If you are able to get newspaper or other publicity on a local level, send it along with your book to the following major chains. If even just one of them likes your book, it could mean sales of thousands of copies, and even a potential best seller:

B. Dalton, Bookseller—P.O. Box 1844, Westbury, N.Y. 11590-9604.

Walden Book Company, Inc.—201 High Ridge Road—Stamford, Connecticut 06904

Doubleday Book Shops, 724 Fifth Avenue, New York, N.Y. 10019

Send the same material to the following wholesalers:

Ingram Book Company, 1125 Heil Quaker Blvd., La Vergne, TN 37086-1986

Baker & Taylor Company, 1515 Broadway, New York, N.Y. 10036

Sales to bookstores generally carry a discount of 40% and terms net/30 days. They also pay the postage. If the book sells for $10.00, their cost is $6.00 plus postage. They should pay in 30 days, but, in practice, it's usually 60 days.

Sales to wholesalers or jobbers are generally at a discount of 50% plus postage. Terms are net/60 days. In practice, it's usually 90 days.

Wholesalers, as a rule, do not sell or promote books. They act as a repository. Many bookstore owners would rather deal with one or two wholesalers than a large number of publishers. It simplifies ordering and paper work. See page 84 for Ingram's computer read-out for one month's sales of my books.

Let us assume that copies of your book have been sent to various newspapers and magazines and that you have received a few favorable book reviews. Photo-copy those reviews and use them in all of your outgoing sales literature. Naturally, the more reviews the better. If you manage to get on television or local radio, see to it that black-and-white photographs are taken of you and the interviewer, and have your book prominently featured. (See page 90.) These photos should also be included in your sales literature. They are an impressive marketing device. It adds excitement to your participation in the project, and, above all, it's great fun.

Pages 91, 92, 93 and 94 contain mailing lists you can purchase from R.R. Bowker Company, 121 Chanlon Road, New Providence, New Jersey 07974. I use its lists and am extremely pleased with the service. They will supply the names on pressure-sensitive labels. This makes it very easy for you to do the mailing yourself. If you're involved with large quantities of mail, contact a professional mailing service for reasonable rates and you'll wind up saving time and money.

On page 92 there is a list of college and paperback bookstores. You can rent any part of it for correspondingly less. This is true of any company that deals in lists. They'll rent you a single state, if you wish.

I'd particularly like you to take note of the lists pertaining to public libraries and libraries of the government, federal, and armed forces. These names could be a veritable gold mine for you.

I would advise you to start with a minimal quantity, tabulating the results. If they're good, continue. If not, stop and analyze your literature.

You can also run ads in *Publishers Weekly, The American Bookseller* and the *Library Journal*.

I developed my business with the book trade mainly through the use of direct mail. Over the years, the entire book trade has come to be familiar with my name. See page 95 for the type of direct mail I have found to be very effective. The mailing piece is made of the same material as the cover of this book and is the same size. On one side, I very clearly state my message; the reverse side has the order form. With this style of mailer, busy bookstore people get the message quickly.

I do not cover expenses with every mailing. My profits result largely from reorders. Your goal should be to get the bookstores to stock your book, and, hopefully, display it with the cover showing. If you have faith in the book and in its salability, be consistent with your mailings. They will pay dividends.

I have one of the best sales representatives working for me. Her territory covers California, Alaska, Hawaii, Arizona and Nevada. She has been representing me for 25 years and I have yet to find anyone to compare to her. Betty Gaskill is known and loved by everyone in the business.

Equally well known throughout the industry, and adored by everyone, is my sales manager and chief executive officer for 25 years. Frieda Freedman runs our multi-million-dollar operation effectively with calm efficiency and with total dedication. She knows all the accounts and is in personal contact with our distributors, not only in the United States but in every part of the world. She has her finger on the pulse of the business and is one of those rare individuals who, by the very nature of her personal makeup, is the best public-relations asset a business could conceivably have. If you want to meet a genuine thoroughbred in the field of professionals, visit our office sometime and ask for Frieda. Enjoy the treat of her engaging personality, but don't try to steal her away!

If you desire sales representation, run an ad in *Publishers Weekly* in the "Weekly Exchange" classified section, or answer an ad for a representative looking for a line of books. Every library carries a copy of *Publishers Weekly*. Don't be hesitant about soliciting representation merely because you have only one book. Who knows, that book might become a million seller. Besides, you won't always be a single-book publisher. Once the book is successful, you'll be on to the next in very short order.

Just as soon as your sales progress in the United States, I'll help you get overseas representation. Contact me before you sign up with any company, and I'll help you select those that will do a good job for you and pay you within a reasonable length of time.

I'm sure this sounds like a lot of work and a great amount of detail. Well, it is. But there is no other way; no short-cuts. You must take it one step at a time. Once you have become successful, you'll get offers from book companies wanting to handle your sales. When that happens, ask yourself these questions: Do I want it? What profits will I be giving up? Is the paper work actually bogging me down to the extent that I need their help? There are plus and minus considerations, but my advice to you is do not accept the offer. You can always get a fulfillment house to handle your invoicing and the shipping of your books, and the rates are reasonable. It is also possible to get capable college students to assist you. In this way, you will be able to free yourself of all the detail work and concentrate on the creative end. The creative aspects of writing your book and arranging for its sale are of prime importance and are the two main elements that will produce big profits.

If you haven't yet experienced it, you will be amazed at the motivational force inherent in profit-taking. Even though I am still in the process of writing this book, I'm already looking forward to my next. In fact, I even have the title. I am also working on new books with some of my established authors.

If your success gives you the desire to publish not only your own books but those of others, you will have a career without equal. From many perspectives, there is nothing from which you will exact greater personal satisfaction. There's always the possibility you will have an idea for a book that could sell millions, or publish someone else's book that could become a runaway best seller. The ever-present prospect of making it to the best-seller list can generate energy to churn the creative juices. For my part I can hardly wait to get to my office each morning to find what book ideas have come in the mail. I can hardly wait for the phone to start ringing—the call could be my next winner.

As far as I know, I am the only publisher who solicits telephone calls from individuals wishing to discuss book ideas. I can immediately indicate to the caller whether I am or am not interested in his idea. All I want to know is the title. Most publishers ask to see an outline, a synopsis, and perhaps three chapters.

On a personal note, I have no desire to be in any other profession. I love my "work," and every day is filled with the magic of creativity and the excitement of opportunity. There are no shackles on my inventive resources. What I choose to dream of doing, I do. I answer to no one or to anything except my own principles of professional integrity. And I can't be fired.

Besides, I'm having a great time. I have a piano and a guitar in my office which provides my staff and me whatever entertainment we can manage to elicit from visitors who know how to play those instruments. We have been entertained in this fashion by seasoned professionals who have come on business but who have stayed to enjoy an impromptu musical session.

The *Los Angeles Times*, Sunday edition, recently carried my picture and a story about me. The paper, with its Sunday circulation of 1,400,000 readers, mentioned the name of my mail-order book and did an article on my seminars. (See page 96.) The results were incredible. We were deluged with orders for the book, and my seminars were subsequently filled to capacity. The phones in the office didn't stop ringing for one solid week. It seemed that everyone in town had suddenly come up with a great mail-order product, and wanted me to become a partner. Had I been a less discriminating person, I could easily have wound up the year with 365 partners.

That newspaper article constituted a perfect piece of "advertising copy." To quote Marcia Grad, my publicist, "Good publicity represents subliminal advertising that money can't buy." She's right. That bit of publicity was actually worth thousands of dollars. You cannot buy such a story—it must appear under the guise of publicity. And that's the job of the publicist.

With regard to the most appropriate method of merchandising your book, my advice is to start in an area of mail order or direct selling in which you feel most comfortable. Start publicity aimed at the proper exposure of you and your book. Become involved conducting seminars, giving informal lectures or just talks in your particular area of accomplishment or expertise. Explore all avenues for the merchandising of your book. Listen to feedback from whatever source, and evaluate it carefully. Be mindful that from even negative feedback there can come clues that point in a positive direction. And from it all, hopefully you'll generate momentum in your campaign that will be self-perpetuating and conducive to excellent sales. Remember, every sale is a good sale even if it's a single book. That purchaser could be responsible for selling hundreds, even thousands, of copies of your book.

Just prior to the Six-Day War, I published two books about Israel. After the war, visiting Israel for the first time on a fact-finding mission, I met the General who led the Israeli forces to victory and had my picture taken with him.

I used this picture in a direct-mail piece sent to bookstores, stating that if the store owner/buyer could name the General, I'd send the two new books to him free. Over 100 bookstore owners/buyers sent the correct name. It was an excellent way to introduce the books; you might want to use a variation of this technique for your own promotion. See page 97.

Can you name the General? If so, send in his name. You'll receive either a free copy of *The Story of Israel in Stamps* or *The Story of Israel in Coins,* or a surprise book.

Feel free to call or write to me at any time to tell me how your overall campaign is progressing. I'll look forward to hearing from you. We'll try to solve the marketing puzzle together.

The next chapter relates to self-publishers who have become extremely successful using the techniques advocated in this book. It will lend credibility to my techniques and demonstrate how they work effectively when properly applied.

Tommy Boyce and Melvin Powers promoting their new book *How to Write a Hit Song and Sell It.*

Here I am on television promoting the third edition of *How to Get Rich in Mail Order.* This picture was taken on August 28, 1981 on Inez Pedroza's "Daybreak L. A." show on KABC-TV, Hollywood.

Bowker Mailing Lists.
A Straight Line to Success

All of the lists included in this brochure are derived from our extensive database resources and are available to you at competitive prices.

LIBRARIES

Libraries are broken down to highlight particular specializations, depending on the type of readership they serve.

☐ **Public libraries in the U.S.** are categorized according to book budget, ranging from annual book budgets of approximately $1000 to the large libraries that spend up to $200,000 and more a year on book buying.

☐ **College and university libraries** are likewise categorized by budget – ranging from $10,000 to $200,000.

☐ **School libraries** below the college level are broken down into two categories:

A) general libraries serving specific grade levels, i.e., public high schools, public junior high schools, etc.

B) school libraries at various levels that employ a full time librarian.

☐ **Special libraries** – medical, law, religious Spanish-language libraries, to name a few – are listed individually.

NAMES	COUNTS	PRICES
Public libraries in the U.S.	9,337	$ 350.00
Public libraries, book budgets over $1,000	6,405	$ 250.00
Public libraries, book budgets over $5,000	3,670	$ 150.00
Public libraries, book budgets over $10,000	2,600	$ 110.00
Public libraries, book budgets over $25,000	1,404	$ 55.00
Public libraries, book budgets over $50,000	760	$ 35.00
Public libraries, book budgets over $100,000	287	$ 35.00
Public libraries, book budgets over $200,000	123	$ 30.00
County and regional libraries	1,584	$ 45.00
Government, federal, and armed forces libraries	1,505	$ 45.00
Branch public libraries (public libraries without their own book budgets)	6,068	$ 195.00
Libraries in Canada of all kinds	2,897	$ 85.00
College and university libraries	1,867	$ 65.00
College and university libraries, book budgets over $10,000	1,492	$ 55.00
College and university libraries, book budgets over $25,000	1,074	$ 40.00
College and university libraries, book budgets over $50,000	647	$ 35.00
College and university libraries, book budgets over $100,000	395	$ 30.00
College and university libraries, book budgets over $200,000	236	$ 30.00
Junior college libraries	1,229	$ 45.00
Public high school libraries	16,173	$ 550.00
Public high school libraries with full time librarian	10,320	$ 375.00
Junior high school libraries	13,471	$ 425.00
Junior high school libraries with full time librarian	8,350	$ 320.00
Elementary school libraries	48,890	$1000.00
Elementary school libraries with full time librarian	14,020	$ 450.00
Catholic high school libraries	1,495	$ 55.00
Catholic elementary school libraries	7,094	$ 260.00
Private high school libraries	1,519	$ 45.00
Private elementary school libraries	1,818	$ 45.00
Law libraries	1,435	$ 45.00
Medical libraries	2,846	$ 80.00
Libraries with record collections	6,687	$ 200.00
Libraries with film collections	3,796	$ 140.00
Libraries that buy Spanish-language books	1,504	$ 45.00

NAMES	COUNTS	PRICES
Religious libraries of all types	1,777	$ 45.00
Catholic libraries	314	$ 25.00
Protestant libraries	952	$ 35.00
Jewish libraries	269	$ 25.00
Special libraries of various kinds (including the following)	11,006	$ 325.00
Libraries with business collections	2,965	$ 100.00
Corporation-owned libraries (this list is included in the above)	1,360	$ 50.00
Technical libraries	4,139	$ 130.00
Corporation-owned technical libraries	2,276	$ 85.00
Business and technical libraries	6,305	$ 225.00
Social and behavioral science libraries	2,707	$ 85.00
Agriculture, botany, fisheries, food, forest libraries	1,493	$ 55.00
Art and architecture libraries	1,209	$ 40.00
Historical society and museum libraries	986	$ 35.00
Music libraries	630	$ 35.00

LIBRARY SCHOOL FACULTY

Library school faculty (name list)	2,023	$ 75.00

LIBRARY NETWORKS, CONSORTIA, AND ORGANIZATIONS

Library networks, consortia, and organizations	370	$ 30.00

BOOKSELLERS

☐ Bowker offers a wide variety of general and specialized bookselling outlets. Bookstores are classified as *general,* by *type* (i.e., college bookstores or chain bookstores) or by *specialization* (i.e., bookstores with especially comprehensive stocks of law, black studies, or religious books).

NAMES	COUNTS	PRICES
Book outlets of all kinds in the U.S.	25,353	$725.00
General bookstores handling new books	10,898	$400.00
Selected bookstores	1,595	$ 80.00
Chain bookstores	1,906	$ 70.00
Dept. store book depts.	1,597	$ 55.00
Canadian bookstores of all kinds	2,142	$ 65.00
Remainder bookstores	3,958	$100.00
Elementary, junior high, high school bookstores	1,808	$ 55.00
College and paperback bookstores	12,706	$475.00
College bookstores	3,675	$160.00
Bookstores handling the following:		
Paperback books	11,888	$410.00
Law, medicine, science, and technology	2,026	$ 75.00
Religious books of all kinds	5,686	$195.00
Protestant books	4,272	$160.00
Catholic books	2,236	$ 80.00
Jewish books	1,255	$ 45.00
Metaphysics	838	$ 35.00
Health sciences (yoga, diet, nutrition)	323	$ 30.00
Science fiction and fantasy	281	$ 30.00
Sexuality	29	$ 20.00
Homosexuality	26	$ 20.00
Feminism	112	$ 25.00
Black studies	1,020	$ 45.00
Bookstores *specializing primarily* in the following:		
General books	5,365	$195.00
Paperbacks	697	$ 35.00
Juvenile books	163	$ 30.00
College	331	$ 30.00
Religion	1,232	$ 40.00
Protestant books	1,010	$ 40.00
Catholic books	180	$ 25.00
Jewish books	66	$ 25.00
Metaphysics	156	$ 25.00
Law	60	$ 25.00

NAMES	COUNTS	PRICES
Medical books	65	$ 25.00
Technical books	55	$ 25.00
Remainders	20	$ 20.00
Used books	429	$ 30.00
Stationers, drug stores, office supplies, etc.	447	$ 75.00
Mail order	1,001	$ 45.00
Antiquarian	1,520	$ 45.00
Second hand and rare book dealers	2,807	$ 95.00
Second hand dealers	2,804	$ 80.00
Rare book dealers	2,363	$ 65.00
Law book dealers	436	$ 30.00
School book dealers	631	$ 35.00
Medical book dealers	670	$ 30.00
Technical book dealers	1,529	$ 45.00
Wholesalers of books	1,186	$ 45.00
Juvenile book dealers	7,461	$225.00
Specialty shops (health foods, feminism, politics)	1,676	$ 60.00

PUBLISHERS

☐ We present three lists in the section *Publishers:* a comprehensive list of over 12,000 companies, a smaller, more refined list of nearly 1,600 selected publishers in the U.S., and a list of Canadian publishers.

Book publishers in the U.S.	12,050	$475.00
Selected U.S. book publishers	1,612	$ 70.00
Book publishers in Canada	167	$ 30.00

CHILDREN'S BOOK SPECIALISTS

☐ This section is broken down into a variety of lists by grade level and specialization. It is possible to target your mailing pieces to the exact person serving schools at the state, faculty, or school board levels. These valuable name lists are updated and cleaned with the the same care as our institutional lists.

Children's book specialists of all kinds (including the following)	8,189	$280.00
School library supervisors (name list)	2,551	$100.00
Young adult specialists (name list)	1,877	$ 65.00
Teachers of courses in library science with an emphasis in children's literature (name list)	1,199	$ 45.00
Selected reviewers, librarians, educators (name list)	3,486	$110.00

SPECIALIZED LISTS

☐ **BOOK REVIEWERS**

Book reviewers for magazines, newspapers (name list)	896	$ 50.00

☐ **ENVIRONMENTALISTS**

Environmentalists (name list)	2,645	$110.00

☐ **AUDIOVISUAL SPECIALISTS**

Selected audiovisual specialists in the U.S. (name list)	9,120	$275.00

☐ **STATE DIRECTORS OF EDUCATION**

State directors of education (name list)	2,625	$110.00

☐ **CURRICULUM MATERIALS PERSONNEL**

Buyers of school materials at the school board level (name list; includes the following)	14,130	$450.00
Directors of media services	5,071	$225.00

☐ **PRE-SCHOOL CENTERS**

Pre-school education centers	7,503	$250.00

Mailing List Information

Our counts
Entries on our mailing lists are counted on the third Friday of each month. Counts vary slightly from month to month and counts cited here are accurate at the time of publication. All counts and prices are subject to change without notice. Before you order be sure to contact the Mailing List Department for the latest counts and prices.

Our format
Each of our computerized lists comes to you in 4-across east-west labels – for affixing by Cheshire mailing equipment – on which are printed up to five lines of address. The arrangement of each list is a single numerical zip code sequence.

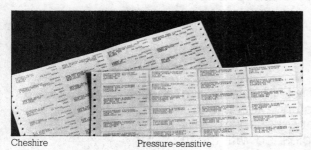

Cheshire   Pressure-sensitive

For those without access to a Cheshire, we can supply 4-across, east-west pressure-sensitive labels, or, for a minimum charge, we can affix your labels for you.

And we will slug (put an "attention" line), at $2.00 per thousand, any title you want on your mailing pieces on any lists that are not name lists – providing it is 25 characters (including spaces) or less.

Our rates and minimum charges
☐ **4-across east-west Cheshire labels:** $40 per thousand for state selections and $50 per thousand for nth selection.
☐ **pressure-sensitive labels:** add $5.00 per thousand
☐ **slug lines:** add $2.00 per thousand
☐ **shipping and handling:** a minimum charge is assigned to each order according to geographic location.
    Eastern states: $5.00/min.
    Central states: $7.00/min.
    Mountain states: $9.00/min.
    Pacific states: $11.00/min.
    Orders from outside the U.S., its possessions, and Canada must be prepaid and must include $5.00 postage per 1M labels.

MAILING SERVICES
We provide a number of mailing services at various rates. These services include: opening flaps of No. 10 envelopes; inserting; sealing; metering; sorting by postal district of matter to be mailed under 3rd class bulk rate; tieing and labeling; bagging and delivery to Post Office; folding one letter, two folds; handling of bulky materials and catalogs; hand inserting; affixing Cheshire labels to envelopes or catalogs.

Rates for these services are available upon request. Phone queries are invited.

Guarantee
We guarantee the accuracy of our lists and will reimburse $.10 for undeliverables in excess of 5% of the total count. These must be returned to us within 45 days of the delivery of labels.

Merge-Purge
A variety of lists can be combined with all duplicates purged. Lists that are ordered in combinations – and are *not* merged into a single zip code sequence – are not purged.

Approval of mailing pieces
We reserve the right to request a sample mailing piece or proposed copy (if material not printed) before agreeing to release any of our lists.

First-time orders
All first time orders must be accompanied by a sample of the mailing piece, and *payment in full in advance.* Any adjustments that may be necessary will be made after completion of order.

Unauthorized use of lists
All lists are for one-time rental and one-time use only. Unauthorized re-use will be billed at the regular one-time rental.

Ordering deadline
Orders must be received by Friday to guarantee processing on that day, and shipping 10 days thereafter. Any orders received after Friday will be processed the following week.

Overseas book buyers
For information about our extensive overseas library, publisher, and bookseller lists, please contact Lawrence N. Masucci at 212-764-5223.

Please note that all mailing lists are printed on demand and are, therefore, nonreturnable.

Wilshire Book Company

8721 SUNSET BLVD.
HOLLYWOOD, CALIFORNIA 90069

The New York Times Book Review

JULY 4, 1965

(c) 1965, by The New York Times Company

SECTION 7

PAPERBACKS   Best Sellers

General

1 **Black Like Me.** *John H. Griffin.* In blackface, a white reporter tours the South.

2 **The Drinking Man's Diet.** *Gardiner Jameson and Elliott Williams.* Cut down on carbohydrates.

3 **I Hate To Cook Book.** *Peg Bracken.* Cooking without carrying-on unduly.

4 **Psycho-cybernetics.** *Maxwell Maltz.* Subtitle, "a new way to get more living out of life."

5 **Heloise's Housekeeping Hints.** *Heloise Cruse.* Assorted tips on how to do it.

An analysis of June's best sellers based on reports from more than 125 bookstores in 64 U.S. communities.

$2

PSYCHO-CYBERNETICS

A New Technique for Using Your SUBCONSCIOUS POWER

By
MAXWELL MALTZ, M.D., F.I.C.S.

Foreword by
MELVIN POWERS

Based on an amazing new scientific innovation, this simple yet practical "New Way of Life" can be the most important influence in your life!

"An invaluable aid to the layman, offering a sound, scientific method of practical self-improvement."

Mark Freeman, Ph.D.
Clinical Psychologist

Los Angeles Times

VIEW

★ Sunday, February 27, 1983/Part VIII

KEN HIVELY / Los Angeles Times

Vince DiMaggio, former major leaguer, now 70, stands among the Fuller Brush products he sells.

Associated Press

The rarely together DiMaggios, suited up for an old-timers' game, are, from left, Dom, Joe and Vince.

A DiMaggio Named Vince . . . and His Brush With Baseball Fame

By DAVE LARSEN, *Times Staff Writer*

You probably don't remember Vince. Not many people do.

They remember Joe DiMaggio, the superstar New York Yankee baseball player who established an impossible consecutive-game hitting streak, who married a movie legend, whose name is still spoken in awe.

Even, especially in New England, they remember Dominic, the brother who had a string of great years for the Boston Red Sox.

But within a modest house on a quiet street in North Hollywood is a gray-haired man who turned 70 a few months ago. He spends his time tending his backyard camellias, reading his Bibles, supplementing his Social Security by selling Fuller Brush products.

For 10 years, Vince DiMaggio had a respectable career in the major leagues. Always, though, he was the third and oldest of the playing brothers, the one who once set a season record by striking out 134 times, the one whose retirement didn't make headlines.

The forgotten DiMaggio.

"It was me who first got Joe and organized baseball together," Vince said. "The San Francisco Seals were coming up to the last day of the 1932 season, and our shortstop, Augie Galan, asked the manager if he could leave early for Hawaii.

"I was an outfielder for the team, and I overheard the conversation. The manager was protesting that he wouldn't have anybody to play shortstop. I commented that I had this kid teen-age brother at home who could do the job.

"The manager shrugged and said OK. I remember it was a Sunday double-header that didn't mean anything in the standings. Joe played short, got a couple of hits, and also proved that he had a strong arm by sailing a couple of throws into the grandstand."

By the time the next spring training arrived, Vince had a sore arm from having made a diving catch, and the Seals' outfield had a different DiMaggio, one who would put the family name in the Hall of Fame.

"I had been released and was sitting in the grandstand one day, very discouraged, when Bill Lane, owner of the Hollywood Stars, came up and said he had a trainer who could fix my arm," Vince said. "He did, and I played for the Stars."

The older DiMaggio went on to a good-enough career in the National League, 10 years with Boston, Cincinnati, Pittsburgh, Philadelphia and New York. He hit 125 homers and had a .249 lifetime average.

By the time it was over in 1946, not only was the sporting world singing the praises of Joe, but the other playing brother, Dominic, was getting the remaining attention.

The Baseball Encyclopedia dutifully records that Joe had the nickname of the Yankee Clipper and that Dom was called the Little Professor. The game never bestowed a nickname on Vince.

Not in Brothers' Shadows

"I'll tell you this, I never felt I played in the shadow of either of them," the elder brother asserted over coffee the other day. "Joe was a better batter, but I could play rings around him as far as knowledge of the game and being in the outfield.

"I could smoke those throws. If you put a dime on second base, I could hit it from the outfield.

"No club owner ever paid me on the basis of what my last name was." In 1946, Vince, released by the New York Giants and apparently through with the sport, began selling sporting goods.

"I missed qualifying for a pension by one year. You had to be on a major league roster as of 1947. All I got after 10 years was a gold card entitling me to free admission to major league games."

While his two brothers were the toast of baseball, Vince would visit the clubhouse of the Oakland Oaks, personally peddling shoes and gloves.

One-Year Reprieve

Unexpectedly, he got a one-year reprieve. Although Vince's right arm had gone bad again, the Oakland manager, a man by the name of Casey Stengel, asked him to come back for one last season.

"I told him I could uncork only one good throw a game," Vince recalled. "He said that was good enough—better than his other outfielders could do—and I found myself playing again."

DiMaggio went on to manage Stockton in the California League, then Pittsburg, Calif., in the Far West League. "And I thought *playing* was tough," he said. "Try pleasing a couple dozen athletes."

By 1951, as with most who make a living from a game, it was over for Vince DiMaggio. After many a summer dies the dream.

Spring training is upon us again. Vince DiMaggio wonders if he will have a good year selling brushes.

Every other week, a white truck from Riverside pulls up in front of his house, and the driver drops off a few cartons containing Fuller Brush Co. products, items already requested by the former ballplayer's customers.

It has been a routine for 11 years now.

"I answered an ad in the paper," Vince said. "I have what is known as a commercial route. I basically call on stores and offices, and I've reached the point where mostly I stick to old customers.

Cold Canvassing

"It doesn't happen often anymore, but sometimes if things get slow I do cold canvassing. I walk door to door with a briefcase, hand out a brochure with my name and phone on the back, and maybe leave a basting brush as a sample.

"Sometimes people don't connect the name until after I've left."

As far as his brother, Dominic, is concerned, Vince missed his calling in the first place.

Please see VINCE, Page 1[illegible]

The Powers of Positive Publishing

By PAT B. ANDERSON

Almost anyone, according to Melvin Powers, can make money in mail-order sales. He says he knows this because he has done it. And then, he says, he makes more money by teaching mail-order techniques at colleges around Los Angeles, offering for sale the tapes of his class and by selling, usually by mail order, a book he wrote, "How to Get Rich on Mail Order."

January to March is the best time for mail-order business because people are at home more during the winter, so they have time to read and to activate their New Year's resolutions for self-improvement, according to Powers.

Hundreds of Ads

He tries to prove his theory by asking a skeptic to recall how many mail-order advertisements run in almost every publication.

"Pick up a newspaper or magazine," Powers, 60, said during an interview at his North Hollywood publishing company. "You see hundreds—thousands—of ads. And they repeat year after year. OK, what does that tell you? You know these people are making money.

"So you do the same thing. The copycat technique, I call it. You find something other people sell successfully, and you do it. Maybe even better. And you make money too."

"You can become the captain of your ship," says Powers.

Writer and Editor

He calls himself a "writer, editor, publisher, lecturer and executive head" of a publishing company employing 18 people and stocking more than 200 self-improvement books sold mainly through mail order.

Making money is no longer his primary aim. Now he is having fun, he says, in a profitable sort of way.

He teaches one-day workshops at Santa Monica, West Los Angeles, Pierce, Valley, Los Angeles City, Glendale and Southwest colleges and is a guest lecturer on mail order

Please see MELVIN, Page 19

LINDA WOLF / Los Angeles Times

Book boosters: Betty Rosenberg, Alan Chabin, Dale Vorreuter, Lewis Perdue, Michael Goth, Jamie O'Toole, Barry Lipton, Herman Hong.

Lend-Lease: Imaginative Plan to Save a Bookstore

By BEVERLY BEYETTE, *Times Staff Writer*

Around the Westwood Book Store, they like to tell this story (nonfiction): An acquaintance of theirs telephoned another bookstore, one of those big chain operations, and asked, "Do you have Gertrude Stein on tape?" To which a baffled young clerk replied, "What group is she with?"

The Westwood Book Store (est. 1936) prides itself on being an independent neighborhood store, a *real bookstore* where the people who sell books also read them, and books are judged more on their literary merit than on whether they hit the best-seller lists.

Financial Problems

Sure, the bookstore has all of Harold Robbins and all of Irving Wallace, but it has as well all of Elias Canetti (the 1981 Nobel Prize winner for literature), all of Joseph Conrad, all of Carl Jung, Dickens by the dozens.

It also has financial problems by the volume.

On Oct. 1, the bookstore, beset by rising book costs, a sinking economy and—most devastating—a forced move to a new location in Westwood Village where the four-digit rent doubled and the foot traffic disappeared, filed for Chapter 11, protection from its creditors.

Bankruptcy appeared to be the end of the line for the Westwood, where once Thomas Mann and Aldous Huxley came to buy books and where today the patrons include Ray Bradbury, Jon Voight, John Houseman, Henry Winkler and Kareem Abdul-Jabbar. But Lewis Perdue, a writer ("The Trinity Implosion," "The Delphi Betrayal," "Queensgate Reckoning"), a resident of Westwood and a devotee of the bookstore, had another idea.

Why, Perdue reasoned, couldn't a nonprofit educational foundation be formed to help the bookstore out of its financial mess? Within weeks, an attorney was drawing up incorporation papers for the Westwood Literary Foundation. Last month, it received its IRS stamp of approval as a tax-exempt corporation.

With the foundation as its angel, an angel whose first order of business will be to establish a vast lending library of at least 10,000 volumes within the store, the store's owner-employees are smiling again.

Opening Scheduled

On March 11, the lending library will have its ceremonial opening in conjunction with a "Come as your favorite California character" costumes-optional party, by invitation, at the bookstore to celebrate publication of "Lotus Land," a novel by Monica Highland (a k a Carolyn See, Lisa See Kendall and John Espey). The authors have promised all proceeds from the evening to the foundation.

The following day, the lending library will open to the public with a nucleus of about 500 specially purchased books, what foundation executive director Herman Hong calls "the beginnings of a library that

Please see BOOKSTORE, Page 12

About Women

Treating Post-Menopausal Bone Loss

By JANICE MALL

Women have always known about osteoporosis, by experience if not medical expertise. It is the post-menopausal loss of calcium in the bones that causes older women to stoop, to shrink, to suffer fractures from slight falls.

A new study at UC San Francisco that followed women after surgical menopause—removal of the ovaries—found that the amount of bone loss was far more than expected. "Almost all women after oophorectomy lose bone rapidly from the spine and they lose a large amount," said Dr. Harry K. Genant, professor of radiology, medicine and orthopedics. "This finding was not expected. We thought it would be a small percentage of bone loss; instead we found the average annual loss was 7% to 9% and some women lost as much as 15% to 20%."

The study was the first ever done of spinal mineral content following oophorectomy. Previous research has studied mineral loss in the peripheral skeleton and indicated a much smaller degree of bone loss. The new information has wide implications for all women since all will go through menopause and suffer some degree of bone loss, Genant said. While the condition is less dramatic in women who undergo natural menopause, a high percentage of menopausal women lose bone rapidly, at a rate of as much as 5% a year, he said.

The study was also of treatment, comparing bone loss in women who were treated with placebos and two forms of estrogen therapy, low-dose and a higher dosage of 0.6mg. An important aspect of the study was that the use of computer tomography measurements of spinal mineral content provided a sensitive method for determining the natural course of the disease and also the effectiveness of various treatments.

Only the higher estrogen dose was effective. Five of six women treated with it showed no bone loss, and the others averaged only 0.5% compared to the 7% to 9% in the other two groups. The women who had been on placebos regained bone mineral, "some of them in significant amounts," Genant said, when they were treated with the higher estrogen dose.

Please see ABOUT, Page 21

Jack Smith is on vacation.

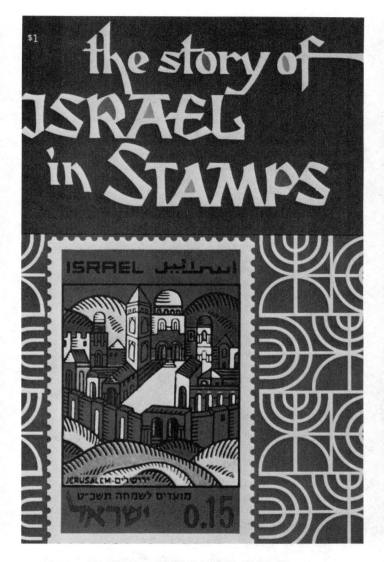

Dear Book Seller:

Here are two excellent books about Israel.
The picture on the left was taken in Israel
one month after the Six Day War. I'm in the
middle. Can you name the General shown in
the picture? Send me his name and I'll send
you a copy of each of the above books with my
compliments.

MODERN ISRAEL contains 130 beautiful pictures.
It's an ideal guide to Israel.

THE STORY OF ISRAEL IN STAMPS is a book for
both young and old interested in stamp
collecting.

                              Shalom
                              Melvin Powers

97

June 1974, at NBC taping of THE GEORGE SEGAL SPECIAL, featuring Miss Teresa Brewer singing an original song, "Willie Burgundy," written by the new and soon-to-be-famous team of Boyce & Powers. From left to right . . . Melvin Powers, Teresa Brewer, Tommy Boyce.

Chapter Nine

Success Stories of Self-Publishers
How to Maximize Your Earning Potential When You Have a Winner.
Think Two or Three Times Before You Allow a Major Book Company to
Publish and Distribute Your Winning Book—It Can Cost You Thousands of Dollars in Profits.

Is there the slightest doubt in your mind that the self-publisher can make it big? If there is, this chapter will allay whatever fear you might have and encourage you to continue your pursuit of success. It will also encourage you to keep control of your book when you have an obvious winner. Unfailingly, a winner somehow sends out a signal to many self-serving individuals and distribution companies seeking to cash in on your hard-won victory by offering enticing representation deals. Enjoy their flattery but exercise sound business judgment before you consider relinquishing control of your book. Don't make the decision in haste.

My vote for one of the smartest self-publishers in the United States goes to Robert J. Ringer, author of *Winning Through Intimidation, Looking Out for #1* and *Restoring the American Dream.* He has sold 10,000,000 copies of his books. An article about him that appeared in *The Wall Street Journal* is well worth reading. (See page 102.) Following the brilliant success achieved publishing his own books, he expanded his operation to accommodate the publication of other authors' books, many of which have reached the best-seller list. Foremost among these is *Crisis Investing,* a non-fiction, hard-cover book of 1980, which sold for $12.50 and reached the best-seller list with the sale of 400,000 copies. The article attributes the success of this book and his others to the compelling nature of his mail-order advertising copy. He used a tested technique that had proved workable for him.

As with a great many success stories, Robert Ringer met with many failures on the road to the top. He was a dropout from dental school, an unsuccessful men's shirt

designer, and an unsuccessful real-estate broker. At one time, he was deeply in debt, but he did not despair. Instead, he wrote and self-published *Winning Through Intimidation,* a book with which he achieved immediate success by utilizing mail-order techniques. He directed the orders to the bookstores rather than to himself. He later sold the mass paperback rights for $800,000. He then wrote his second book, *Looking Out for #1,*and, again, using the same mail-order techniques, sold 200,000 copies in two months. It was all due to his brilliant advertising and publicity campaign. (See pages 103 and 104.)

The third Ringer book was *Restoring the American Dream,* for which former Secretary of the Treasury William Simon wrote the foreword. The book was on the *New York Times Best-Seller List* for 16 weeks. Apropos of the foreword, this is an excellent example of how the persuasive force of a foreword written by a man of accomplishment can benefit sales and add to the book's prestige.

At the present time, Robert Ringer is publishing a newsletter, *The Tortoise Report.* It contains examples of the author's remarkable insight, his ideas and recommended strategies. The newsletter is a natural outgrowth of Ringer's philosophy and gives him the enviable opportunity to communicate with his millions of readers on a one-to-one basis regularly each month. The annual subscription cost is $59.00.

Robert Ringer is the perfect example of a man who is doing everything just right. And can you believe that he is actually managing to accomplish all this without having had the benefit of reading this book! Well, just to make sure that his good fortune continues unabated, I'm going to send him a copy of this book when it's finished. I want very much to encourage him to get into the seminar business for both pleasure and profit. Hopefully, he will find seminars a source of great personal satisfaction.

At this point I'd like you to turn to page 105, where you'll find an interesting article on self-publishing.

Among other highly successful self-published books are the following:

How to Avoid Probate by Norman Dacey. After the author had sold 10,000 copies, it was picked up by Crown and sold over 1,000,000 copies.

How to Be Your Own Best Friend by Mildred Newman and Bernard Berkowitz, Ph.D. The book was sold mainly on the West Coast. Random House bought it for $60,000.

John Muir sold more than 1,000,000 copies of *How to Keep Your Volkswagen Alive.*

How to Flatten Your Stomach by Coach Jim Everroad was originally self-published. The book has now sold over 2,000,000 copies and has been copycatted many times with similar titles and similar formats. I copycatted the format and title myself with a humorous book called *How to Flatten Your Tush* by an imaginary coach named Marge Reardon. The book took one day to write and one day to photograph. I sold 100,000 copies in a short period of time. See page 22.

The Taming of the C.A.N.D.Y. Monster by Vicki Lansky is another best-selling, self-published book.

The Dieter's Guide to Weight Loss During Sex by Richard Lewis was inspired by his self-publishing activities. (See page 105.)

One of the truly classical success stories in the self-publishing genre is that of Mary Ellen, author of *Mary Ellen's Best of Helpful Hints.* She published her first book, *Best of Helpful Hints,* in 1976. It was a spectacular success, selling more than 500,000 copies almost overnight. She then published three more "helpful hints" books. They were all best sellers, with a combined readership of over 3.5 million. She became a national celebrity and in 1979 joined the "Good Morning America" television show, an affiliation which lasted for two years. She writes a syndicated column that is carried by over 125 newspapers,

has been profiled in almost every major magazine, and continues to be a favorite guest on national talk shows.

Self-publication is one of the few avenues of communication where the importance of the subject matter or the title of the book supersedes the importance or reputation of the author. Initially, the author is usually unknown, and it is amazing how quickly he becomes widely read through the use of topics dealing with how to have better health, how to improve sex life, how to improve relationships, how to make money — all kinds of "how to" books. These are subjects that have the best chance of making it in the market place.

Currently, the latest highly successful self-published book is *The One Minute Manager* by Drs. Spencer Johnson and Kenneth Blanchard. Seven-hundred-thousand copies have been sold at $15.00 a copy; it is #2 on the best-seller list; and it has been on the list for 56 weeks. It's a very small book with a production cost of about $1.50. See page 106. It's now in paperback as well at $6.95.

Until Dr. Johnson met his co-author at a cocktail party, he had intended to write *The One Minute Plan* as a parenting book. But Blanchard, a well-known management consultant, convinced Dr. Johnson that his techniques would be far more marketable as a management book. The two agreed to work as a team.

An interesting sidelight to the collaboration is that Dr. Johnson was so sure it would result in a best seller, he bought Blanchard a copy of a book, *Jackpot,* written by Dr. Jim Fixx, the author of *The Complete Book of Running.* The book deals with Dr. Fixx's problems when it came to handling his sudden success and wealth.

Dr. Johnson has followed this success with three books, and you can be sure they'll become best sellers. The titles are *The One Minute Mother, The One Minute Father,* and *The One Minute Salesman.* The one-minute theme is suited ideally to a series of humor books. It's sure to happen. Put yourself to the test. Can you think of a few funny titles?

Dr. Johnson says, "Most self-help books are complicated, which is ironic. All people want is something that works, and works fast."

Dr. Johnson's book, *The One Minute Manager,* did not receive good reviews from the critics, but the public loved it. This brings to mind some pertinent questions I'd like you to think about. Is a good review absolutely necessary for a book or movie to become a hit? Is the public influenced by what the critics have to say? Would the sale of Dr. Johnson's book have been significantly strengthened by favorable reviews? What made the book sell so well at a price of $15.00 when, judging from its physical appearance, it would seem that the price should be about $5.00? Would the book have sold better at $5.00 than at $10.00?

Interestingly, Dr. Johnson wanted to charge twice as much as that charged for any book its size. "Books should be priced by their value, not their size," says Dr. Johnson. "If it's not worth $15.00, why am I writing it?"

He realized that traditional publishing companies would not accept his premise, so he and Dr. Blanchard first published the book themselves. They sold 20,000 copies in a very short time. Later, 17 publishing companies bid for the publishing rights.

I must admit, I would not have priced the book at $15.00. I adhere to a philosophy that advocates selling the maximum amount of books at the lowest price but enabling me to realize a small profit. It's a policy that has worked remarkably well for me. The projected value of my books has always been accurate. Even bookstore owners have asked me how I can publish quality books and sell them as reasonably as I do. From an altruistic point of view, the fact that my books have had an enormously positive influence on a broad segment of the reading public has given me great satisfaction. I am a self-improvement publisher and any way I can help the reader's personal image helps me to fulfill my professional purpose in life.

I want you to pay particular attention to the following figures, because when you have a winner, *I want you, the prospective self-publisher, to maximize your potential earnings.* Don't give them away; you deserve to keep them. As a rule, the general public has no interest in which company is publishing a particular book—a well-established, well-known house or a self-publisher. Sales would not be affected.

Let's suppose the authors received from a publishing and distribution house a royalty of 15% on the retail selling price of the book. Priced at $15.00 each, 700,000 copies would amount to retail sales of $10,050,000. The royalties would amount to $1,507,500. Here is how the authors could have made $3,500,000 on the same amount of sales!

Let us split the sales discount the publishing house gives in half, from 40% to the regular trade bookstores and 50% to the wholesalers. This gives us an average discount of 45%. A 45% discount off $10,050,000

amounts to $4,522,500. This leaves us with $5,527,500. From that figure, let's deduct the cost of the book at $1.50 each, or $1,507,500. This leaves a figure of $4,020,000. Let's suppose, again, we had a fulfillment house filling the orders and doing all the invoicing, billing and collecting, and a special person to oversee the account. The fee for doing this would be somewhere about 25 cents per book, depending on the company. Deduct $175,000 from $4,020,000. That leaves $3,845,000. Let's spend another $345,000 for advertising and publicity. The authors are now left with $3,500,000 to divide. How nice!

So, with very little effort and added work on their part, the authors could have collected another $2,000,000 on the $1,507,500. Had they been students of mine, I would have advised them against making the decision they did. There are numerous fulfillment houses throughout the country that would gladly have handled the shipments and paper work. The authors would have received a weekly computer read-out on all the books shipped, monies owed and monies received. The fulfillment houses even bank the money in an author's account with the right to withdraw funds limited strictly to him. When ready to re-order books, he would simply call his printer.

It is not necessary to hire a single employee for the operation. An advertising agency can be engaged to write and place ads; a publicist hired to keep the publicity in high gear. It requires a minimal amount of your time once the operation is set in motion.

But, for the moment, let's say my estimate was wrong and the sales would have been 25% lower if the authors had handled the sales themselves. This means they would have sold 525,000 copies. Deducting expenses proportionately, but keeping the same advertising and publicity figure of $345,000, the authors would have made $3,330,000. They would have doubled their royalty payment and made another $1,822,500. See page 108 for an interesting article about business books.

I've explained in detail the dollars-and-cents aspect of the authors' business decision because I think it's important to post warnings to protect you against the pitfalls you may encounter. Potential earnings on a winning book could be depleted through a wrong business decision.

Opportunities abound for the entrepreneur self-publisher. There is nothing difficult or complicated about any facet of it. Don't hesitate to ask questions. Develop an intellectual curiosity about those areas you don't understand. Use the expertise of others to accomplish your goals. Concentrate on the marketing of your book and all of its ramifications. That's where the money is made.

THE WALL STREET JOURNAL, TUESDAY, MARCH 24, 1981

*Sex, Fear and Big Ads
Are a Winning Trio
For New Publisher*

* * *

Advertising Gets Much Credit
For 2 Straight Best Sellers;
Are All Generations 'Me'?

By LAUREL LEFF
Staff Reporter of THE WALL STREET JOURNAL

"A mundane sex life can be compared to a frozen TV dinner: It will keep you alive but it's not a gourmet banquet served in a posh restaurant."

So teases a newspaper advertisement for "Nice Girls Do—and Now You Can Too!" a frothy sex guide by a Hollywood psychologist, Irene Kassorla. The ad is also chock-full of specific advice on how to share in the feast. So specific that several newspapers refused to run it. "We didn't think it was the right kind of copy for a family newspaper," says the general advertising manager for the Pittsburgh Press.

But newspapers' skittishness doesn't seem to have slowed sales of the book, which is near the top of the New York Times best-seller list. Nor has it intimidated the book's publisher, Robert J. Ringer, the controversial author of the 1970s book "Winning Through Intimidation." Mr. Ringer dismisses the newspapers' action as "relatively insignificant."

A few ads in a few markets may not be crucial to the success of "Nice Girls Do," but Mr. Ringer's overall advertising strategy certainly is. Largely as a result of flamboyant marketing maneuvers, Mr. Ringer's publishing house, Stratford Press of Beverly Hills, Calif., now is two for two—two books and two best sellers in just one year. The company was founded in January 1980.

Manhattan Amazed

Using a hard-sell approach, unabashed appeals to Americans' self-interest and an unusual form of advertising, Mr. Ringer pushed both Stratford books to the top of the best-seller lists in a matter of months. Stratford's first book, "Crisis Investing," a dour chronicle of "opportunities and profits in the coming great depression," was the best-selling nonfiction hard-cover book of 1980, selling over 400,000 copies. Priced at $12.50 for "Crisis Investing" and $9.95 for "Nice Girls Do," the two books have reaped about $5.4 million in revenues for Stratford.

The Manhattan publishing establishment is amazed. "Two books from a small West Coast publisher on the New York Times best-seller list at the same time, it's just remarkable," says Susan Ginsberg, executive editor of Gulf & Western Industries Inc.'s Pocket Books unit. "People were very surprised."

Mr. Ringer, however, wasn't. Ever since 1973, when he published "Winning Through Intimidation" himself, after all the major publishing houses had turned it down, Mr. Ringer has been beating his own path to the best-seller list. After "Winning Through Intimidation," he wrote "Looking Out for No. 1" and "Restoring the American Dream." They were all best sellers and were published by Mr. Ringer's Los Angeles Book Publishers Co., a forerunner of Stratford.

Sitting in Stratford's makeshift Beverly Hills office, the 43-year-old Mr. Ringer doesn't look or sound intimidating. (He does, however inform this reporter at the outset of an interview that he intends to tape it.) The former real-estate broker and all-around promoter doesn't even sport the "dress for success" look one would expect from the man who wrote that "posture is everything." Instead, he looks like an accountant on his day off, wearing a velour pullover, corduroy pants and gray suede shoes.

Reams of Words

If his manner is nonchalant, his marketing approach isn't. Mr. Ringer uses basically the same carefully executed strategy to promote all his books. First, he introduces the book with expensive full-page newspaper ads, each cooperatively financed by Stratford and a bookstore chain, usually B. Dalton Booksellers or Waldenbooks. Unlike most ads, which emphasize pretty pictures and splashy slogans, Mr. Ringer's ads feature reams of words and one small photo of the author. It's what the ads say—Mr. Ringer writes them himself—that counts.

"The ads are a remarkable piece of persuasion," says Oscar Dystel, formerly Bantam Books Inc.'s chairman and currently a consultant. "Once you're hooked into reading the ad, you figure you might as well try the book."

Mr. Ringer also makes it as easy as possible to get the book. While many publishers run cooperative ads with the chain stores, and others sell books through mail orders, Mr. Ringer is one of the few to combine the two methods: Each of his ads contains a mail-order coupon that the reader can clip and send to the store. "To be a legitimate publisher you have to sell through bookstores," Mr. Ringer says. "You can sell thousands of books through mail order, and the general public will never hear about it."

This merchandising method permits Stratford to concentrate sales in two major chains with best-seller lists of their own that are highly visible in the publishing trade. The method also provides, through the chains' computerized weekly sales lists, a quick measure of consumers' response to the ads.

The theory is that once the books appear on the chains' best-seller lists, other retailers will be encouraged to stock them and the authors will be invited to local talk shows and other promotional forums. Then it's only a matter of time before the books appear on more-widely-circulated best-seller lists.

J. Kendrick Noble, a publishing analyst for Paine Webber Mitchell Hutchins Inc., sees an additional reason for Mr. Ringer's success. "He has a gift for identifying books that buyers have a need for," Mr. Noble says. Mr. Ringer agrees and asserts that the public's appetite for self-interest books won't slacken.

"People in the media keep insisting that we're going through a period, that the 1970s were the 'me generation,'" Mr. Ringer says. "Every generation since neolithic times has been the 'me generation.'"

Mr. Ringer is particularly adept at identifying and playing on people's fears. Ads for "Crisis Investing," which he picked up from a small publisher who had sold it through mail orders, warn that you will probably "lose everything in the coming depression." But they assure you that if you read the book, you might be one of the "canny few that will not only survive, but prosper."

"Nice Girls Do" isn't exactly "my cup of tea," Mr. Ringer says, but he contends "there's a need for this kind of book." The book was in its fourth rewrite, and had been rejected by several publishers, when Mr. Ringer met Irene Kassorla at a party. He suggested that she borrow his editor, Ellen Shahan, to help with the book. The psychologist-author describes the resulting collaboration as "a miracle."

She is less pleased with the book's advertisements. "They're too, well, sexy," she says. "The book isn't sexy. I wanted to be represented as a research scholar with a revolutionary approach to female sexuality. I'm making one of the most important statements about sex in this century." She apparently hasn't been upset enough, though, to demand that Mr. Ringer alter the ads.

Based on the success of his first two books, Mr. Ringer plans to double his staff to 20 and move from his cramped quarters. He also plans to publish about a book a month beginning with an economics book, "The Alpha Strategy," in May. Mr. Ringer, who tends to talk in advertising slogans, describes "The Alpha Strategy" as "the greatest book ever written on the free-market philosophy."

Next summer he plans to publish a book for divorced fathers and another entitled "Living Alone and Liking It." He says he is "seriously negotiating" for six other books.

PAGE 100   CALENDAR   *Los Angeles Times*   SUNDAY, OCTOBER 30, 1977

103

BEHIND THE BEST SELLERS
By Herbert Mitgang

Richard Smith ✓

Smith.

At last count, there were 3,000 diet books, 2,000 self-improvement treatises and 1,000 sex manuals, give or take a few hundred. Inevitably, someone had to come along to combine the three categories in one all-purpose book called "The Dieter's Guide to Weight Loss During Sex" — as Richard Smith has, in his new trade paperback best seller from Workman Publishing Company.

Included in the book are a "Height Report" for men and women (if you weigh 271 to 285 pounds, your partner ought to be 7 feet 7 inches tall), data about weight loss resulting from various sexual plays and ploys. For readers in a hurry, there's a pocket calorie counter with the book that gives information about sex and fat. Examples: Seducing partner if you are shy (15 calories); if you are rich (5 calories); if you are poor (164 calories).

Richard Smith, the 37-year-old author, who stands "6 feet 1 and change," says he was a 256-pound weakling until he discovered that shedding pounds in the most interesting way devised by mankind could bring him fame and a best seller. He now weighs 198.

Mr. Smith grew up on a farm in Parksville, N.Y., in the northern Catskills. In his youth, he worked as a busboy and waiter at resort hotels. He became "a good eater" while serving four meals a day (the fourth was a "midnight snack"), sampling between the kitchen and dining hall. The germ of the idea for the book was nurtured on the Borscht Circuit.

He discovered that waiting on tables for the big eaters and small tippers ("doctors and dentists — the worst") was not his glass of tea. But the Catskills, as one or two *tummlers* before him learned, were the mother lode for a would-be humorist; where no one was a straight man and anyone worth a half-sour pickle had to make out where it really counted — in the dining room and casino.

Mr. Smith went on to Orange County Community College, in Middletown, N. Y., where his main activity was playing the trombone in his own dance band. He became a dropout, drove a tractor-trailer for Pepsi-Cola, enrolled as an executive trainee at Alexander's department store in Manhattan and worked his way up to women's underwear buyer, became publicity director for an association whose aim was to persuade men to dress better. Somewhere along the line he was married once, a state of grace that no longer binds him. He is now a full-time humorist for several magazines.

Four years ago he devised a poster, "The Sensuous Dieter's Guide to Weight Loss During Sex." Privately printed, it sold tens of thousands of copies. The book, his first, followed inevitably.

Mr. Smith keeps in trim, for the most part, not as one might imagine from the author of "The Dieter's Guide to Weight Loss During Sex," but by running 60 miles a week in Central Park. He has to, because his favorite foods are pizza and halvah — "God, do I love halvah." He's been running for 11 years and is now preparing for a New York marathon. "There are two kinds of runners," he says, "the real ones and the civilians."

Mr. Smith is now working on a sequel to his book for Workman, in addition to other books. Two may turn out to be fiction: "About a man who is terribly afraid of women, and what will be the first Jewish Gothic. I've already got the title — 'The Isle of Murray.' "

His main activities now are writing, running and "keeping company with nice women." He was mortified when a woman reader proposed that they try out some of the weight-reduction activities in his book. "I said, 'Of course not,' but I took her telephone number, anyway." You can take the boy out of the Catskills, but not the busboy. ■

July 2, 1978/The New York Times Book Review

Paperback Best Sellers

MASS MARKET

Mass-market paperbacks are softcover books sold at newsstands, variety stores and supermarkets, as well as in bookstores. This listing is based on computer-processed reports from bookstores and representative wholesalers with more than 40,000 outlets across the United States.

1 **THE THORN BIRDS**, by Colleen McCullough. (Avon, $2.50.) Australian family saga: fiction.

2 **JAWS 2**, by Hank Searls. (Bantam, $2.25.) Female great white shark returns to familiar waters.

3 **THE LAWLESS**, by John Jakes. (Jove/HBJ, $2.25.) The Kent family saga reaches the glittering, corrupt 1890's.

4 **LOOKING OUT FOR #1**, by Robert J. Ringer. (Fawcett/Crest, $2.50.) Getting yours.

5 **TWINS**, by Bari Wood and Jack Geasland. (NAL/Signet, $2.50.) Twin doctors and their relationship in life and death: fiction.

6 **DAMIEN Omen II**, by Joseph Howard. (NAL/Signet, $1.95.) Evil child returns; sequel to "The Omen."

7 **THE INVESTIGATION**, by Dorothy Uhnak. (Pocket, $2.50.) Woman accused of murdering her children: fiction.

8 **THE BASTARD**, by John Jakes. (Jove, $2.25.) First book in the Kent family chronicles: basis of the recent TV series.

9 **THE DRAGONS OF EDEN**, by Carl Sagan. (Ballantine, $2.25.) How intelligence evolved.

10 **THE PROMISE**, by Danielle Steel. (Dell, $1.95.) Lovers separated by a tragic set of circumstances: fiction.

11 **CONDOMINIUM**, by John D. MacDonald. (Fawcett/Crest, $2.25.) Disaster hits a Florida key: fiction.

12 **DELTA OF VENUS**, by Anaïs Nin. (Bantam, $2.50.) Elegant erotica written for a wealthy patron: fiction.

13 **YOUR ERRONEOUS ZONES**, by Wayne W. Dyer. (Avon, $2.25.) Self-help pep talk.

14 **LOVE'S DARING DREAM**, by Patricia Matthews. (Pinnacle, $2.25.) From the Irish potato famine to romance in the Pacific Northwest: romantic fiction.

15 **SPLINTER OF THE MIND'S EYE**, by Alan Dean Foster. (Ballantine/Del Rey, $1.95.) The further adventures of Luke ("Star Wars") Skywalker.

TRADE

Trade paperbacks are softcover books usually sold in bookstores and at an average price higher than mass-market paperbacks. This listing is based on computer-processed reports from bookstores and wholesalers with more than 2,500 outlets across the United States.

1 **THE COMPLETE RUNNER**, by the Editors of Runner's World Magazine. (Avon, $4.95.) Advice by professionals.

2 **THE DIETER'S GUIDE TO WEIGHT LOSS DURING SEX**, by Richard Smith. (Workman, $2.95.) Spoof on diet and sex manuals.

3 **CROCKETT'S VICTORY GARDEN**, by James Underwood Crockett. (Little, Brown, $9.95.) Month-by-month guide.

4 **THE RUNNER'S HANDBOOK**, by Bob Glover and Jack Shepherd. (Penguin, $3.95.) Fitness guide for men and women.

5 **THE AUDUBON SOCIETY FIELD GUIDE TO NORTH AMERICAN BIRDS (Eastern Region)**, by John Bull and John Farrand Jr. (Knopf, $7.95.) Illustrated.

6 **THE PEOPLE'S PHARMACY**, by Joe Graedon. (Avon, $3.95.) Guide to prescriptions, over-the-counter drugs and home remedies.

7 **THE JOY OF SEX**, by Alex Comfort. (Simon & Schuster/Fireside, $6.95.) With illustrations.

8 **STALKING THE PERFECT TAN**, by G. B. Trudeau. (Holt, Rinehart & Winston, $1.95.) Shifting political winds caught in cartoon form.

9 **ON DEATH AND DYING**, by Dr. Elisabeth Kübler-Ross. (Macmillan, $2.25.) Lessons to be learned from the terminally ill.

10 **OUR BODIES, OURSELVES**, by the Boston Women's Health Book Collective. (Simon & Schuster/Touchstone, $4.95.) Illustrated guide.

11 **THE TAMING OF THE C.A.N.D.Y. MONSTER**, by Vicki Lansky. (Meadowbrook Press, Wayzata, Minn., $3.95.) Warning about "Continuously Advertised Nutritionally Deficient Yummies."

12 **IRELAND: A Terrible Beauty**, by Jill and Leon Uris. (Bantam, $7.95.) A "love song" in words and photographs.

13 **SHANNA**, by Kathleen Woodiwiss. (Avon, $3.95.) A stormy marriage: historical romance.

14 **BORN TO WIN**, by Muriel James and Dorothy Jongeward. (Addison-Wesley, $5.95.) How to apply Transactional Analysis.

15 **LIVE LONGER NOW**, by Jon N. Leonard, J. L. Hofer and Nathan Pritikin. (Grosset & Dunlap/Today Press, $2.95.) Diet-and-exercise regime.

PAPERBACK TALK

Continued from Page 19

women's historical romances.

Stomach flattener. Every year a thousand brave souls publish books of their own composition and attempt to sell them by mail or on consignment through bookstores. Every year several of them have a stroke of luck and achieve bestsellerdom. A recent example is Vicki Lansky's "The Taming of the C.A.N.D.Y. Monster," now on our trade paperback list.

The latest lucky self-publisher is Jim Everroad of Columbus, Ind. In 1974, after losing his job as a high-school athletic coach, Mr. Everroad thought he'd like to become a sportswriter. He spent the summer writing an article about something that had concerned him since he was a boy — his potbelly and the exercises he'd devised to flatten it. After selling it to a newspaper, he arranged to print an expansion of it in paperback — 6,000 words illustrated with two dozen photographs — and sold out his 3,000 copies quickly. Euphorically, he then ordered 50,000 more copies, advertised the work more widely and persuaded a number of bookstores to stock it. After he'd disposed of 35,000 copies he was compelled to take a number of odd jobs, such as driving a Pepsi-Cola truck.

Then came his moment of luck. Late last year a new employee of Price/Stern/Sloan, the Los Angeles publisher, told its sales manager, Chuck Gates, about the many copies of Mr. Everroad's book she had sold while working in a bookstore back in Indiana. Mr. Gates investigated, found it to be just the sort of checkout-counter item that is P/S/S's specialty.

P/S/S published "How to Flatten Your Stomach" last January and promptly discovered that America is full of people worried about their potbellies. The book hopped onto our Best Seller List last week. Sales to date: 225,000. ■

Best Sellers

October 23, 1983/The New York Times Book Review

This Week	Last Week	Weeks On List	NONFICTION
1	2	5	**MOTHERHOOD: The Second Oldest Profession,** by Erma Bombeck. (McGraw-Hill, $12.95.) A humorous look at the biggest on-the-job training program ever.
2	1	41	**IN SEARCH OF EXCELLENCE,** by Thomas J. Peters and Robert H. Waterman Jr. (Harper & Row, $19.95.) Lessons to be learned from well-run American corporations.
3	5	2	**THE MARY KAY GUIDE TO BEAUTY.** (Addison-Wesley, $19.95.) An illustrated guide for women prepared by the staff of a cosmetic firm.
4	6	3	**THE BODY PRINCIPAL,** by Victoria Principal. (Simon & Schuster, $16.95.) Exercises for women by a television personality.
5	3	8	**ON WINGS OF EAGLES,** by Ken Follett. (Morrow, $17.95.) The rescue of two Americans from an Iranian prison.
6	4	50	**MEGATRENDS,** by John Naisbitt. (Warner, $17.50.) Predictions about America in the next decade based on an analysis of conditions today.
7	7	4	**FATAL VISION,** by Joe McGinniss. (Putnam, $17.95.) The case of Jeffrey MacDonald, Ivy League graduate, respected physician and convicted killer of his wife and daughters.
8	9	6	**THE BEST OF JAMES HERRIOT.** (St. Martin's Press, $19.95.) Selections from the writings of the Yorkshire veterinarian.
9	11	4	**THE PETER PAN SYNDROME,** by Dan Kiley. (Dodd, Mead, $14.95.) A psychologist's analysis of the plight of men who have never grown up.
10	8	(56)	**THE ONE MINUTE MANAGER,** by Kenneth Blanchard and Spencer Johnson. (Morrow, $15.) How to increase the productivity of those with whom you work, as well as your own.
11	10	22	**CREATING WEALTH,** by Robert G. Allen. (Simon & Schuster, $15.95.) Making money in real estate.
12		1	**VIETNAM: A History,** by Stanley Karnow. (Viking, $19.95.) Profusely illustrated history of the war; tie-in with the current PBS television series.
13	13	4	**OUTRAGEOUS ACTS AND EVERYDAY REBELLIONS,** by Gloria Steinem. (Holt, Rinehart & Winston, $14.95.) Essays by a leading feminist writer.
14	14	15	**OUT ON A LIMB,** by Shirley MacLaine. (Bantam, $15.95.) The actress tells of her mid-life "journey to find her true self."
15		1	**A HERO FOR OUR TIME,** by Ralph G. Martin. (Macmillan, $19.95.) The life and legend of John F. Kennedy.

Paperback Best Sellers

December 25, 1983/The New York Times Book Review

MASS MARKET

Mass market paperbacks are soft-cover books sold at newsstands, variety stores and supermarkets, as well as in bookstores. This listing is based on computer-processed reports from bookstores and representative wholesalers with more than 40,000 outlets across the United States.

1 **CHRISTINE,** by Stephen King. (NAL/Signet, $3.95.) A car that kills is at large among a Pennsylvania town's high school set: fiction

2 **ONCE IN A LIFETIME,** by Danielle Steel. (Dell, $3.95.) A young woman copes with the problems of widowhood and motherhood: fiction.

3 **TRULY TASTELESS JOKES THREE,** by Blanche Knott. (Ballantine, $2 25.) Humor.

4 **SPACE,** by James A. Michener. (Fawcett/Crest, $4.95.) The space program: fiction.

5 **MISTRAL'S DAUGHTER,** by Judith Krantz. (Bantam, $4.50.) The art world of the 20's and the fashion business of the 80's: fiction.

6 **AND MORE BY ANDY ROONEY,** by Andrew A. Rooney. (Warner, $3.95.) Essays by the columnist and television commentator.

7 **FOUNDATION'S EDGE,** by Isaac Asimov. (Del Rey/Ballantine, $3.95.) The struggle to keep civilization alive in a crumbling empire: fiction.

8 **UTAH!** by Dana Fuller Ross. (Bantam, $3.95.) Pioneering in the land of the Mormons: fiction.

9 **GROSS JOKES,** by Julius Alvin. (Zebra, $2.50.) Raunchy humor.

10 **THE VALLEY OF HORSES,** by Jean M. Auel. (Bantam, $3.95.) A fictional saga of human survival at the dawn of civilization.

11 **TRULY TASTELESS JOKES,** by Blanche Knott. (Ballantine, $2.25.) Humor.

12 **THE CLAN OF THE CAVE BEAR,** by Jean M. Auel. (Bantam, $3.95.) The beginning of the saga continued in "The Valley of Horses."

13 **THE RIGHT STUFF,** by Tom Wolfe. (Bantam, $3.95.) Basis of the film about the space program.

14 **TRULY TASTELESS JOKES TWO,** by Blanche Knott. (Ballantine, $2.25.) Humor.

15 **LOVELY LYING LIPS,** by Valerie Sherwood. (Warner, $3.95.) The turbulent lives of three beauties in 17th-century Somerset: fiction.

TRADE

Trade paperbacks are soft-cover books usually sold in bookstores and at an average price higher than mass market paperbacks. This listing is based on computer-processed reports from about 2,000 bookstores in every region of the United States.

1 **THE ONE MINUTE MANAGER,** by Kenneth Blanchard and Spencer Johnson. (Berkley, $6.95.) How to increase your productivity.

2 **GARFIELD SITS AROUND THE HOUSE,** by Jim Davis. (Ballantine, $4.95.) Cartoon humor.

3 **GROWING UP,** by Russell Baker. (NAL/Plume, $5.95.) The New York Times columnist recalls his boyhood and youth.

4 **THE SECOND GARFIELD TREASURY,** by Jim Davis. (Ballantine, $7.95.) Cartoon humor.

5 **THE COLOR PURPLE,** by Alice Walker. (Pocket/Washington Square Press, $5.95.) Black men and women in the South: fiction.

6 **MORE ITEMS FROM OUR CATALOG,** by Alfred Gingold. (Avon, 4.95.) A second spoof of the L. L. Bean catalogue.

7 **COLOR ME BEAUTIFUL,** by Carole Jackson. (Ballantine, $8.95.) Beauty tips for women.

8 **LIVING, LOVING & LEARNING,** by Leo F. Buscaglia. (Fawcett, $5.95.) Inspirational talks by a California professor.

9 **BEYOND THE FAR SIDE,** by Gary Larson. (Andrews and McMeel, $3.95.) Cartoon humor.

10 **GARFIELD ON THE TOWN,** by Jim Davis and Lorenzo Music. (Ballantine, $4.95.) Cartoon humor.

11 **BLOOM COUNTY,** by Berke Breathed. (Little, Brown, $6.95.) Cartoon humor.

12 **WILD BELLS TO THE WILD SKY,** by Laurie McBain. (Avon, $6.95.) Perils and romance on the high seas and at the court of Elizabeth I: fiction.

13 **MARY ELLEN'S 1,000 NEW HELPFUL HINTS,** by Mary Ellen Pinkham. (Doubleday/Dolphin, $5.95.) Tips for housekeepers.

14 **THE ROAD LESS TRAVELED,** by M. Scott Peck. (S&S/Touchstone, $7.95.) Psychological and spiritual inspiration by a psychiatrist.

15 **THURSTON HOUSE,** by Danielle Steel. (Dell, $7.95.) Three generations of a wealthy San Francisco family: fiction.

Business Is Hotter Than Sex, Book Publishers Find

Manager's Journal

by Harriet Rubin

No one, least of all publishers, ever expected business books to top diet, fitness and sex on the best-seller charts.

Yet for nearly half a year, the three leading sellers have been "In Search of Excellence," by Thomas J. Peters and Robert H. Waterman Jr.; "The One-Minute Manager," by Kenneth Blanchard and Spencer Johnson, and "Megatrends," by John Naisbitt. Sales of the three books together have approached two million copies in less than a year. Each has been matching the initial sales pace of "Gone With the Wind."

In a period of declining revenues for publishers, business has been the industry's biggest growth category. In 1981, there were 50,000 business titles in print and sales of about $492 million. An analysis of Publishers Weekly best-seller lists going back through 1979 shows about two dozen or more long-lasting best-seller titles on everything from selling to money to investments to negotiation to careers. Moreover, these books' buyers don't seem sensitive to price. Most business books appear as hardcovers with an average price of $25, compared with $14.95 for general-interest works, making business one of the most expensive categories after textbooks and luxury art books. The recent success has been greatest in management books. Sales of books on money, real estate and job-finding are slackening. In their place is practical advice on how to manage and lead people for the best results.

All this is a far cry from the 1930s, when Peter Drucker embarked on research for his "Concept of the Corporation." General Motors' vice chairman, Donaldson Brown, told him: "I don't think you'll find a publisher—I don't see anyone interested in a book on management." Mr. Drucker agreed. "There was not then, it seemed, even a management public for a book on management, indeed, most managers did not realize they were practicing management. The general public, while very interested in how the rich made their money, never heard of management."

Business books back then dealt with pricing theory or the allocation of scarce resources. Thus, when "Concept" was finally published in 1946, one reviewer offered Mr. Drucker his sympathies: "It is hoped that this promising young scholar will soon devote his considerable talents to a more serious subject."

Mr. Drucker, of course, defied the skeptics and found an eager market for management literature. His 15 titles together have sold more than 1.2 million hard-cover copies in the U.S. The more typical commercial fate of management books is a backlist; life of five to 10 years, with cumulative sales that generally peak at 20,000 copies. But there also are books—such as "The Management of Time," by James T. McCay, 300,000 copies to date—whose sales of tens of thousands of copies a year have made them silent best sellers, seldom heard of by the public because best-seller lists are based on weekly retail sales.

This year's management best sellers are speaking to nontraditional business-book readers. Individual success has become strongly identified with business—as well as with diet, fitness and sex—and management naturally has become the newest self-help discipline. In varying degrees, the new best sellers all partake of the standard pop self-help styles: "Having caught America doing something right, these books make people feel good about themselves; they provide positive reinforcement," says Pat Blakely, buyer at the B. Dalton chain.

In addition, there is a new readership that thinks of itself as managerial. Says Prof. John Kotter of Harvard Business School: "Never before has there been such a ready market for these books, a population of around five million primed by some amount of business-school education—as undergrads, MBAs or executives in training programs—turn to business books for advice and information."

Publishers always have been suspicious that many books sold to business people weren't read so much as bought, a peculiarity of the business-book market, where sales are encouraged by tax deductions.

But today's best sellers *are* being read: Often they are required reading in corporations. A decade ago, Publishers Weekly reported that pop business books were avoided by most corporations "in favor of more specialized items." Suddenly, top executives are taking an evangelistic interest in promoting the popularizers. AT&T's chairman, Charles Brown, distributed two of the top sellers and a personal memo to his company's managers. The reason:

"We're all looking for answers," says Myron Goff, manager of management education and methods at AT&T. Companies of all sizes are turning their conference rooms into mini-universities with required reading.

The investment in books has its attractions, particularly in a smaller economy. Bob Wallace, a senior editor at Macmillan's Free Press, says: "Instead of buying a consultant's services for $5,000, you buy a consultant's book for $15." The books also are well packaged. Each of the three best sellers has abandoned the scholarly, technical, data-ridden format that has been typical. The new style "makes business simple," according to Ms. Blakely of B. Dalton, by means of anecdotes, parables and an emphasis on people's "feelings rather than on hard analysis." Some observers have even asked whether some of the new best sellers are merely cleverly packaged collections of aphorisms and anecdotes.

Publishers are competing vigorously for business manuscripts, for everything from business how-tos and psychological studies of success, to "kiss-and-quit" tales of partnerships and divestitures. Business is becoming the glamour category, moving into celebrity biographies. The management lessons of Lee Iacocca, Akio Morita and Mary Cunningham are only the, most recent instances of books commanding high six-figure contracts. Consulting firms, too, are suddenly disgorging their secrets in print. Other business categories also are benefiting: The rights to a primer on selling, which two years ago would have gone begging, recently sold for more than $200,000 in a heated, two-day auction.

Will management books continue to dominate the best-seller lists? No, says Claire Wyckoff, publishing and marketing director of Amacom: "The business book market has been strong for the last 10 years. The best sellers are a culmination of a long trend, the top of the swell. But the popular culture tends to move on."

But the best sellers certainly are having an impact. Says Robert E. Finley, director of the American Management Association's Book Clubs Division: "All of a sudden you have over a million and a half people reading these three books. These people have been given an insight into how management works and a realization that the whole publishing industry is taking their interests to heart. They'll be back for more."

Chapter Ten

How to Copyright Your Book
How to Secure a Library of Congress Catalog Card Number
How to Obtain an International Standard Book Number (ISBN)

The title page of the book is usually on the right-hand page and is numbered "page one." The copyright page is usually on the back of the title page and is numbered "page two."

To secure copyright Form TX, write to the United States Copyright Office, Library of Congress, Washington, D.C. 20559. Since the form is free, ask for several and you'll be ready for your next book.

When you print your book, or photo-copy your manuscript, inscribe in print on the copyright page the word "copyright," followed by the year, followed by your name. (See page two of this book.) This is done *before* you actually receive the copyright. Once the book is printed, it is required that you send two copies of the book, together with a properly filled-out copyright Form TX and a check for $20.00, payable to the Register of Copyrights, Library of Congress, Washington, D.C. 20559. You are not required to pay the postage when sending books to be copyrighted. (See Postal Manual 137.22.)

The use of the copyright notice is the responsibility of the copyright owner and does not require advance permission from the Copyright Office. The required form of the notice for copies generally consists of three elements: (1) the symbol "©", or the word "Copyright" or the abbreviation "Copr.", (2) the year of first publication, and (3) the name of the owner of the copyright. For example: "Copyright 1983 by Melvin Powers."

See pages 111 through 114 for very important information pertaining to the duration of the copyright. Also see pages 115 through 120 for the actual copyright form, including instructions.

When the copyright office receives your two books, together with your TX Form and your check, you will in turn, be sent a registration number and an indication of the effective date of your registration. Additionally, you will receive the copyright form you submitted, and it will contain the registrar's signature and photocopy of the official seal.

Library of Congress Catalog Card Number
The Card Division of the Library of Congress pre-assigns Library of Congress catalog card numbers for forthcoming books. This service is free. The card number is requested before the book is printed and is included on the copyright page of your book. (See the copyright page of this book.) (See page 121 for the form.) For the official form, write to: CIP Office, Library of Congress, Washington, D.C. 20540

Thousands of libraries around the world are subscribers, receiving the index cards to which you refer when looking for a particular book in the library. Some may request specific areas of interest. Your card will reach the attention of the librarians, who, if interested, will order your book.

International Standard Book Number—ISBN
The numbering system is intended to simplify clerical work, billing, inventory control and royalty accounting. It also simplifies the process of ordering books by libraries, bookstores and wholesalers.

The first part of the number identifies the geographical or linguistic group; the second part, the publisher; the third part, the author and title. The last number is a single-check digit which the computer links with the other digits in a lightning-speed multiplication process to eliminate error.

The identifiers 0 and 1 have been allotted to the major English-speaking countries: the United States, Great Britain, Canada and Australia.

Wilshire Book Company has been assigned the number 0-87980. "0" stands for an English-language publisher. We assigned this book the number 406-8. The last number, 8, represents a computerized, mathematical function to make sure the rest of the numbers are correct.

The ISBN number is included on the copyright page of your book, as well as on the back, outside, lower-right-hand corner. Put the number in at least 10-point type so that it can be easily read.

To become an official publisher with recognition all over the world, you will need the Title Output Information Request Form. Write to: International Standard Book Numbering Agency, 121 Chanlon Road, New Providence, New Jersey 07974.

In summation, when you publish your book, be sure to include the following: (1) your copyright notice, (2) your Library of Congress Catalog Card Number, (3) your ISBN number on the copyright page, as well as on the back outside cover, and (4) under the copyright notice include "All Rights Reserved." This is a requirement of the Buenos Aires Convention. The United States and the majority of Latin American countries belong to it. Most countries are members of the Universal Copyright Convention as well.

A word of caution. Be sure to include the title of your book and your name on the spine of the book. Many self-publishers fail to do this. When the book is displayed in the bookstore, chances are it will not be positioned with the face out, but on the shelves with the spine showing. So print your title and name as large as you can on the spine.

Circular **R15a**

**Duration
of Copyright**

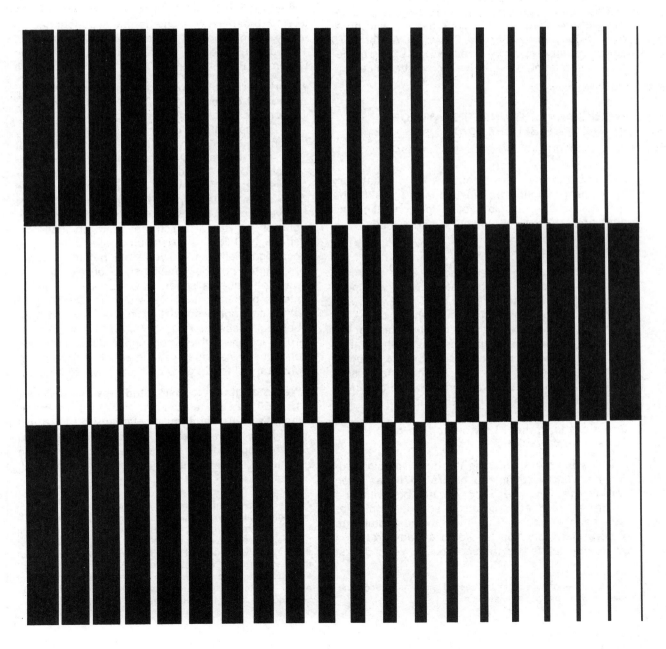

Duration of Copyright

Provisions of the Law
Dealing With the Length
of Copyright Protection

SCOPE

This circular provides you with a general summary of the statutory provisions dealing with duration of copyright under the Copyright Act of 1976 which became effective January 1, 1978. For detailed information, write to the Copyright Office.

WORKS ALREADY UNDER STATUTORY PROTECTION BEFORE 1978

For works that had already secured statutory copyright protection before January 1, 1978, the new law retains the old system for computing the duration of protection, but with some changes.

Duration Under the Old Law

Under the law in effect before 1978, copyright was secured either on the date a work was published, or on the date of registration if the work was registered in unpublished form. In either case, the copyright lasted for a first term of 28 years from the date it was secured. During the last (28th) year of the first term, the copyright was eligible for renewal. If renewed, the copyright was extended for a second term of 28 years.[1] If not renewed, the copyright expired at the end of the first 28-year term.

Effect of the Present Law on Length of Subsisting Copyrights

This system of computing the duration of protection for works copyrighted before 1978 has been carried over into the 1976 statute, but with one major change: the length of the second term is increased to 47 years. Thus, the maximum total term of copyright protection for works already protected by federal statute is increased from 56 years (a first

term of 28 years plus a renewal term of 28 years) to 75 years (a first term of 28 years plus a renewal term of 47 years).

The specific situation for works copyrighted before 1978 depends on whether the copyright had already been renewed when the Copyright Act of 1976 came into effect, or was still in its first term on December 31, 1977.

- **Works originally copyrighted before 1950 and renewed before 1978:**[2] These older works have automatically been given a longer copyright term. Under the statute, copyrights that had already been renewed and were in their second term at any time between December 31, 1976, and December 31, 1977, inclusive, do not need to be renewed again. They were automatically extended to last for a total term of 75 years (a first term of 28 years plus a renewal term of 47 years) from the end of the year in which they were originally secured. **NOTE:** This extension applies not only to copyrights less than 56 years old, but also to older copyrights that had previously been extended in duration under a series of Congressional enactments beginning in 1962. As in the case of all other copyrights subsisting in their second term between December 31, 1976, and December 31, 1977, inclusive, these copyrights will expire at the end of the calendar year in which the 75th anniversary of the original date of copyright occurs.

- **Works originally copyrighted between January 1, 1950 and December 31, 1977:** Copyrights in their first 28-year term on January 1, 1978 will **still have to be renewed** in order to be protected for the second term. If a valid renewal registration is made at the proper time, the second term will

---

[1] For a number of copyrights, the second term was extended beyond 28 years by special legislation.

[2] A special transitional situation arose with respect to first-term copyrights that were originally secured in 1950, and that became eligible for renewal during the calendar year 1977. If renewal registration was made before January 1, 1978, the duration of the copyright was extended to the full period of 75 years without the need for further renewal. However, even if renewal registration was not made before January 1, 1978, renewal for the second 47-year term could be made under the new law at any time between January 1, 1978 and December 31, 1978.

last for 47 years (19 years longer than the 28-year renewal term under the old law). However, if renewal registration for these works is not made within the statutory time limits, a copyright originally secured between 1950 and 1977 will expire on December 31st of its 28th year, and protection will be lost permanently.

Example: A work copyrighted in 1960 will be eligible for renewal in 1988. If renewed, it will be protected until 2035, but if renewal registration is not made at the proper time, copyright protection will expire permanently at the end of 1988.

Forms for renewal registration (Form RE) are available from the Information and Publications Section, LM-455, Copyright Office, Library of Congress, Washington, D.C. 20559. For further information about the time limits and other requirements for renewal registration, write for Circular R15, *Renewal of Copyright*. For specific information about the extension of copyright terms for works already under statutory protection before 1978, write for Circular R15t, *Extension of Copyright Terms*.

WORKS ORIGINALLY CREATED ON AND AFTER JANUARY 1, 1978

For works that are created and fixed in a tangible medium of expression for the first time after January 1, 1978 the Copyright Act of 1976 does away with all renewal requirements and establishes a single copyright term and different methods for computing the duration of a copyright. Works of this sort fall into two categories:

• **Works created on or after January 1, 1978:** The U.S. copyright law, for works created after its effective date, adopts the basic "life-plus-fifty" system already in effect in most other countries. A work that is created (fixed in tangible form for the

first time) after January 1, 1978 is automatically protected from the moment of its creation, and is given a term lasting for the author's life, plus an additional 50 years after the author's death. In the case of "a joint work prepared by two or more authors who did not work for hire," the term lasts for 50 years after the last surviving author's death. For works made for hire, and for anonymous and pseudonymous works (unless the author's identity is revealed in Copyright Office records), the duration of copyright will be 75 years from publication or 100 years from creation, whichever is shorter.

• **Works in existence but not copyrighted on January 1, 1978:** Works that had been created before the new law came into effect but had neither been published nor registered for copyright before January 1, 1978, automatically are given federal copyright protection. The duration of copyright in these works will generally be computed in the same way as for new works: the life-plus-50 or 75/100-year terms will apply to them as well. However, all works in this category are guaranteed at least 25 years of statutory protection. The law specifies that in no case will copyright in a work of this sort expire before December 31, 2002, and if the work is published before that date the term may be extended by another 25 years, through the end of 2027.

YEAR-END EXPIRATION OF COPYRIGHT TERMS

The new law provides that all terms of copyright will run through the end of the calendar year in which they would otherwise expire. This not only affects the duration of copyrights, but also the time limits for renewal registrations. From now on, the last day of a copyright will be December 31st of that copyright's last year; and, for works originally copyrighted between 1950 and 1977, all periods for renewal registration will run from December 31 of the 27th year of the copyright and will end on December 31 of the following year.

TERMINATION OF GRANTS

As explained above, for works already under statutory protection before 1978, the length of the renewal term has been increased to 47 years. This means that, in most cases, 19 years have been added to the end of a renewal copyright. The new statute also contains special provisions allowing an author, or specified heirs of the author, to file a notice terminating any grant of rights made by the author and covering any part of that added period of years. This right to reclaim ownership of all or part of the extended term is optional; it can be exercised only by certain specified persons in accordance with prescribed conditions and within strict time limits.

With respect to copyrights that are nearly 56 years old, and those that are already older than 56 years, the option of serving an advance notice of termination is now a possibility. The Copyright Office has issued final regulations on this subject, and you can obtain a copy of them by writing for

ML-161, *Termination of Transfers and Licenses Covering Extended Renewal Term.*

SPECIAL POINTS TO REMEMBER:

- Initial Registration of Works Published Before January 1, 1978: Works published with notice of copyright prior to January 1, 1978, must be registered and renewed during the first 28-year term of copyright to maintain protection.
- Copyrights originally secured between 1950 and 1977 must still be renewed. If not, they expire at the end of their 28th calendar year.
- Copyrights in their second term on January 1, 1978, are automatically extended up to a maximum of 75 years, without the need for further renewal.
- Works already in the public domain cannot be protected under the new law. The Act provides no procedure for restoring protection for works in which copyright has been lost for any reason.

Copyright Office • Library of Congress • Washington, D.C. 20559

August 1982 - 50,000

☆ U.S. GOVERNMENT PRINTING OFFICE: 1982 - 361-279/509

APPLICATION FOR COPYRIGHT REGISTRATION
for a
Nondramatic Literary Work

FORM TX

UNITED STATES COPYRIGHT OFFICE
LIBRARY OF CONGRESS
WASHINGTON, D.C. 20559

HOW TO APPLY FOR COPYRIGHT REGISTRATION:

- **First:** Read the information on this page to make sure Form TX is the correct application for your work.

- **Second:** Open out the form by pulling this page to the left. Read through the detailed instructions before starting to complete the form.

- **Third:** Complete spaces 1-4 of the application, then turn the entire form over and, after reading the instructions for spaces 5-11, complete the rest of your application. Use typewriter or print in dark ink. Be sure to sign the form at space 10.

- **Fourth:** Detach your completed application from these instructions and send it with the necessary deposit of the work (see below) to: Register of Copyrights, Library of Congress, Washington, D.C. 20559. Unless you have a Deposit Account in the Copyright Office, your application and deposit must be accompanied by a check or money order for $10, payable to: *Register of Copyrights.*

WHEN TO USE FORM TX: Form TX is the appropriate application to use for copyright registration covering nondramatic literary works, whether published or unpublished.

WHAT IS A "NONDRAMATIC LITERARY WORK"? The category of "nondramatic literary works" (Class TX) is very broad. Except for dramatic works and certain kinds of audiovisual works, Class TX includes all types of works written in words (or other verbal or numerical symbols). A few of the many examples of "nondramatic literary works" include fiction, nonfiction, poetry, periodicals, textbooks, reference works, directories, catalogs, advertising copy, and compilations of information.

DEPOSIT TO ACCOMPANY APPLICATION: An application for copyright registration must be accompanied by a deposit representing the entire work for which registration is to be made. The following are the general deposit requirements as set forth in the statute:

Unpublished work: Deposit one complete copy (or phonorecord).

Published work: Deposit two complete copies (or phonorecords) of the best edition.

Work first published outside the United States: Deposit one complete copy (or phonorecord) of the first foreign edition.

Contribution to a collective work: Deposit one complete copy (or phonorecord) of the best edition of the collective work.

These general deposit requirements may vary in particular situations. For further information about copyright deposit, write to the Copyright Office.

THE COPYRIGHT NOTICE: For published works, the law provides that a copyright notice in a specified form "shall be placed on all publicly distributed copies from which the work can be visually perceived." Use of the copyright notice is the responsibility of the copyright owner and does not require advance permission from the Copyright Office. The required form of the notice for copies generally consists of three elements: (1) the symbol "©", or the word "Copyright", or the abbreviation "Copr."; (2) the year of first publication; and (3) the name of the owner of copyright. For example: "© 1978 Constance Porter". The notice is to be affixed to the copies "in such manner and location as to give reasonable notice of the claim of copyright." Unlike the law in effect before 1978, the new copyright statute provides procedures for correcting errors in the copyright notice, and even for curing the omission of the notice. However, a failure to comply with the notice requirements may still result in the loss of some copyright protection and, unless corrected within five years, in the complete loss of copyright. For further information about the copyright notice and the procedures for correcting errors or omissions, write to the Copyright Office.

DURATION OF COPYRIGHT: For works that were created after the effective date of the new statute (January 1, 1978), the basic copyright term will be the life of the author and fifty years after the author's death. For works made for hire, and for certain anonymous and pseudonymous works, the duration of copyright will be 75 years from publication or 100 years from creation, whichever is shorter. These same terms of copyright will generally apply to works that had been created before 1978 but had not been published or copyrighted before that date. For further information about the duration of copyright, including the terms of copyrights already in existence before 1978, write for Circular R15a.

HOW TO FILL OUT FORM TX

Specific Instructions for Spaces 1-4

- The line-by-line instructions on this page are keyed to the spaces on the first page of Form TX, printed opposite.
- Please read through these instructions before you start filling out your application, and refer to the specific instructions for each space as you go along.

SPACE 1: TITLE

- **Title of this Work:** Every work submitted for copyright registration must be given a title that is capable of identifying that particular work. If the copies or phonorecords of the work bear a title (or an identifying phrase that could serve as a title), transcribe its wording completely and exactly on the application. Remember that indexing of the registration and future identification of the work will depend on the information you give here.

- **Periodical or Serial Issue:** Periodicals and other serials are publications issued at intervals under a general title, such as newspapers, magazines, journals, newsletters, and annuals. If the work being registered is an entire issue of a periodical or serial, give the over-all title of the periodical or serial in the space headed "Title of this Work," and add the specific information about the issue in the spaces provided. If the work being registered is a contribution to a periodical or serial issue, follow the instructions for "Publication as a Contribution."

- **Previous or Alternative Titles:** Complete this space if there are any additional titles for the work under which someone searching for the registration might be likely to look, or under which a document pertaining to the work might be recorded.

- **Publication as a Contribution:** If the work being registered has been published as a contribution to a periodical, serial, or collection, give the title of the contribution in the space headed "Title of this Work." Then, in the line headed "Publication as a Contribution," give information about the larger work in which the contribution appeared.

SPACE 2: AUTHORS

- **General Instructions:** First decide, after reading these instructions, who are the "authors" of this work for copyright purposes. Then, unless the work is a "collective work" (see below), give the requested information about every "author" who contributed any appreciable amount of copyrightable matter to this version of the work. If you need further space, use the attached Continuation Sheet and, if necessary, request additional Continuation Sheets (Form TX/CON).

- **Who is the "Author"?** Unless the work was "made for hire," the individual who actually created the work is its "author." In the case of a work made for hire, the statute provides that "the employer or other person for whom the work was prepared is considered the author."

- **What is a "Work Made for Hire"?** A "work made for hire" is defined as: (1) "a work prepared by an employee within the scope of his or her employment"; or (2) "a work specially ordered or commissioned" for certain uses specified in the statute, but only if there is a written agreement to consider it a "work made for hire."

- **Collective Work:** In the case of a collective work, such as a periodical issue, anthology, collection of essays, or encyclopedia, it is sufficient to give information about the author of the collective work as a whole.

- **Author's Identity Not Revealed:** If an author's contribution is "anonymous" or "pseudonymous," it is not necessary to give the name and dates for that author. However, the citizenship or domicile of that author **must** be given in all cases, and information about the nature of that author's contribution to the work should be included.

- **Name of Author:** The fullest form of the author's name should be given. If you have checked "Yes" to indicate that the work was "made for hire," give the full legal name of the employer (or other person for whom the work was prepared). You may also include the name of the employee (for example, "Elster Publishing Co., employer for hire of John Ferguson"). If the work is "anonymous" you may: (1) leave the line blank, or (2) state "Anonymous" in the line, or (3) reveal the author's identity. If the work is "pseudonymous" you may (1) leave the line blank, or (2) give the pseudonym and identify it as such (for example: "Huntley Haverstock, pseudonym"), or (3) reveal the author's name, making clear which is the real name and which is the pseudonym (for example, "Judith Barton, whose pseudonym is Madeleine Elster").

- **Dates of Birth and Death:** If the author is dead, the statute requires that the year of death be included in the application unless the work is anonymous or pseudonymous. The author's birth date is optional, but is useful as a form of identification. Leave this space blank if the author's contribution was a "work made for hire."

- **"Anonymous" or "Pseudonymous" Work:** An author's contribution to a work is "anonymous" if that author is not identified on the copies or phonorecords of the work. An author's contribution to a work is "pseudonymous" if that author is identified on the copies or phonorecords under a fictitious name.

- **Author's Nationality or Domicile:** Give the country of which the author is a citizen, or the country in which the author is domiciled. The statute requires that either nationality or domicile be given in all cases.

- **Nature of Authorship:** After the words "Author of" give a brief general statement of the nature of this particular author's contribution to the work. Examples: "Entire text"; "Co-author of entire text"; "Chapters 11-14"; "Editorial revisions"; "Compilation and English translation"; "Illustrations."

SPACE 3: CREATION AND PUBLICATION

- **General Instructions:** Do not confuse "creation" with "publication." Every application for copyright registration must state "the year in which creation of the work was completed." Give the date and nation of first publication only if the work has been published.

- **Creation:** Under the statute, a work is "created" when it is fixed in a copy or phonorecord for the first time. Where a work has been prepared over a period of time, the part of the work existing in fixed form on a particular date constitutes the created work on that date. The date you give here should be the year in which the author completed the particular version for which registration is now being sought, even if other versions exist or if further changes or additions are planned.

- **Publication:** The statute defines "publication" as "the distribution of copies or phonorecords of a work to the public by sale or other transfer of ownership, or by rental, lease, or lending"; a work is also "published" if there has been an "offering to distribute copies or phonorecords to a group of persons for purposes of further distribution, public performance, or public display." Give the full date (month, day, year) when, and the country where, publication first occurred. If first publication took place simultaneously in the United States and other countries, it is sufficient to state "U.S.A."

SPACE 4: CLAIMANT(S)

- **Name(s) and Address(es) of Copyright Claimant(s):** Give the name(s) and address(es) of the copyright claimant(s) in this work. The statute provides that copyright in a work belongs initially to the author of the work (including, in the case of a work made for hire, the employer or other person for whom the work was prepared). The copyright claimant is either the author of the work or a person or organization that has obtained ownership of the copyright initially belonging to the author.

- **Transfer:** The statute provides that, if the copyright claimant is not the author, the application for registration must contain "a brief statement of how the claimant obtained ownership of the copyright." If any copyright claimant named in space 4 is not an author named in space 2, give a brief, general statement summarizing the means by which that claimant obtained ownership of the copyright.

FORM TX

UNITED STATES COPYRIGHT OFFICE

```
REGISTRATION NUMBER



        TX            TXU
```

```
EFFECTIVE DATE OF REGISTRATION


. . . . . . . . . . . .    . . . . . . . . . . .
     (Month)          (Day)         (Year)
```

DO NOT WRITE ABOVE THIS LINE. IF YOU NEED MORE SPACE, USE CONTINUATION SHEET (FORM TX/CON)

(1) Title

TITLE OF THIS WORK: | **PREVIOUS OR ALTERNATIVE TITLES:**

If a periodical or serial give: Vol. . . . . . . No. . . . . . Issue Date . . . .

PUBLICATION AS A CONTRIBUTION: (If this work was published as a contribution to a periodical, serial, or collection, give information about the collective work in which the contribution appeared.)

Title of Collective Work: . . . . Vol. . . . . . No. . . . . . Date . . . . Pages. . . . .

(2) Author(s)

IMPORTANT: Under the law, the "author" of a "work made for hire" is generally the employer, not the employee (see instructions). If any part of this work was "made for hire" check "Yes" in the space provided, give the employer (or other person for whom the work was prepared) as "Author" of that part, and leave the space for dates blank.

1

NAME OF AUTHOR: | **DATES OF BIRTH AND DEATH:**
Born . . . . Died . . . .
(Year)   (Year)

Was this author's contribution to the work a "work made for hire"?   Yes. . . . . .   No. . . . . .

AUTHOR'S NATIONALITY OR DOMICILE: | **WAS THIS AUTHOR'S CONTRIBUTION TO THE WORK:**
Citizen of . . . . } or { Domiciled in . . . .
(Name of Country)   (Name of Country)

Anonymous?   Yes . . . . . .   No . . . . . .
Pseudonymous?   Yes . . . . . .   No . . . . . .

AUTHOR OF: (Briefly describe nature of this author's contribution)

If the answer to either of these questions is "Yes," see detailed instructions attached.

2

NAME OF AUTHOR: | **DATES OF BIRTH AND DEATH:**
Born . . . . Died . . . .
(Year)   (Year)

Was this author's contribution to the work a "work made for hire"?   Yes. . . . . .   No. . . . . .

AUTHOR'S NATIONALITY OR DOMICILE: | **WAS THIS AUTHOR'S CONTRIBUTION TO THE WORK:**
Citizen of . . . . } or { Domiciled in . . . .
(Name of Country)   (Name of Country)

Anonymous?   Yes . . . . . .   No . . . . . .
Pseudonymous?   Yes . . . . . .   No . . . . . .

AUTHOR OF: (Briefly describe nature of this author's contribution)

If the answer to either of these questions is "Yes," see detailed instructions attached.

3

NAME OF AUTHOR: | **DATES OF BIRTH AND DEATH:**
Born . . . . Died . . . .
(Year)   (Year)

Was this author's contribution to the work a "work made for hire"?   Yes. . . . . .   No. . . . . .

AUTHOR'S NATIONALITY OR DOMICILE: | **WAS THIS AUTHOR'S CONTRIBUTION TO THE WORK:**
Citizen of . . . . } or { Domiciled in . . . .
(Name of Country)   (Name of Country)

Anonymous?   Yes . . . . . .   No . . . . . .
Pseudonymous?   Yes . . . . . .   No . . . . . .

AUTHOR OF: (Briefly describe nature of this author's contribution)

If the answer to either of these questions is "Yes," see detailed instructions attached.

(3) Creation and Publication

YEAR IN WHICH CREATION OF THIS WORK WAS COMPLETED: | **DATE AND NATION OF FIRST PUBLICATION:**

Date. . . . .
(Month)   (Day)   (Year)

Year. . . . .

Nation . . . .
(Name of Country)

(This information must be given in all cases.) | (Complete this block ONLY if this work has been published.)

(4) Claimant(s)

NAME(S) AND ADDRESS(ES) OF COPYRIGHT CLAIMANT(S):

TRANSFER: (If the copyright claimant(s) named here in space 4 are different from the author(s) named in space 2, give a brief statement of how the claimant(s) obtained ownership of the copyright.)

- *Complete all applicable spaces (numbers 5-11) on the reverse side of this page*
- *Follow detailed instructions attached*   • *Sign the form at line 10*

```
DO NOT WRITE HERE

Page 1 of . . . . . . . pages
```

INSTRUCTIONS FOR FILLING OUT SPACES 5-11 OF FORM TX

SPACE 5: PREVIOUS REGISTRATION

• **General Instructions:** The questions in space 5 are intended to find out whether an earlier registration has been made for this work and, if so, whether there is any basis for a new registration. As a general rule, only one basic copyright registration can be made for the same version of a particular work.

• **Same Version:** If this version is substantially the same as the work covered by a previous registration, a second registration is not generally possible unless: (1) the work has been registered in unpublished form and a second registration is now being sought to cover the first published edition, or (2) someone other than the author is identified as copyright claimant in the earlier registration, and the author is now seeking registration in his or her own name. If either

of these two exceptions apply, check the appropriate box and give the earlier registration number and date. Otherwise, do not submit Form TX; instead, write the Copyright Office for information about supplementary registration or recordation of transfers of copyright ownership.

• **Changed Version:** If the work has been changed, and you are now seeking registration to cover the additions or revisions, check the third box in space 5, give the earlier registration number and date, and complete both parts of space 6.

• **Previous Registration Number and Date:** If more than one previous registration has been made for the work, give the number and date of the latest registration.

SPACE 6: COMPILATION OR DERIVATIVE WORK

• **General Instructions:** Complete both parts of space 6 if this work is a "compilation," or "derivative work," or both, and if it incorporates one or more earlier works that have already been published or registered for copyright, or that have fallen into the public domain. A "compilation" is defined as "a work formed by the collection and assembling of preexisting materials or of data that are selected, coordinated, or arranged in such a way that the resulting work as a whole constitutes an original work of authorship." A "derivative work" is "a work based on one or more preexisting works." Examples of derivative works include translations, fictionalizations, arrangements, abridgments, condensations, or "any other form in which a work may be recast, transformed, or adapted." Derivative works also include works "consisting of editorial revisions, annotations, elaborations, or other modifications" if these changes, as a whole, represent an original work of authorship.

• **Preexisting Material:** If the work is a compilation, give a brief, general statement describing the nature of the material that has been compiled. Example: "Compilation of all published 1917 speeches of Woodrow Wilson." In the case of a derivative work, identify the preexisting work that has been recast, transformed, or adapted. Example: "Russian version of Goncharov's 'Oblomov'."

• **Material Added to this Work:** The statute requires a "brief, general statement of the additional material covered by the copyright claim being registered." This statement should describe all of the material in this particular version of the work that: (1) represents an original work of authorship; and (2) has not fallen into the public domain; and (3) has not been previously published; and (4) has not been previously registered for copyright in unpublished form. Examples: "Foreword, selection, arrangement, editing, critical annotations"; "Revisions throughout; chapters 11-17 entirely new".

SPACE 7: MANUFACTURING PROVISIONS

• **General Instructions:** The copyright statute currently provides, as a general rule, and with a number of exceptions, that the copies of a published work "consisting preponderantly of nondramatic literary material that is in the English language" be manufactured in the United States or Canada in order to be lawfully imported and publicly distributed in the United States. At the present time, applications for copyright registration covering published works that consist mainly of nondramatic text matter in English *must*, in most cases, identify those who performed certain processes in manufacturing the copies, together with the places where those processes were performed. *Please note:* The information must be given even if the copies were manufactured outside the United States or Canada; registration will be made regardless of the places of manufacture identified in space 7. In general, the processes covered

by this provision are: (1) typesetting and plate-making (where a typographic process preceded the actual printing); (2) the making of plates by a lithographic or photoengraving process (where this was a final or intermediate step before printing); and (3) the final printing and binding processes (in all cases). Leave space 7 blank if your work is unpublished or is not in English.

• **Import Statement:** As an exception to the manufacturing provisions, the statute prescribes that, where manufacture has taken place outside the United States or Canada, a maximum of 2000 copies of the foreign edition can be imported into the United States without affecting the copyright owner's rights. For this purpose, the Copyright Office will issue an import statement upon request and payment of a fee of $3 at the time of registration or at any later time. For further information about import statements, ask for Form IS.

SPACE 8: REPRODUCTION FOR USE OF BLIND OR PHYSICALLY-HANDICAPPED PERSONS

• **General Instructions:** One of the major programs of the Library of Congress is to provide Braille editions and special recordings of works for the exclusive use of the blind and physically handicapped. In an effort to simplify and speed up the copyright licensing procedures that are a necessary part of this program, section 710 of the copyright statute provides for the establishment of a voluntary licensing system to be tied in with copyright registration. Under this system, the owner of copyright in a nondramatic literary work has the option, at the time of registration on Form TX, to grant to the Library of Congress a license to reproduce and distribute Braille editions and "talking books" or "talking magazines" of the work being registered. The Copyright Office regulations

provide that, under the license, the reproduction and distribution must be solely for the use of persons who are certified by competent authority as unable to read normal printed material as a result of physical limitations. The license is nonexclusive, and may be terminated upon 90 days notice. For further information, write for Circular R63.

• **How to Grant the License:** The license is entirely voluntary. If you wish to grant it, check one of the three boxes in space 8. Your check in one of these boxes, together with your signature in space 10, will mean that the Library of Congress can proceed to reproduce and distribute under the license without further paperwork.

SPACES 9, 10, 11: FEE, CORRESPONDENCE, CERTIFICATION, RETURN ADDRESS

• **Deposit Account and Mailing Instructions (Space 9):** If you maintain a Deposit Account in the Copyright Office, identify it in space 9. Otherwise you will need to send the registration fee of $10 with your application. The space headed "Correspondence" should contain the name and address of the person to be consulted if correspondence about this application becomes necessary.

• **Certification (Space 10):** The application is not acceptable unless it bears the handwritten signature of the author or other copyright claimant, or of the owner of exclusive right(s), or of the duly authorized agent of such author, claimant, or owner.

• **Address for Return of Certificate (Space 11):** The address box must be completed legibly, since the certificate will be returned in a window envelope.

HOW TO COPYRIGHT YOUR BOOK

<table>
<tr><td rowspan="3"></td><td>EXAMINED BY: . . . .
CHECKED BY: . . . .</td><td>APPLICATION RECEIVED:</td><td rowspan="4">FOR
COPYRIGHT
OFFICE
USE
ONLY</td></tr>
<tr><td>CORRESPONDENCE:
☐ Yes</td><td>DEPOSIT RECEIVED:</td></tr>
<tr><td>DEPOSIT ACCOUNT
FUNDS USED:
☐</td><td>REMITTANCE NUMBER AND DATE:</td></tr>
</table>

DO NOT WRITE ABOVE THIS LINE. IF YOU NEED ADDITIONAL SPACE, USE CONTINUATION SHEET (FORM TX/CON)

PREVIOUS REGISTRATION:

- Has registration for this work, or for an earlier version of this work, already been made in the Copyright Office?   Yes . . . . No . . . .
- If your answer is "Yes," why is another registration being sought? (Check appropriate box)
  ☐ This is the first published edition of a work previously registered in unpublished form.
  ☐ This is the first application submitted by this author as copyright claimant.
  ☐ This is a changed version of the work, as shown by line 6 of this application.
- If your answer is "Yes," give: Previous Registration Number . . . . Year of Registration . . . .

(5) Previous Registration

COMPILATION OR DERIVATIVE WORK: (See instructions)

PREEXISTING MATERIAL: (Identify any preexisting work or works that this work is based on or incorporates.)

{ . . . .

MATERIAL ADDED TO THIS WORK: (Give a brief, general statement of the material that has been added to this work and in which copyright is claimed.)

{ . . . .

(6) Compilation or Derivative Work

MANUFACTURERS AND LOCATIONS: (If this is a published work consisting preponderantly of nondramatic literary material in English, the law may require that the copies be manufactured in the United States or Canada for full protection. If so, the names of the manufacturers who performed certain processes, and the places where these processes were performed *must* be given. See instructions for details.)

NAMES OF MANUFACTURERS	PLACES OF MANUFACTURE
. . . .	. . . .
. . . .	. . . .
. . . .	. . . .

(7) Manufacturing

REPRODUCTION FOR USE OF BLIND OR PHYSICALLY-HANDICAPPED PERSONS: (See instructions)

- Signature of this form at space 10, and a check in one of the boxes here in space 8, constitutes a non-exclusive grant of permission to the Library of Congress to reproduce and distribute solely for the blind and physically handicapped and under the conditions and limitations prescribed by the regulations of the Copyright Office: (1) copies of the work identified in space 1 of this application in Braille (or similar tactile symbols); or (2) phonorecords embodying a fixation of a reading of that work; or (3) both.

a ☐ Copies and phonorecords   b ☐ Copies Only   c ☐ Phonorecords Only

(8) License For Handicapped

DEPOSIT ACCOUNT: (If the registration fee is to be charged to a Deposit Account established in the Copyright Office, give name and number of Account.)

Name: . . . .

Account Number: . . . .

CORRESPONDENCE: (Give name and address to which correspondence about this application should be sent.)
Name: . . . .
Address:. . . . . (Apt.)
. . . .
(City)   (State)   (ZIP)

(9) Fee and Correspondence

CERTIFICATION: ✱ I, the undersigned, hereby certify that I am the: (Check one)

☐ author ☐ other copyright claimant ☐ owner of exclusive right(s) ☐ authorized agent of: . . . .
(Name of author or other copyright claimant, or owner of exclusive right(s))

of the work identified in this application and that the statements made by me in this application are correct to the best of my knowledge.

☞   Handwritten signature: (X) . . . .

Typed or printed name. . . . . Date . . . .

(10) Certification (Application must be signed)

. . . . (Name) . . . . (Number, Street and Apartment Number) . . . . (City) (State) (ZIP code)	**MAIL CERTIFICATE TO** (Certificate will be mailed in window envelope)

(11) Address For Return of Certificate

✱ 17 U.S.C. § 506(e): Any person who knowingly makes a false representation of a material fact in the application for copyright registration provided for by section 409, or in any written statement filed in connection with the application, shall be fined not more than $2,500.
☆ U.S. GOVERNMENT PRINTING OFFICE: 1978-261-022/22

Sept. 1978 - 500,000

CONTINUATION SHEET FOR FORM TX

FORM TX/CON

UNITED STATES COPYRIGHT OFFICE

- If at all possible, try to fit the information called for into the spaces provided on Form TX.
- If you do not have space enough for all of the information you need to give on Form TX, use this continuation sheet and submit it with Form TX.
- If you submit this continuation sheet, leave it attached to Form TX. Or, if it becomes detached, clip (do not tape or staple) and fold the two together before submitting them.
- **PART A** of this sheet is intended to identify the basic application. **PART B** is a continuation of Space 2. **PART C** is for the continuation of Spaces 1, 4, 6, or 7. The other spaces on Form TX call for specific items of information, and should not need continuation.

REGISTRATION NUMBER
TX   TXU
EFFECTIVE DATE OF REGISTRATION
. . . . (Month)   (Day)   (Year)
CONTINUATION SHEET RECEIVED
Page _____ of _____ pages

DO NOT WRITE ABOVE THIS LINE: FOR COPYRIGHT OFFICE USE ONLY

(A) **Identification of Application**	**IDENTIFICATION OF CONTINUATION SHEET:** This sheet is a continuation of the application for copyright registration on Form TX, submitted for the following work: • TITLE: (Give the title as given under the heading "Title of this Work" in Space 1 of Form TX.) . . . . • NAME(S) AND ADDRESS(ES) OF COPYRIGHT CLAIMANT(S): (Give the name and address of at least one copyright claimant as given in Space 4 of Form TX.) . . . .

(B) **Continuation of Space 2**	**NAME OF AUTHOR:** Was this author's contribution to the work a "work made for hire"? Yes...... No......	**DATES OF BIRTH AND DEATH:** Born .... Died .... (Year) (Year)
	AUTHOR'S NATIONALITY OR DOMICILE: Citizen of .... } or { Domiciled in .... (Name of Country) (Name of Country)	**WAS THIS AUTHOR'S CONTRIBUTION TO THE WORK:** Anonymous? Yes...... No...... Pseudonymous? Yes...... No......
	AUTHOR OF: (Briefly describe nature of this author's contribution)	If the answer to either of these questions is "Yes," see detailed instructions attached.
	NAME OF AUTHOR: Was this author's contribution to the work a "work made for hire"? Yes...... No......	**DATES OF BIRTH AND DEATH:** Born .... Died .... (Year) (Year)
	AUTHOR'S NATIONALITY OR DOMICILE: Citizen of .... } or { Domiciled in .... (Name of Country) (Name of Country)	**WAS THIS AUTHOR'S CONTRIBUTION TO THE WORK:** Anonymous? Yes...... No...... Pseudonymous? Yes...... No......
	AUTHOR OF: (Briefly describe nature of this author's contribution)	If the answer to either of these questions is "Yes," see detailed instructions attached.
	NAME OF AUTHOR: Was this author's contribution to the work a "work made for hire"? Yes...... No......	**DATES OF BIRTH AND DEATH:** Born .... Died .... (Year) (Year)
	AUTHOR'S NATIONALITY OR DOMICILE: Citizen of .... } or { Domiciled in .... (Name of Country) (Name of Country)	**WAS THIS AUTHOR'S CONTRIBUTION TO THE WORK:** Anonymous? Yes...... No...... Pseudonymous? Yes...... No......
	AUTHOR OF: (Briefly describe nature of this author's contribution)	If the answer to either of these questions is "Yes," see detailed instructions attached.

(C) **Continuation of Other Spaces**	**CONTINUATION OF** (Check which): ☐ Space 1 ☐ Space 4 ☐ Space 6 ☐ Space 7

REQUEST FOR LIBRARY OF CONGRESS CATALOG CARD NUMBER

To receive a PREASSIGNED card number please supply fullest information possible:

Publisher: _____

Author(s): _____

_____

Title: _____

_____

_____

Edition (e.g., 1st, 2nd, revised, etc.): _____

U.S. place of publication (city and state): _____

Proposed date of publication: Month _____ Year _____

Series Title: _____

Number of pages (approximate): _____

Will this publication appear at regular intervals under the same title (i.e., is it a serial publication)?

Yes _____   No _____

Although there is no charge for a PREASSIGNED card number, the Library of Congress requires one copy of the best edition of the completed book for cataloging purposes. A postage-free, self-addressed label will be sent with the preassigned card number for your convenience in mailing the required copy of the work. NOTE: This form may be used ONLY for requesting a PREASSIGNED card number, IN ADVANCE OF PUBLICATION. Once a work has been published, a card number can no longer be PREASSIGNED and can be obtained only by DONATING one copy of the published work to the Library.

Name and address to which preassigned card number should be sent:

Contact person: _____

_____

_____

_____

Phone number : _____

Send this form to: Cataloging in Publication Division
Library of Congress, Washington, D.C. 20540

607-7 (rev 12/78)   ☆U.S. Government Printing Office: 1980—311-423/3525

Copyright Office · Library of Congress · Washington, D.C. 20559

Announcement

NEW HOTLINE ESTABLISHED AT THE COPYRIGHT OFFICE

If you need application forms for registration of a claim to copyright, you may now call (202) 287-9100 at any time, day or night, to leave your request as a recorded message on the Forms HOTLINE of the Copyright Office in Washington, D.C.

The Copyright Office has established this new service to speed up service to callers who know what application forms they need and who do not need the services of a Public Information Specialist.

Requests made on the HOTLINE number are filled and mailed promptly.

If you do not know what forms you need or if you need additional information about copyright, you may call the Copyright Public Information Office at (202) 287-8700 weekdays between 8:30 a.m. and 5:00 p.m. Calls will be answered in sequence.

WHAT APPLICATION FORMS YOU WILL NEED

If you wish to apply to register your work for copyright, you will need one of the following application forms: Form TX, Form SE, Form PA, Form VA, Form SR, Form RE, Form CA, or Form GR/CP.

Use Form TX for Nondramatic Literary Works.

Class TX includes all types of published and unpublished works written in words or other verbal or numerical symbols, except for dramatic works and certain kinds of audiovisual works. You will need this form if your work is fiction or nonfiction, poetry or prose, or a textbook, reference work, directory, catalog, advertising copy, computer program, data base or other "nondramatic literary work."

Use Form SE for Serials.

Class SE, serials, includes all works issued or intended to be issued in successive parts bearing numerical or chronological designations and intended to be continued indefinitely (periodicals, newspapers, magazines, newsletters, annuals, journals, etc.).

ML-255

Chapter Eleven

How to Write a Winning Advertisement—Your Strategy for Success

The challenge in writing effective advertising copy is to present your statement in a way that is designed to elicit a favorable response from the reader. It is far more than a combination of words. In proper proportions, it should combine creative skill, writing and psychology. Then, the finished product produces the impact that motivates the reader. As with all other forms of writing, so it is with this—a craft in which you develop your skills in an unending growth process. Writing is an art form, but not an exact science. Even when we know what the important elements are that go into a winning ad, there is no guarantee of success. It is comparable to knowing all the necessary elements for writing a best-selling novel. Using them as effectively as you can, there's still no promise that you'll come up with the award-winning book. The guarantee to success in writing anything, whether it be an advertisement, a novel, a movie, a television script, a song or a theatrical play, relies on creativity. Will the story or ad hold the interest of the reader? Is it believable and original? Will it, in the case of advertising copy, be so compelling that a favorable response becomes inevitable?

I think it will be interesting and informative for you to know how I created an entirely new ad for Melvin Powers' *How to Get Rich in Mail Order.* For several years, we had been running variations of the ads shown on pages 45, 46 and 47 in numerous magazines and newspapers. The response was beginning to diminish—a clear signal that it was time to change the ads or the slant (story line). Perhaps we had exhausted readership response, or possibly, due to the length of time the ads had been running, they were no longer sufficiently captivating to generate reader interest. Furthermore, by this time the readers were possibly so familiar with the ad that upon recognition they immediately turned the page without reading it. But whatever the reason, I knew I had a problem, and that was how to make changes that would significantly increase the pulling power of the ads.

After considerable deliberation, I suggested to Melvin that I write what is known in advertising circles as a "blind ad"—an ad that makes no disclosure of the content of the book. Benefits to be derived from reading it are stressed, and the reader is encouraged to order the book because it carries a money-back guarantee.

One of the problems in stating at the outset what the book is all about is the possibility that the reader might have been exposed to similar ads and has concluded, with or without valid reasoning, that what the book has to offer will not suit his needs. Whereupon he might dismiss the ad and turn to the next page.

The blind ad, on the other hand, is intriguing, fascinating and mysterious. In effect, it's comparable to the "sneak preview" of a movie. There are many who find more excitement and entertainment in the element of surprise than in being totally aware. See pages 127 and 128.

Logically, such an ad prompts the question, "Why doesn't the ad specifically state what the book is all about?" In my ad copy on page 127, column two, under *Your Secret Dreams Come True,* I state what the book is *not* about. In fact, I don't even disclose that what the reader will receive is a book. I talk about "a program." My ad copy makes the statement, "My program for riches has nothing to do with franchising, real estate, stock market, precious metals, diamonds, pyramid schemes, oil wells, energy conservation, salesmanship, multi-level selling, positive thinking, door-to-door selling, telephone sales, or calling on businesses, neighbors, family or friends."

Clearly, the psychology behind the technique of stating what the offer is *not* about is to arouse the curiosity of the reader to a point where he says to himself, "What could it possibly be that will enable me to make all that money?"

Please take the time to read the ad in its entirety. At a later time, I'll break it down into its component parts.

Having now read the ad, do you like it? Do you object to the blind-ad principle? If the ad appeals to you, what is there about it that you especially like? What are its strong points? What are the weak points? How would you improve the ad? If the ad is not to your liking, can you come up with a different or better story line?

All answers can be correct. The validity lies in running a new ad incorporating your changes to test the response.

The headline is the most important part of your ad. It must have the power to arrest the reader's attention, causing him to pause in his perusal of the magazine or newspaper. If it is not able to do that, he will never read the body of the ad. Just as you must have a good title for your book, so must you have a good headline for your ad.

Originally, my headline for the new ad was "*How to Get Rich Starting from Zero.*" Later, I came up with a better headline by incorporating the all-important element of time. It then read, "*How to Get Rich This Year Starting from Zero!*" I liked that better.

"Don't wait for success. Make it happen!" "You are not only what you are today, but also what you choose to become tomorrow!" These two statements attributable to Melvin Powers are representative of his philosophy as forerunners to success. I might add that I have adopted the philosophy inherent in those statements into my own philosophy. From a standpoint of reader-impact, I can readily conclude that the effectiveness of Melvin's headline plus the influence of those two statements will cause the reader to pause and take notice.

The philosophy of making success happen is actually the prime thrust of this book. What Melvin is saying is "You should not wait for success to step up and greet you, but, rather, through your own initiative, bring about the encounter." He further states that our perspective

must be broad enough in range to provide for what we will become tomorrow. "We are not only what we are today, but also what we choose to become tomorrow." And I, for one, couldn't agree more. My own personal game-plan calls for the attainment of certain goals which I know I'll achieve because of my attitude and the motivation behind it. A similar positive mental attitude will underwrite the success of your book.

Blind ads usually employ the formula of telling the reader how a person starting from nothing can make a ton of money after he has discovered "the technique." The ad will then go on to say that the reader can do the same thing by following the prescribed technique. Our ad does the same thing. However, I added a component that was never used before. I asked Melvin for permission to list his actual bank deposits for a period of time covering several months. These figures would tell the story more persuasively than all the advertising copy in the world. A factual documentation cannot be disputed nor faked, because the Federal Trade Commission would interfere. Melvin's willingness to give the reader an inside look at the dollar-and-cents ledger resulted in instant readership confidence and interest.

Because of the average reader's skepticism, I urge him to "Take a minute to read this ad with an open mind. It could readily change your life and make your secret dreams come true." You'll find this stated above the testimonials. In column one, I ask him to spend one evening judging the contents of the material. (Note that I do not refer to it as a book.)

I also reveal the names and complete addresses of some of the people who made money using Melvin Powers' techniques. To my knowledge, no one has ever done that before. Ads usually give the person's initials and city of residence. The inclusion of the individual's actual street address gives credibility to our testimonials. Some of the readers who had provided testimonials later asked us to eliminate mention of last name and street address because they were barraged with phone calls from people wanting to know about the book. An amusing fact is that some people were spending more on phone calls than the price of the book. There's no denying that testimonials make powerful copy. Use as many as you find appropriate for your advertising copy. Notice that the advertising copy is broken up with subtitles. This device helps to tell the story and to facilitate reading.

In a subtle way, the illustration showing $20.00 bills suggests to the reader what he can expect.

I like the subtitle, *Still Skeptical? Be My Guest*. And I especially like the statement in the body of the copy that reads, "Put your mind at ease, and post-date your check 30 days from today." The idea originated with Joe Karbo and is used to gain the reader's confidence when it comes to sending for a book.

Guard against the curse of illegibility by telling the reader to print or type his name on the coupon. Use a key number in your ad so you can count your orders and have an indication of their origin.

The last part of the ad calls for the reader to take action. In a persuasive manner, he is asked to send for the material, fortified with the understanding that if he is not satisfied his check will be returned to him.

I am not convinced that the acceptance of credit cards, such as VISA or BankAmericard, would increase the sale of the book. It would entail more paper work, plus a cost of six percent (72¢ in this case) on every order. *Stay away from C.O.D. orders.* From 40 to 50% of the books are returned as undeliverable.

I would very much like to include Melvin Powers' picture in the ad. But try as I might—and he gives me a totally free hand when it comes to writing advertising copy—I have not been able to persuade him to let me do so. He maintains that it's unimportant; that people are interested in the book, not the author. I'm not at all sure he's right. I think the photo would contribute a personal note to supplement the already personal aspect of the book. What are your feelings in the matter?

We ran parts of the ad in color, but it made no difference as far as the response was concerned. I also changed the layout and the typography of the ad several times. It still made no difference.

To insure maximum readership, I usually ran our newspaper ads on the front page of the classified section. I placed a number of ads on what is known as "standby space," which means that the ad will run sometime within a period of several weeks on any page where there is an opening in the paper. This is known as ROP (run of the press) and the rate is usually half the usual rate. However, under this arrangement there is no way for the ad to command top readership. It might appear in a section of the paper read by relatively few people, resulting in marginal response. We no longer subscribe to this practice.

Because of the enormous expense of a full-page ad, I usually recommend a two-step approach to a new author. One, use a classified ad or a one-inch display ad telling the reader what the book is about and directing him to send for free details. Two, follow this with a four-page sales letter, testimonials, circular, order form, return envelope, photograph or illustration of the book, and perhaps a photograph of yourself with biographical material. This provides a complete selling job without the restrictions imposed by the physical limitations of a classified or small display ad. It has been my experience that one sixth of a page (one-half column) is the least amount of magazine space you can run and receive results. It's very difficult to motivate the reader to buy your book with a small amount of advertising copy. Your ad cannot be adequately developed. A classified ad becomes prohibitive in cost because you are paying for each word.

When your sales literature produces interest, construct a full-page ad using the key elements. When this ad proves successful, you are ready to expand to a variety of magazines and newspapers.

With your sales literature pulling in orders, you might want to consider the use of direct mail as well. There is no limit to the number of names you can rent of potential buyers for your book. You can, if you wish, experiment with 40,000 different business lists and 15,000 consumer lists containing millions of names.

Study ads and direct-mail literature for the sale of books. Using your ingenuity, see if you can improve on them. This practice will benefit you tremendously when it comes to writing your own ad.

Carefully study book ads that you know to be repeaters. They are winners. Incorporate some of the ideas for layouts, typography, guarantees, copy and illustrations into a new ad for your book. It is common practice for copywriters to read weekly and monthly advertising trade magazines for new ideas. I do it myself. I am in constant touch with mail-order advertising agencies and copywriters in order to keep my finger on the pulse of the market. When I place an ad in a magazine or newspaper, I invariably speak with the representative to find out what is happening in the market place.

Just as development of a writer's skill is an unending growth process, the same is true when it comes to the development of ability to construct an effective ad. The accomplished ad writer is skillfully adroit in the art of positioning and juxtaposing words. It's like solving a puzzle.

According to Melvin, a good ad is like a good song. It sounds good. My advice is read your ad aloud, as though you were selling it on TV or radio. Do you like the sound of it? Does it have rhythm? Do the words move along smoothly? Are they holding the listener's interest? Objectively, would the ad motivate you to buy the book? If you can answer all those questions in the affirmative, you might have a winner.

In working with clients who have become successful, I find the more input I receive from them, the better the chances for success. It means they have done their homework.

The following check-list should prove useful to you when it comes to writing your own ads:

1. Write a strong headline. In importance, it's 75% of your ad.
2. Decide on either short or long copy.
3. Be specific about benefits.
4. Accentuate the positive.
5. "Sell the sizzle and not the steak."
6. Use subheadings to help sell and to break up the copy.
7. Include photos and illustrations.
8. Request testimonials.
9. Offer guarantee.
10. Ask for readers' orders.
11. Test split-run for copy and price.
12. Add P.S.—it is additional chance at message.
13. Perhaps use "Read this only if you have decided not to order."
14. Read ad aloud.
15. Live with ad for a few days.
16. Do your own market research with ad copy, trying it on family, friends and associates.

I wish you success as you embark on your self-publishing adventure.

Don't wait for success. Make it happen!

How to Get Rich this Year Starting from Zero!

You are not only what you are today, but also what you choose to become tomorrow!

Absolute Proof

Here are the figures of my actual bank deposits for the months of Jan., Feb., and March 1983.

I reveal these confidential figures not only to prove to you the practicality of what I'm doing but, mainly to encourage you to do the same. With the material I am going to send you, these could be your bank deposits. There's no mystery to it — I tell you exactly what to do.

Jan. 4	$26,661.38	Mar. 1	151.08
Jan. 7	9,914.46	Mar. 2	15,453.65
Jan. 11	29,118.99	Mar. 3	18,761.11
Jan. 14	12,750.54	Mar. 4	18,761.11
Jan. 18	14,363.37	Mar. 8	16,818.82
Jan. 21	10,368.58	Mar. 11	19,491.69
Jan. 25	5,582.63	Mar. 12	9,368.09
Jan. 28	26,650.23	Mar. 15	9,368.09
Jan. 31	29,820.29	Mar. 16	867.57
Total	$165,230.47	Mar. 18	10,539.55
Feb. 3	109.00	Mar. 21	115.00
Feb. 4	8,787.73	Mar. 22	14,343.48
Feb. 8	12,014.33	Mar. 23	1,739.30
Feb. 11	4,590.40	Mar. 25	12,044.77
Feb. 15	56,606.91	Mar. 29	5,079.49
Feb. 18	26,016.06	Mar. 31	45,891.19
Feb. 22	13,533.04		
Feb. 25	67,880.66		
Total	$189,538.13	Total	$170,664.79

Three months' total: **$525,433.39**

"I certify the bank deposits listed above are correct and are on file as required by the United States Federal Trade Commission."
— MELVIN POWERS

My Personal Story

Twenty-five years ago, I was having a rough time making it with the various jobs I had. I was so bogged down making a living that I didn't have time for anything else. At times, I even worked two jobs. Everything was going up except my earnings. Since I didn't have a college education, a trade, or any special training, I took whatever jobs I could get trying to "find myself." Like you, I worked hard and felt that I deserved a break. My mistake was in hoping and waiting for someone to give it to me. It never happened.

Out of desperation, I accidentally discovered a way of making extra money in my spare time. It was the beginning of a wonderful new direction to my life. The results were better than I had anticipated, even in my wildest dreams. Soon I was able to quit my dead-end jobs and devote full time to being my own boss. It was the end of my financial worries.

At last I had the money, peace of mind, and time necessary to really enjoy life and my loved ones. I had the freedom to fish, loaf, vacation where and when I wanted, play golf and tennis frequently, pursue my hobbies, and do all the things I always wanted to do. It was my dream come true.

The bottom line to this true personal story is that I've made millions of dollars with my success plan, have taught others how to do it, and am willing to share with you my money-making knowledge. Are you willing to spend one evening to judge what I have to say? I hope so.

You Can Trust Me!

Why? Because I've accomplished the personal and monetary goals that I've set for myself. I have all the material things one could reasonably wish for, including ownership of property, good investments, and even Arabian horses. I want to share my success plan for making money with those who are ambitious and willing to follow my instructions. It can make you rich.

Follow My Success

You may be wondering if you can really believe what I'm saying. My answer is, "Absolutely yes." I've even revealed my confidential business deposits. Those figures are factual. My information for you is not based on abstract theories — it's based on cold, hard facts which have been successfully proven and tested over many years.

Sure — times are tough and making money is harder than ever – but the people listed below are raking in the dollars after having sent for my material. You can do the same if you have a sincere desire for extra income. Take a minute to read this ad with an open mind. It could really change your life and make your secret dreams come true!

$7,000 In 2 Months
— James Best, Levittown, PA

$8,230 In 1 Month
— Thomas Ciola, Utica, NY

$18,000 In 3 Weeks
— Victor W., Carpinteria, CA

$20,000 In 6 Months
— Steve Murphy, Manhattan Beach, CA

$40,000 In 1 Month
— George Bowman, Canton, MI

$93,000 In 28 Days
— Steve H. Nowlin, Indianapolis, IN

$100,000 In 4 Months
— Barrie K., Grand Rapids, MI

$1,000,000 In 5 Months
— George Campion, Los Angeles, CA

Certified Success Stories:

Here is authenticated proof my system works. You can duplicate the success of these persons. It's been effective for them — why not for you? Testimonials are on file as required by the United States Federal Trade Commission.

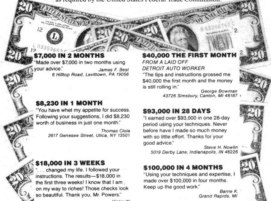

$7,000 IN 2 MONTHS
"Made over $7,000 in two months using your advice."
James F. Best
6 Hilltop Road, Levittown, PA 19056

$8,230 IN 1 MONTH
"You have whet my appetite for success. Following your suggestions, I did $8,230 worth of business in just one month."
Thomas Ciola
2617 Genesee Street, Utica, NY 13501

$18,000 IN 3 WEEKS
". . . changed my life. I followed your instructions. The results—$18,000 in the first three weeks! I know that I am , on my way to riches! Those checks look so beautiful. Thank you, Mr. Powers."
Victor W.
Carpinteria, California 93013

$20,000 IN 6 MONTHS
"By using only a couple of your suggestions, I personally made $20,000 in a six-month period. Melvin . . . priceless and I highly recommend it to anyone."
Steve Murphy
1142 Manhattan Ave.
Manhattan Beach, CA 90266

$40,000 THE FIRST MONTH
FROM A LAID OFF
DETROIT AUTO WORKER
"The tips and instructions grossed me $40,000 the first month and the money is still rolling in."
George Bowman
43726 Simsbury, Canton, MI 48187

$93,000 IN 28 DAYS
"I earned over $93,000 in one 28-day period using your techniques. Never before have I made so much money with so little effort. Thanks for your good advice."
Steve H. Nowlin
5019 Derby Lane, Indianapolis, IN 46226

$100,000 IN 4 MONTHS
"Using your techniques and expertise, I made over $100,000 in four months. Keep up the good work."
Barrie K.
Grand Rapids, MI

$1,000,000 IN 5 MONTHS
"I was completely broke and in the depths of depression when I read your material. Believe it or not, in five months I did $1,000,000 worth of business, and I am now in the process of purchasing a building worth close to $500,000. My whole life has been changed due to you. How can I ever thank you?"
George Campion
6314 Santa Monica Blvd., L.A., CA 90038

Your Secret Dreams Come True

My program for riches has nothing to do with franchising, real estate, the stock market, precious metals, diamonds, pyramid schemes, oil wells, energy conservation, salesmanship, multi-level selling, positive thinking, door-to-door selling, telephone sales, or calling on businesses, neighbors, family or friends.

It's perfectly legal and requires no previous business experience. It is equally good for both men and women of any age, and you can begin just as soon as you receive my material.

Now is the time to do something about your future. Everyone has secret dreams — and yours are about to come true. Use my know-how for making money.

Room For Everyone

Why would I invite competition? The fact is, I don't look at it as competition. The money-making opportunities are so tremendous that there's plenty of room for all who are motivated to improve their situations. Do you have the motivation?

Pick My Brains

Give me the opportunity to show that I can help you achieve financial security.

My material clearly explains my money-making technique with easy-to-follow, step-by-step instructions. To convince you that it works, you get a one-year, 100%-money-back guarantee. Do you know any other offer to match that? Here is your golden opportunity to invest in your success.

Money-Making Formula

My material reveals in detail my success-money formula and how I keep hitting the jackpot again and again, making millions of dollars. You can, too! In fact, I give you a practical, proven, tested guide that will help you realize your financial goals. Is it easy? Yes, once you have the information I give you in my enlightening guide on how to achieve riches. You will learn to duplicate my technique for your own success.

You may wonder why I am sharing my technique for riches if my business is so profitable. To make more money, of course. That's just part of my business — sharing knowledge that will make money for you and at the same time make money for me. Read the happy success stories of people such as yourself who took my material seriously.

Praise from Experts

"A comprehensive guide on how to make it big by an outstanding entrepreneur, Melvin Powers, who did starting from zero. How he did it is clearly explained. He shares with you his knowledge and successful experience in making money . . . could repay its cost a thousandfold."
— Paul Muchnick

Take the First Step

This is the moment of truth. Do you really want to be rich? If your answer is "Yes," follow your impulse now and order my material. Remember, it is sold on a 100%-money-back guarantee basis. You can improve the quality of your life. It's really up to you. It's an exciting prospect that can come true for you. Give it priority. Take the first step on the exciting road to riches.

You'll be pleasantly surprised and delighted with your newly-found knowledge, especially when those beautiful, green dollars start rolling in as they have for others.

Still Skeptical? Be My Guest

I guarantee you'll be completely satisfied and excited with the illustrated material that I send you. Furthermore, I will not even cash your check or money order for 30 days. If, for any reason, you feel the material will not bring you riches, I'll return your uncashed check or money order immediately. No questions asked.

I'll go even one step further. I realize you don't know me and you may still be skeptical about my offer. Put your mind at ease and post-date your check 30 days from today. You have everything to gain by cashing in on my unique know-how for making money.

Good luck as you take the first step on the road to riches.
© 1983 by Melvin Powers

Los Angeles Times

You

Consumer VIEWS

Getting to the Art of 'Get Rich' Schemes

By DON G. CAMPBELL, *Times Staff Writer*

Question: I'm sure I'm not alone in my skepticism when I read all of these full-page ads in your paper, and in others, about how some millionaire (for $10 or $20) is going to share his "secret" with me. I've enclosed a sample of a modest one—not how to "make a million dollars over the weekend" but just a mere $30,000 to $100,000 a year, and all of it without leaving the house.

Am I right in thinking these are all rip-offs, and, if they are, why do you let them advertise with you? Isn't anybody watching them? —T.J.

Answer: It is frequently thought that a writer's greatest challenge is the epic narrative poem.

Not so. Try writing a 10,000-word, full-page newspaper advertisement without once giving the reader the tiniest hint of what you are talking about. Except that by suggesting that if the reader does exactly the same thing (whatever it is), he, too, can end up filthy rich and have his picture taken draped over the hood of a $150,000 Rolls Royce in front of his French chateau.

Just what in the world are all of these people *selling* with so much apparent success?

At the risk of disillusioning you, we must reveal that the majority of these hush-hush secrets have to do with either (1) inspiration, (2) the secret of direct-mail selling or (3) a combination of these. You say you have no interest in direct-mail selling, and would never send away for information on the subject? Yes, that's the way most people feel, so that's why the ads are written so skillfully that the phrase *direct mail* never actually appears. (Melvin Powers' recent ad: "How to Get Rich this Year Starting from Zero," touts his $12 book, "How to Get Rich," but the full title of the book is actually "How to Get Rich in Mail Order.") And there's nothing illegal about the practice, unless it is blatantly false and misleading and the promise is made that you definitely *will* make $100,000 over the weekend without even getting out of bed.

The pioneer in the you-can-get-disgustingly-rich-without-really-trying industry, according to both Herschel Elkins, of the Los Angeles office of the U.S. Attorney General, and Don Clark, director of classified advertising for the Los Angeles Times, was the late Joe Carbo and his "The Lazy Man's Way to Riches." And there was never any question about how Carbo did, indeed, get rich—by selling hundreds of thousands of copies of "The Lazy Man's Way to Riches."

"Actually," Clark adds, "it's a fairly decent little book—part of it inspirational and part of it on selling."

What the cynics reading such ads (and Carbo's success inspired dozens of imitators) fail to take into account, Clark says, is that a newspaper (or radio or TV station) "isn't in a position to sit in judgment on the value (or lack of it) in any of these offerings. Who can say, 'Well, this isn't really worth the $5, $10 or $15 that you're asking for it?' "

Some Ads Rejected

But this doesn't mean that every such offer isn't screened, nor that a lot of related advertising isn't flatly rejected, Clark insists.

"We don't take work-at-home ads," Clark emphasizes, "nor would we take one where the 'secret' turns out to be advice that the buyer also buy a full-page ad offering a secret way to wealth."

Not infrequently, however, says Frank Hobart, The Times' classified production coordinator, "we'll contact the advertiser and tell him, flatly, that we don't think the material he's offering is worth the $12.50, or $15, or whatever, that he's asking for it. That the buyers are going to be disappointed. We'll ask him to adjust his price or whatever else is needed."

Where the media, the Attorney General's office and the Federal Trade Commission *will* descend on the advertiser, breathing fires of wrath, however, is when the material isn't sent, as promised, or when a dissatisfied buyer doesn't get his money back as advertised.

"It's a very odd thing," Elkins of the Attorney General's office observes. "We would have control here if anyone bothered to complain, but no one does. People will occasionally complain about the ads, as such, but they don't after they've received the merchandise."

And, skeptical or not, no one is really injured by an advertisement as such.

"Most of this material people send away for," Elkins adds, "isn't usually worth very much. But that doesn't seem to make much difference. As long as they get *something*, they don't ask for their money back, even when it's guaranteed. Maybe all they get is a booklet saying: 'Have confidence in yourself! Wake up every morning saying *today* I'm going to *do* it!' "

Paradoxically, though, Elkins continues, the complaints come fast and furious—"even if the money involved is only a buck or two—if something promised doesn't show up in the mail. But, once it does, it's an entirely different matter.

Under $30

"Our experience has been," he adds, "that you don't start getting complaints about the *value* of what they've bought until the price is about $30 or more. That's why you'll always find these 'get-rich' promotions priced well under that."

While the Federal Trade Commission does have some rules governing the use of testimonials in such ads, according to the FTC's local spokeswoman, Ann Guler, these rules are quite complicated and, obviously, not too difficult to sidestep.

"I think most people don't complain about being taken," Guler says, "because they feel sheepish about it. They don't like to admit what we've been telling them all the time: 'If it sounds too good to be true, then it probably is.' "

The full-page ad that you enclosed—which is headed "What's This Woman Doing" and which is illustrated with a large photograph of a woman in goggles apparently hand-wrestling a small, but evil-tempered, squid—is so typical of the genre that we risked $9.95 for the book, entitled "Home Money Projects Starter Guide," a product of Green Tree Press of Dunkirk, N.Y.

What did our $9.95 buy us? A rather slick, 90-page, 8½x11 booklet that explores 38 home-based money-making projects with heavy, but not exclusive, emphasis on, sure enough, direct-mail projects.

Several of the projects, however, are purely and simply personal services that can be operated out of the home—a telephone checkup service on elderly parents living alone and paid for by their absentee children . . . a baby-sitting placement service. Whatever the project discussed, several vital points are covered: the training or skills needed, the market, what you need to get started, how to advertise (sell) the product or service and pitfalls to be avoided.

Do we feel ripped-off? No, not really. Neither in the full-page ad, nor in the booklet received, are any flamboyant money claims made. Most of the projects are relatively small, part-time endeavors aimed at generating a few hundred dollars a month in extra income. No claims are made that any of the projects can be undertaken without some work, and many require some skills or expertise.

While we don't feel particularly motivated at the moment to open a cat-sitting service, we're also not going to demand our money back.

We feel cheated on only one score: What in the blue-eyed world *is* that woman doing in the Green Tree Press advertisement? No explanation is ever given.

Chapter Twelve

Publicity Represents Advertising
That Money Can't Buy

by
Marcia Grad, Freelance Publicist

Other than a bad press, no greater disaster can befall a book or an author than no press at all. True, word-of-mouth is a persuasive marketing factor, and favorable comment from the lips of satisfied readers can hype sales to soaring heights. But in the beginning, it is the publicity pitch that really counts. Millions are spent on seemingly innocuous phrases to bring a product to the attention of the consuming public. Radio and television advertising costs have pyramided to the point where only the financial giants can buy time during the prime-time advertising hours. The final episode of the fabulously successful super-series, *M*A*S*H,* carried a price-tag to advertisers of $450,000 for each 30-second commercial, a total of more than $10,000,000 for the single two-hour episode. Not even professional football's super-bowls bring in that kind of money.

The extent to which agencies and network representatives will go to accent the importance they attach to advertising their product was convincingly demonstrated in a conversation I had a while back with a remarkably successful and knowledgeable television producer of prime-time shows. One of his shows had been consistently among the Top Twenty in the Neilsen ratings. The Neilsen ratings are, in effect, the official industry barometer—a device which, by computerized samplings of homes across the nation, enables the Neilsen people to make a reasonably accurate judgment as to what percentage of the viewing populace each of the particular shows has attracted in that specific week. Considering that the ratings cover approximately 80 shows, a position in the Top Twenty is considered to be very good. In short, the show in point was a popular and highly regarded quality production. In spite of this, the show was

dropped by the network. The producer was understandably enraged and demanded to know why a show that was so consistently pleasing to audiences should be dropped. He was told by a network representative that a survey had been made and the viewers who watched his show were not the kind of people who "*obey* the commercials." So, obviously, as far as the network was concerned, the entertainment factor was secondary. What was of prime importance was the advertising factor—will the viewer, when the closing credits have been run, remember not the statement that the show was trying to make, but the statement that the network was trying to make as to where and how he should spend his money and on what merchandise.

In varying degrees, this, of course, is what all forms of advertising seek to accomplish. It is not possible to overemphasize the role of advertising as a viable component of national marketing.

Of equal importance is the phenomenon known as publicity. In fact, it is considered by some to be even more important because it is advertising "bought" without dollars. How often have you heard it said, "Not all the money in the world could get you that kind of advertising?"

That's where I fit into the picture. As a freelance publicist, it is my responsibility to my clients and their products to get the kind and quality of exposure that money cannot ordinarily buy. The degree to which fulfillment of that responsibility is possible depends largely on a good working relationship with the client.

Servicing Melvin Powers' publishing company has been accomplished without the frustrations so common to the trade and with genuine pleasure and satisfaction. Melvin approaches his work as a publisher with the same care with which he serves his community as an educator. He is dedicated, caring, always ready to help, and governed by the same discipline that he expects of the many people who relate to him professionally. The thousands of books stacked to overflowing in his warehouse and shipping department represent a wide variety of self-improvement literature, and they are all characterized by a singleness of literary posture—honesty of words and credibility of author. This is no accident. It is in keeping with Melvin's penchant for selectivity and the implied good-faith warranty that goes with every book that bears the logo of the Wilshire Book Company.

Knowing the emphasis Melvin places on integrity in his business, I once asked him what he regards as total integrity on the part of a publisher, or anyone else who deals in the printed word. Without a moment's hesitation, he responded, "To me, integrity means print the truth and trust to the effect; never print the effect and trust to the truth."

In my capacity as a publicist, it is my ongoing responsibility to secure as much meaningful publicity as I possibly can for Melvin and his hundreds of authors. This includes setting up book reviews, arranging for guest appearances on radio and television, appearances at various trade and public functions, as well as the highly important function of planting supportive articles in widely circulated newspapers and magazines.

Here is a list of some of the major publications to which I regularly send books for review and publicity. Be sure to do likewise with your book.

Publishers Weekly
249 W. 17th Street
New York, New York 10011

Library Journal
249 W. 17th Street
New York, New York 10011

Booklist
American Library Association
50 East Huron Street
Chicago, Illinois 60611

The Kirkus Reviews
200 Park Avenue South
New York, New York 10003

Weekly Record
Publishers Weekly
121 Chanlon Road
New Providence, New Jersey 07974

Cumulative Book Index
H. W. Wilson Company
950 University Avenue
New York, New York 10452

Book Review Editor
New York Times
229 W. 43rd Street
New York, New York 10036

Book Review Editor
Los Angeles Times
Times Mirror Square
Los Angeles, California 90053

Book Review Editor
Washington Post
1150 15th Street N. W.
Washington, D. C. 20071

The publication of each new book is met with excitement and hopeful expectation. My immediate function is to arrange for a book review, and this might be done in a number of ways, depending on the nature of the book. With the publication of *How to Get Rich in Mail Order*, I sent out a letter and card to numerous book review editors, *without* return pre-paid postage, informing them that this book was available for review, and that if they were interested we would make the necessary arrangements. Return of the postcard would indicate their interest. I explained that solicitations were going to a select and limited number of reviewers by direct mail, aimed at having the book receive the kind of careful and prestigious assessment I believed it deserved. I'm sure the meaning implied in the letter was at once apparent—I was not seeking a slanted review but was entrusting it to astute and sophisticated reviewers who would give it an honest appraisal. (See page 134 for my letter and page 135 for my return postcard.)

The response was excellent and resulted in many reviews, the most gratifying being a full-page review in the April, 1981, issue of *Success Unlimited* by Og Mandino, a famed author distinguished for many widely heralded books, including the million seller, *The Greatest Salesman in the World.* (See page 136 for the review.)

At last count, Mr. Mandino's review generated more than 1,600 orders at $11.00 each, or $17,600 in sales—a profit of over $13,000. To produce this dollars-and-cents result through paid advertising, rather than through the kind of publicity that was occasioned by Mr. Mandino's review, would have cost a small fortune.

Equally impressive were the results of a review in *Entrepreneur's Magazine*, a periodical ideally suited to this particular kind of book. Because of the large number of sales stemming from the review, the Wilshire Book Company ran monthly ads in the magazine for an entire year with excellent results.

Wilshire Book Company has just published a new book, *Kantar for the Defense*, by Edwin B. Kantar. I succeeded in getting wide review coverage on the book, with the result that the first edition of 5,000 copies was sold out immediately. This, again, underscores the value of gratis publicity as opposed to paid advertising. Psychologically, the reader attaches considerably more credibility to the gratuitous assessment of a learned reviewer than to the enticing statements of a paid copywriter.

Nowhere is there a more graphic example of the resounding impact of publicity in the raw than that which prevails in the New York theater. Broadway plays rise and fall on the judgment of a small handful of reviewers. Actually, with the demise of so many of New York's newspapers, the fate of a play rests in the hands of barely more than a single reviewer. It is not at all a rare occasion for playwrights to devote years of research, hard work and discipline to creating a piece of entertainment, only to see their efforts fail in a single night. Unlike a book which can remain on the bookstores' shelves and eventually at least cover its initial cost, the economics of the Broadway theater are such that a bad review means instant death to the production. This is largely due to the fact that the houses look to theater parties for their profits and long-term survival—large organizations taking huge blocks of tickets and selling them to their members at a profit. Obviously, no organization will take the chance of being unable to sell an expensive block of tickets for a play that has suffered a bad review.

What do you imagine it's worth to get someone like Dr. David Schwartz, author of *The Magic of Thinking Big*, to appear on Dr. Robert Schuller's television program? (See page 15.) It just isn't possible to buy that kind of exposure. But you can get it for absolutely nothing with an author who is particularly suited to the program and has an interesting message to convey.

I never had a client who did not aspire to appear on the Johnny Carson show, the Merv Griffin show or the Phil Donahue show. It can be accomplished if there is determination and perseverance on the part of the writer or his publicist. But the subject matter must be interesting and provocative, and, more importantly, the author must be personally engaging to audiences. No matter how brilliant the book, its author must be able to project personal magnetism to the audience.

To get on the show, make a phone call to the program director and find out who is in charge of guests. Send your book to him with publicity material that will convince him you would be a perfect guest for the show. Wait a week or two, then follow up with another pitch.

To expedite matters, I have recently started making video tapes of authors, imitating the kind of interview they would be subjected to at the hands of a moderator or panelist. I then send the tape to program directors, giving them the opportunity to determine in advance whether or not the author would make a suitable guest for the program. Program directors place great emphasis on the guest's personality, his stage presence, his ability to converse easily, and his appearance.

Television programs are deluged by publicists, publishers and authors with requests for guest appearances. As it is not possible to accommodate them all, the screenings are intense and highly selective. If you are not a celebrity, I advise you to make your presentation as unique as possible.

A good press release for your book is highly essential, so prepare it with care and design. See pages 137 and 138 for the press release for *A Guide to Personal Happiness*. Use it as a guide in constructing your own press release. See page 139 for review of book.

When Melvin first published *How to Get Rich in Mail Order*, I was able to get him on more than 100 radio talk shows. The interviews were conducted by telephone, most of them live, with the listeners at home calling in questions. Other interviews, lasting half an hour or an hour, were taped for later broadcast, and some shows invited him to appear a second time. Mail order is a fascinating subject, and that, coupled with the fact that I had a dynamic guest, formed a potent combination that got us virtually all the shows we wanted.

To give added impetus to interviews, I arranged with the interviewer to ask the author how to get a copy of his book. If it is to be found in the B. Dalton and Walden bookstores, that point should be mentioned. If those stores do not carry the book, the author should give his name and address and the amount of money to be sent to buy the book.

It is advisable for the guest to prepare approximately 25 questions he would like to be asked by the interviewer. Strange as it may seem, the interviewer will welcome this, rather than regard it an encroachment on his duties. Interviewers are among the busiest of all people, so these sample questions will be a welcome assist. It's even possible he will not have had an opportunity to read the book. The author should not consider this an insult—the book may be a priority with the author; it is not always a priority with the interviewer.

Not all publicity is productive. There are times when the effort, like everything else in life, encounters total resistance. For example, the Wilshire Book Company published a humorous book, *How to Make Love to Yourself*, written by a husband-and-wife team, Ron Stevens and Joy Grdnic. I called it "the world's funniest book," and sincerely believed it to be just that. It was a hilarious spoof in the tradition of such best-selling books as *How to Make Love to a Man*, *How to Make Love to a Woman*, and *How to Make Love to Each Other*. The entire Wilshire staff and manuscript readers tabbed it a hit. I was able to get the authors on television and radio shows across the country. All this coverage was acquired by sending out a copy of the book, a publicity release, and a copy of the ad that had run in the Los Angeles *Herald-Examiner*. (See page 140.) The interviewers were delighted with both the book and the authors.

The book even got counter displays. But the one thing it did not get—at least not in abundance—was reorders. The public took the book title seriously, and that spelled doom. Sales were good in college bookstores; however, the book did not move in the regular trade bookstores. Finally, it became apparent that there was no point in continuing the publicity. It was a disappointing experience.

But such occurrences are not uncommon. In lesser or greater degree, they happen in every area of communication with the consumer public. Not too many years ago, Richard Zanuck, one of the most knowledgeable of all of the current filmmakers, decided it was time to produce another blockbuster embodying the magic of *Sound of Music*. The vehicle chosen to accomplish this feat was a picture called *Star*. For added insurance, Robert Wise and Julie Andrews, the fine director and the fabulous star who sent *Sound of Music* skyrocketing through every theater roof in town, were chosen to re-

prise their roles in *Star*. The first preview of the film was such an explosive success that Richard Zanuck sent his father Daryl Zanuck a telegram stating in effect that further previews were unnecessary. He was convinced that *Star* was a smash hit, destined to surpass *Sound of Music* in every respect, especially box-office. Well, to make a long sad story short, *Star* turned out to be the Edsel of the motion picture industry. After that first preview, no one went to see it. And no matter what changes and re-editing they did to the film, people avoided it.

As a self-respecting publicist with a good track record and an objective approach to the potential of new material in work, I am eagerly looking forward to seeing this book in print. Self-publishing is an extremely interesting subject, and its proper management can result in enormous profits for the authors. I have not the slightest doubt that this book will enable me to keep Melvin busy for at least a year making television and radio appearances. I have already written the publicity release for this book and have the initial campaign ready to go. Added to the book's many other fine attributes, there is an unlimited potential for seminars dealing with the subject matter. Melvin has started teaching the self-publishing seminars and I am already working with various colleges and universities to coordinate the publicity. These schools welcome freelance publicists because of the publicity it gives the institutions, the students it attracts, and the increased enrollment fees that result.

To those authors who are planning to conduct seminars in their communities, I would advise you not to depend on the schools for your publicity. Schools, as a rule, are understaffed, and, when it comes to priorities, publicity is not at the top of the list. Make it your business to call your local newspaper and provide it with your own publicity.

With newspapers and magazines, it is important to have an interesting focal point for the article. Call your local newspaper and talk to the person whose department deals with authors. Do the best you can to gain a personal interview, but if this is not possible, send the person your book and whatever publicity you have prepared on your own. Follow up in two weeks. Remember, these editors are not there to defeat or reject you; they need material for their newspapers and magazines. It's a two-way street.

Another ideal avenue of approach is the convention. Annually, there are thousands of conventions looking for speakers, and the author of a book is a highly desirable candidate. If your subject is appropriate to the philosophy of their meeting, convention administrators are very apt to contract you for a speaking engagement. This affords you an excellent opportunity to sell your book and garner the kind of publicity that can set you off and running to important goals.

So, as you might have surmised by now, there is no end to the amount of publicity you can generate for yourself once you have made up your mind to go after it. And take my word for it—it's worth all the effort it takes.

The August, 1982, issue of *Reader's Digest*, with a readership of 18 million, carried a four-page article about Melvin's favorite charity, Johnny Carpenter's "Heaven on Earth Ranch for Handicapped Children" in Lake View Terrace, located just outside Los Angeles. (See pages 141, 142, 143 and 144.) You cannot *buy* that kind of publicity. So, if you have an interesting story to tell, flavored with the kind of humanitarian dedication that underscores Johnny Carpenter's work, your chances of acceptance are excellent. It's not easy, of course. But if you have an article that could be of interest to millions, stay with it. Don't ever tell yourself it's beyond the realm of possibility. You must believe that you can accomplish whatever you really want to do.

That is not to say that guidance from others should not be encouraged. We can all use it to advantage. For example, I recently mentioned to Melvin that I was interested in the subject of charisma. His immediate reaction was that it could be an intriguing subject for both a seminar and a book, and suggested that I send a synopsis and an outline to the colleges where he teaches. I took his advice, was interviewed, and now teach classes on *Charisma—How to Develop It and Use It Effectively.* See page 145 for picture of yours truly on the Joseph F. Puccio television show promoting my charisma classes and forthcoming book.

As author of the book, *A Taste for Life,* published by Charles Scribner's Sons, New York (see page 146), I understand the writer's point of view as well as I do that of the publicist. In everything I do as a publicist, I am mindful of the writer's problems and govern myself accordingly. I am also sympathetic to his needs, and one of those needs is publicity. There are no secrets in getting good publicity. It is strictly a matter of knowing what you want to accomplish and then going after it using logic, style and imagination.

As an example, I was very eager to get excerpts from the book *Think Your Way to Success* by Dr. Lew Losoncy into various magazines. I sent the book to the appropriate publications whose readers would logically find Dr. Losoncy's philosophy to be of interest. I followed this up with personal telephone calls. To my great delight, as well as the delight of everyone else concerned, the January, 1984, issue of *Science of Mind* magazine ran a 14-page excerpt from one of the chapters in the book. See pages 147 to 150 for part of the excerpt as it appeared in the magazine. This resulted in thousands of subscribers becoming acquainted with Dr. Losoncy's writing and subsequently ordering his inspirational book, *Think Your Way to Success.*

My guest chapter in this book is titled "Publicity Represents Advertising That Money Can't Buy." The excerpt in *Science of Mind* represents a perfect example of receiving *free* publicity—publicity that is impossible to buy at any price. Hopefully, you'll be able to accomplish the same thing and boost the sales of your book onto the best-seller list.

Wilshire Book Company

12015 Sherman Road, North Hollywood, California 91605

(818) 765-8579
FAX (818) 765-2922

NEW BOOKS

Re: *How to Get Rich in Mail Order* by Melvin Powers
336 pages, 8½" x 11", $20.00

How to Write a Good Advertisement by Victor O. Schwab
256 pages, 8½" x 11", $20.00

Dear Book Review Editor:

An increasing number of companies are turning to mail order for marketing their products and services to combat the escalating cost of using traveling salespeople.

These two books, full of proven nut-and-bolts techniques, will help your readers to be successful in direct marketing.

How to Get Rich in Mail Order was written by a mail order consultant and publisher who has used mail order techniques to sell millions-of-dollars worth of inspirational books and products. He is publisher of such bestselling titles as *Psycho-Cybernetics, The Magic of Thinking Big,* and *Think and Grow Rich.*

How to Write a Good Advertisement, written by one of the outstanding advertising men of our time, is a compilation of winning advertising ideas and techniques, based on years of experience.

If you are interested in either or both of these books, please request review copies by returning the enclosed form.

We look forward to hearing from you.

Sincerely,

Marcia Grad

Marcia Grad
Publicity

Marcia Grad, Publicity
Wilshire Book Company
12015 Sherman Road
No. Hollywood, CA 91605

Please send me the following books for possible review:

_____*HOW TO GET RICH IN MAIL ORDER*

_____*HOW TO WRITE A GOOD ADVERTISEMENT*

Name_____
               (Please print)
Magazine represented_____

Address_____

City_____ State_____ Zip_____

OG MANDINO REVIEWS

APRIL 1981/SUCCESS UNLIMITED

How to Get Rich in MAIL ORDER
by Melvin Powers

Published by
Wilshire Book Company, Dept. 123
12015 Sherman Road
North Hollywood, California 91605
336 pages, 200 illustrations
$11 postpaid

I have always been fascinated by those individuals who begin with little more than an idea and a dream and eventually convert those two unrefined bits of ore into a fortune.

Leonard Carlson took a $1 personalized rubber stamp and parlayed it into Sunset House, the multimillion-dollar catalog-sales firm.

Anastasios Kyriakides came here from Athens at age 15 with only $72 in his pocket and is now the "father" of the *Lexicon*, that amazing little computer translator which can be a lifesaver when you're traveling in a foreign country.

Frederick Mellinger, nearly broke in 1947, decided to design women's clothes from a man's point of view, and now his California-based Frederick's of Hollywood grosses millions.

Joseph Sugarman failed, time and again, until he began to sell low-cost pocket calculators and digital watches, and now this young marketing guru is the head of a $50 million-plus consumer-electronics organization.

These four entrepreneurs, and hundreds of others in our country, have something in common. They became success stories after they learned how to sell their products to the consumer by *mail order.*

Selling by mail (either through advertisements in the media or direct mail) is one of the last American outposts of free enterprise where an individual can begin on little more than a shoestring and, with persistence, motivation and luck, become wealthy. How wealthy? Estimates vary, but it's safe to figure that approximately $200 billion of merchandise is being sold directly to consumers at home each year, and that may be conservative.

If you've ever had an itch to look into this lucrative field and didn't know how to begin your exploration, let me recommend a new book that will answer every question you ever had about mail order and plenty you never thought about. *How to Get Rich in Mail Order,* unlike many books on the subject that are so replete with charts and diagrams that one dozes before page nine, was written by a talented mail-order expert with a long and successful track record. Listen to him, from his opening chapter:

I am Melvin Powers—writer, editor, publisher, lecturer and executive head of the Wilshire Book Company, specializing in self-improvement books. I have been a book publisher and mail-order entrepreneur for more than 25 years, selling millions of dollars' worth of books and products, utilizing mail-order techniques almost exclusively.

During those years, I have learned that the mail-order business, despite its mundane image, is a highly creative endeavor. You will better understand this once you start to open the envelopes and watch the money pour out.

Like most businesses, the world of mail order is one in which there is a direct correlation between what you are prepared to put into it and what you will eventually take away from it. But unlike many, it is a game unfettered with restrictions and qualifications—and for that reason, it could be the best game in town. The opportunity for success is available to all. There is no distinction in terms of social background, job or affluence. No particular skills are necessary, nor is education required beyond that which is provided in my book and the supplemental-reading program suggested. Play by the rules, follow the guidelines, meet the challenges squarely, and the only limit on how much you can earn is that which you set.

As with anything else, the prime catalyst for accomplishment in the mail-order field is *motivation.* Given this incentive, the determination to succeed and the guiding hand of one who has already successfully established a business, and you are well on your way.

In this large-format book, crammed full with fascinating examples and illustrations as well as sage advice, the author provides a firm guiding hand while mincing no words. If you're looking for an easy way to earn a fast buck, this is not the book for you. Throughout the book, you

will, again and again, encounter statements that sound as if they sprang from a master of self-help, and that's only natural, I guess, when you consider that Mel Powers's publishing company, Wilshire, over the years, has published such success classics as *Think and Grow Rich, I Can, Psycho-Cybernetics* and *The Magic of Thinking Big.* For example:

Each of us is unique. Each of us has a personality and temperament distinct from others. We each have individual hopes, desires and ambitions. It is by virtue of these individualities that each of us brings to a business venture a different approach from that used by someone else. It is this uniqueness I want to encourage and develop, for it is the element which will eventually spell success. If you have not yet been as successful as you would like to be, don't be discouraged. In reading this book, at least you are doing something about it—taking constructive steps to bring it about. A failure in the past does not preclude a future that can be extremely successful. Monetary and personal success begins with a correct mental attitude. Knowing someone is successfully mail ordering lobsters from Maine ... or selling apples from the state of Washington should be good news for you. If he can do it, so can you.

Just a few of the chapter titles will give you some idea of how much this book can teach you: "How to Make Money With Classified Ads," "The Unlimited Potential for Making Money With Direct Mail," "How to Start and Run a Profitable Mail-Order Special Interest Book or Record Business," "Melvin Powers's Mail-Order Success Strategy—Follow It and You'll Become a Millionaire," "How to Get Free Display Ads and Publicity That Will Put You on the Road to Riches," "Questions and Answers to Help You Get Started Making Money in Your Own Mail-Order Business." After you have read this book, written in a style that is never dull or stodgy, you just might get the urge to try what you've been talking about for years—starting a business of your own. And here's one that you can test while you're still working at your regular job. If it clicks, you can tell "them" to stuff their pension plan.

One more thought. Here's an author willing to go "the extra mile." If you want to know more about mail order, just drop him a line at his publishing address, and he'll put you on his mailing list to receive the *Melvin Powers Mail-Order Newsletter.* He makes this gracious offer in the last chapter of his book.

Send for *How to Get Rich in Mail Order,* or pick it up at your local bookstore. It just may change your life—for the better! □

Melvin Powers

Wilshire Book Company

12015 Sherman Road, No. Hollywood, California 91605

Press Release

A GUIDE TO PERSONAL HAPPINESS
by Dr. Albert Ellis and Dr. Irving Becker

192 Pages . . . . Price $5.00

Who, today, is the psychologist's psychologist? Not, as you might guess from the mass media, Freud, Jung, or Adler. Nor, as you might also imagine, Carl Rogers, Abe Maslow, or Rollo May. All these popular writers still exert strong influences over psychological therapists. But the psychologist whose name now seems to lead all the rest as a profound influence on psychotherapists and counselors is Albert Ellis. Evidence of Ellis's emerging leadership among therapists is shown in three studies that have just appeared in psychological journals.

1. According to a study published in the latest issue of the Journal of Counseling Psychology (1982, 29, 400-405), Classics and Emerging Classics in Counseling Psychology, the most frequently cited authors of works published before 1957 in three major counseling psychology journals were Carl Rogers, Donald Super, and Albert Ellis; and the most frequently cited authors of works published after 1957 were Albert Ellis, Robert Carkhuff, and J. L. Holland. The school of therapy, moreover, that Dr. Ellis originated and fathered, rational-emotive therapy (RET) and cognitive behavior therapy (CBT), was the mode most cited by researchers since 1957.

2. In a study, Trends in Counseling and Psychotherapy, by Darrel Smith, which appeared in the July 1982 issue of the American Psychologist, the three most influential psychotherapists mentioned by 800 clinical and counseling psychologists (all members of the American Psychological Association) were Carl Rogers, Albert Ellis, and SigmundFreud. Again, rational-emotive therapy (RET) and cognitive behavior therapy (CBT) was the main therapeutic orientation of the ten most influential therapists found in this study.

3. In a study by Douglas Sprenkel, Bradford Keeney, and Philip Sutton published in the July 1982 issue of the Journal of Marital and Family Therapists, it was found that the four most influential theorists on 600 clinical members of this Association were Virginia Satir, Sigmund Freud, Carl Rogers, and Albert Ellis.

All this tends to show that although Freud and Rogers are still definitely in the running as far as having important influences on today's psychotherapists and counselors, the emerging Zeitgeist or spirit of the age clearly favors Ellis and RET.

What is RET and how can ordinary people achieve personal happiness through using it? Dr. Albert Ellis and Dr. Irving Becker, in their new book, A GUIDE TO PERSONAL HAPPINESS, show their readers exactly how they can achieve personal fulfillment through using rational-emotive therapy as a self-help procedure. This book shows people how they can unblock themselves and increase their pleasure by clearly and simply explaining what they do to create their own disturbances and what they can now do to eliminate them. It specifically demonstrates how to use the ABCs of RET to undo the main blocks to personal happiness; and it illustrates a number of intellectual, emotive, and behavioral methods to gain self-actualization. It succinctly tells how almost anyone can overcome shyness, feelings of inadequacy, guilt, and sex problems, as well as cope with depression, low frustration tolerance, hostility, mating, and work difficulties. It closes with a unique chapter on the RET approach to forging an upward and onward path to satisfaction and joy.

A GUIDE TO PERSONAL HAPPINESS includes two unique parts. In the first part, Drs. Ellis and Becker show why it is legitimate to search for personal happiness, give the ABCs of RET and their application to self-fulfillment, indicate the main blocks to happiness, explain how to dispute and uproot emotional disturbance, present important emotive and behavioral methods of achieving one's own goals, and give ten summary rules for achieving personal happiness.

In the second part of A GUIDE TO PERSONAL HAPPINESS, Drs. Ellis and Becker present verbatim excerpts from RET psychotherapy sessions with actual clients who are shown how to deal with their problems of self-downing, guilt, depression, anger, sex, and work; and they show, by their comments during these sessions and their subsequent analyses of what was done during therapy, how almost anyone can quickly and efficiently deal with life difficulties by using the down-to-earth, no-nonsense RET approach. The book also includes a special section giving scores of suggestions for enjoyable pursuits.

Dr. Albert Ellis, as the studies cited above show, is a world-famous psychologist, marriage and family counselor, and sex therapist, and is the founder of rational-emotive therapy (RET). He is Executive Director of the Institute for Rational-Emotive Therapy in New York City, has been an officer of several professional societies, including President of the Division of Consulting Psychology of the American Psychological Association, has won many awards, such as the Humanist of the Year award of the American Humanist Association, and has published more than 500 scientific and popular articles and 45 books, including How to Live With a "Neurotic," Sex Without Guilt, Reason and Emotion in Psychotherapy, and A New Guide to Rational Living. Dr. Irving Becker has written his doctoral dissertaion about RET, holds a doctorate in psychology from Temple University, has worked as a psychologist for the Trenton, New Jersey board of education, currently works for the New York City board of education, and is in the private practice of psychotherapy in New York City.

Recommended Texts

A GUIDE TO PERSONAL HAPPINESS. Albert Ellis and Irving Becker. *North Hollywood, California: Wilshire Book Company, 1982, Pp. 188, $7.00, soft cover.*

Drs. Albert Ellis and Irving Becker have collaborated to produce a delightful short volume, *A Guide to Personal Happiness*. It is just as the authors describe it—a "guide." A rationale for making the choice to search for personal happiness is proposed, followed by a blueprint for achieving such a goal.

The approach is primarily cognitive in emphasis with additional focus on emotional and behavioral aspects of human functioning. In the first part of the volume, basic Rational Emotive Therapy (RET) philosophy and principles are described. Ellis and Becker identify what they consider to be the three primary irrational ideas that cause emotional disturbance and their concomitant maladjustment responses. They describe how an individual combats inappropriate emotional responses and behavior using such cognitive methods as "disputing," "problem solving," "imaging." Also included in the change process are emotive methods such as "shame attacking" and behavioral methods such as "self-management."

The second part of the book is devoted to the presentation of actual verbatim transcripts of therapy sessions with clients who display a variety of disturbances including feelings of inadequacy, guilt, depression, anger, sexual and work problems. A brief description of each case precedes the transcripts, followed by a discussion (in RET terminology) of what takes place. Not only are the explanations valuable, but excellent insights concerning RET are found in the therapist-client discussions. One such discussion involves the apparent simplicity of RET.

The book concludes with a summary statement and with some ideas for new pursuits to enhance our lives.

Albert Ellis and Irving Becker have provided the reader with a clearly stated, concise, easy to understand self-help tool in the cognitive therapy field. It is frank, fresh, and stimulating. Such a volume can serve as a useful adjunct to ongoing therapy. I highly recommend it to therapists, clients and "lay readers" alike. It is an interesting, brief but comprehensive presentation of the basic philosophy and style of Rational-Emotive cognitive therapy.

Tamara R. Cohen, Ph.D.
Hollywood, Florida

The World's Funniest Book is Guaranteed to Keep You Laughing for Days!*

My name is Melvin Powers and I'm president of the Wilshire Book Company. Over the past 25 years, I've published multi-million best sellers, such as *Psycho-Cybernetics, Magic of Thinking Big,* and *Think and Grow Rich.*

I've read thousands of manuscripts, including hundreds devoted to humor. Several years ago, I published the best seller, *How to Flatten Your Tush,* by Coach Marge Reardon which poked fun at all the exercise books.

Two months ago, a young husband-and-wife comedy team left a manuscript with me to read and review for possible publication. Routinely, I gave it to one of my editors. Within minutes, I heard continuous laughter coming from her office. My curiosity, as well as that of others on my staff, was aroused and we went to her office. She blurted out, between her fits of tear-producing laughter, "This is the funniest book I've ever read!"

She began to read parts of it aloud and her laughter became contagious. The men and women in the adjoining warehouse, hearing the commotion, came in to investigate. Soon, we had 24 people laughing uncontrollably at the funny material. I had never witnessed such a reaction.

It was evident to all that we had another best seller. This book could bring laughter into the lives of many persons, I thought — laughter which would be a welcome change from the seriousness of the times in which we live.

What's It All About?

During the past few years, there have been books on love, improving relationships, love making, and sex. Every one of them seeks to enhance a person's life in one or more of these areas. *The Joy of Sex,* a perennial best seller, gives explicit directions for improving one's sex technique and for becoming a virtuoso in the bedroom. The books, *How to Make Love to a Woman* and *How to Make Love to a Man,* represent two more cookbook approaches to sexual recipes.

You've heard of . . .
**HOW TO MAKE LOVE TO A MAN
HOW TO MAKE LOVE TO A WOMAN
HOW TO MAKE LOVE TO EACH OTHER**
Now at last—the ultimate experience!

$3

How to Make Love to Yourself

STEVENS AND GRDNIC

*Works at night, too!

These and other books, such as *The Sensuous Woman, The Sensuous Man,* and the latest best seller, *The G Spot,* strive to educate the public by providing instructional information in the area of human sexuality.

But the problem is that people, in general, cannot fulfill the wondrous expectations of exotic delight so graphically illustrated and described in these manuals. Often, the result is complete frustration from trying to reach calisthenic heights of ecstasy that, in truth, might exist only in the minds of the authors.

Here It Is

Sure, loving relationships and sex are serious matters. However, perhaps it's time to laugh at our universal love-making frustrations. It's comparable to the baseball player

trying to hit a home run every time he's at bat. Relaxing, poking fun at ourselves, and finally, realizing the folly of trying to reach an unattainable goal each time are good psychological releases for one's psyche. This is exactly what the authors had in mind when they wrote the book, *How to Make Love to Yourself.* Professional comedians have dubbed it "The World's Funniest Book." There isn't a serious thought in the entire content. Stevens and Grdnic wanted you to laugh your way through every page and they have expertly accomplished just that.

Everyone Needs a Good Laugh

I guarantee hours of hilarious laughter — laughter you'll be able to share with family and friends. That's why I've taken out this full-page newspaper advertisement to acquaint you with a marvelously funny new book. It is the perfect gift for friends whom you know would enjoy a side-splitting parody.

At All Bookstores Everywhere

You can purchase *How to Make Love to Yourself* by Ron Stevens and Joy Grdnic, priced at only three dollars, published by Wilshire Book Company of North Hollywood, CA, at all bookstores listed below.

Send this coupon to your favorite bookstore or to Wilshire Book Company.

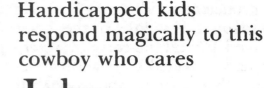

Handicapped kids respond magically to this cowboy who cares

John Carpenter and His Miracle Ranch

By Earl C. Gottschalk, Jr.

Carpenter and Randy Horton at the Heaven on Earth Ranch

THE SIGN ON THE GATE read: "John Carpenter's Heaven on Earth Ranch for Handicapped Children." And, as Marie and Armando Perello stood at the end of the corral, a sturdy cowboy with a weather-beaten face and a white hat strode over, picked up their seven-year-old son Carl and set him on a big black horse. "Okay, cowboy, let's take a ride," he said and began to lead the horse around the corral. The boy grasped the saddle horn and meekly followed John Carpenter's instructions.

Carl was an autistic child, who from age two had spoken only gibberish and was given to fits of screaming. His wild behavior caused even close friends and relatives to shun the Perellos, who lived in a state of constant fear and isolation. Marie Perello had tried everything to control Carl and teach him to talk properly, but nothing worked. Neither doctors nor speech therapists had been able to help. Finally she heard about Carpenter, who let handicapped children ride horses at his ranch in Lake View Terrace, Calif., 20 miles northwest of Los Angeles.

One weekend, after months of regular visits, Marie left the family at the corral and went off to do errands. When she returned, her husband and their two other children were shouting with glee. It seemed that Carl had wanted to ride the horse outside the corral and, as Carpenter led the horse near the gate, the boy had said clearly and unmistakably his first meaningful

READER'S DIGEST

words: "Open the door, Carpenter."

Not only did Carl continue to talk more and more, but he became calm. By age eight he had become so proficient a rider that he could stand on the saddle as the horse walked around the corral. Carpenter had provided Carl with something that doctors and specialists couldn't: the feeling that he was normal. *There was something in the mystique, the magic of the horse, rider and teacher,* Marie thought.

Carl is only one of dozens of autistic and spastic children who have spoken their first words at the ranch. An incredible total of 750,000 handicapped persons have visited since Carpenter opened the ranch in the early 1940s.

Among them was Randy Horton, whose motor functions were so impaired by cerebral palsy that he could not walk and could speak only a few words. His hip sockets had been damaged, and doctors said they might have to be replaced with plastic-lined metal sockets. The Los Angeles teen-ager had spent all his life indoors—at home, in special schools and hospitals. A sullen figure crouched in his wheelchair, Randy never smiled. His mother brought him to the ranch to see if that might cheer him up.

At first Randy just sat watching the activity: spastic children riding horses; handicapped children leading other handicapped children around on horses; children wearing braces and protective helmets riding in a stagecoach.

Then Carpenter appeared. With his usual greeting, "Hi, cowboy," he slapped a Stetson on Randy's head. During his first stagecoach ride, Randy's twisted body was tense; his features were contorted in fear. But as Carpenter snapped the reins and the mules pulled the coach, Randy began to relax.

At the end of half an hour a smile spread across the youngster's face. With every subsequent visit, he was involved in more phases of riding. He started on a mule sidesaddle. Later Carpenter got him astride a well-trained horse. Leather straps held Randy upright. He tilted strangely in the saddle, his head cocked. But slowly, through Carpenter's patient commands, the boy learned to direct the horse. Soon he was riding alone around the corral.

One December Randy performed at the ranch's Christmas party. Sitting stiffly but proudly in the saddle, Randy trotted his horse for the audience. He tugged on the reins, and his horse turned left. Another tug, and the horse moved smartly to the right.

"Okay, cowboy, show them what you can do!" Carpenter shouted. Randy tugged the reins again, and the horse pranced forward and backward, then pirouetted. The crowd cheered, as Randy's mother beamed. *A miracle,* she thought. *John Carpenter accomplishes miracles here.*

Carpenter also puts on shows for the handicapped. Vans and buses arrive at the ranch, and nurses roll

JOHN CARPENTER AND HIS MIRACLE RANCH

wheelchair patients down the dusty streets of a ramshackle western town Carpenter built. In Gruesome Gulch, the clock is turned back 100 years. A rinky-tink piano plays in the Mangy Dog Saloon. A dance-hall gal in a frilly red-and-black dress strolls out through the swinging doors. Pack mules wait in front of Higgins General Store.

Suddenly hoofbeats echo through the town. Gunshots ring out. Astride a black horse, Carpenter thunders into view, his six-gun blazing. Hot in pursuit are two scroungy bad guys. Carpenter turns and fires. One mustachioed villain—a stunt man donating his time—falls from his horse into a pile of hay. His horse does a trick fall, too, onto its side. The kids cheer!

Carpenter would be performing a great service even if he charged for such outings. But the children pay nothing. Carpenter's Social Security plus donations from friends, relatives and organizations pay the $42,000 annual operating costs. But coming up with the money is a constant struggle.

The ranch is a one-man operation. Carpenter, who looks 15 years younger than his 68 years, labors seven days a week. He feeds the animals, mucks out the stalls and corrals, prepares cookout meals and handles reservations. The only time he gets a day off is when it rains. Some days Carpenter is so tired that friends have to help him onto his horse. It has been that way ever since he started the ranch.

John Carpenter grew up in Dardanelle, Ark., and learned to ride horses on his father's farm. An incident back then helped form the philosophy he has practiced all his life. Besides the farm, John's father ran a butcher shop. One day a neighbor with nine children stopped in, said he had no money and asked the elder Carpenter if he would buy his milk cow. John's father gave him $40 for the animal.

Later he asked John to return the cow. John was puzzled. "Someday you'll understand," his father said. "They need that cow a lot more than we need the forty dollars."

A close brush with death also helped develop John Carpenter's empathy for the handicapped. When he was 18, a car careened out of control and ran over him. His left leg was broken in seven places, his back in two places, and he had internal injuries. In a body cast for 119 days, Carpenter experienced the isolation of the handicapped. As he lay helpless, he made a pact: if God would let him walk again, he would spend his life helping the handicapped. When the cast came off, his father suggested that he strengthen his leg by riding. Even though he couldn't walk without crutches, he could still ride.

Carpenter then moved to California and found work at a stable. The riding slowly strengthened him, but eight years passed before he was able to throw away his crutches.

In time, he gained a reputation

READER'S DIGEST

around Los Angeles as a handsome cowboy who had skill with a horse. He began stunt riding in movies. Carpenter also started writing, directing and producing his own "B" westerns—and he opened a stable. One day four young blind men came to the stable and asked if they could ride. Despite misgivings, Carpenter saddled up four horses and, to his surprise, the men rode slowly around the corral.

Timing and balance turned out to be more important than sight in horseback riding. The horse, after all, *can* see. The blind men came back three or four times a week and kept getting better. Eventually, with Carpenter's training, they became quite a sensation at rodeos and parades.

By the 1960s B westerns were passé, and Carpenter's avocation became his full-time, nonpaying job. Visitors are impressed with his achievements. "It's hard to put your finger on just what it is," says Hal Hubbard, a sociologist at California State University at Long Beach. "John creates a mood, and the kids relax. Sometimes we forget that kids need to have a good time."

Carpenter believes that, deep down, handicapped kids want to participate in the same kind of action sports as normal children do. "Just like the rest of us, they'd like to jump on a horse, shoot the bad guys and ride off into the sunset," he says.

The horse is just a device Carpenter uses to help handicapped children grow. Says Marie Perello, "The kids respond to horses. If only we could get state institutions for the handicapped and retarded turned into ranches, we might see some real progress."

The handicapped youngsters know what Carpenter has done for them. Carl Perello has now grown into a strapping 18-year-old who speaks well. Rated "high functioning," he lives at a home for autistic young adults. His parents believe Carl eventually will be independent, a big achievement for a person afflicted with autism.

The ranch has been a miracle not only for thousands of youngsters but also for John Carpenter himself. "The Bible says, 'As you sow, so shall you reap.' Well, I've reaped two-hundredfold," he explains. "I've gotten more satisfaction out of this ranch than anything else I've ever done. Everything I own is on my back. Yet because of the ranch, I can get up every morning and walk down the street like a king. The ranch, for me, is a spiritual thing. If I get to heaven, it'll be on the coattails of these kids."

Here is Marcia Grad promoting her charisma classes and forthcoming book on the Joseph F. Puccio television show on Group W Cable.

A TASTE FOR LIFE

Marcia Grad, like some 15 million other Americans, suffers from hypoglycemia—low blood sugar. Her husband, Jerry Grad, was told that he was overweight and that his cholesterol and triglyceride levels were dangerously high. Marcia and Jerry needed to follow special diets, but as a family they all wanted to eat the same foods. Could the children follow the same regimen?

As Marcia Grad collected, tested and refined dozens of high-protein, low-sugar recipes, she divided them into two groups, one for the Strict Diet and one for the Liberal Diet. She submitted them to her doctor, R. Paul St. Amand, and to several other medical authorities, who approved them for the whole family. Using these recipes has helped Jerry lose weight, kept Marcia on her high-protein, low-sugar diet and started a lifetime of good nutrition for the Grad children.

The more than 300 dishes she describes in this book are easy to prepare and all the ingredients are readily available. Included are recipes for dozens of soups, main dishes, sauces, desserts, snacks and beverages. A substitution chart is provided to help you convert your own favorite recipes to fit your high-protein, low-sugar diet. The book also includes suggestions for eating in restaurants, traveling, food for youngsters and party fare. Everyone—whether on a special diet or not—can eat any of these delicious dishes and enjoy better health, happier mealtimes and good nutrition.

Marcia Grad taught school in California and has worked with hypoglycemics on a one-to-one basis for several years. Through her personal interest she has become deeply involved in the problems of metabolic disorders, with special interest in diet and the effects of sugar in the diet.

Dr. R. Paul St. Amand, a Tufts graduate, practices internal medicine in Los Angeles.

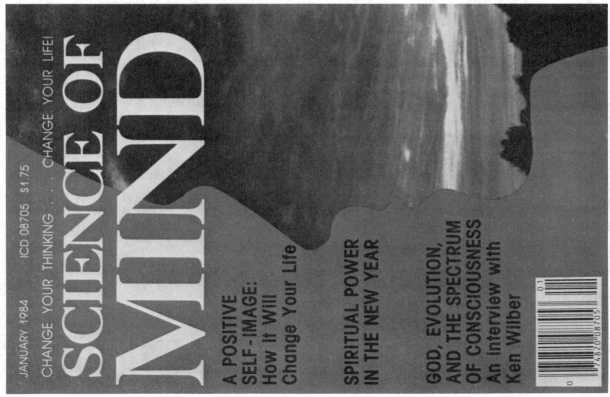

The End of Failure

Dr. Lew Losoncy

You can change — *now*. You can make your move towards success at this very moment. You can reach any dream that you have in mind by using the other 95% of your potential that you have left lying dormant. How? By building your positive self-image.

As you will soon see, when your self-image changes, everything in your life changes. Researchers have shown that students have gone from "F" to "A's" in a matter of weeks. Salespeople have literally doubled their income; shy people have become respected leaders; depressed people have developed a renewed enthusiasm for life. All of these changes have occurred because of one thing — a change in self-image.

Self-image is the ultimate determiner of personal success or failure. Your self-image is so important that one study after another concludes that your view of yourself is the key factor regulating your life. And the

Dr. Lew Losoncy is Director of the Institute for Personal and Organizational Development in Reading, Pennsylvania, and co-creator of the Encouragement Training Program. He lectures and presents workshops nationwide on motivation, communication, and encouragement, and is a consultant to business and industry as well as to many schools, hospitals, and prisons. Dr. Losoncy is the author of Turning People On, You Can Do It, and Think Your Way To Success, and he is co-author of The Encouragement Book. This article is from his book Think Your Way To Success, copyright © 1982 by Dr. Lewis Losoncy, published by Wilshire Book Co. North Hollywood, CA 91605. Used with permission.

"....the person envisions success and

great news is that your self-image can change. Before getting you into the fun work of developing [...] a positive self-image, immerse yourself in some of these interesting findings that researchers have discovered on the unparalleled power of your self-image.

In my search for the answer to the question, "Why do people fail?", I chanced upon a writer who could be considered the first advocate of the self-image psychology. In his insightful book, *Self-Consistency: A Theory of Personality*,[1] the educator Prescott Lecky argued that people fail to succeed not because they are incapable of success, but because of their failure self-image. Lecky showed how negative preconceived beliefs and expectations build up resistances and convince people ahead of time that it would be impossible for them, with their limited capacities, to succeed. For example, if a person believes that learning a foreign language would be impossible, that person's self-image will fight to the bitter end to keep him or her from achieving success in speaking the new language. The second that the foreign language teacher enters

the room, this convinced person resists the teacher's words.

To disprove the conclusion this person could not possibly learn the new language, note that even retarded people have learned foreign languages. But they only learn when they believe they can. If, however, their self-images resist, they will not learn. And, as a more humbling fact, even chimpanzees have learned to understand and respond to the English language! But chimps are lucky. Our hairy friends have an advantage over us. We spend all of our intelligence, reasoning power, and mental energies convincing ourselves that we cannot learn. We conclude that it would be too difficult to learn or perhaps too humiliating to try and maybe fail. If we used just half of that volcano of misdirected failure energy to actively tackle the task, we would succeed. So fear of failure as a result of a negative self-image is a sure guarantee of failure. With a positive self-image, however, the person envisions success and proceeds ahead to achieve that success.

Expand Your Self-Image, Expand Your Possibilities

Think about your own self-

1. Island Press, New York, 1945

proceeds to achieve that success . . ."

image. Have you ever limited your social possibilities by believing that there were certain men or women who were out of your social class? If you held these beliefs, what behavior would your failure beliefs dictate? You probably did not even get the relationship off the ground. Or, if you did approach them, perhaps you said some self-defeating things that sabotaged your chances of developing a relationship. Your self-image actually limited your pool of romantic possibilities. Imagine the number of romantic possibilities you would have just by expanding your self-image.

Did your self-image tell you that you deserve to live in a certain kind of house or that you deserve to have a certain level of income? Did you listen to your self-image and buy that house or work to that exact level of income? And nothing more?

Evidence of the power of self-image is seen everywhere. For example, in the field of organizational development a common explanation used to demonstrate why promoted people sometimes fail is the well-known Peter Principle, developed by Dr. Lawrence Peter. People who are competent at one level are sometimes promoted to a higher level. The Peter Principle suggests that because the new level demands different skills, they often fail due to their lack of these new skills. The reason they fail, according to the Peter Principle, is because they were promoted to their level of incompetence.

I believe the Peter Principle is only partially correct. As a consultant to a few corporations, I found another reason to explain why some promoted people fail. If someone is promoted to a new position but his or her self-image views the position as too difficult or overwhelming, this person will fail. With expanding responsibilities must come expanded self-image. So people who are promoted, especially those who are promoted quickly, frequently need self-image expansion. Any organization wishing to tap the potential of its people needs to provide some sort of self-image expansion for its family members.

The owner of a major barber and beauty salon in Florida wanted to raise his prices for haircuts, but the barbers working for him resisted the price in-

(Continued on page 79)

THE END OF FAILURE
(Continued from page 35)

crease. His employees feared that a price raise would result in a loss of customers. I consulted with the owner, advising him that the barbers' resistance was not do to fear of losing customers, but rather their resistance was a result of their low self-image. They saw their styling abilities at too low a level. Their comment that they would lose customers was simply a comment on their self-image. They believed that they were not worth the new service charge. I advised the enthusiastic owner to help the barbers expand their self-images. This would help them to see their worth in new ways. I asked, "Have you asked your barbers how much they would pay, not for a hair style, but essentially for confidence, courage, and hope? Have you helped them see their profession, not their jobs, in a new light? If you do, and you help the barbers to develop a more positive and expanded self-image, they will beg you for the price increase. The price increase is your comment of respect for them. It shows that you believe in them."

As a college professor, I would often hear students make dogmatic comments such as, "I'm a B student," or "I'm an average student." I would always be tickled when one of these "B" students or "average students" would receive a great grade and share it almost apologetically with me. When I would proudly glance over the student's "A" grade, I would click my heels together and say, "Great job!" Strangely enough, with a self-image lower than the grade the student received, I'd hear something like, "Well, the only reason I received an A was because the professor was easy. I really should have earned a B, because I'm a B student."

Incredible, isn't it? Have you ever done the same? Why did the student need to apologize for the "A"?

Do You Initially Reject New Positive Ideas?

Prescott Lecky explained why the self-image always initially rejects a new view of itself. Lecky wrote, "The center of the nucleus of the mind is the individual's idea or conception of himself. If a new idea seems consistent with the ideas already present in the system, and particularly with the individual's conception of himself, it is accepted and assimilated easily. If it seems to be inconsistent, however, it meets with resistance and is likely to be rejected."[2]

2. Ibid., p. 246

"Believe you can or believe you can't — either way you'll be correct..."

Lecky's theory of self-consistency was further supported by researchers who found that people's self-images of their abilities were better predictors of how they would achieve than were their I.Q.'s. Imagine that. It is not your ability but your beliefs about yourself that hold controlling interest in determining whether you will or will not succeed. Imagine the devastating cost of a negative self-image, because, in the end, if you believe you are incapable of success, your self-image will work overtime to make sure that success will not happen.

Other researchers, including W.B. Brookover and his associates, concluded from their studies that changes in a person's self-image lead to changes in achievement.[3] Again, this is powerful and exciting news. Your success is preceded by the belief that you can succeed. K.L. Harding, an educational researcher, showed that it could be predicted with reasonable certainty whether a student would or would not quit school just by knowing the student's self-image.[4]

In fact, a better gauge than any test devised of how a person will perform in a position is the person's self-image. On these astounding findings, the father of self-image research, William Purkey, writes in relation to school achievement and self-image:

The conclusion seems unavoidable — a student carries with him certain attitudes about himself and his abilities which play the primary role in how he performs in school.

Lecky wondered why educators gave students remedial training when what the pupils really needed was an altered and positive vision that reflected the belief, "I can and will learn."

Did you ever see a person labelled "retarded" by one person in the presence of another person who believed in him or her? This person is like two different people in these different relationships. He or she performs much more successfully in the presence of the "believer." Consider yourself. Did you ever have a supervisor who didn't believe in you? Everything you did was viewed negatively. What happened? You probably began to feel incompetent. Conversely, did you ever have a supervisor who enthusiastically encouraged you to recognize your strengths and contributions? What happened? You performed — remember, the same you — probably more productively because of the person's beliefs and expectations!

Keep in mind that what you have just read is not opinion — it is scientifically researched fact. What you see is what you will be!

Concurring with Adler, Lecky, and others, Maxwell Maltz, the world-renowned plastic surgeon, wrote on this topic of self-image:

The self-image is the key to human personality and human behavior. Change the self-image and you change the personality and behavior. But more than this. The self-image sets the boundaries of individual accomplishment. It defines what you can and cannot be. Expand the self-image and you expand the area of the possible. The development of an adequately realistic self-image will seem to imbue the individual with new capabilities, new talents, and literally turn failure into success.[5]

It is perhaps no news to you that Maltz's book, *Psycho-Cybernetics*, is one of the best selling psychological classics of all time. Literally millions of people have been successfully influenced by this "self-determined psychology." Henry Ford's comment, "Believe you can or believe you can't," is in tune with Maltz's and Lecky's and Adler's observations. In fact, Melvin Powers, the publisher of [the book from which this article is taken] and the paperback publisher of *Psycho-Cybernetics*, upon reading the book for the first time, predicted that *Psycho-Cybernetics* would sell millions of copies. And it did! Powers didn't have that positive success insight by looking into a crystal ball. No, Melvin Powers concluded ahead of time that the book without a doubt was going to be a winner. And he proceeded to make it happen. He looked to the skies and set his goals high!

Just how do these powerful ideas of self-image psychology work to create success?

3. Brookover, W.B., A. Patterson and S. Thomas. "Self-Concept of Ability and School Achievement." U.S. Office of Education, Cooperative Research Project No. 845. East Lansing; Office of Research and Publications, Michigan State University.

4. Harding, K.L.A. "A Comparative Study of Caucasian Male High School Students Who Stay in School and Those Who Drop Out." Ph.D. dissertation, Michigan State University, 1966.

5. Maltz, M. *Psycho-Cybernetics*. North Hollywood, California: Wilshire Books, 1960, p. xix.

SCIENCE OF MIND

Think Your Way to Success is available at $6.00 postpaid from Melvin Powers, 12015 Sherman Road, No.Hollywood, CA 91605.

80

Chapter Thirteen

Questions and Answers to Help You Get Started As a Self-Publisher

Question: What are my chances of succeeding as a self-publisher?

Answer: It depends largely on your subject matter and on the character of your commitment. Wishing won't make it so, unless you back it up with action. Proceed in a logical businesslike way to be constructive, and with total dedication on your part, the chances for success are excellent.

Question: How can I get my book translated into foreign languages?

Answer: Go to your local library and refer to a publication called *International Literary Market Place*. The publication covers 160 countries with listings of thousands of book publishers and their particular areas of interest. Select the publishers you believe would be interested in your book, and send them a letter describing the book, the ads, the publicity, and any other pertinent information you think will enable them to assess the value of your book. See page 154 for some of my books which have been translated into foreign languages.

Question: How can I increase my chances of appearing on television shows or obtaining speaking engagements?

Answer: This is where your publicist can be an enormous help. He knows, as you should, that great importance is placed on physical image and personality. Personal appearance and charisma are potent factors, possibly necessitating a change of hair style, a dieting regimen, a change in manner or a change of wardrobe.

Be receptive, not sensitive and defensive, toward constructive suggestions that will help your chances. I have seen my publicist, Marcia Grad, transform authors into new personalities through her expertise in grooming and her ability to instill confidence in the person involved. If there is an initial reluctance to change, it gradually turns to delight as the transformation takes over.

Question: Why is so much importance attached to the author's personal image? Doesn't the book speak for itself?

Answer: In an important way, yes. But the book isn't the beginning and the end. You are its chief spokesman with the possibility of reaching millions of potential readers via television and radio. In effect, you are the chief marketing factor—the real sales representative. The manner in which you impress your audience and project an image of confidence, credibility and competence is the manner in which your sales will be affected. Communication skills are not acquired overnight. They take study and coaching. Think of every interview and speaking engagement as a learning experience. Be totally objective about how they went, and seek whatever feedback you can acquire to improve them.

Question: I'm apprehensive about my chances for success. Can you give me some encouragement?

Answer: The perceived inability to succeed is a common apprehension among neophytes in any field of endeavor. In the early stages of any undertaking, success seems far down the road. Set minimal challenges for yourself in the beginning. You'll soon experience elation when the first order for your book puts you in the publishing business. At that moment, you'll be convinced that there isn't a thing on earth you can't accomplish. And it's valid. Your potential for success is as great as anyone's. You don't have to be a genius to reach your goals and achieve financial freedom. How many are? But you must have perseverance. That's the key that opens the door.

Question: How can I develop an instinct, or a sense of evaluation, as to what topics could put a book in the best-seller class?

Answer: The answer is initiative and research. Analyze the best-seller lists. Spend time at your local bookstore and see what books are being prominently displayed. Develop rapport with the owner, the manager, the personnel, and tell them you're looking for ideas to help you get into self-publishing. You'll be delighted with the information you get. You might also speak with your librarian. When people are solicited at the authority level, they are delighted to share their knowledge. Ask if there is a trend toward any particular type of book. Track various mail-order ads for books. If the ads continue, you know the books are making money. Get on the mailing list so you can receive and study the follow-up.

Question: Are popular interview shows receptive to self-published authors?

Answer: Absolutely! The publisher of the book is not important—it's the content and the author. As instruments of public communication, they have a responsibility to inform and entertain their viewers and listeners. Accordingly, they want authors who are interesting and articulate. To insure that you meet their qualifications in this regard, the major shows will conduct interviews in advance. When that happens, be relaxed, and turn on the personality.

Question: What is the most common reason for failing to become a successful self-publisher?

Answer: The most common reason is a definite lack in the appeal of your subject matter. And this might be because you are not experimenting enough with mail order ads and direct mail and not getting enough publicity about your book and yourself. You simply are not "beating the drums" to let people know about your book.

Question: What can I do if I have already published my book and am having difficulty selling it?

Answer: Call or write to me, giving me complete details on your advertisements and publicity. Send a copy of your book, and I'll get back to you with some appropriate suggestions.

Question: From the standpoint of learning about book publishing, what do you recommend as the best of the trade publications?

Answer: I suggest you read *Publishers Weekly.* It's available at all libraries.

Question: Can you give a good example of someone who has achieved success by following your self-publishing techniques?

Answer: Indeed I can. Probably the most outstanding example of the Melvin Powers technique at work is that of Tomi Ryan and James H. Ryan, M.D. Tomi is my protégé. Dr. and Mrs. Ryan have self-published a book called *The Meatless Meal Guide.* It contains over 200 delectable and nutritional recipes. The book retails for $5.00, and the sales have exceeded 250,000 copies. The Ryans are doing everything according to plan.

Tomi gives seminars at many of the colleges in the Los Angeles area, and she has done numerous radio and television shows. Her book can be found in all the major bookstores. See page 155 for a picture of Tomi and me. It was taken on August 28, 1981 on Inez Pedroza's "Daybreak L.A." show on KABC-TV, Hollywood. Tomi is holding one of her beautiful vegetable-floral arrangements.

Now here comes an unsolicited mail-order pronouncement: If you want to enjoy delightful, vegetarian recipies, write for *The Meatless Meal Guide.* The price is $7.00 postpaid. Address your letter to: Wilshire Book Company, 12015 Sherman Road, No. Hollywood, California 91605. I can personally attest to the fact that her recipes are positively delicious and scrumptious. (I'm secretly hoping this unexpected publicity will get me another invitation *tout de suite,* for one of her fabulous Chinese dinners!)

Question: Is there a tax advantage in publishing your own book?

Answer: Absolutely. All the expenses incurred in publishing, marketing and publicizing your book are fully deductible from your income. The cost of this book, other books needed for reference work, subscriptions to magazines such as *Publishers Weekly and Writer's Digest,* and expenses incurred during your attendance at seminars are also fully deductible.

If you use one room of your apartment or home exclusively for your publishing business, you can deduct that portion of your rent or mortgage. Book publishing offers you an excellent legal method for sheltering pre-tax dollars. Confer with your accountant about this. He'll save you money.

Uncle Sam wants you to be successful, and, to that end, offers you these incentives. He knows what he is doing, and it isn't entirely altruistic. Don't forget, when you start making money, he becomes your partner. Call your local Internal Revenue Service office and ask for IRS Publication 587—*Tax Information on Operating a Business in Your Home*.

Question: Should I publish my book with a hard cover?

Answer: No. It only adds great expense to your printing and to the eventual selling-price of the book. For example, if I had published this book with a hard cover, it would have been necessary for me to increase the cost of the book by at least five dollars. Paperback books have universal acceptance. Libraries employ a service to put hard covers on their paperbacks.

Question: What size books are most economical to run?

Answer: 5½″ × 8½″ and 8½″ × 11″. Stay away from 6″ × 9″ books.

Question: What is the minimum economical run?

Answer: 3,000 books. You pay the same price for 1,000 books. The main cost is in getting the plates and equipment ready to run your book.

Question: Where can I find the best reasonably priced printer?

Answer: Look no further. For 25 years, I have been running a printing service for self-publishers. It is possible to offer extremely good prices because of the million-dollar printing volume for my own publishing company. In addition, I lend my expertise and act as a consultant in the publishing of the book. This is included in the price, and is of enormous advantage because of the many details that have to be watched. You are welcome to call or write me for an immediate quotation: Melvin Powers, 12015 Sherman Road, North Hollywood, California 91605. Telephone: (818) 765-8579.

Question: Can you recommend a reasonably priced typesetter?

Answer: Yes. Contact me, and I'll be pleased to recommend someone who is suited to your particular requirements.

Question: How can I sell to the armed forces?

Answer: Send a copy of your book and literature to the following addresses:

Acquisitions Librarian
Air Force Libraries Section
U. S. A. F. Military Personal Center
Randolph A.F.B., Texas 78148.

Acquisitions Librarian
Chief of Naval Education
General Library Services Branch N32
Pensacola, Florida 32509

Acquisitions Librarian
Department of the Army
Washington, D. C. 20314

Question: Do I need a model release if I use a photograph of a friend in my book?

Answer: Absolutely. Do not use any photograph without a proper model release. See page 156 for the correct form. Copy the form and have the friend/model sign it.

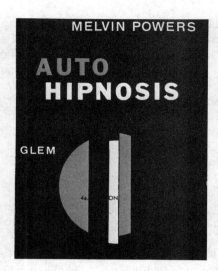

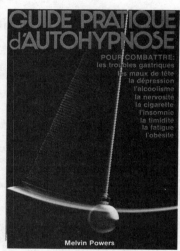

Tomi Ryan and Melvin Powers on the Inez Pedroza's "Daybreak L. A." show on KABC-TV, Hollywood. Tomi is holding one of her beautiful vegetable-floral arrangements.

MODEL RELEASE

TIME ARRIVED . . . .   HOURLY RATE . . . .

DEPARTED . . . .   TOTAL . . . .

In consideration for value received, receipt whereof is acknowledged, I hereby give

. . . .

the absolute right and permission to copyright and/or publish, or use photographic portraits or pictures of me, or in which I may be included in whole or in part, or composite or distorted in character or form, in conjunction with my own or a fictitious name, or reproductions thereof in color or otherwise, made through any media at his studios or elsewhere, for art, advertising, trade or any other lawful purpose whatsoever.

I hereby waive any right that I may have to inspect and/or approve the finished product or the advertising copy that may be used in connection therewith, or the use to which it may be applied.

I hereby release, discharge, and agree to save:

. . . .

from any liability by virtue of any blurring, distortion, alteration, optical illusion, or use in composite form, whether intentional or otherwise, that may occur or be produced in the taking of said pictures, or in any processing tending towards the completion of the finished product.

DATE . . . .

MODEL . . . .

ADDRESS . . . .

PARENT OR GUARDIAN . . . .

WITNESS . . . .

Chapter Fourteen

Self-Publishing and the Midas Touch

What are your chances of becoming a successful self-publisher? What are your chances of attaining secondary goals as a self-publisher? What are your chances of accumulating wealth as a self-publisher?

The answer to these questions is contingent upon several things: the subject matter you have selected for your book; the manner in which the book is merchandised; the effectiveness of your publicity campaign; the employment of good business judgment; the willingness to accept and act upon constructive suggestions; and the insight to profit from mistakes as well as successes. If the triumphant sense of well-being that goes with enthusiasm and excitement about your project is topped off with a winning attitude, you've got it made!

We are all familiar with the legendary success stories of people who immigrated to America and, without knowing the language or receiving a formal education, became extremely successful in business. I personally know many such people. They seem to have the "Midas Touch." Whatever they undertake is done in a methodical way and with a long-range point-of-view. They are industrious, self-assured, and unalterably committed to the belief that the future is what they make it.

The first step in developing the Midas Touch is to adopt the attitude that if others have done it, so can you. The second step is to develop a positive mental attitude based on reality. And what that reality is to be is entirely up to you. Each of us must work within the sphere of reality as perceived by ourselves. The point is effectively illustrated in newspaper articles about Peter McWilliams. (See pages 159 to 162.)

Teresa Valenti self-published her 44-page illustrated book, *How to Kiss with Confidence*, using her daughter, Jeanette, and a friend, Mark Freedman, as models.

The author ran ads in teen-age magazines, an obviously good choice, and hit the jackpot. The ad on page 163 pulled 3,500 orders (at $5.00 each) the first time it ran! Moreover, Bantam Books bought the book trade rights and stimulates sales each Valentine's Day with a big promotion.

Because of the interest in the subject, Ms. Valenti has done over 80 radio and television interviews in the United States, Canada and Australia. She has appeared on most of the major television shows in Los Angeles and has received numerous favorable book reviews. See pages 164 and 165 for two of the reviews. The book has been translated into Japanese, Dutch and Swedish—indicative of the universal appeal of the subject.

Anne Anthony self-published her 112-page illustrated book, *Win at Bingo*, the first edition of 5,000 copies (at $6.95 each) selling out in several months. Anne writes a monthly guest column for various bingo publications and, taking advantage of an opportunity for excellent placement, runs her ads immediately following her articles. The result—Bingo! See page 166.

How does one develop the Midas Touch? One of the best ways I know is to start a reading program in the positive-thinking field. I have consistently recommended books on positive thinking as one of the very best investments you can make for yourself. Success begins with a proper mental attitude—a fact that is indisputable. Positive-thinking books are based upon the wisdom that the ages have given to those who seek success. Allow yourself to absorb that wisdom from your reading until it becomes a part of your psyche. Once you have developed your success consciousness, nothing can deter you from achieving your goals. Developing a positive mental-set makes you a winner in everything you do.

Success breeds success. Given the right set of circumstances, motivation and guidance, you can succeed as a self-publisher. Success in any field demands effort.

Do you remember the song, *You Light Up My Life?* It was sung and made popular by Debbie Boone and in 1978 won the 20th Annual Grammy Award for its writer, Joe Brooks. In accepting the award, Brooks said, "This song was turned down by every firm that is out there tonight. Some turned it down twice . . . this tastes so sweet."

Joe Brooks sustained belief in his song in spite of what the experts said, and it paid off in big dividends.

Success can be yours if you make a sustained effort to attain it. The results will be commensurate with the effort you expend. And before you know it, you will have developed the Midas Touch.

I am listing a series of books with the suggestion that you read one a week. These books are psychologically motivational and comprise one of the most inspirational reading programs I know. Taking the material seriously could give you the success lift-off that you need.

I wish you good luck in the pursuit of your self-publishing goals.

The Midas Touch Library

BRAINSTORMING Charles Clark	$7.00
CHARISMA--HOW TO GET "THAT SPECIAL MAGIC" Marcia Grad	7.00
DYNAMIC THINKING Melvin Powers	5.00
GUIDE TO PERSONAL HAPPINESS Albert Ellis, Ph.D. & Irving Becker, Ed.D.	7.00
HOW TO ATTRACT GOOD LUCK A.H.Z. Carr	7.00
HOW TO DEVELOP A WINNING PERSONALITY Martin Panzer	7.00
HOW TO DEVELOP AN EXCEPTIONAL MEMORY Young & Gibson	5.00
HOW TO SUCCEED Brian Adams	7.00
HUMAN PROBLEMS & HOW TO SOLVE THEM Dr. Donald Curtis	5.00
I CAN Ben Sweetland	7.00
I WILL Ben Sweetland	7.00
KNIGHT IN RUSTY ARMOR Robert Fisher	5.00
KNIGHT IN RUSTY ARMOR (Hard Cover) Robert Fisher	10.00
MAGIC IN YOUR MIND U.S. Andersen	10.00
MAGIC OF THINKING SUCCESS Dr. David J. Schwartz	7.00
MAGIC POWER OF YOUR MIND Walter M. Germain	7.00
NEVER UNDERESTIMATE THE SELLING POWER OF A WOMAN Dottie Walters	7.00
NEW GUIDE TO RATIONAL LIVING Albert Ellis, Ph.D. & R. Harper, Ph.D.	7.00
PSYCHO-CYBERNETICS Maxwell Maltz, M.D.	7.00
SALES CYBERNETICS Brian Adams	7.00
SECRET OF SECRETS U.S. Andersen	7.00
SUCCESS CYBERNETICS U.S. Andersen	7.00
10 DAYS TO A GREAT NEW LIFE William E. Edwards	3.00
THINK AND GROW RICH Napoleon Hill	7.00
THREE MAGIC WORDS U.S. Andersen	7.00
TREASURY OF THE ART OF LIVING Sidney S. Greenberg	7.00
YOUR SUBCONSCIOUS POWER Charles M. Simmons	7.00
YOUR THOUGHTS CAN CHANGE YOUR LIFE Dr. Donald Curtis	7.00

Please add $2.00 postage for the first book and 50¢ for each additional book.
Send your order to: Melvin Powers, 12015 Sherman Road, No. Hollywood, CA 91605

He put hardware into softback

By MARY KASDAN
Daily News Staff Writer

Y ou could call Peter McWilliams an opportunist. If so, he picks the right opportunities.

McWilliams dived into Transcendental Meditation (TM) before everybody else and surfaced in 1975 with "The TM Book," a guide for the skeptical masses.

He penned lightweight love poetry when relationships were the rage, then co-authored "How to Survive the Loss or a Love" when they were not. One million copies of the book are currently in print.

Now that the "Me" generation is all abuzz about computers, McWilliams is right out in front again with "The Personal Computer Book" and "The Word Processing Book." Coming this fall is "The Personal Computer and Business Computer Book."

"I don't look at something and say, 'Well, I'll get involved with that so I can write about it,'" says McWilliams, who describes himself as an "all-or-nothing" kind of guy. "I am curious and seem to be slightly ahead of the general population."

But he does not write just for the pure pleasure of writing. "I'm going to write about the thing that is going to sell the most," he admits.

He says he became attracted to word processors three years ago because of his twin faults of bad spelling and even worse typing.

"Here was this wonderful new thing that would correct my spelling and required no new typing," recalls McWilliams, who is, nevertheless, a talented and humorous writer. "I knew I had to have one."

It took him eight months to research his purchase because no buying guides existed. That is when the light bulb went on in McWilliams' head. The rest is becoming publishing history.

"The Word Processing Book," which made its debut in May of 1982, has sold 170,000 copies. Almost that many more are now being printed.

But when McWilliams sensed the future would lie in personal computers, he introduced "The Personal Computer Book," which has already sold 190,000 copies since last September. An even bigger batch is on the way.

"It would have been throughly inappropriate to invite you into this room a few years ago," he says, gesturing around the bedroom of the West Hollywood condominium that now serves as the

Please see McWILLIAMS Pg. 4

When Peter McWilliams wanted to buy a word processor and a personal computer he did enough research to write a book.

Daily News photo by Roger W. Vargo

Author is computing what book buyers need most

McWILLIAMS from Pg. 1

executive office of his Prelude Press.

When the publishing company — named for his Honda — sprawled throughout the condominium, McWilliams moved a few doors down in the same complex.

He still writes at home on his first purchase, a NorthStar Horizon with a TeleVideo 950 terminal. But his current favorite is the KayPro II personal computer, which holds the place of honor on his office desk and can connect with all the other KayPros in the building.

"My first book went on and on about how wonderful the Osbourne (personal computers) were," McWilliams says. "Then the KayPro came along with a much better machine, so I sent out postcards ... I had to come up with some way of updating the material."

As he speaks, staffers downstairs are licking envelopes containing sophisticated updates that McWilliams mails to readers who send in a self-addressed, stamped envelope.

"These are the only two books in history to go through a new edition every two months to try to keep them current," he adds.

Computers sit in cartons and on the kitchen counter downstairs, waiting to be reviewed. Nearby, his staff scans the page proofs of the upcoming business and personal computer book.

McWilliams, who will be 34 on Friday, confidently presides over all the activity, happy that there is no end in sight.

These days, he recommends buying a personal computer that can run a word processing software program, rather than a word processor alone. The latter, he explains, tends to be more expensive and more limited.

We will not be sitting at "dumb terminals" that hook up to a Big Brother terminal in 1984 or thereafter, he says.

The future lies in less expensive but full-featured, powerful personal computers, he adds. They will occasionally hook up to larger computers, as they do today, through a modem, a machine that turns computer signals into beeps and signals that can be transmitted over telephone lines.

But more often, the "stand alone" personal computer of the future will be linked by modem with other personal computers, allowing users to send messages and files back and forth.

"Within a year, you will be able to buy a laser disc (like those that record film for videodisc players) for $30 that will hold four times the information contained in the Encyclopaedia Britannica," McWilliams says. "You won't even have to contact another computer. Imagine what you can do with that."

The field will become even more exciting when this information becomes available, he adds. "Think of kids being able to get all they need to know for four years of college or the first year of medical school from a disc."

We will not be able to legally trade software programs in the foreseeable future, though Congress is now trying to decide what people can and cannot share, McWilliams explains.

"I am sympathetic with the people who do it (share programs)," he says. "As long as computer companies continue to charge high prices, there will be rip-offs. Five hundred dollars a program is a lot of temptation."

Now that there is a huge market, it would make sense for software companies to make more copies of the same program and sell it for less, he says.

He believes that small software and programming companies that move quickly can still capture a corner of that ancillary market. But entering the field of personal computers proper would be virtually impossible for most small companies at this point.

"In order to make a dent in the market with a new computer," he says, "you would probably have to spend $100 million in advertising in the first six months."

He says the IBM Personal Computer, which

was introduced with a great deal of fanfare, is comparable to a lot of other personal computers, many of them costing less than IBM's.

But, adds McWilliams, "IMB has support like you cannot believe. They've established their computer as the standard so that people are writing software for it." And, as a result, even a lot of big companies are saying, "We're not going to make a personal computer," according to McWilliams.

He still believes people can get more computer, dollar-for-dollar, in the KayPro II than anything else. His is a 26-pound transportable, with a disc drive and videoscreen, costing $1,595.

The NEC Spinwriter is McWilliams' favorite letter-quality printer, retailing at about $1,300. But Smith Corona makes the TP-1, an admittedly slower and noisier letter-quality printer, for as little as $550.

On more technical matters, however, McWilliams remains intentionally ignorant. If he became an expert or hobbyist, he would lose his value as an educated consumer, he notes.

"I know nothing about graphics and couldn't program a computer to save my soul," he says. "I still marvel when I see people in the supermarket playing 'Pac-Man.'"

L.A. Author Strikes It Rich With Computers

By PAUL RICHTER, *Times Staff Writer*

There is a pattern to the hundreds of computer books for beginners that crowd bookstore shelves.

In their opening paragraphs, the books promise to explain all points clearly. And simply. And a few lines later, they plunge the reader into a Mariana Trench of technical text, leaving him to thrash around among dynaturtles, I/O interfaces and complementary metal-oxide semiconductors.

One exception to the pattern has been the series of quirky paperbacks that are apparently earning a Los Angeles writer a small fortune.

Peter A. McWilliams has shipped 410,000 copies of his chatty, pun-filled "The Word Processing Book" and "The Personal Computer Book," and this month launched a third, "The Personal Computer in Business Book." The first two have made the 34-year-old McWilliams a top-selling computer writer in a year when computer books are among the hottest items in the bookseller's inventory.

"I'm not a millionaire yet," he offers. "But, hopefully, that's coming soon."

The quotable McWilliams has appeared on several television news shows as a personal computer guru; his face recently grinned from the pages of People and Playboy magazines. Since he began writing a personal computer column last spring, it has been snapped up by more than 60 newspapers, including the Washington Post and the Philadelphia Inquire

In addition to the column, he publishes a $100-a-year computer newsletter and cranks out regular updates to the books. Columnist William F. Buckley, a McWilliams acquaintance and admirer, refers to these enterprises as "McWilliams' Industries."

All of it comes from a writer who started his own tiny publishing business after most publishing houses rejected his first manuscript. And from a computer "expert" who doesn't know a lick of programming and dropped out of Eastern Michigan University at 19. ("It was

Please see AUTHOR, Page 16

IRIS SCHNEIDER / Los Angeles Times

Author Peter A. McWilliams hams it up—top, in his bathroom filled with computer equipment, and with a complicated manual.

AUTHOR: Rich

Continued from Page 1

fashionable to drop out then—especially from EMU," he says.)

No matter, say those who have watched his rise. Writer-entrepreneur McWilliams has succeeded on the strength of his writing and his talent as a self-promoter.

"He's been able to cut through the clutter and get across to people what they need to know," says Ron Jeffries, publisher of the Jeffries Report, a Santa Barbara-based microcomputer newsletter. "And McWilliams markets McWilliams very well," he says, referring to the writer's ability to keep his name before the public.

He has cashed in on popular trends before. McWilliams won his first following in the early 1970s, when he wrote the first of nine volumes of Rod McKuenesque love poems. (One title: "I Love, Therefore I Am.") So far, 3 million copies of the books have been shipped.

Before PCs, TM

McWilliams reached the New York Times trade-paperback best-seller list in 1975 as co-author of a transcendental meditation primer called "The TM Book." One million copies of the book have been shipped to date, and more than 1 million have been shipped of another, "How to Survive the Loss of a Love."

None of the past enterprises have been as successful as his current ones, however. "McWilliams Industries" has grossed $2 million in the first nine months of this year, compared to less than $200,000 during the first nine months of last year.

McWilliams' latest moneymaking plan is to sell the publishing business to a major publisher, then contract with the buyer to write several more computer books. He hopes to get about $1 million in the deal, and says 10 publishers have expressed interest.

Despite his apparent knack for trend spotting, McWilliams insists that he didn't become a computer writer because he thought there was a gold mine in readable books for beginners. "I'd be a lot richer if my vision was that clear," he says.

He will take credit for the nonstop jokes that have endeared his books to some readers, but alienated a few critics. Among them was a quip that the personal computer's "yes/no circuits" are capable of saying no "faster than Debby Boone."

A product of the sooty Detroit suburb of Allen Park, Mich., McWilliams began selling love poetry in 1968. Sandwiched between his successful books were two less successful ventures.

McWilliams wrote, produced and directed a film starring rock singer Bette Midler, after the two met in a Windsor, Ont., nightclub where Midler was singing. The film, titled "The Greatest Story Overtold," lost $50,000. On an attempt to launch a line of romantic greeting cards, he lost about $500,000.

In 1979, licking his wounds from that loss, McWilliams moved from Manhattan to Watts, where he rented a $200-a-month apartment.

It was laziness, actually, that drove him to the personal computer. He heard that he could avoid retyping drafts by using a computer as a word processor. "And I *abhor* retyping," he said.

After eight months of researching word processing, he bought a Northstar Horizon computer and set out to write a review of "The Word," a word-processing program, for Byte magazine. McWilliams was instructed to keep it to 3,000 words. In the exuberance of his first effort on a word processor, however, the article had soon grown to 16,000 words.

McWilliams was snubbed when he tried to get publishers to sell his overgrown article as a book. Nobody's interested in computer books, they told him—and even if they were, they wouldn't be interested in *funny* ones.

"Their argument was, 'If God had wanted technical books to be funny, he would have put jokes in the Bible,' " the writer says.

Happily, McWilliams one day got an Internal Revenue Service notice reminding him of taxes due on a New York bank account that he had forgotten. That account held $11,006—enough for him to set up his own tiny publishing concern (named Prelude Press after his Honda), and print the first 3,000 copies of "The Word Processing Book."

Buckley Liked It

McWilliams reaped a publicity windfall the day columnist William F. Buckley called to chat about word processing and praise the book. With Buckley's permission, McWilliams turned the praise into a book-jacket endorsement. Other endorsements and reviews followed, including four in the New York Times.

McWilliams' "Word Processing Book" and "Personal Computer Book" now head the national computer-book best-seller list maintained by Crown Books. That makes him "one of the best selling of all the authors we carry " says Robert M. Haft, president of the Maryland-based chain.

Along with praise, McWilliams has gotten a few knocks from those who have reviewed his work. Some have suggested that the books are too repetitious, particularly in the brand-name buying guides that appear in the back. "He keeps on writing the same book," says newsletter publisher Jeffries. "He ought to go on to another one."

How to Kiss with Confidence.

The most complete guide to creative kissing for teenagers.

See these and many more descriptive photos thoughout the book.

You'll know that you know how!

Learn about other teens' first kiss experiences, how to flirt, how to touch, and many more ideas on how to kiss with confidence.

We know just how you feel about kissing. Maybe you're afraid to get close to someone or to kiss someone - scared you'll be rejected or, worse, laughed at or put down. Worry no more. **"How to Kiss with Confidence"** was written especially for you to overcome these fears and to give you new self-assurance.
Hint: Send it anonymously to a friend who needs it - or make sure you're doing it right. Chapters uncover many sensitive areas that no one ever tells you about. But we tell it like it is with humor and warmth. You won't put it down until it's finished.

Terry & Mike

For each beautifully designed book, shipped in a plain envelope, (great gift item), send $5.00 with the following information to:

P.H.D. UNLTD., Dept G
19750 Ventura Blvd. • Woodland Hills, Calif. 91364

Name: _____

Address: _____

City: _____ State: _____ Zip: _____

PHILADELPHIA, PA.
PHILADELPHIA DAILY NEWS
D. 229,981 S. 153,220

OCT 6 1981

Osculation Won't Make You Crazy

I know it had to be in sixth grade at St. Francis of Assisi School in Harrisburg, because in fifth grade, I wore braces and my brother called me 'buck tooth buzzard.' I know I was not into kissing then.

In sixth grade, my braces were removed and I discovered a nice Italian boy who had been in my class as long as I could remember. For some reason, one day we decided to rendezvous during recess in the empty second-grade classroom that separated the girls' lavatory from the boys' in the basement of the school.

We planned to kiss, a daring act, especially in a Catholic grammar school.

There was a china closet filled with books in the corner of the room, and Danny and I slipped behind it. Both of us wore heavy winter coats. He put his arms around my bulky wool wrap, we closed our eyes, pursed our lips, and suddenly, we heard a stern, authoritarian voice: "What do you think you're doing?"

I thought it looked pretty obvious, but the eighth grader, a self-appointed policeman, did not. She marched us off to the principal.

What reminded me of this encounter was Teresa Valenti, 43, of Canoga Park, Calif., who has re-discovered the Great Teenage Dilemma of Our Time. Not Brooke Shields' bluejeans, not teenage pregnancy, not the sexual sophistication that everyone would have us believe about teenagers.

No, this is it: teenagers don't know how to kiss.

Valenti, whose lips were "too stiff" during her first kiss at 12, learned this by eavesdropping on kids in her living room. One of her daughter's friends was panicked about kissing for the first time and friends wanted to buy her a gag gift for her "sweet sixteen" party — a book on how to kiss. None existed, and so the hair stylist decided to sit down and write her very first booklet, "How to Kiss with Confidence." She published it herself.

One night, her son came home from a date and he said, "Mom, hurry up and write the book, because I just kissed someone and they really need it." Her daughter, then 17, volunteered to pose for the accompanying photos in the book.

Valenti advertised it for $5 in the back of Cosmopolitan and Teen Magazine, and was flooded with 13,800 orders, including one who wrote: Please rush, emergency. Another boy wrote back he was told he kissed like a baby, and he didn't kiss anyone for another three years.

With a market like that, Bantam Books decided to grab reprint rights and will publish an expanded version on Jan. 9 for $1.98.

Included was such erotic advice: "When he advances toward your mouth, keep your lips slightly parted. When your lips touch his, respond by putting your arms around him. Following his lead, gently move your lips and head — avoid nose bumping, this could be embarrassing. If he extends his tongue into your mouth, do the same, trying to follow his tongue movements..."

"Another good technique is to caress the face, lips, eyelids, cheeks and nose slightly with your fingertips. This may send chills up and down your spine or your partner's. Don't be alarmed, enjoy the sensation."

Valenti insisted last night she is not adding to the already explosive teenage pregnancy rate: "You don't get pregnant from kissing. I had kissed from 12 to 20 and I had a good time. I just feel you don't have to go further. It worked for me, but now," she paused, adding, "I don't know."

Were kids still having problems with kissing?

I decided to check with my friend, Kathryn "Kitsi" Watterson Burkhart, who just spent 2½ years talking to more than 250 teenagers about sexuality. Her book,

Kitty Caparella

called "Growing into Love: Teenagers Talk Candidly about Sex in the 1980s," will be published by G.P. Putnam Sons on Oct. 19.

Indeed! She found kids feel just as vulnerable, and just as scared during their first embrace as we were. In fact, an 18-year-old from Pomona, Calif., wasn't sure he wanted anything to do with it.

"Personally, I don't know why a lot of people go through all the hassle," he told Burkhart. "...I been hurtin' my tongue."

Another boy, Louis, 14, of Hartford, Conn., and his girlfriend walked and walked for hours outside a dance while he mustered up his courage. They sat down on a park bench, they got up, they walked around, they sat down again.

"It's really tough," he said. "In my mind, it's so smooth and easy, but in real life all these other things happen...When all you're thinking about is how you're going to get around to kissing her, you can't think of anything else to say... Once you get used to it, it's a breeze. It's just getting there that's hard."

Kitty Caparella's column appears on Tuesdays.

Bob Greene

Who's behind that hot kisser guide? It's mom

IF YOU BELIEVE the conventional wisdom, the life of the average American teen-ager is a cross between Penthouse magazine, the Kama Sutra, and "Debbie Does Dallas." Today's teen-age boys and girls are supposed to be so sexually sophisticated and precocious that they will have nothing left to look forward to in the bedroom by the time they reach the legal voting age.

But a 43-year-old California woman has put her money on the theory that the conventional wisdom is wrong. And every indication is that she's going to make a modest fortune off her hunch.

"The main thing you should understand about today's teen-agers is that they don't know how to kiss," said Teresa Valenti. "That's where I come in."

Mrs. Valenti arrived at her realization when she was eavesdropping on a gathering of teen-agers in her neighborhood. They were getting ready to go to a party, and some of the girls wanted to get another girl a copy of a book on how to kiss. But they had discovered that no such book existed.

On the spot, Mrs. Valenti decided to go into the business of teaching teen-agers how to kiss.

"I'm a very good kisser myself, and I thought if no one else was going to teach the kids how to do it, then I would," she said.

SHE SAT DOWN and wrote a book called "How to Kiss With Confidence." She saw it as a "guide to creative kissing" for teen-agers: "Everyone has all kinds of advice for today's kids, but no one had taken the time to teach them how to kiss."

Mrs. Valenti's advice was not exactly what you would expect to find in "Dear Abby" or "Ask Ann Landers." Some excerpts from her guidebook:

● "Your behavior will signal a guy as to when you want to be kissed. When he advances toward your mouth, keep your lips slightly parted. When your lips touch his, respond by putting your arms around him. Following his lead, gently move your lips and head—avoid nose bumping, this could be embarrassing. If he extends his tongue into your mouth, do the same, trying to follow his tongue movements.

● "During your kissing encounter, the lips are sometimes the first place of contact but not necessarily so. Different areas become aroused, and kissing them can cause sweet sensations. Another popular place to kiss is the neck. Passionate pressure is acceptable in this area. If you girls are wearing a tube top or strapless dress, and you guys are wearing a tank top, you may continue your creative kissing by moving to the shoulders and upper chest.

● "A beautiful touch is cupping your partner's face in your hands and kissing lightly all over—the face, that is. This is a delicate, caring, caressing action, sure to cause a warm, loving response. Another good technique is to caress the face, lips, eyelids, cheeks, and nose lightly with your fingertips. This may send chills up and down your spine or your partner's. Don't be alarmed; enjoy the sensation."

MRS. VALENTI had her handbook published herself. Inserted between the instructions were photographs of a teen-aged girl getting her lips kissed off.

"That's my daughter, Jeanette," Mrs. Valenti said, with pride in her voice.

Next Mrs. Valenti took out small advertisements offering the booklets for $5 apiece. She placed the ads in magazines aimed at teen-age girls.

To her surprise, almost immediately she received 13,500 orders for the book. Many of the orders were accompanied by letters from the teen-agers, thanking her for instructing them in an area no one had addressed before.

Mrs. Valenti realized that her project had gotten out of hand. So she sold reprint rights to her book to Bantam Books, the mass-market paperback company. Early next year, Bantam is going to try to sell "How to Kiss With Confidence" to millions of potential teen-age buyers around the country.

"They've even given me $900 extra to have more pictures taken of my daughter kissing," Mrs. Valenti said.

WHEN I SPOKE with Mrs. Valenti the other day, she said that the secret to her book's appeal is that "there are a lot of teen-agers who are afraid of kissing. Everyone assumes that they know how, but they are very insecure about it."

She thought a moment, then added:

"I'm 43, and I kiss a lot of people who don't know how to kiss right."

I asked her if—with all the publicity about teen-age sex—she can't be accused of adding to a national problem.

"No one ever got pregnant from kissing," Mrs. Valenti said. "Having one beer does not lead to alcoholism, and kissing does not lead to sex.

"I advise my readers to go only so far, and then to stop. I don't believe in teen-age sex, but I do believe in teen-age kissing."

MRS. VALENTI said her own life history is a case in point:

"I started kissing when I was 12. But I wouldn't go any further until I got married.

"These kids watch kissing all the time. It's all over the TV. So they might as well learn to do it right. All I'm trying to tell teen-agers is that kissing is fun, and that they should learn how to enjoy a good kissing session."

Mrs. Valenti said that, although her book is being marketed toward teen-agers, some people her own age can learn from it, too.

"I have a friend who is 40 years old, and she never knew you weren't supposed to bite a man on the lips until she read it in my book," Mrs. Valenti said. "I guess she'd been biting men's lips all her life, and they had all been too embarrassed to tell her to stop."

BINGO TALK©

by ANNE ANTHONY
Author of
How To Win At Bingo

Pet Peeves vary in degrees of intensity and importance depending on the emphasis given to them by individual players. Most are merely momentary inconveniences and are not really ingrained peeves at all. Like flashbulbs, these flash suddenly and disappear almost as fast. But, there are those of a more persistent nature that occur, time and time again, on a regular basis and do become "pets(?)."

What player has not upset a cup of coffee or soft drink, drenching hardcards, chips or paper sheets... or dropped a dauber in the middle of a game...or scattered a handful of chips, displacing those already covering called numbers? To be sure, these "incidents" are disconcerting to neighboring players, but, most Bingo players can relate to them and willingly assist and help the hapless one back into the game, quickly, so they, too, can pay attention to their Bingo squaes.

The fast-paced tempo of the games does demand a certain amount of concentration and manual dexterity. Some players have more of each than others. One night, one player, indeed, proved he did have both. He ate a neighbor's sandwich before the owner realized it was gone, or, the diner was aware that he had eaten it. Such ability is not common.

Sustained concentration coupled with dexterity is even harder to achieve, especially when influences and actions, by others, manage to create involuntary mental hurdles. This is the fertile field for pet peeves to develop and gain momentum. The serious player is more discomforted by them than the lack-a-daisical player. However, both are affected by them.

The most common ones are not confined to one Bingo Hall but surface wherever Bingo games are played. Understandably, they are always "caused" by the behavior of "others." However, human voices get more than their share of blame. Not so surprisingly, they top the list.

PLAYERS WHO:
Talk incessantly, drowning out the Caller's voice and then asking everyone around them what number was called or what the next pattern game will be.
Repeat the last number called, over and over again, while searching for it on their Bingo squares...sometimes, even in in a foreign language..."OCHO"... "OCHO"..."OCHO"..."OCHO", repeated for every card the player has, can sound more like a tribal chant than a number.
Let loose an explosive "BINGO!" that not only rattles chips but

scares the socks off everyone within earshot.
Proclaim loudly, "I'm On," "I'm On," "I'm On," unnerving the calmest players around them.
MONITORS WHO:
Shout "PAPER!," wave the paper sheet like a banner, and then, let it float down, covering a purchaser's card and chips during the progress of a game.
Engage in private conversations and jokes, with each other, just loud enough to compete with the Caller's voice.
CALLERS WHO:
Call numbers so fast that only a quad-armed player can keep up.
Use the delayed calling technique, splitting double digit numbers in half, giving all players the frustrating pause of anticipation.
Bingo, assuredly, must be a mecca for "talkers," based on the voiced pet peeves, but where else can so much talk go on, offering such a liberal education of the human comedy----its foibles----its humor and certainly its surprise element of entertainment?

GOLDEN CHIP AWARD
Goes to Rita, a Caller who blithely announced, "Monitors are now selling the floor on paper."
©1983 Anne Anthony

Wednesday night at Temple Emet in Woodland Hills, you will find courteous volunteers like Frances Heyman and Alice Rosman. It's volunteers like Frances and Alice that help make Temple Emet a pleasure to play at. Check Temple Emet's ad for further information.

CHICKEN DINNER AND SUPER BINGO

Temple Ahavat Shalom serves Super Bingo with a tasty Chicken Dinner, July 30th, doors open at 4 p.m. and the chicken will be served 4:30 to 6 p.m. Admission is only $15, this includes 15 Hard Cards and the Chicken Dinner. After dinner you can get ready for Super Bingo, with E.E. Birds starting at 6:30 p.m. Temple Ahavat Shalom is located in Northridge, one block south of Rinaldi St., between Reseda Blvd. and Zelzah, just off the 118 Simi Valley Freeway. For information call: Stu 892-0079; Ray 360-0223; Buddy 993-0852 or Lin 360-9034

BINGO TALK is a first for Bingo Bugle and will cover the various aspects of the game(s), the highlights, the insights, and other player's interesting methods that can make playing Bingo challenging, exciting and fun for you.

BINGO TALK

by ANNE ANTHONY
Author of
How To Win At Bingo

Is Winning At Bingo "just plan Luck"?

The vast majority of Bingo players are convinced that it is. After all, and rightfully so, they reason that there is a winner or winners at each of the 35 to 40 games played during a Bingo Session and somebody has to win. If they win they attribute it to "Luck". BUT, what about those players who win more often than others? They are, as a rule, regular Bingo players and stand out in Bingo Halls. You will find them not only at one Bingo Session or one location. They usually play at different places during the week and have a tendency to win wherever they play. Their winning is not confined to any one location because they move around.

During the research for my book HOW TO WIN AT BINGO, this phenomena and enigma surfaced very early and became more and more pronounced as time went on. My curiosity led to conversations with a select and rare group of Bingo players who did not believe their winning was entirely all luck. Many tried to analyze why this happened to them and their answers, being subjective, differed from one to another; yet, there was an unspoken underlying thread that did link them together. See if you can find it in their answers. Here are some that I chose at random:

"I dreamed one night of a Bingo card with all the numbers covered except one—the number I-16. I woke myself up shouting "BINGO!"

I kept thinking about winning the Cover-all all the next day. That night I just had to play Bingo and chose several cards with 16 on them. I did win the Cover-all, but on the number 61."

The individual numbers were there, only in reverse. The dream was significant. She did win the Coverall that particular evening.

"When a card starts filling up for any pattern and only one number remains, mentally I concentrate on that number coming up, and more often than not it does. The more I do this, the more it happens.

"I pick cards at randon (?) and manage to win often enough. This works for me."

"I expect to win and I do, at least one game of an evening when nothing interferes with that expectation during any one game...such as social conversations of neighboring players."

"I have winning streaks and then dry periods. but those dry periods happen mostly when I allow negative influences on TV, at home or at the office to dominate my thinking and behavior while playing Bingo. I found that out just recently...by changing that mental attitude, the dry spells have been fewer in duration." (This lady realized what was occuring and made an attempt to correct it.)

Have you found the common link yet? The next few statements may uncover it.

"Many times I 'know' the next number before it is called...especially when I can see the color of that ball."

"I'm lucky. I've known that all my life."

I am sure you have the answer by now. Interesting, isn't it?

THE GOLDEN CHIP AWARD OF THE MONTH:

Goes to a lady named Alice. Upon winning a Bingo game, she bought three extra paper sheets for the next game and gave them to each of the three players at her table.

It's the little unexpected things people do that warm the heart.
©1983 Anne Anthony

"COUPONS" "COUPONS"
PLAYERS; please use the coupons that our advertisers have supplied for you. This lets the manager know you are reading the Bingo Bugle. Thank you and GOOD LUCK.

Update 1992

It has been eight years since I first published this book. During that time, many of my readers have had outstanding success as self-publishers, which is truly gratifying to me. Book publishing is a fascinating business and a constant challenge they've grown to love.

The difference between being a successful or unsuccessful self-publisher usually has to do with one's advertising campaign. You can have the greatest book in the world—but if you don't convince potential readers of this, they'll never know how great it is, and they won't spend their money to purchase it.

How to Get Rich in Mail Order
In chapter five of this book, I gave you numerous examples of advertising copy that helped sell over $2,000,000 worth of my book *How to Get Rich in Mail Order*. I have now sold over $7,000,000 worth and have made hundreds of thousands of dollars on a mail order audio cassette program based on the book. I ran full-page magazine and newspaper ads. I also produced two-minute television commercials and half-and one-hour infomercials, called *Mail Order Millionaire*. After several years of airing the shows, sales slowed down and I took them off the air. Other people, who assumed the advertising was still going great, went on the air with mail order ads and infomercials—and they were successful.

It's interesting that when you think you have saturated a market and have stopped advertising, sometimes someone else comes along and rekindles the public's interest in the product. This is true of all forms of advertising. Of course, all ads and infomercials eventually wear out and need to be redone or replaced.

I know I should run new mail order print ads and shoot a new infomercial, but I prefer to work on a new book or product. I enjoy the challenge of trying to produce another winner.

I was written up in a Los Angeles magazine. (See pages 168 and 169). I send out this reprint with literature on my book and course, thus increasing my sales. Many customers comment on the article, saying that they enjoyed reading my success story. When you get publicity about yourself, be sure to use it as an enclosure whenever you can.

I continually test ad copy. I include circulars in every outbound book order. At the end of each month, I have an exact count of the circulars sent out, orders received, and percentage of sales. My goal, naturally, is to improve the response.

I also produce a continuous flow of direct mail to book buyers. Here too, I tabulate monthly how many orders I have received for each book, and I calculate the percentage of sales. You should be doing the same thing when you start selling your book.

In this update, I'm including some of my current successful book ads. Your job is to study them carefully and use or adapt portions of them to sell your book.

When you do a mailing for a single book, the rule is to

167

MELVIN POWERS:
The Man with the Midas Touch

Skeptics might scoff at a self-help book like
"How to Get Rich in Mail Order," but its
author is living proof that these theories work.

By Randall D. Schultz

Make no mistake about it, Melvin Powers has the Midas touch. Sure, he does things differently—some would even say he does things wrong. Yet in the process of doing everything "wrong," he's made himself a very rich man.

Melvin Powers publishes books. Not just any kind of books, special interest books. Books about bridge, chess, pets, sports and hobbies. But his Wilshire Book Company is best known for its line of self-help and inspirational books, the kind that most other publishers don't quite know how to handle. And the world headquarters for Wilshire Book Company is located not in a fancy New York City high-rise, but in a modest office/warehouse building in North Hollywood.

In an age of million-dollar advances and lavish book tours for superstar authors, Melvin Powers's Wilshire Book Company inauspiciously sells more than half of its books by mail. Mail-order selling is Powers's first love, and it's how his multimillion dollar publishing empire began.

As a teenager in Boston, Powers subscribed to *Popular Science* magazine, and occasionally read the classified ads in the back. An avid chess player, he noticed an ad for a chess book and mailed away for it. When it arrived, he decided he should sell books by mail, too.

"I started in the mail-order business when I was 16 years old," says Powers. "It was my hobby, running classified ads

in the same magazines that I was reading—*Popular Science* and *Mechanix Illustrated*. I began selling books on chess, then one-by-one, added new titles and new subjects."

At first, he bought books from publishers at wholesale cost and sold them for retail. When he got one order, he sent it out with a flyer advertising the other books that he had. And he's still basically doing the same thing—running almost the same ad. "The formula is still working after all these years," he says, with a chuckle.

His first venture into publishing was a book called *"Hypnotism Revealed,"* which he wrote himself. "There's no money in having someone else publish your book," Powers explains. "I was an entrepreneur, so instead of getting a small percentage as a royalty from another publisher, I decided I might as well print the book and sell it myself."

It was a good decision. Now, 40 years after moving to Southern California to start Wilshire Book Company, Powers publishes all of the books he sells. Wilshire Book Company, which began on Wilshire Boulevard near downtown Los Angeles (hence the name), is privately held by Powers, and he is reluctant to release financial information. The company employs 21 people, and sells "a couple million books a year," says Powers.

Powers's first big publishing success came in the early 1960s with *"Think*

and Grow Rich" by Napoleon Hill. Even though it had been published in hardcover years before, it was Powers who first asked the question, "Why isn't this book available in paperback?" He bought the "trade paperback" rights and has since sold more than 7 million copies of the book. This trade paperback format—a larger size than the "mass market" paperbacks that fit into racks in supermarkets and drugstores—accounts for virtually all of Wilshire Book's sales.

His biggest coup, however, was snatching up the trade paperback rights to *"Psycho-Cybernetics"* by Dr. Maxwell Maltz.

"'Psycho-Cybernetics' wasn't doing anything in hardcover," says Powers. "Zero. But, I read a couple a pages of the book while standing in a bookstore and said to myself, 'This is a multi-million best-seller.'"

He was right. The Wilshire Book trade paperback edition of *"Psycho-Cybernetics"* jumped onto the best-seller lists, and to date has sold more than 3 million copies. It's still one of the company's steady sellers. And ever since the back-to-back mega-successes of *"Think and Grow Rich"* and *"Psycho-Cybernetics,"* self-help and inspirational books have been the company's primary editorial focus and biggest selling line of books.

Powers still goes to bookstores every week or two to read the hardcovers, looking for his next big find. He knows that the big New York publishers, with hundreds and sometimes thousands of books on their lists, sometimes let a good one slip through the cracks without being properly promoted. But bookstores aren't the only places he finds new books to publish.

Twenty years ago, when a friend asked him to buy an Arabian horse, Powers went to the Calabasas Saddlery and asked to see the horse books. He was shown a section of hardcover books.

"Where are your paperback books?" he asked.

"There aren't any," said the salesperson.

"There aren't any?" he asked, incredulously. "How come?"

"Everybody who has horses has money," said the salesperson. "They can afford to buy hardcover books."

When Powers heard that, he knew he had found another gold mine. He quickly wrote to the publishers of the hardcover books, negotiated the paperback rights and brought out a line of 70 horse-related books as fast as he could. He sold them by mail, in bookstores, in the 17,000 riding goods stores across America and Canada and got sales reps to sell them at the major riding goods trade shows. Mr. Midas had struck again.

Powers has also demonstrated his golden touch in the music business. When songwriter Tommy Boyce came into his office 15 years ago with a manuscript called *"How to Write a Hit Song and Sell It,"* Powers not only published the book but decided to try his hand at songwriting. With some personal coaching from Boyce, and some classes in composition and lyrics at U.C.L.A., Powers co-wrote some songs with Boyce that made it onto the country and western charts. Teresa Brewer recorded his "Willie Burgundy," and he was invited to Nashville to accept an award for his song, "Who Wants a Slightly Used Woman."

He also used his songwriting experience to get into the *"Guinness Book of World Records"*—for getting the world's smallest royalty check.

"It was for a song called 'San Antonio, Texas,'" he says. "I got this check for four cents. Other people might have hidden it, but I got a big kick out of it. So I called the Guinness people and made it in the 1980 edition of the book." The four-cent check is still proudly displayed on his office wall.

As you might expect from someone who has made millions of dollars by selling books by mail, Powers is now a renowned expert in mail-order sales. The book he wrote and published, *"How to Get Rich in Mail Order"* is the all-time best-seller on the subject, and is considered the bible of the mail-order industry. He has taught seminars on mail-order techniques at virtually every community college in the Los Angeles area. Despite his understated approach and low-key personal style, he is truly a super salesman.

So, it isn't surprising that his newest endeavor is called "Melvin Powers Television Marketing," which sells products on TV. For many years he has been sought out as a consultant, working behind-the-scenes to help the companies that offer Ginsu steak knives, exercise equipment, vegetable slicers and other hard-to-resist goodies on TV. Now he's actively seeking products that his new company can sell on cable TV.

"That means traveling to housewares and food shows, trying to find a product with the potential for mass appeal," says Powers. "It might be a new kitchen gadget or small appliance, or even an automotive product or a course of instruction in a book or on tape. Believe it or not, sometimes television exposure generates so many orders that the manufacturers can't keep up."

In other words, Melvin Powers may be about to open up another gold mine.

Not that he's giving up the publishing business. Far from it. Last year Wilshire Book Company published 12 new books to add to its total list of about 450. This year, if he can find another dozen good books he'll publish them, too. But he's not on any quota system, so he'll only publish the books that he cares about.

Of all the books he's published, he's proudest of *"How to Get Rich in Mail Order."* "It's helped a lot of people leave their jobs and start a business for themselves and become financially independent," he says. He also mentions *"New Guide to Rational Living"* by Albert Ellis, and of course, *"Psycho-Cybernetics."*

"I'm happy with the books I've published because every week people tell me how their lives have been changed by them," says Powers. "It's a nice feeling." WM use a four-page circular, which provides ample opportunity to get the message across and convince recipients to buy. Because I usually send from six to twelve circulars in a direct mail package and think that most people will not read that many four-pagers, I sometimes instruct my copywriters to try doing the job in two pages. It's like crowding a 30-minute infomercial into a two-minute commercial. Can you do it successfully? At times, yes.

Brainstorming

Here is an example of a two-page circular that's pulling in the orders. (See pages 171 and 172). Note that I do not have subheads, a table of contents, or a coupon. That's breaking the rules of advertising copy for books, but the point is, it's working. I love the headline, and the copy is strong. When I included the one-page book review on page 173, sales increased. Whenever you can, use testimonials, endorsements, publicity write-ups, and book reviews.

Note that the book is also available on cassette. Many orders are for the cassette program, rather than for the book. This happens often. Some time ago, I was running ads for the book and audio cassette program *Sales-Cybernetics* by Brian Adams. The book sold for $7.00 and the tapes for $25.00. A very high percentage of the orders were for the cassette program. I attribute this to salespeople's desire to listen while driving in their cars. I, too, find listening to tapes while driving to be a great time saver.

I'm breaking another important rule by not offering a 30-day money-back guarantee. Every book on advertising copy admonishes you to include a guarantee. Generally speaking, I do include it in my advertisements. It's a must for newspaper, magazine, and television. But I had an instinctive feeling that it should not be included in this ad. I've sold thousands of copies of the book and tape program and have never had even one copy of either returned. Most customers end up buying additional copies for their associates.

Consider putting your material on audio and video cassettes. It's highly profitable. "Put your driving time to good use" is a phrase used to sell a wide variety of information. Foreign language and motivational programs have done particularly well.

Sales-Cybernetics

I knew this book would have excellent sales because of my success with *Psycho-Cybernetics* by Maxwell Maltz, M.D. and *Success-Cybernetics* by U.S.

Andersen. I had the audience targeted perfectly. I sold thousands of these two books to multi-level companies. All I did was send out samples of the *Sales-Cybernetics* by Brian Adams to my regular customers and back came the orders for thousands of books. It was that easy. I wrote a four-page foreword for the book that served as a strong endorsement. (See pages 174 and 175.) And I designed the cover to look like *Psycho-Cybernetics*. (See page 74.) How could I miss?

Grow Rich with Your Million Dollar Mind

This book is also by Brian Adams. It's selling extremely well because of the author's name and the success of his previous books, *Sales-Cybernetics* and *How to Succeed*. Multi-level marketing companies are constantly looking for new books to motivate their people. There's a very high drop-off rate. (See pages 176 and 177 for the two-page circular I am using.)

The Magic of Thinking Success

Having sold over one million copies of his book *The Magic of Thinking Big*, I encouraged David Schwartz to write *The Magic of Thinking Success*. I edited the book myself. (See page 178.) It is enjoying phenomenal sales to both multi-level companies and the general public. I couldn't miss because of Dr. Schwartz's reputation and the success of his previous book. *The Magic of Thinking Success* has been translated into French, Spanish, and Portuguese. Worldwide sales are especially strong in Canada, Great Britain, Australia, New Zealand, and South Africa.

My motivational books have tremendous sales all over the world, because people are hungry for the material. The books encourage readers to succeed, to develop self-confidence in their personal and business relationships, and to feel good about themselves.

The point is that once you have a book that is selling well, you have a ready-made audience for the author's next book. Whether you are self-publishing or publishing the work of others, this will work for you as well as it does for me.

How to Attract Good Luck

The ad on page 179 did not pull well, so I decided to use a technique that has invariably worked for me. I reproduced the foreword I had written and used it along with the ad in my direct mail solicitations. That worked beautifully. (See pages 180 through 182.) Aren't we all interested in good luck and how to get it?

You may believe that the foreword is too long and

Wilshire Book Company

12015 Sherman Road, North Hollywood, California 91605

(818) 765-8579
FAX (818) 765-2922

THE SECRET
OF
BECOMING A MILLIONAIRE

Dear Mail Order Entrepreneur:

For years I have been fascinated by how some people become millionaires while others in the same business or profession never really reach the pinnacle of success. I wanted to know what millionaires think or do that set them apart from individuals who never quite seem to make it no matter how hard they try. I wondered if, perhaps, millionaires share a secret of success.

Over the years, I studied every success book I could find, and I interviewed over a hundred millionaires who had made it big in various fields of endeavor. What did I learn? That there are, indeed, specific attitudes and behaviors that helped make these people winners. Most were highly-motivated, positive thinkers who avidly read motivational and positive thinking books. And they had learned how to originate creative ideas that they diligently put into action. How did they come up with the ideas that made them millionaires? Their answers were always the same--by using a technique called brainstorming.

Brainstorming is a dependable, effective method of stimulating one's creative thinking. And creative ideas are a major component of success. Without them, achieving millionaire status is only an unlikely dream.

Let me share a few personal experiences with you. I spent a year as a songwriter. Although I had never before written lyrics or music, I came up with original song ideas and developed them into hits that made the charts. For one of those hits, I won a prestigious ASCAP award. I even sold an album to MGM Records for which I received a $15,000 advance. How did I do it?--by brainstorming.

I was in the Arabian horse business for many years. One of the horses I owned was a famous Arabian, double champion stallion named Asdar. I paid $20,000 for him and three years later was offered $175,000. Again, I have brainstorming to thank for my success. This time I used it to help me be creative in training, grooming, and developing Asdar, and in marketing his services.

My nephew, Fred Powers, bought a restaurant in downtown Los Angeles, now called Gorky's Cafe and Russian Brewery. He had never before been in the restaurant business, yet, in less than three years, he tripled both his profits and the physical size of his restaurant which now has additional seating, a bakery, and a micro-brewery. To what does Fred owe his astounding success? He attributes it to brainstorming.

A good friend of mine has a 23-year-old son, Robert Grad, who is bass-guitarist for "Kik Tracee," one of the thousands of rock bands trying to make it in Los Angeles. After five years of practicing nights and weekends, the band members began brainstorming sessions that in a few months produced an exciting, unique new sound for their music, a dynamic new image, and over a dozen original songs that incorporate the winning elements of current rock hits. Their efforts culminated in a major record contract with RCA. They are on their way to stardom thanks to brainstorming.

My success as a mail order entrepreneur and book publisher (I have sold millions of copies of such books as *Psycho-Cybernetics*, *The Magic of Thinking Big*, and *Think and Grow Rich*) is directly related to my use of brainstorming techniques. Where did I learn how to brainstorm?--from a book entitled *Brainstorming* by Charles Clark. I have used it as my business bible for the past 30 years. Fred Powers, "Kik Tracee," and an impressive list of well-known businesses and major corporations, such as General Motors, have done the same.

If you are serious about becoming a successful mail order entrepreneur or about achieving success in any business endeavor, you owe it to yourself to read *Brainstorming*. It can make the difference between success and failure.

Order your copy of *Brainstorming* now for only $9.00 postpaid. California residents send $9.57. It could be the best investment you've ever made in your future success. The book is also available on cassette tape for $55.00. California residents send $59.54. Or if you prefer to order by telephone, call (818) 765-8579 and use your Visa or MasterCard.

Feel free to call me when you finish reading the book and/or listening to the cassette tapes. I would be pleased to discuss specifically how you can use the brainstorming techniques you learned to join the ranks of millionaire entrepreneurs.

Good luck on your exciting new road to riches.

Sincerely,

Melvin Powers

Melvin Powers

P.S. Don't let this opportunity slip away. Brainstorming can make you a winner. It's helped others. Why not you?

Brainstorming

By Charles Clark (in book and audiocassette formats)

Reviewer: Bob Greene — Human Resources Development

While driving to the AQP Spring Conference in Baltimore I was accompanied by a friend of many years, Charles Clark. Well, Charles didn't actually ride with me, but cassette tapes of the reissued book, Brainstorming *did. The book was first published in 1958 and was a popular bestseller back then. Charles Clark was a research associate for Alex Osborn, the originator and popularizer of brainstorming.*

Joseph A. Anderson, a division general manager for General Motors, writes in the foreword of this book, "I can think of no finer way to enrich a person's life than to stimulate them to a greater use of their creative talents. The ability to be creative — in which the techniques of brainstorming play such an important part — is largely a state of mind. It is a state of mind that we all can cultivate." Charles Clark tells us how we can cultivate that creative state of mind.

He shows us how ideas make a difference and how ideas can change our lives. As he puts it, the one quality that turns the ordinary into the extraordinary is ideas. Before taking us into brainstorming we are given some interesting anecdotes on how our subconscious mind impacts creativity.

After years of working with his book and now having these audiocassettes to work with, I have this message for quality and participation practitioners — if you aren't coming up with literally hundreds of ideas in your brainstorming sessions you should get a copy of this book.

Even if you are getting hundreds of ideas, get the book anyway because it will improve your ideation ability. Ideas are still more powerful than any other force known to mankind.

Why do I say this? Because most of our knowledge of brainstorming comes from a quick run–through of the rules and then someone quickly asks for our ideas and lists them on flip chart paper. This is not the whole idea of brainstorming.

Charles does a great job discussing ways a team can narrow the problem statement from a steam shovel question to a spade question. He gives examples and hints on how to make the problem statement broad enough to elicit a large number of alternatives, which is what the team is looking for in a brainstorming session. He also shows us how steam shovel questions can be brainstormed to give the team a list of spade questions or opportunity statements which then can be further brainstormed for solid results.

In the quick training on brainstorming we learned that brainstorming is only for small groups. That's not written in stone. Charles believes limiting a brainstorming group to 10–15 is an unnecessary restriction. He tells us that successful brainstorming techniques can be used by one, two, three, or several hundred people. There is even a chapter on how to make your home life richer using brainstorming with your family.

There are a number of good tips in the book on what to do after the brainstorming session is over. Best among them are a number of good ideas on how to sell your boss on brainstorming. There are also some excellent examples of brainstorming sessions from different unrelated companies. This gives the first time or novice brainstormer as well as the experienced team member some useful examples to see how well the methodology works in the "real world."

The chapter on The Complete Brainstormer has the reader look at the world creatively: ways they can solve their problems creatively; how to start an idea bank, an idea museum and idea traps.

This book, Charles tells us, is not an end but the summing up of the art of brainstorming. It is a beginning and an inspiration to discover what we can do with our brain power to make our world a better one. He ends by offering us a challenge to try brainstorming — and find our how to think up ideas that make a difference in your life and our world.

Every team member should have a copy of the book, *Brainstorming*. It will make good teams better. The tapes can be used as gifts (or prizes) to excellent teams ◆

SALES CYBERNETICS
320 pages - $8.00 postpaid
by Brian Adams
Foreword by Melvin Powers

It isn't often that a publisher can honestly say that the book he is introducing is the best one on a particular topic that he has ever read. This is one of those rare occasions. *Sales Cybernetics* is the best book that I've read on the psychology of selling. And I've read a lot of them.

Sales Cybernetics draws its foundation from the "bible" of self-improvement — the classic *Psycho-Cybernetics* by Dr. Maxwell Maltz. Now the powerful principles of self-image psychology are focused by Brian Adams into the scientific techniques of motivational selling. It is my hope that the millions of persons who gained new ways of improving their personalities and erasing negative habit patterns from *Psycho-Cybernetics* will reap the same benefits from this new offering. In short, I hope it will open the way to new riches in your life, personally and financially.

Few things contribute more to an individual's well-being and sense of self-worth than his ability to stand on his own two feet, to achieve independence for himself and the ones he loves. Personal independence is difficult to attain without financial independence. Such independence can only come from your ability to make money. The more you make, the more your self-image will rise. I don't mean this to sound crass or mercenary, but it is undeniably true that one of the greatest joys in life is knowing that you are financially secure. I want you to be worth more by the time you finish reading this book. I want you to be able to make a lot more money; not just a fraction of what you earn at present, but *many times* more.

1

If you are content drawing an average salary for the rest of your life, accepting the fact that you will only have just enough to "get by," this book is not for you. But if you want your self-image *and* your bank balance to soar, study the time-proven, thoroughly researched methods of *Sales Cybernetics.*

There is only one area in the work force where you stand an excellent chance of making big money. That area is *business.* The great success stories of men like Carnegie, Rockefeller, Ford, and now Iacocca all spring from the field of business.

When I was starting in business, the giant corporations of America seemed overwhelming. There was no way I thought I could achieve the same greatness. But today, I have achieved some of that status for myself. I own a publishing company valued at millions of dollars.

How did I do this? By realizing two all-important things. First, I saw that success in business is primarily related to sales. All the rest is window dressing. The buildings, the staff, the logo, the letterhead, the image, and the advertising are there for only one reason — to sell a product.

Second, I saw that the art of sales is the art of interpersonal relationships. If people believe in you, they will believe in your product. I found that *Sales Cybernetics* explains how to sell both yourself and your product better than anything I've read. It so validated what I personally had learned, and so inspired me, that I was eager to share its secrets with the millions of persons who have bought my other books.

Written by an internationally acclaimed trainer in salesmanship at all levels of business, *Sales Cybernetics* exhaustively covers sound professional advice while putting sales techniques into a new, dynamic framework that works to produce electrifying results. It is action-oriented from the very beginning, a masterful synthesis of 15 proven formulas for getting people to say "yes" to you and your product. This "yes" can translate into untold dollars to anyone who puts the principles to work.

2

The first two formulas lay the groundwork by using computer programming principles to increase your sales productivity. Effective sales communication comes about through programming persuasive attitudes into your mental computer. An extremely important point is brought out in the discussion of the third formula; namely, that a poor concept of yourself is the biggest contributor to your failure. The chapter devoted to this formula shows you how to raise your self-image and match it with a better reality.

What you believe manifests itself in what you do. This is also true of your customer. If you wish to make a sale, it's important to know the belief system of your client — what motivates him to buy. Mr. Adams presents one of the best analyses of buying motives I have ever seen, and a powerful listing of the traits necessary to being a dynamic seller.

Further formulas tell you how to "get through" to people by making them like you; analyze the changing public tastes and preferences to make certain your product is always in demand; and prospect the market to find new avenues of business.

A truly extraordinary section is the one on how to handle objections through the psychology of harmonious human relationships. Blocks to your making a sale can be eliminated by using such techniques as *capitalizing*, making objections work in your favor, and *indirect denial*, a "yes-but" formula that lets you outflank your prospect's reasons for not buying by diverting his attention to why he *should* buy.

A book such as this is the result not only of many years of the author's experience, but lifetimes of experience of the most successful people in the business world. It is full of practical tips and secrets from leading authorities on how to increase sales. Following this advice can save you years in costly mistakes and help you start making big money. I believe that there is no substitute for experience in the field. This book is not meant to be such a substitute but, rather, a guide to potentiating your experience—making it maximally

3

effective and giving you time to make more sales and more money than you ever dreamed possible.

Sales Cybernetics contains aids to sales of every description, including many illuminating case histories. Read it carefully. Follow precisely the principles laid down and deliberately program yourself to sell until your subconscious mind takes over and makes you an "automatic" supersalesperson.

Brian Adams has written a book to show you how to *help yourself* to make more sales. You will have to exert the effort required to implement the principles. If you do, I can promise that the results will come back manyfold in proportion to the effort needed to produce them. These principles have helped thousands, and I have every confidence that they will now help you. Get ready. You are about to embark on the road to riches.

Melvin Powers
Publisher, Wilshire Book Company

*12015 Sherman Road
North Hollywood,
California 91605-3781*

4

175

Wilshire Book Company

12015 Sherman Road, North Hollywood, California 91605

(818) 765-8579
FAX (818) 765-2922

GROW RICH
WITH YOUR MILLION DOLLAR MIND

Wealth Strategies For Those Who Want to Achieve Financial Success
by Brian Adams

Today's successful entrepreneurs are amassing larger-than-life fortunes and achieving success where so many are failing because, whether they know it or not, they are tapping the extraordinary creative power of the human mind -- the same power that you can use to achieve and attain everything you've ever wanted.

YOU CAN CHANGE YOUR LIFE

The power that controls your destiny is part of the creative you and can be used to turn failure into success. *Grow Rich With Your Million Dollar Mind* reveals how to release your subconscious power to quickly change the direction of your life. You will discover how to tap your creative power to attract opportunity, resulting in prosperity.

PUT PROVEN WEALTH-BUILDING TECHNIQUES TO WORK FOR YOU

Thousands of men and women from all parts of the world have amassed wealth by using Brian Adam's techniques. He has taught these techniques to great numbers of people in the United States, Canada and Australia and has witnessed the amazing changes in lifestyle of those who have diligently applied them. These same techniques are now available to you in a remarkable step-by-step guide, *Grow Rich With Your Million Dollar Mind*. This is your opportunity to learn these proven wealth-building secrets and how to use them for immediate results.

STIR THE GENIUS WITHIN YOU

You will discover how to release the creative genius within you. It doesn't matter who you are, what you are, or where you are. You can be rich through the scientific use of your mental powers. This book shows you the way.

YOUR BLUEPRINT FOR FINANCIAL INDEPENDENCE

You'll learn how to become a success thinker, a shaper of your own destiny, a winner. You'll raise your self esteem and expand your desire and capacity to achieve financial independence. With your creative mind operating at peak efficiency, your dreams and aspirations can become a reality. If you want to achieve more, accumulate wealth, and enhance your lifestyle -- this book is for you. It's for every man and woman determined to start living a meaningful, rewarding, and outstandingly successful life.

Learn how to tap the power of your million dollar mind. Send today for your copy of *Grow Rich With Your Million Dollar Mind*.

$9.00 postpaid (CA residents $9.58)

GROW RICH
WITH YOUR MILLION DOLLAR MIND

Contents

THE MAGIC
OF THINKING
$UCCE$$

Your Personal Guide to Financial Independence
by Dr David J Schwartz, author of

—— THE ——
MAGIC OF
THINKING
BIG

Foreword by Melvin Powers

Even if you're a hard-nose skeptic, I can prove how you can
ATTRACT GOOD LUCK & LIFE'S RICHES

One of the most startling scientific breakthroughs of our time in which it is proven that Good Luck can actually be made to order...attracted to you like a magnet...exploited and pyramided to become one of the most powerful success-tools ever invented!

"Based upon a very sound and substantial philosophy of life"—**Dr. Norman Vincent Peale.**

"One of the most helpful and worthwhile books I know"—**Edwin A. Locke, Jr.,** noted industrialist and former U.S. Ambassador.

HERE'S THE SECRET

Yes, it's true! Good luck is NOT a gift...NOT just a matter of chance...NOT anything at all to do with superstition. *The Art of Attracting Good Luck is a skill, and can be learned just as you'd learn any other skill!*

This is now a proven scientific fact, and this great new authoritative book brings you—for the first time—*the simple but incredibly powerful techniques of attracting—recognizing—and exploiting good luck to the fullest!*

YOU CAN BE A WINNER

Here, for instance, you learn the one unconscious mistake that MAKES most people unlucky—and how it can be eliminated overnight. Dozens of actual cases are presented in which chronic bad luck has been changed to good luck *in a matter of hours!* Nothing was demanded but a simple change in point of view—*a magnetic short cut to good luck that turned these men and women into WALKING RESERVOIRS OF GOOD FORTUNE!*

Here are the exact step-by-step methods (so simple that they will astound you) that enable you to set up *luck-channels*, where good luck can come to you automatically. How to turn *strangers* into sources of good luck, from the very first moment you meet them! The *Seven Golden Actions* that attract good luck—and the *Three Fatal Mistakes* that drive it away! How to recognize *hidden luck* in situations where ordinary people see nothing but disaster!

GOOD FORTUNE CAN BE YOURS

How to make every stroke of good luck do *double duty*—actually pyramid your good luck—make each stroke of good fortune actually produce another! *How to turn "bad luck" into good luck by TWISTING its results to your benefit!* How to develop *luck antennas* that can give you the reputation of being the luckiest man in your town!

Let me repeat: This is NOT a matter of superstition. This is a new psychological breakthrough—discovered only recently—and released to you only through this great new book! *The very first stroke of good luck it brings to you is worth years of hard work!* If you choose to put good luck to work on your side—success, happiness and riches can be yours!

Try It Entirely At My Risk!

So you won't hesitate about trying this new approach to luckier living and **who knows how lucky you can get**, I make the following offer.

TRY THE INSTRUCTIONS FOR 27 DAYS. If you aren't in a lucky cycle and on your way to riches in just 27 days, simply return the book for every cent of your money back. Fair enough?

This can be your lucky day if you act today!

FOREWORD

Scientific literature concerning the element of luck in achieving success is extremely rare, yet luck's bright thread runs through the fabric of every victorious venture. Conversely, luck in its malignant aspect is often blamed by those who fail or meet with a seemingly inexplicable series of reverses.

We all know people who are admiringly (and perhaps a little grudgingly) said to be lucky in everything they undertake, and we are also familiar with those whose every effort is apparently plagued by bad luck. Inasmuch as many individuals in the latter group seem as highly motivated and as tirelessly active as those in the former, we have come to accept the idea that luck is an unpredictable attribute raising those who are blessed with it to the heights, and plunging those whom it eludes to the depths.

This myth has become a fixed idea, almost a conditioned response, for millions of Americans who thankfully accept the superstitious folklore that luck is beyond their control. It allows their egos to survive, and in many cases attracts pity, a face-saving emotion almost as attractive as success for some individuals. The fact is, though, you can make good luck a constant factor in any project you wish to bring to fruition if you will take positive steps to attract it. It need not be variable if you will acquaint yourself with the rules of the game, the chief of which is preparedness—the knowledge to shape it to your ends.

Barring natural catastrophes—floods, earthquakes, and other uncontrollable examples of misfortune for which we have not, as yet, found satisfactory solutions—you can attract luck with almost mathematical certainty. It is simply a matter of your personality. An adequate self-image, a capacity for hard work, a careful self-evaluation and certain other attributes can change a negative and failure-prone personality to a positive one that admits no defeat and recognizes that good luck is not an accident. To put it paradoxically, "good luck" is not a matter of luck in the sense most people use the word. In ordinary usage, "luck" has become interchangeable with "chance," but as Mr. Carr shows in this book there is a world of difference in the real meaning of the words.

The insecurity and timidity that keeps one from developing his highest potentialities for success is in large part of his own making. It is euphemistic to say—despite our bill of rights—that all people are created free and equal, but you can do a great deal to conquer genetic, social and environmental handicaps that cause inequalities if you will study the factor of luck. It is the one thing, barring random chance, that can make kings out of paupers and paupers out of kings. And happily, very few individuals enter the world a born loser. We are, with few exceptions, the captains of our fate, and luck is the helmsman. You can point for any direction on the compass, provided you give up your antiquated ideas about luck.

We go far to shape our own luck, not only in the economic side of our lives, but in the domestic side as well. Today, many Hollywood notables blame their successive failures in marriage on "bad luck," but it would be more accurate to say they knew too little about the true nature of their partners, and the odds are against two individuals staying in love when their first and last love is all too often likely to be themselves. In the language of psychiatrists, they do not seek to give or share their love, but find an "altar ego" to continually reassure them that their excessive self-love is not unreasonable. Their "misfortunes" are predictable, and bad luck seldom plays a role in their immature actions.

The information in this excellent book has been the subject of some scientific research by mathematicians, psychologists and even gamblers, but Mr. Carr has done the non-professional reader a great service by proving that luck can be bent to the average person's will if he keeps himself in constant readiness for its appearance.

It has been said with accuracy that one man's meat is another man's poison, and the same ancient truism applies to luck. The sudden breeze, for instance, that fills the sails of one racing contestant will not affect those who have embarked on a different tack, and they will be left becalmed and far astern. Very often, however, the sailor who catches the freshening breeze is the one who has made an exhaustive study of the wind patterns of the locality in which he is sailing.

In a recent international race a veteran skipper confounded even his own crew by pointing his craft on a tack which left his sails flapping aimlessly while the rest of the racers took advantage of a spanking breeze which urged them forward in what seemed to be a better direction for achieving their objective. Within two minutes, however, the wind veered around to fill the sails of the craft which spectators felt had been eliminated by the bad judgment of the skipper. Before he had to change to another tack, he had piled up a 20-minute time advantage the other contestants were unable to reduce.

Practically every spectator attributed this shift in the wind as another astounding manifestation of the good luck that always seemed to come to the aid of the winner. But was it luck? Not at all. It wasn't even an educated guess. The "lucky" skipper had carefully studied the regional weather charts for the preceding decade, and saw his only opportunity for victory. He actually had an inferior boat in the race, but he had ascertained that

he had a far better than even chance of benefiting from a wind that often veered about around 2:00 p.m. He pointed on his "hopeless" tack at that hour, and scarcely had time to break out his spinnaker before the wind bellied it out along with his main sails.

Briefly, he was in the right place at the right time, but he had created his own luck by a thorough evaluation of the situation, from recognizing the limitations of his craft to calculating the odds of a shift in wind. Mr. Carr's book provides many examples of this sort of "luck," and they provide ample evidence that luck is not the determining factor in the result although superficial reasoning may indicate this is the fact.

In speaking of odds one really is estimating the inherent risk of a certain event occurring. Any dice player can tell you that if the number you must throw to win is ten, you would do well to curtail the money you bet that you will succeed. This is because a ten can be rolled in only two ways (5-5 or 6-4) while seven, a winning number if it is your first throw, is a disaster thereafter because it can be made in three ways (5-2, 4-3 and 6-1), losing you both the dice and your money. It is said that all horse players die broke, but you can make an excellent start in this direction by betting you will roll a ten before you turn up a seven because of the higher inherent risk involved.

I intend no moral judgment for or against gambling here, but if you do gamble I suggest you learn the odds against you in any form of wagering. Many amateurs who lose money are quick to say the game they chose was rigged against them, but this is seldom the case. Professional gamblers follow the inexorable laws of probability, and if you play with them, sooner or later you will be out of pocket. Of course, hunches win at times, but this is the exception, not the rule. As a visitor (a non-gambling one) in Las Vegas, I can offer you a money-saving rule in poker known to many Americans but often disregarded. If you are tempted to try to fill an inside straight, forget it. The odds against this accomplishment are astronomical.

As Mr. Carr points out, professional gamblers know the inherent risk in every hand they are dealt, and do not have to cheat to win. They capitalize on your mistakes and lack of knowledge of the mathematical probabilities involved. They may lose a battle, but they will never lose the war. Incidentally, most of them feel the same contempt for the petty crooks of their profession as you do. They rely on absolutely proven percentages, and their egos would not allow them to stoop to trickery. You could do far worse, whether you gamble or not, to follow the rules of their profession in which random chance is reduced to a minimum. They, like the skipper mentioned earlier, make their own luck, except it is not really luck because the term has become misused by the increasing erosion of our language.

If you read this book carefully, I am sure your ideas about the uncertainty of luck will change. I freely confess mine did, for I, too, frequently used the term interchangeably with chance, a variable which cannot be wooed. They are only distant cousins, far removed in every aspect except ignorance.

In conclusion, in determining the odds (and this applies to any objective) you cannot lose in the long run if you "go by the book," if all other factors are equal.

There is a great deal of little known scientific advice in this book, and you can be on the high road to success if you follow it. It has been ranked with *Psycho-Cybernetics** a runaway best seller in 1965 that has enabled more than 900,000 persons to better cope with their problems, and in many cases has changed despair to hope. It has also permitted the attainment of goals many individuals had dismissed as impossible.

How To Attract Good Luck will give you another weapon to aim on to aim on success, and when you have completed this book you will recognize its power. You have a luck-potential which can carry you to any reasonable ambition. It is my sincere hope that you will do so. You are fortunate that this book furnishes you a blueprint you can follow to attain any realistic goal.

Few books on self-improvement furnish such explicit and workable details. Mr. Carr is to be congratulated. Most books in this field present only repetitious platitudes. I wish you the best of luck in whatever you wish to achieve, but if you succeed I am quite sure you will deserve what many will call your good luck.

In most cases a generous dose of pluck is needed to obtain the help of luck, but people tend to overlook the many qualities needed before one can become known as one of the lucky ones. Luck, in its real meaning, is the determining factor in most successful or unsuccessful ventures. It is a dynamic force that you can bend to your will for better or for worse. This may sound like a strange statement, but it is a sad fact that many people have a will to fail and spurn all approaches of Lady Luck. In evaluating your potential, make sure you are not one of them. *You can improve your luck*—and this book shows you how!

Melvin Powers
Publisher

*PSYCHO-CYBERNETICS by Maxwell Maltz, M.D. Published by Melvin Powers, 12015 Sherman Road, No. Hollywood, California 91605.

people won't read it, but they will if they are interested in the subject matter. I wrote a 16-page foreword for the book *Cybernetics Within Us* by Y. Saparina. (See page 75.) Why? Because at the time I published it, I had sold 2,000,000 copies of *Psycho-Cybernetics* and wanted these readers to perceive the new book as a follow-up. Besides using the foreword in my direct mail, I used it to interest bookstores in purchasing the book. I should be in the *Guiness Book of World Records* for writing the world's longest foreword—one that helped me to sell over 500,000 copies of *Cybernetics Within Us*.

Don't be afraid to do something unusual in merchandizing your book. Ad copy represents a creative challenge. I work at improving my advertising all the time, often taking the risk of doing something different. Although not every piece I write is a winner, I have developed a sense of what "feels right." When I was writing music, I knew which songs were going to make it even before I finished writing them. The flow felt right and I just "knew" I couldn't miss. The same thing happens when I write ad copy. When it's going right, I instinctively know it. In time, you will experience the same feeling.

Free Magazine Publicity
Magazines usually pay to excerpt material from books. I offer my books to magazines in exchange for mentioning the price of the book and the name and address of my company. I include a key or department number so I know where the orders originated. Over the years, this has proven to be a very successful technique. As examples, I'm including some recent excerpts that appeared in the magazine *Spare Time Money Making Opportunities*. (See pages 184 through 190.) Excerpts can pull better than ads. They are like book reviews. I have sold thousands of books this way at no expense. The magazine sometimes wants to run several excerpts from the same book over a period of months. When they do, it's like hitting the jackpot.

Coping with Alzheimer's
A Caregiver's Emotional Survival Guide
A book review for this book in the *Clinical Gerontologist* launched a successful campaign. I sold several hundred books directly to psychologists as a result of the review. They, in turn, recommended it to others. As a result of this and other reviews, I sold out the first edition of 5,000 copies. This is a very important book. I feel good about publishing it, and although the sales are nice, they are not my primary concern. I am much more interested in getting the book into the hands of those who can be helped by it. (See page 191.)

Slick 50
At one time, I was aggressively advertising an engine product called Slick 50. Besides running full-page newspaper and magazine ads, I produced a 30-minute infomercial that was aired nationally on cable TV.

One of the magazines I advertised in every month was *Western Horseman*. I asked for and received an editorial on the product that pulled thousands of dollars in orders. I asked for the editorial knowing the magazine would probably do it, because as a book publisher I routinely request and often get reviews for the books I advertise. Don't be bashful about doing the same thing.

My winning full-page ad for Slick 50 is on page 192. Note the lengthy advertising copy. The ad follows a logical sequence and has all the winning elements necessary to hook the reader. Interestingly, 50% of all orders were for two bottles. You can use the same layout and structure for a book.

I previously mentioned that the sale of your book is like your calling card. It's just the first step in a continuum of products and/or services to offer the buyer. In advertising terms, that's known as the bounce-back. All mail order success is based on it.

Knowing this, what else would you have done to sell more product to your Slick 50 customer? Think about it for a moment before I tell you what I did.

Knowing that the buyer was concerned about his car, I inserted in every order a two-sided circular selling Slick 50 Automatic Transmission Treatment and Slick 50 Gear Treatment for Manual Transmissions. Back came the orders, 50% of which were for two bottles.

I also included a circular for a book called *How to Save up to 50% or More on Gasoline and Car Expenses*. It produced one of the highest rates of return I have ever had. (See page 193.) One customer bought 8,000 copies to be used as a premium. That was an unexpected sale. As you can see, one product or book can be the basis of a thriving business. I want you to start thinking about where your book can take you.

In the next section, I tell you all about one of my authors, Charles Prosper, entrepreneur *par excellence*. He is a perfect example of someone who has become very successful by following the Melvin Powers success plan—the same plan that I'm teaching you in this book.

How to Attract Good Luck

by A. H. Z. Carr

This article has been excerpted, with permission, from the book of the same name, published by the Wilshire Book Co.© 1965 by A.H.Z. Carr. **See the end of the article for a special offer.**

GOOD LUCK, it has been remarked, usually strikes into the world of men (and women) with the suddenness of lightning.

And the question which confronts us is: How can we attract this beneficent lightning into our own lives?

Remembering that Benjamin Franklin caught nature's lightning when he sent a metal-laden kite soaring toward the clouds, we cannot do better than to borrow his principle:

In order to attract luck, we must first expose ourselves to it.

This phrase, "exposure to good luck," is much more than a metaphor. It describes realistically the way in which we find most of our luck—a way so obvious that we often overlook it.

Over many years, hundreds of people have related the luckiest experiences of their lives to the author of this book. Many of the stories were the stuff of everyday experience. But others told of strange, almost unbelievable twists and turns of fortune.

An analysis of the cases, however, showed that more than half of them had one thing in common: the lucky episode began for the person concerned at a time when he was exposed to others—*when someone else unexpectedly said something important to him.*

Often the thing said was, in itself, trivial. Only by touching precisely the right conditions could it possibly have produced the luminous spark of luck.

We see a simple illustration of the process in an example contributed by a Catskill farmer, who reported:

"A fellow from the city came up to our house last January and said his car was stuck in the snow. My son and I went out to give him a hand. We got to talking and he said he was manager of a new store in Kingston. Said he was going to open up a farm-equipment department. It just happened my son was looking for a job, and this was right down his line. Worked out fine. Started as a salesman and now he is managing the department."

Commonplace? Perhaps. But unmistakably lucky! An everyday remark, uttered by chance, meshes with a person's interests—and the result is an important new fulfillment in life.

(Continued on page 40)

Good Luck
(Continued from page 32)

portant new fulfillment in life.

We must, of course, recognize that the roots of such pieces of luck go far deeper than the incidents themselves. If the farmer and his son had not been the sort of men who are willing to go out in a snowstorm to help a stranger, the luck outside their door would have passed them by.

But here we need only concentrate on the first important steps in attracting luck: *to recognize that most of our good luck*—the beneficial effect of chance upon our lives—*comes to us through other people.*

Between ourselves and those who cross our path, chance spins an invisible thread of awareness: a "luck-line."

It is not too much to say that any new acquaintance to whom we throw out a luck-line represents a possible gain in our future luck and happiness.

Not that we can tell which luck-lines will carry a live current of luck. Of the men and women to whom we talk, perhaps not one in ten, or one in a hundred, will make the unexpected remark that significantly touches us. But sooner or later, someone does—and that one remark can transform a life.

To expose ourselves to luck, then, means in essence to come into healthy human relationships with more people.

The more luck-lines a person throws out, the more luck he is likely to find.

In enabling us to throw out luck-lines to strangers and old acquaintances alike, one quality beyond all others has almost magical power—the quality of zest.

To be zestful is to have within our minds a secret and inexhaustible fountain of youth. But zest, while it keeps the mind fresh and resilient, needs to be distinguished from the sheer exuberance and animal spirits of childhood.

In a very real sense, true zest is a short cut to luck, for it quickly brings us within range of a far greater number of favorable chances than could otherwise reach us. To follow this short cut, we need to take an explorer's interest in the world we live in.

The zestful person, while he may be occasionally angered or disquieted by events, loves life with all of its pains, absurdities, and follies. His curiosity on meeting new people is directed, not to learning what they may think of him or how much money they make or what they can do for him, but to the discovery of their personalities and their ways of life.

How a zestful person unconsciously brings luck into his life is suggested by an experience that befell the celebrated sports announcer of the 1920s, Graham McNamee. This was at a time when the radio industry had hardly been fledged,

and McNamee was a young, unknown, and unhired singer.

One day he received a call to jury duty at the Criminal Courts Building in New York City. During a recess he observed a sign being put up on a building across the street. It had four meaningless letters on it—nothing more.

Curious, he went over to the workmen who were hauling it into place, and learned that the sign comprised the call letters for a broadcasting station. He knew nothing about radio, but it occurred to him that just possibly they might have use for a singer.

A moment later he was in the small office, speaking with the manager. The answer was a shake of the head. Accepting the refusal good-naturedly, McNamee took the occasion to ask some sensible questions about the mechanics of the business. At this display of genuine interest, the manager looked up. He was going into the control room, he said. Would McNamee care to see what it looked like?

Zest, at this stage, had enabled McNamee to throw out a fresh luck-line to a stranger, and the current of good luck was not long in flowing. After their tour of the station, the manager remarked thoughtfully that McNamee had a good speaking voice. They might need another announcer. In 10 minutes, the test was made. In 10 more, McNamee was hired. And one of the notable careers of radio was launched.

In McNamee's case, we have a quick completion of the luck-cycle: the zestful man—the stranger—the favorable chance—the stroke of luck.

But often, zest shows its influence on luck much more subtly, and over a much longer period of time. Its immediate reward may be merely a piece of information or a new idea—a seed of luck that only later flowers into reality.

The preceding article was excerpted from the 191-page paperback book, *How to Attract Good Luck.* The book explains how generosity invites luck, how one's abilities have an effect on luck, and how intuition (not wishes) can bring better luck—to mention just a few of the topics covered.

"If you read this book carefully," says publisher Melvin Powers in the foreword, "I am sure your ideas about the uncertainty of luck will change.... There is a great deal of little-known scientific advice in this book, and you can be on the high road to success if you follow it. *How to Attract Good Luck* furnishes you a blueprint you can follow to attain any realistic goal."

For a copy of the book, send $8.50 to: Wilshire Book Co. • Dept. ST-491 • 12015 Sherman Road • North Hollywood, CA 91605.

Book Excerpt

The Magic of Thinking Success:
Your Personal Guide to Financial Independence

by David J. Schwartz, Ph.D.

**The Successful LIfe
Begins With a Dream**

Successful people do not look at their families, their jobs, their health or their net worth as they are.

They jump ahead of the masses and do one simple but profound thing: *They look at life as it can be, not as it is.*

They perceive life as it will be after application of their persistent, intelligent, "I-will-win" efforts.

Progress in any activity is made only when its potentiality is envisioned, not when it is restricted by reality.

Great architects, construction people and investors don't see the reality of big city slums and worn-out buildings. They see potential possibilities in converting slums into new communities where people can live, work and play.

Every business, school, institution and building is a dream someone made happen.

A great life always begins with a great dream.

Winning *vs* Losing

Whether we spend life winning or losing depends on how we use our mindsight—what we choose to "see" or to dream.

Each of us has the power to make this life a heaven or a hell, depending on how we choose to dream about it. Those who see life as a heaven are the winners; those who view life as a hell are the losers.

Some believe luck or chance determines their destiny. These people think that fortunes, success and the good life depend on the roll of the dice, on the spin of a wheel, or on a randomly selected number in a state lottery.

How foolish.

The statistical odds of winning a million dollars in a lottery are many millions to one. Lotteries appeal to people who believe wealth can be had with an investment of only a few dollars. The target market for lotteries, or any kind of gambling, are people who think they can acquire wealth by chance or luck.

Wishing *vs.* Dreaming

Wishing is different from dreaming. Wishing is passive and inactive. Wishing is an idle pasttime with no brains or effort behind it.

But dreaming—*when backed up with an action plan*—can produce re-

sults.

Jim "wishes" he would be promoted. But Jim never volunteers to do extra work, he avoids helping co-workers who need help, and he never submits an idea, asking, "Why don't we try this?"

Will Jim's wish for more money come true? Of course not.

Mary "wishes" she could become a partner in the accounting firm where she works. But Mary "doesn't have time" to take advanced accounting courses in school, nor does she volunteer to help out when 12- and 14-hour days are needed. And Mary does not go out of her way to pass on tax-saving ideas to clients.

Result: Mary's wish is wasted.

Tim and Susan "wish" they could have their own successful business. But Tim and Susan place weekend recreation first. Something—parties, trips, entertainment—always exhausts their time. And their wish remains only a wish.

You see, anyone can wish. *But a dreamer takes action on what he or she wants.*

Which category are *you* in?

You can divide the people you know into two categories: the winners and the losers.

Winners are active dreamers working to convert their dreams into positive, tangible accomplishments.

Losers are inactive faultfinders who believe the "system" is against them, and luck or fate determines what will happen.

Losers are cynical. "June got her promotion because of her 'extra curriculars' with the boss." "Fred got the big order because he bribed the buyer." "Pete and Sara have a new Mercedes, but they probably had to finance it for five years."

Winners are people of good will.
(Continued on page 32)

SPARE TIME

Thinking Success

(Continued from page 8)

"I'm glad for John. He worked hard and deserves his reward." "Betty's promotion proves there is reward when you give the job your best."

People who dream big think, "Regardless of how good or bad the economy is now, it will get better. It always does. I'm banking on a great future. Besides, I can't control what happens to the nation's economy, but I can control *my* economy."

Winners are generous. "The more I help other people make money, the more money I'll make in return."

Winners know "There is no free lunch," "Sacrifice means investing for my future and those I love" and "Hard work makes happy people."

How to Grow a Dream

It's easy to dismiss someone else's achievements with he or she "was lucky," "had superior athletic ability," "was born a genius," "got in on the ground floor" or, in some way, lucked into success.

But success, wealth and happiness do not come from luck. All accomplishments stem from dreams courageous people convert into reality. The great structures we work in, the agricultural enterprises that feed us, the industries that entertain us, the institutions that educate and inspire—evolved from the ideas and dreams of productive individuals.

When you see a successful business, school, entertainment product, or political institution, you are looking at an individual's dream grown into reality.

Think of life as a garden.

At one time, the great valleys of California were deserts. But some people with dreams saw the "useless" land as irrigated areas used to grow food people need. Acting on their dreams, many who bought this land became wealthy.

Successful people are individuals who convert their dreams into services and products other people desire.

Growing a dream into success is like growing a garden. Six steps are involved:

1. Select your dream seed (the basic idea). Decide what you want to do and estimate the profit potential of your dream.

2. Prepare your mind to accept the seed. Wash away memories (of failed endeavors) that hold you back, and develop a positive mental attitude toward your dream.

3. Plant your dream seed. Take action—now. Don't wait for perfect conditions or until "after the holidays" or "after I'm out of debt." Start *today.*

(Continued on page 42)

Thinking Success

(Continued from page 32)

4. Nourish your dream seed. Use imagination, encouragement and ideas to help it grow and make you prosper. Make a commitment. Set aside, say, three hours during the week and all day Saturday or Sunday. Give up TV, bowling or other time-wasters. Attend seminars. Go to school if necessary. Join trade associations. Talk to and affiliate with successful people. *Read.* Keep out the weeds and the bugs— negative comments from friends, relatives and co-workers and negative news about business failures and the economy. Divorce yourself from those who are bad-mouthing everything and want to see your dream die.

5. Focus your energy. Put "I will" to work. Don't say, "I'll try." Say, "I will." When someone says, "I'll try," translated it means, "I'll go through the motions, but I'm sure I'll fail." To achieve any dream—wealth, admiration, business, success—total dedication to the objective is required. "Zero in," "get your act together," and focus your "I will" energy.

6. Hire time to work for you. Invest your time and talent now for a higher reward later, instead of living only for today.

Remember, "The largest journey begins with one step." A giant fortune can begin with only a few dollars. A happy life is built one day at a time.

The above article has been excerpted from the first chapter of *The Magic of Thinking Success: Your Personal Guide to Financial Independence.* Other chapters include: Whistle While You Work (breaking the chains of career slavery) • The Magic of Thinking Big! • How to Build Confidence for Success • Give 100% for Success • Successful Techniques for Motivating People to Do What You Want • Enthusiasm Plus Action Equals Success • Appeal to Others' Self-Interest to Achieve Your Goal • 5 Sure Steps to Success Through Leadership • 5 Never-to-Be-Forgotten Keys to Success and Wealth.

For a copy of this inspiring 202-page book (for yourself or as a gift), send $8.50 ($7 + $1.50 shipping) to: Wilshire Books, Dept. ST-1090, 12015 Sherman Road, North Hollywood, CA 91605. Please mention that you read the excerpt in *Spare Time.*

How to Program Your Ambitions

Your future success can be brought forward at an accelerated rate via a specific plan of action which pinpoints your desires and outlines a sensible proposal for their fulfillment.

An action plan is very much like a road map. It's a guide to your destination offering the most *direct* route in the shortest possible time.

The reason many people do not participate in the riches of life is because they are vague about what they really want and have no definite plan to bring about success.

Vagueness in achievement-building is to be avoided at all costs. Until you formulate clearly in your mind *what* you want, *when* you want it, and *how* you plan to become successful, you will make little progress.

The degree of your progress is tied to the degree of your strategic planning. The more detailed information-base you can assemble, the easier and faster your ambitions will be realized.

• Establish that *what you seek* is available to you.

• Commit yourself to a workable plan of action.

• Then pursue your dreams until you experience them, rejoice in them and benefit from them.

This procedure reduces wasted energy...saves valuable time...and stimulates you to grasp opportunity and take on bigger and better challenges.

How to Eliminate Confusion and Frustration from Goal-Striving

Be precise when making a list of your aims. Write down exactly what it is you desire to be...what you want to have...and what you want to do in life. Think goals through. Assess them in your mind. Visualize them. This process reduces (or eliminates) confusion and frustration in goal-setting and goal-striving.

It is important to detail every aspect of a goal you desire to achieve. It is not enough to say, "I want to be rich." You must state an actual amount, *why* you want it, and *when* you want to receive it.

Wealth does not fall into your bank account just because you think it should or

This article is an edited excerpt from the new book, **Grow Rich With Your Million Dollar Mind:** *Wealth Strategies for Those Who Want to Achieve.* ©1991 by Brian Adams and used with permission of the publisher, Wilshire Book Co. *Please see the end of the article for a special offer to our readers.*

dream that it will. Wealth-attractors know that a detailed plan of action must be prepared, and then actively worked on.

Surround each goal with information. Call for facts, opinions and ideas, and intelligently use this information to arrive at workable strategies and tactics to accomplish your dreams.

How to Go About Expanding Your Bank Balance

Bank-balance builders will need to specify, in actual terms, the size of each deposit they wish to make...when each deposit is to be made...and the action that needs to be taken to accrue wealth.

Name the bank you desire to do business with. Meet the manager or other executive. Open an account. Fill out deposit slips with the amounts you intend to bank and forward-date them. Visualize your monthly statement showing the desired balance.

Accept that you are entitled to be financially independent and *will* be through goal-planning and positive goal-striving.

How to Prepare Your Goals List

Prepare a Goals Chart, listing your aims and objectives clearly and concisely. Place your personal goals list where it can be read every day. Don't file it away where it is out-of-sight and out-of-mind. Use it as a stimulus to keep you on track.

Audit your progress at regular intervals and revise your strategies and tactics if necessary. Be flexible in this regard. Don't stick to an unworkable strategy, if there is an easier and better way to achieve a particular project. Learn from your setbacks and use the information to enhance your next move.

The two rules to follow when preparing your goals list are these:

1. Identify aims and objectives in specific terms.

2. Prepare a detailed strategies and tactics achievement formula.

(Continued on page 34)

SPARE TIME

How to Set and Achieve Your Goals

(Continued from page 14)

Establish a Priority Goals List

Goal-striving can be a time-consuming and energy-draining exercise. Therefore, it is wise to give serious consideration as to whether a particular desire is really worth pursuing.

If you aren't totally committed to a project, chances are you will run out of steam when approaching the first hurdle. Establish that what you presently *think* you want is, in fact, what you actually *need* and want before embarking upon a campaign which could result in wasted effort.

The foundation of your goals success rests on the *commitment* you make to your detailed plan of action. You must be prepared to persevere when problems confront you; do not give in easily.

If you aren't prepared to see a project through to a positive conclusion because it isn't especially important, then don't waste valuable time and energy chasing it. Your weak commitment will destroy your incentive to win. This, in turn, targets your project for failure.

When your goals list is complete, analyze it. Give each goal a rating from 1 to 10. If goals with a low rating aren't of benefit to you, eliminate them. Spend your time wisely. Go after important, valuable and beneficial needs, wants and desires which will greatly add to your enjoyment, growth, well-being and financial independence.

Why You Should Establish an Objectives Time-Frame to Succeed

Many people wish to be financially well-off long before retirement. Others wish to gradually accumulate a nest egg they can rely on after retiring from business or the work force.

Decide *when* you need financial independence, and when you should start to taper-off your activities. Calculate the age you will be when you expect to complete your goals.

Allow plenty of time to *enjoy* the fruits of your labor. Having accumulated a sizeable bank balance, some people go to their final resting place without benefit or enjoyment of the riches they've earned. Winning the riches of life doesn't always come easy. Plan your empire-building activities judiciously. Leave plenty of time to bask in the glory of dreams realized.

3 Basic Time-Frames to Follow

Separate goals into three time-frames. Short-term desires are those that are easiest to accomplish—usually under one year.

Medium-term aims may require up to five years to complete.

Long-term goals are those of a complex variety which could take up to 10 years or more to achieve.

Give each goal a commencement and completion date. Within each time-frame, establish progress check-dates at intervals of three months (or less) to audit your goals direction.

It's best to remember that you do not have time to do everything. It's sensible to take on aspirations that can be won within a certain time-frame and have a worthwhile value. Some inconsequential aims may not be worth even a minimum expenditure of your time. Neither undertax or overtax your time, energy and capability.

How to Convert Your Dreams into Reality

Some people, at a very early age, know exactly what they want to do, want to have and want to become. They begin dreaming early. Sadly, some of these same people allow their dreams to remain dormant like unlit charcoal lying in a barbecue pit.

Dreams have the *potential* to manifest if ignited. Drifting through life— dreaming about wealth and success—is, for them, far easier than chasing opportunity, confronting challenges, and facing up to responsibility.

It's axiomatic that you need a dream to make a dream come true.

However, a dream doesn't come true until *action* is taken to *make* it come true.

Support your dreams with a burning desire to accomplish them. Get them up-and-running. Be enthusiastic, joyful, energetic and courageous as you set about attracting a triumphant life.

You have an awesome power, which you can use to *make* your dreams come true.

The realization of your dreams begins and ends with *you*. Make the first move. Take the first step on your journey into lavish living, ever-expanding personal growth, self-actualization, and financial independence.

The preceding article was excerpted from the inspiring, 192-page paperback, **Grow Rich With Your Million Dollar Mind**, by Brian Adams. Topics include: How to acquire a millionaire mentality to grow rich • How to command the power of your million dollar mind • How to increase your personal assets • How to rise from follower to leader • *and* How to duplicate the wealth-gathering assets of millionaires.

For your copy of this new book, send $8.50 ($7 + $1.50 shipping) to Wilshire Book Co. • Dept. ST-11 • 12015 Sherman Road • North Hollywood, CA 91605.

SPARE TIME

How to Make Money with Classified Ads
by Melvin Powers

One of the easiest and least expensive ways of starting your mail order business is to place classified ads for your product or service.

Go to the library and study the classified ads in a large variety of magazines. Also study the classifieds in the weekly tabloids found at supermarket checkout counters. (*Editor's Note:* And, of course, read the classifieds in this issue of *Spare Time.*) Notice whether the ads ask you for money or ask you to send for further information.

As a rule, you'll be asked to send for further information. The classified ad is designed to arouse your interest. The principal function is to solicit inquiries, and then convert these inquiries into sales by the use of direct mail. The direct mail will usually take the form of literature about the product or service, personal letters, testimonials, photographs or other illustrations, an order form, a return envelope, and a guarantee.

Classified ads for products in newspapers generally do not pay off. The reason for this is two-fold: **1.** The life expectancy of a newspaper is, at the most, one day. **2.** As a rule, the general public is not in the habit of looking for mail order merchandise in the newspaper's classified section.

The first few words of the classified ad are usually set in capital letters, and you should try to make these words count by giving them impact. Make them attention-grabbers. The advantage of classified ads is you have reader curiosity working in your favor.

You might want to change the classification under which your ad appears. Such headings as PERSONAL and MISCELLANEOUS are two classifications to consider if you are not getting anticipated results from the section where you would normally expect to find your ad.

When you get excellent results from your ads, run them on a "T.F." basis. T.F. means "til forbid." The publication will continue to run your ad until you cancel. It saves you time and paperwork.

Learn to write tight copy–succinct...to the point. A good practice is to pretend you're writing a telegram where every word is expensive. Eliminate the extraneous. By the end of the year, this can add up

to a savings of hundreds, maybe thousands, of dollars.

You can sell your product on either a one-step plan or a two-step plan.

One step means you want to sell right from the ad. The problem here is you are paying for each word of the ad, and that can become prohibitive in terms of anticipated orders.

I use the two-step approach in selling the books in my catalog. Many mail order companies prefer to sell a single item, and then include a catalog in the shipping carton for further orders. Experiment with both techniques.

Either way, keep a record of the responses—how many inquiries you receive from each ad, how many were converted into sales, the amount of the sales, and the amount of the average order. I also want to know what percentage of inquiries turned into orders.

When studying the classified sections, you'll learn to recognize certain repeat ads, indicating these ads are paying their way and making money. Mail order advertising must pay off or the ads will stop. A non-paying ad doesn't pull any better because of repetition.

Perhaps you have, on occasion, made the statement, "How could anyone make money selling that?" Be assured they are (if the ad is repeated frequently), and to satisfy your mind on that score, send away for the offer. When you do, note the date you send away for the product, and the date you receive it. See if you get follow-ups. Keep a record of it. It's all valuable information, and you'll begin to appreciate it as you progress in your own mail order operation.

Let's say you are making money with your classified ad. Run the ad again in the same magazine, and gradually expand your coverage until your ad is running in as many magazines as you can manage and still have them pay off. As a general rule, I would advise placing your ads in publications with long classified sections. They have a proven track record.

(*Continued on page 34*)

Make Money with Classified Ads
(*Continued from page 22*)

Assume you are making money with your classified ads. Try to get an even better response by adding a few descriptive words. Study other classified ads and see what key words they are using. Your opening words are very important.

Assume you are not making money on your ad; now what do you do? Try to improve the ad just as you would if the ad were making money. These are the variables to consider: you may be advertising in the wrong publication for your kind of offer; you have too much competition for the same product and sales are watered down; your price is either too high or too low; your follow-up literature doesn't tell the story effectively or succinctly; the offer isn't believable; your advertising copy doesn't generate excitement; you didn't answer the inquiry immediately, or your offer just doesn't initially make it.

Here's a mail order tip for you: Answer your inquiries the same day you receive them. As a mail order beginner, working at it in your spare time, you might be tempted to wait for the weekend to answer. You are busy and might be tired after a full day's work, but you can miss the boat by waiting. Your competition might be getting his literature to the same potential customer before you. By the time he receives your literature, he's already made his purchase. The rule is: Catch the prospect when he's interested and hot. Don't let him cool off.

In my office, literature to inquirers steming from my classified or display ads is the first mail to go out every day. The orders and correspondence can wait a day or two, but new business is what keeps things rolling. I've checked my competitors and some don't answer for several weeks. I'm sure you've had similar experiences with information you've sent for.

The following are questions and answers that most often come up in regard to running classified ads. The answers would also apply if you were running small display ads.

Question: In what magazines do I advertise?

Answer: In those patronized by other mail order companies. The magazines which consistently run their ads are the survivors of trial and error. The advertisers have tested the various magazines, and you can learn from their experience which are the best. That doesn't mean that you can't experiment. Hunch bets have been known to pay off. But customers, by habit,

(*Continued on page 36*)

Make Money with Classified Ads
(*Continued from page 34*)

have become programmed to look in certain publications for various classified offers, and you would be well advised to use them if you wanted the largest audience.

Question: How do you find out about advertising rates?

Answer: Many times, the publication will carry that information at the beginning of the classified section. It will read something like this: Classified rates based on 300,000 copies of each issue printed and mailed. $4.50 per word. Minimum of 15 words—$67.50. First four words in first line set in CAPS. Name, address and numbers must be included in word count. No charge for Zip Code. First-time advertisers: Please include response material (copy of offer) and your telephone number with your order. Classified section closes on 1st of month preceding date of issue. For example: April issue closes March 1.

[*Editor's Note:* When comparing ad rates of two or more magazines, compare the cost per thousand, based on each magazine's circulation. For example, let's say Magazine B has a classified ad rate of $4 per word and a circulation of 200,000. This means the cost per thousand (CPM) readers is $0.02 (2¢) per word. To get this figure, divide $4 by 200. By comparison, *Spare Time* has a classified rate of $4.50 per word, with a circulation of 300,000. This means the CPM is $0.015 (1½¢) per word ($4.50 divided by 300). So even though you're paying more per word, you're getting a better buy with *Spare Time* because you're paying less per reader. And please don't confuse circulation with "readership." Circulation means the actual number of copies that are printed and mailed. *Spare Time* and other ethical magazines will provide copies of postal receipts on request, showing the true circulation figures. "Readership" is usually an inflated figure derived by multiplying the number of copies printed by five or ten or more, supposedly because more than one person reads each copy. Pure fiction!]

Question: Should I charge for the catalog or literature that I send to people who answer my ad?

Answer: For your initial ads, and until such time as you are really making money in your mail order business, I'd strongly recommend you do not. The SASE (self-addressed stamped envelope), stamp, 25¢ or $1 you receive isn't going to spell the difference between failure and success. You want to receive as many requests as possible, and your job is to find out if you

(*Continued on next page*)

(*Continued from preceding page*)

have a viable product or service to sell. Put your energy into the important part of your program. Asking for money for your literature will definitely cut down on your responses. Good advertising literature (sent to those who answer your ad) can turn curiosity seekers into buyers. The very fact that they send for your literature indicates some interest. Take that interest seriously and do whatever you can to capitalize on it.

Question: I'm using the two-step approach to selling my product. What is the optimum sales literature package?

Answer: Your objective is to develop a mailing package that will generate maximum response at the lowest cost. It may not be necessary to mail the optimum literature in response to an inquiry because of the expense in printing, envelopes and postage. Keep testing to satisfy yourself you are getting the best return at minimum cost. As an example, you might not need 4/color circulars to sell your product. Black-and-white might suffice. And you might not need (expensive) coated stock for your mailing pieces.

Here's the literature that should comprise the classic response to an inquiry: a sales letter, advertising literature including illustrations of the product, testimonials, guarantee, credit card option, postage-paid reply envelope, and incentive for prompt response. But you *can* succeed with less.

The preceding was excerpted from the 352-page, 8½"x11" book, **How to Get Rich in Mail Order**, by Melvin Powers (a highly-successful publisher and marketer of how-to books and other products). Other topics in this well-illustrated book include: How to find a unique product or service to sell • How to make money with display ads • How to copycat successful mail order ads • How to start and run a profitable mail order special-interest book, record or video cassette business • Some of his successful—and not-so-successful—ads and circulars • How to sell your products to mail order companies, retail outlets, jobbers and fund-raisers • How to get free publicity • *and* How to make your advertising copy sizzle.

For a copy of this best-selling book, send $22 ($20 + $2 shipping) to: Wilshire Books • Dept. ST-292 • 12015 Sherman Rd. • North Hollywood, CA 91605.

FEBRUARY 1992

Clinical Gerontologist™

THE JOURNAL OF AGING AND MENTAL HEALTH

BOOK REVIEWS

COPING WITH ALZHEIMER'S, A CAREGIVER'S EMO-
TIONAL SURVIVAL GUIDE. *North Hollywood, California:
Melvin Powers Wilshire Book Company, 1987, 230 pp., $7.00.*

This is a practical as well as philosophical guide to the caregivers
of patients stricken with an incurable disease. The premise is the
psychotherapeutic view that individuals are capable of restructuring
their lives if they alter their perception of the critical events that
severely reduce their coping energies. The primary approaches to
such restructuring are the practical, the behavioral and the cognitive.

The book undertakes a difficult task to explain the logic of feeling in an effort to convince the reader that one can change emotions
if one chooses to do so. The caretakers' feeling about a given prob-
lematic situation is subject to rational explanation that should result
into an altered perception of the problem at hand. Respectively, the
perception of the problem can be modified to improve the coping
difficulty that may arise in care of a hopelessly ill patient.

The authors repeatedly impress upon the reader that Alzheimer's
is a disease, not a disgrace. Several concepts in care giving are
identified and elaborated: denial, anger, shame, self pity, guilt,
threat, depression, stress, acceptance. The concepts are logically
analyzed and practical guides on how to deal with them are provided by an abundance of examples presented effectively in the
form of a dialogue with various caregivers.

Perhaps the most poignant part is a message to the caregiver that
he/she needs to realize and accept the fact that the patient is no
longer the same person he/she used to be. In order that the caregiver
is able to continue to be useful to this new "stranger" he/she needs
to practice and accomplish emotional distancing from the one human being whom he/she may have loved a life long.

The book is presented in a compassionate as well as rational manner; it is well suited not only for the lay persons who are caregivers
but for professionals who give counseling in situations involving an
Alzheimer's.

192

Charles Prosper, Balloon Artist Extraordinaire

Charles Prosper took my self-publishing class at a community college in Los Angeles. He was unsure of his ability to sell his prospective book, *How to Become a Balloon Artist and Make Up to $100,000 a Year.* I told him that I'd be pleased to guide him every step of the way and that if he followed my instructions, he'd be teaching seminars full time, showing people how to make money, making a carload of money himself, and having a great time doing it. Charles was puzzled by my enthusiasm, but I knew I had successfully accomplished this feat myself in several areas of expertise—and I had helped others to do the same thing.

The student was ready and the teacher appeared. Charles was an adept student. His business has grown beyond anything he ever imagined possible. He teaches all over—even at colleges out of state. (See page 195 for a full-page ad for his book, page 196 for a newspaper announcement of his class, and page 197 for newspaper publicity.) Charles has been interviewed many times on local television as an entrepreneur who is making a valuable contribution to the community. He now has his own successful half-hour television show, which is being syndicated nationwide to hundreds of cable stations.

His phone rings continually with calls from viewers seeking information. As a result, he is selling tens-of-thousands of dollars worth of books, video tapes, balloons, and supplies. He even offers a newsletter giving the subscriber valuable tips on building a balloon business and other pertinent information, including announcements of forthcoming workshops. Charles and I still brainstorm on how to increase his business and what new directions to take. With all of his success, he's still listening and ready to explore new pathways.

Charles is high on selling his books, tapes, products, and seminars; high on his television show; high on helping other people to make money and be successful; and he's high on life.

Your goal is to follow my successful techniques. They will work perfectly if you work the plan. It's like having a gold mine at your disposal. The only question is, How much of it do you want to mine?

Marcia Grad, Ms. Charisma

Marcia Grad, senior editor at Wilshire Book Company, wrote a book called *Charisma—How To Get that Special Magic.* We conducted a flawless campaign. She was on numerous television and radio shows and did many newspaper interviews. Marcia had a fun, exciting time promoting her book. The book opened the door to becoming a paid, professional speaker for all types of business organizations, and it helped her to develop an impressive clientele from all walks of life, who wanted to develop charisma and improve their image. (See newspaper article on page 198.)

For eight years, she taught self-development classes (with the same title as her book) at community colleges and in high school adult education programs and private schools. Her classes were well-attended and well-received. Marcia had a wonderful time sharing her expertise, and she gained much pleasure and satisfaction from seeing the remarkable changes in people's lives when they put her program of self-development into practice.

The multi-level companies have purchased large quantities of her book. Interestingly, it has sold extremely well in Great Britain. The book has been translated into Portuguese and Norwegian. (See page 199.) See my foreword on page 200.

I did an extensive mail order campaign because I believed in the book and had seen firsthand the positive results of her program. Here's a challenge. On pages 201 through 203, I've included three ads for the book. These were sent out by the thousands in all of my outgoing mail over a period of years. Try to determine which ad pulled best and write to me, telling me why you chose the one you did. If you don't choose the right one, I'll give you the answer.

Note that we have an audio cassette program, consisting of one of Marcia's three-hour seminars. We have sold tens-of-thousands of dollars worth. Once again, many people order the tape program without the book. It always seems a bit strange to me as I invariably expect people to buy both.

Finding Your Niche and Audience

My niche is books that deal with psychological growth. This is my main area of sales. It's easy for me to get distribution because of the contacts throughout the world I've made over a long period of time. As you develop a network of contacts for your particular book or books, the same thing will happen to you.

According to a recently released *Consumer Research*

How To Become A Balloon Artist And Make Up To $100,000 A Year!

This is the book you've been waiting for!

HOW TO BECOME A BALLOON ARTIST & MAKE UP TO $100,000 A YEAR . . .

Written by **Charles Prosper**, of Balloons by Prosper, nationally acclaimed balloon artist who started from an apartment living room and moved on to build one of the most successful and lucrative balloon decoration businesses in the world. You read about him in *Balloons Today*, *Flowers &*, *Souvenir*, and *Entreprenuer* magazines, as well as in numerous nationwide periodicals and newspapers. Now for the first time, you have the ideas and designs of this world-class balloon artist at your fingertips.

HEAVILY ILLUSTRATED

with nearly **100 exciting photographs** and illustrations of proven money-making designs with step-by-step instructions that show you how to do them.

☐ **ITEM: BK-1 $35.00** (plus shipping).

WHAT PEOPLE HAVE TO SAY ABOUT THE BOOK . . .

"This book is a Godsend. A constant source of money-making ideas." —
Barbara Morrill, Balloon Images, Mechanicsburg, PA

"A long-awaited contribution of invaluable information." —
Joe Del Vecchio, Balloon Bouquets, Inc., Washington, D.C.

"The best written and illustrated document we have received to date. Well worth the price." —
Dave Finegold, Society's Pages Balloon Deliveries, Fort Worth, TX

"I enjoyed Mr. Prosper's book immensely. I found it extremely useful and valuable. All explanations and illustrations are done in a very professional and easy to understand way." —
Rosa Banchs, Balloons of Clowns, Mayaguez, Puerto Rico

"Charles Prosper is the King of the balloon business." —
Michel Baget, The Petal Pusher, Los Angeles, CA

20 INFORMATION-FILLED CHAPTERS:

1. The History of Balloon Decorating
2. Selecting Your Balloons, Tanks, and Accessories
3. The 7 Don'ts of Balloon Decorating
4. The Balloon Arrangement
5. The King-7
6. The Single Arch
7. The Weave
8. The Art of Color Combination
9. Techniques of the 5-Inch Balloon
10. Doing Floating Numers and Letters
11. Doing Balloon Flowers
12. Doing Balloon People
13. Techniques of Creative Thinking - How Ideas Come
14. Operating From Home vs. Operating From a Store-Front
15. Starting Your Photo Album
16. Specialize in Weddings
17. How to Get Decoration Contracts
18. Keeping a File and Keeping In Touch With Your Customers
19. How to Sell a Decoration to a Client
20. The Lucrative Future of the Balloon Decoration Profession

Balloon art is one of many classes offered at Glendale College.

Up, up and away!

If you can learn to make balloons and dolls at GCC, you can make money, too.

By Melinda Jensen
Glendale News-Press

Charles Prosper and his creations.

When Charles Prosper was laid off from his job as a substance abuse counselor more than 12 years ago, he joked with his colleagues that he was going to sell balloons on street corners to make money.

Twelve years later, selling balloons is no joke for Prosper — as a balloon artist who owns his own Los Angeles-based business, Prosper said he earned more than $100,000 last year by designing balloon sculptures for special events.

Prosper will be an instructor for one of more than 70 business-related courses offered this summer by Glendale Community College's Community Services Department.

The non-credit courses, which vary in cost, range from launching new careers to "Everything You Always Wanted to Know About Computers and Software."

According to Community Services spokesman Eric Carlton, a wide range of city residents normally sign up for the department's business classes.

"The computer classes are popular for businesspeople," Carlton said. "And some people take the classes just for fun."

See Class / **A4**

Author Grad spreads happiness through her book, lectures, life

NORTHRIDGE — Marcia Grad is going to be a June divorcee, her marriage of 23 years fractured beyond repair.

She doesn't have a boyfriend.

So, is she depressed because, on Valentine's Day, she is not likely to be receiving cards, flowers and candy from a beau? Heck no.

"As a single person, I really see Valentine's Day as an opportunity to celebrate my love of life," Grad said enthusiastically. "And with the person I've become through much effort, (I can) appreciate and enjoy the lovely relationship I have with my family and friends. I think it's wonderful to celebrate whatever love you have in your life."

If she sounds unusually upbeat, don't be surprised. The 43-year-old Northridge resident is somewhat of an expert on being happy, something she taught herself to be.

Grad has been passing this trait on to others for more than four years via seminars at community colleges, and is aiming for a broader audience as the author of "Charisma, How To Get That Special Magic."

Grad did not always have an abundance of personality, so she knows how painful it can be to think you are not popular, loved or liked, especially at times like Valentine's Day when the emphasis is on being with someone special.

"I think very often (people) do get depressed," she said of these types of occasions. "I hear that very often in class, and certainly on a day when everyone focuses on that."

Whether people are upbeat or downbeat depends on the attitude they take toward life in general, she said. Grad makes it clear in conversation, her seminars and her book that the attitude should always be positive.

Charisma is something a person can be born with and lose or not be born with and acquire, she points out in her book. The Greeks originally thought it was favor or divine gift, like the ability to heal the sick or peer into the future. German economist and sociologist Max Weber defined charisma as the quality of people with innovative personalities to amass followings.

Grad says there are three types of charisma: pseudo charisma, exemplified by actors, politicians, professional speakers, auctioneers and sales people; situational charisma, which develops when a person gets turned on by an event; and genuine, sustained charisma.

To develop or expand charisma, she endorses a five-step program of thinking and speaking non-critically for 30 minutes, making a list of your good qualities and past successes and reading it at least three times daily, doing one thing you've been embarrassed to do in the past, participating in a child-like activity and greeting at least one new person a day.

Once a person has acquired charisma, Grad suggests hanging onto it by developing a "treasured self-friendship," making a habit of being happy, projecting positive energy and surrounding yourself with positive people.

Grad has not always followed her own advice. She had polio as a child and was not as outgoing as some of her classmates. Her first child died, then she and her husband separated once before eventually agreeing to a divorce.

But she does not believe that once a person develops a personality it is set in concrete. "It's not true that people cannot change," she said. "The (charisma development) program really evolved out of testing and trying and getting feedback from people over a period of nine years."

Grad received a degree from California State University, Los Angeles, and taught school off and on over the years. Then she went to work promoting the authors of self-help books for Wilshire Publishing Co. in North Hollywood, the house that published her book.

"I wanted to be around that (atmosphere) and work with those types of authors," she said. "Very often they were not quite what I expected. There are some who are the very embodiment of what they are preaching and teaching, and of course there are some that are not."

About four years, ago Grad started conducting three-hour seminars each Saturday on different community college campuses. Three years ago, she decided to put her ideas in a book.

MARCIA GRAD

She began practicing what she preached out of a sense of self protection.

"The whole thing started out as a self-development program for myself," she said. "I wasn't happy. I was kind of disappointed with the way my life was going."

Her marriage has evaporated since then, but she is not about to dwell on any negative aspects of the situation.

"This (the divorce) is something I've thought about for several years," Grad said. "I know it was right for me. I have a full, beautiful life and I like to make every day as full and rich and beautiful as I can."

She might not have a date on Valentine's Day, but she'll be smiling.

THE SECRET OF CHARISMA

proach. She explores the many pieces of the charisma puzzle, each essential to its solution — thoughts, attitudes, perceptions, social behavior, sexuality, physical presentation, and personal habits. We are urged to probe, to question, and to change longtime beliefs about ourselves, about others, and about the world that may be blocking the flow of our natural charisma. Then we are ready to start cultivating habits basic to building "that special magic." You will gain some surprising insights into how you behave in your daily life, and will be given specific techniques which will help to make charismatic feelings, behaviors, and qualities become second nature to you. Once mastered, these techniques work automatically, on a subconscious level. They become an integral part of your total being.

This book reflects the personal flair of its author whose enthusiasm and conviction that people can and do change have served as an inspiration to her many students and clients. The same expert guidance and continuous encouragement that have been invaluable to them are now available to you, the reader.

I'm especially pleased to endorse Marcia's book because I've seen the amazing results of her techniques. They work. Her students are now out in the world realizing their dreams. And what happened to them could happen to you.

You needn't become reconciled to remaining as you are. You can be as you've always wished to be — self-assured, in control in social and business situations, energetic, and stimulating to others. You can be noticed, be liked, and be sought after. You can meet the people you want to meet and bring them into your life. You can become involved in relationships you previously thought were beyond you, and you will be able to reach for business opportunities never before within your grasp.

If you've previously believed that only a select few individuals are capable of powerful personal magnetism and that, unluckily, you are not one of them, you are about to embark upon a unique and eye-opening journey. It's exhilarating just to imagine what is waiting for you — achievement of all those goals and aspirations you once thought impossible. This is your chance for a new beginning, for a new and better you, for a new and better life. I wish you success in achieving your goals.

Melvin Powers
Publisher, Wilshire Book Company

CHARISMA
How to Develop the Power to Attract & Influence People

Can you really get "that special magic"? Emphatically, "Yes!" says Marcia Grad, author of *Charisma*. And she has impressive research, clinical evidence, years of experience, and common sense bolstering her claim. She is a well-known image consultant who conducts workshops and lectures at seminars on the subject of charisma and how to get it. Marcia has turned numerous shy, introverted, and unpopular adults into magnetic personalities. How this magic is accomplished is the main subject of this book.

Her message is dazzlingly clear: Charisma is neither an accident of genes, nor is it luck. The potential for charisma is our birthright — a natural gift given to each of us. But if this is the case, why do so few seem to possess it? Because most often it lies quietly dormant deep within the individual — held down, undeveloped, and hidden from view.

Until now, we have found it difficult to explain what charisma is and why some people seem to have it in abundance while the majority of others seem to have little or none at all. And we have been curious about how some people have charisma as children, then lose it, while others first get it later in life. And what about those who have it only at certain times — when at work, for example, but not in social situations, or, as is the case with many entertainers, when on stage but not when off?

This book first unravels these mysteries and then teaches us how to awaken the charismatic force within us, how to enhance its power, and how to sustain its magic. Development of our potential for charisma is a skill, we are told — a skill we can study, practice, master, and absorb as a part of ourselves. Anyone can do it and many individuals already have, simply by following Marcia Grad's highly effective, step-by-step Charisma Development Program.

What is this program that can help a shy person to become confident, an apathetic person to become enthusiastic, a dull person to become exciting, and everyone to have command of his or her own innate magnetism? The author uses a multidimensional ap-

How to Develop Charisma
The Art of Attracting and Influencing People

Have you ever wondered why some people seem to have incredibly attractive personalities? Why they draw others to themselves like a magnet? You know the kind of persons I mean—the natural spellbinders, the men or women whom everyone likes and who always make a lasting impression. In their personal lives everything seems to come their way; friends, lovers, followers, and mates all seem to gravitate towards them. Are these people born with the gift of charisma, the power to influence others, and the overwhelming good fortune to achieve their most cherished goals by the very force of their personalities? Or are these desirable qualities available to all of us if we are truly motivated to attain them?

I am firmly convinced that you can learn to be liked, to command attention, and to persuade others; in short, to have a magnetic personality. Some lucky individuals seem to have inherited their charismatic qualities but the truth of the matter is that most people, either consciously or otherwise, develop those captivating selves we so admire and wish to be like.

HOW DOES CHARISMA WORK?

Consider the following examples of how charisma operates in everyday life. There seems to be a certain undefinable, almost mystical, sense of power emanating from people who have developed magnetic personalities. Haven't you seen a guest on a TV talk show or a TV personality you'd never previously heard of, who kept your attention intensely focused on him or her the whole time he or she appeared on the show? You intuitively felt that that person possessed star qualities. To recognize this is the same job as that of the Hollywood talent scout whose aim is to discover future stars and superstars—the people with latent charismatic qualities. A superstar, in simple terms, is someone using charismatic power to its ultimate degree. We respond forcefully to that power, and a star is born.

Let's take a situation a little closer to home—the person you're introduced to for the first time. It could be a salesperson, a potential business associate, a potential friend or lover—a person in just about any capacity. The point is, you've only just met the person and yet—isn't it amazing?—you often have a good sense of whether you like or dislike him or her. I would like you to reflect for a moment on how utterly remarkable this phenomenon is, and how important it can be to understand its value. What made you form your instant opinion of this person you've just met? Can you really explain it? In most cases it probably had little or nothing to do with what he said or how he dressed. In the case of disliking the person, you were no doubt getting "negative vibrations." That's charisma working in reverse. If you liked the person, chances are you were responding to the subtle mystique of power that the likeable, attractive personality effortlessly exudes.

Do you see why this phenomenon of first impressions is a matter of such importance? How you are perceived, both consciously and subliminally, by the people with whom you come in contact is one of the keys to success in your personal and business life.

LEARN THE SECRETS OF CHARISMA

The secrets of developing a charismatic personality that will generate others' interest in you are yours now to learn and implement. Encompassing all areas of human development, various psychological techniques, intuition and powers of observation, the study of personal magnetism can result in great benefits to those of you who seek to change your life in dramatic ways by becoming "captivating." You'll learn from history's charismatic individuals as well as from living examples. Those seemingly magical qualities of power, the tremendous influence exerted upon others, will become clear to you as you begin to apply this wonderful knowledge to your own life.

MOTIVATION PLUS ACTION EQUALS SUCCESS

Does all this sound too good to be true? When I say you can actually learn to develop a charismatic personality do your shake your head in disbelief? Perhaps you've already tried to be popular, charismatic or to develop certain desirable character traits and failed to see any results. With the instruction available to you you'll have a far greater opportunity to succeed.

ACHIEVE PERSONAL HAPPINESS

Once you've felt the magnificence of your own charisma, your entire life will be changed. The warm glow of the sunshine of life will permeate everything you do. Its subtle influence will be felt in all your interpersonal relationships. When you develop yourself to the fullest, much becomes possible; your secret dreams can come true. This exciting prospect derives from the fact that no one can predict what your potential really is.

It's in constant flux as you develop your vibrant charismatic powers. Once you set your mind to it, every goal becomes attainable. The thrust of a positive mental attitude, combined with the powerful propellant of charisma, makes for sheer explosive dynamism. To be lyrical, it can take you to the moon; you can touch the furthest stars.

MAKE THE MOST OF YOURSELF

This is the era of self-development. So why not live life to the fullest? Why not be a leader and decide right now to give yourself the chance to discover your potential. Successful people set goals for personal happiness and then go after them in a logical way. They are dreamers first, then they are doers. You can discard the limitations that you may have consciously or unconsciously imposed on yourself. You can succeed beyond your wildest expectations. You'll have an expert to guide you, and, with the proper motivation, your success is guaranteed.

EXPERT SHOWS YOU THE WAY

To help you achieve your charismatic powers to the utmost, we offer a book on developing a winning personality and three hours of cassette tapes on which you will hear Ms. Marcia Grad, an acknowledged expert in personality development, instruct you in the fundamentals, techniques and procedures of developing your charismatic powers and potential. These tapes were recorded live at one of Ms. Grad's stimulating college seminars. I urge you to take advantage of this remarkable opportunity to expand your horizons. It's exhilarating just to imagine what this material could mean to you. Provided you're motivated for success, we can positively help you. So get set for a thrilling adventure!

100% MONEY-BACK GUARANTEE

The book and tapes must dramatically and substantially help you to achieve your most secret and treasured aspirations or we'll refund your money. With your new charismatic vitality and awakened zest for life, you'll find that even goals that have always been elusive will become a reality. Yes, dare to dream because your dreams are about to come true!

Send today for the book, *Charisma—How to Get "That Special Magic,"* $8.00 postpaid and for *Marcia Grad's Three-Hour Charisma Seminar on Cassette Tapes,* $25.00 postpaid.

Mail to: Melvin Powers
12015 Sherman Road
No. Hollywood, California 91605

How To Be Charismatic
&
Brighten Up Your Love Life

Dear Friend:

Have you been waiting for a special person to come into your life and fill it with love?

Why let love elude you when you can embrace it? Slip away when you can save it? Grow old when you can rejuvenate it?

Whether you are entering a new relationship or continuing in one you have had for years, you can now have one that is deeper, warmer, fuller, and richer than any you have ever experienced.

You can create love

Have you noticed the elusive way love can go from being overwhelmingly intense to being nearly non-existent—then returning as if it had a mind of its own?

You can sustain love

Do you wish your lukewarm love relationship were piping hot?

You can enhance love

You needn't succumb helplessly to love's whims. How we think and feel and what we say and do produces, maintains, augments or diminishes our other emotions. And so it is with love. The power to create, sustain, and enhance loving feelings is yours to use as you wish.

Have the love you've only dreamed of

There are people who enjoy the full, satisfying love relationship you'd like to have. Perhaps you've seen these happy couples—together for years, and still very much in love. They didn't find the perfect partner and live happily ever after just by luck. Rather, they learned how to get the most from their relationship and then did the things that made and kept it special. You can have their kind of love simply by learning what to do and putting that knowledge into practice.

You can have it all

Don't be one to compromise your dreams of love because you think a comfortable relationship must be dull. Don't expect or accept a disappointing facsimile of the relationship you really want. You need not give up excitement for security, freshness for reliability, or exhilaration for stability. You can have realistic, sensible, mature love that is enlivening and stimulating—even thrilling!

Why go through life enduring colorless love relationships? Why settle for black-and-white love when you can have Technicolor? Don't let another day pass without doing something to spice up your bland love life.

Your love fantasy can come true!

What else can you do after you've read all the books on love and on improving relationships you can find, used the information both directly and indirectly, but still do not experience the results you yearn to see? You know the right things to do and have tried them. You've learned communication skills and how to fight fairly. You've practiced your intimacy training and experimented with the newest sexual techniques. Still, your relationship doesn't sparkle.

Don't despair. You needn't resign yourself to an occasional weak spark of excitement. You can learn to enhance your partner's level of response and love as well as your own. You can boost his or her feelings of love. You can learn how to have your partner fall in love with you and feel the excitement and "cloud nine" feeling of being in love once again.

It sounds like an impossible dream. But that's exactly what we promise because our course of action is based on extensive, sound, and practical information and not just theory.

You can be charismatic, have the love relationship you really want, and be the person you have always secretly wanted to be.

You can put your charismatic power to work by employing special techniques based on widely accepted, sound psychological principles. Learn how from an exciting new, three-hour cassette tape, MARCIA GRAD'S CHARISMA-DEVELOPMENT SEMINAR. It is filled with suggestions on how to be charismatic. You'll learn to put the sizzle back into a relationship that's gone flat and how to turn the tide should love be ebbing. Listen to this exceedingly helpful cassette that can really change your life. Start immediately to feel your newly-found power and start to brighten up your love life.

You are what you choose to become tomorrow.

Send for the cassette tape, MARCIA GRAD'S CHARISMA-DEVELOPMENT SEMINAR, $25.00 postpaid. It's sold on a 100% money-back guarantee basis. It must accomplish what we promise or we'll refund your money.

---------------- **Order Form** ----------------

Please send me one MARCIA GRAD'S CHARISMA-DEVELOPMENT SEMINAR cassette tape $25.00 postpaid.

Enclosed is my check ( ) money order ( ) for $25.00.

Name _____

Address _____
(Please print)

City _____

State _____

Zip _____

Please send your order to:

Melvin Powers
12015 Sherman Road
North Hollywood, California 91605

CHARISMA
How to Develop the Power to Attract & Influence People

Charismatic people are not necessarily more interesting, talented, intelligent, or attractive than you, but it is true they are noticed, liked, and sought after. Material, professional, and personal success seem to gravitate toward them. What exactly do they possess that sets them apart from ordinary people? What is their secret of attracting and influencing people?

These questions really used to baffle me. For years I hung around the sidelines of life wondering what popular people had that I lacked. I thought certain people were born to be special, that they were innately endowed with a mysterious "something" that brought them more than their fair share of the good things in life —appreciation, love, and recognition. How I wished I could be like them. I longed to be the center of attention —poised, confident, and exciting to others. Instead, I became reconciled to my life style. I worked at a routine job, had little excitement in my personal life, and was puzzled as to why I was missing the sizzle.

Then something happened that changed my life dramatically. It was a rainy Saturday night and I was spending the evening curled up on the couch with nothing but my television set for company. My mind kept wandering as I aimlessly switched from one channel to another.

Suddenly I was captivated by a talk show devoted to personality development in which outgoing, stimulating men and women were being interviewed. Their personal stories had a common theme. They had once been shy, had had few friends, had not been getting what they were seeking out of life, and had seen no way to relieve their frustration until they became highly motivated to do something about it.

They told fascinating stories of how dramatic personality changes had gradually come about as a result of reading self-improvement books or by taking personality-development seminars. They developed one common characteristic. Each radiated what I would call —charisma.

To me that was dynamite —their stories were what I needed to hear. From that night on I was excited about the possibility that I, too, could develop charisma and a new life style.

I became determined to learn how I could become charismatic. I talked to people I considered to have charismatic traits. I asked how they had developed charisma, how it felt to have it, and how they used it. I spoke to psychologists and psychiatrists. I researched various psychological and image-enhancement techniques I thought might help me develop charisma.

Finally, my quest paid off. I discovered the secret of creating charisma—the magic I had yearned to possess all my life. From then on, every day became exciting, stimulating, and enjoyable because I became relaxed and self-confident.

Family and long-time friends were amazed by the new me. They said I had defied the axiom that people don't change. I no longer had to be concerned about how and where to meet new people. I met them everywhere and felt at ease. My relationships and life itself began to change for the better. Business and professional opportunities abounded as never before.

As a book publicist, I shared the secret with numerous authors as we worked together to build their charismatic qualities. Interestingly, their personal lives began to flourish. What had worked for me obviously worked for others.

Eager to share the secret with more people, I began teaching college classes throughout the Los Angeles area on how to develop charisma. I now conduct workshops and lecture to all types of groups. From this evolved a step-by-step charisma-development program that has been used successfully with people from all walks of life, including entertainers, politicians, and business and professional people.

You can do exactly as my authors, students, clients, and I have done. You can be as you've always wished to be—self-assured, in control in social and business situations, and energetic and stimulating to others. You can be popular, noticed, liked, and sought after.

It's exhilarating just to imagine what is waiting for you. Get set for a thrilling adventure—the development of the charismatic personality within you.

The cassette tapes I offer were recorded live at one of my three-hour college seminars on charisma. They outline the highly effective charisma-development program that has helped so many people change how they feel about themselves and how others feel about them. Also offered is a supplementary book on how to develop a winning personality.

Take that first step toward your secret dream by ordering now.

Study on Book Purchasing: A Study Inquiring into the Nature of Book-Buying Habits of the American Public, sponsored by the American Booksellers Association and the Association of American Publishers, bookstores accounted for only 53 percent of adult book sales while non-bookstores represented 47 percent.

Although my books in all categories are sold in regular bookstores, I always look for additional outlets that would logically be interested in them. You should do the same. For example, I publish five books in the field of calligraphy. I developed a list of art supply stores that were waiting for my new books. I had standing orders. I publish a list of 60 horse books, most of which are sold through the 20,000 riding goods stores in the United States. I have a list of bridge books, many of which are sold through bridge clubs. My line of metaphysical and occult books are sold primarily through the 2,000 metaphysical bookstores throughout the country. You can rent a list of these bookstores.

I've developed a clientele of multi-level companies who have purchased millions of books from me. Because they have been pleased with the books, they wait eagerly for the next one I recommend. It's great to sell to multi-level companies because they consistently reorder in large quantities, which creates a ripple effect. People who read these books recommend them to friends and associates, who request the books from bookstores and libraries. The result is that we receive additional orders. Along with every order, I send a Wilshire Book Company wholesale catalog and sample covers of other books. This is a must.

I write a letter thanking new accounts for their order and pointing out books in the same genre that they might want to consider. I often send a complimentary copy of one of our books that they might be particularly interested in. A week later, my sales manager, Frieda Freedman, calls to introduce herself and tells them we are looking forward to being of service to them. She chit chats about business in general and always gets a warm reception.

Many of our accounts now fax their orders, rather than sending them by mail. I still get excited every time I hear the fax machine. Somehow the fax orders are more fun than those that come in the mail. Before we got the fax machine, I wondered if we would ever use it, but from the first day, we've used it daily to communicate all over the world.

Once you have an author whose work sells well, you have a ready made audience for successive books. Be sure to keep a mailing list of all your customers.

For ten years, I taught a class called "How to Start and Operate a Successful Mail Order Business." When I started teaching "How to Self-Publish Your Book and Have the Fun and Excitement of Being a Bestselling Author," hundreds of students from my mail order class enrolled. They had seen my name in the school programs and wanted to take another class from me. I felt good about that.

You can be a successful self-publisher if you have a valid idea for a book and you research the best methods to sell it. That means finding your audience. The next section will show you exactly how I continue to fuel sales for the book *The Knight in Rusty Armor* by Robert Fisher. I'm on the way to selling millions of copies of it. I also have exciting plans for an animated television program based on the book.

Getting the Midas Touch
My emphasis in this book, especially in the next section, is to help you learn to write good advertising copy. There are dozens of books at the library on the subject. Read them. You'll get valuable information that will translate into riches. Save and study newspaper and magazine ads and all the direct mail you receive. They don't necessarily have to pertain to books. You can adapt the layout, style, and flow to your book.

If you are interested in selling your book and audio cassette program on television, start taping two-minute direct response commercials and half-hour infomercials. These cost a lot of money to produce, and you can follow the exact format to produce a winning show for yourself.

You can also use the commercials to help you write your own ad copy. The material in a successful television show will produce a winning ad in print or direct mail. The reverse is also true. Good ad copy works on television. I based a television show on a successful one-page ad for Slick 50.

Four-Page Circulars
I love to write four-page circulars for books, products, and services. As I said previously, they usually pull better than two-pagers, and four-page circulars are standard in professional copywriting. However, as a mail order consultant, I've had clients object to the four-page format. Their usual cry is, Who's going to read it? My response is that if we can whet the recipient's

appetite with a provocative headline and strong beginning paragraphs, we stand a good chance of having him read the entire circular.

I use four-page circulars for a variety of purposes in addition to selling books. I recently joined a multi-level health product company. Since I don't have the time to sell or offer the business opportunity on a one-to-one basis, I include a four-page circular in all of my outgoing mail for these purposes. (I'm not limiting the mailing to opportunity seekers.) The results are exceptional. Study the ad and adopt the style for your book. (See pages 206 through 209.) Note the typeface, headline, subheads, copy, and order form.

I teach those who join my multi-level team how to sell the products using mail order techniques, and I immediately get them on a reading program of self-development books and audio cassettes. Once a person develops a positive mind-set, he can sell anything. It's reflected in ad copy. It sweetens the message. It's like sweetening music with violins and guitar licks. I never met a successful entrepreneur who didn't exude confidence. Even people who don't start out with self-confidence develop it one step at a time as they become increasingly successful.

My Creative Challenge
One of the great joys of my life has been helping people to become financially independent and enjoy the life they have always wanted for themselves and their families.

Ralph Waldo Emerson said, "It's one of the most beautiful compensations of life that no man can sincerely try to help another without helping himself." I found that to be true for me when I taught classes in personal development and entrepreneurship.

Who wouldn't feel good receiving a letter like the one on page 210? It validates what I've been doing as a teacher of entrepreneurs and as a motivational author and publisher.

I enroll people in various business opportunities, primarily using mail order techniques. The four-page circular espousing the business opportunity on pages 206 through 209 is very successful. I tried following the same formula for Hotel Express—and it worked well. Study pages 211 through 214 for Hotel Express and pages 215 through 218 for an effective technique to sell a book. An entirely different format that's also working is on pages 219 and 220. Here's an assignment I'd like

you to complete. It will stimulate your creative juices. Can you tell my why the formats are working so well? Can you pinpoint the sizzle and winning elements? Send me your analysis. I would enjoy hearing from you.

Before I recommend a particular business opportunity, I check carefully to make sure that it really is a money maker, and I do as much as possible to ensure the success of those who get involved at my suggestion.

Keith Monen, CEO of Hotel Express requested that I join his program and make his business opportunity available to my students and readers of my books. I have had extensive talks with Keith about my involvement. He agreed to help me provide my students and readers with tested, money-making techniques and to guide them every step of the way with a blueprint for success. We want everyone to be a winner, and we're committed to helping them become one.

In this update of my book, I've been concentrating on helping you to recognize and emulate successful advertising—not only for books, but for products as well. Your success as a self-publisher depends upon your learning to write advertising copy that sells the sizzle, rather than the steak. That's what infomercials do. Make it one of your creative challenges to become an expert in advertising and marketing. It's fun and pays great dividends.

I have subscriptions to numerous business magazines. One that I read every week from cover to cover is *AdWeek's Marketing Week*. It has nothing to do with books. It's strictly about creative marketing of products and services, and it helps to keep my creativity flowing.

I published 50 books before I published *Psycho-Cybernetics* by Dr. Maxwell Maltz. When the book hit the New York Times Bestseller List, colleagues, family, and friends congratulated me on my success. Success didn't come overnight, however, it was a gradual learning process, filled with trial and error. My goal, as that of every publisher, was to get a book on the bestseller list. One success leads to others. Keeping your short and long range goals in proper perspective will lead to success. At one time, I had three books on the bestseller list. It was the pinnacle of my success in publishing.

Announcing...

THE PERFECT ANSWER TO A MAIL ORDER ENTREPRENEUR'S DREAM

Dear Friend,

I'm going to give you some great news that will make it possible for you to make more money, sooner than you ever thought possible. But first I want to tell you about the three elements that can guarantee your success.

Three Golden Keys to Getting Rich

How do so many people who start with nothing become financially successful?
1. They look for a good opportunity until they find one.
2. They get someone to teach them what to do.
3. They do it.

You can do what they have done. But just any opportunity won't do...and neither will just any teacher. Your chances of success are best if the opportunity is unique, powerful, easy, and proven to work...and if the teacher is experienced, successful, and dedicated to helping you make it.

Here's your chance to seize the right opportunity and the right teacher. It couldn't be any easier...I've already found them both for you! All you have to do is take advantage of the opportunity being offered to you.

Your Own Personal Multi-Millionaire Teacher
Will Stand at Your Side and Help Make You Wealthy

Have you ever had a business opportunity that included the help of a multi-millionaire who said, "I'm going to teach you how to become financially successful and guide you every step of the way"? I never did, but that's exactly what I am saying to you.

I can positively make your dream of financial success come true. How am I so sure? Because I've taught many people who once only dreamed of riches how to get their bank accounts to overflow with cash, checks, and money orders—just as mine has every single day for over 40 years.

Many of the people I guided along the road to riches have achieved success beyond their wildest fantasies—yet, they are just "ordinary people" who started out with dreams probably much like yours. Today these "ordinary people" are living their dream lives. And so can you.

My Expertise Will Ensure Your Success

As president of Wilshire Book Company, I have published such multi-million best sellers as *Psycho-Cybernetics* by Maxwell Maltz, M.D. (over 3,500,000 copies sold); *The Magic of Thinking Big* by David Schwartz, Ph.D. (1,000,000 sold); *A New Guide to Rational Living* by Drs. Albert Ellis and Robert Harper (1,000,000 sold); and *Think and Grow Rich* by Napoleon Hill (7,000,000 sold).

For over 30 years I have been a mail order consultant to major businesses, corporations, and advertising agencies. I have seen them flourish as a result of using my techniques. As a college instructor, I taught my techniques to thousands of students. Many who started with little or no money now have enviable annual incomes. As an author, I shared my techniques in my book *How to Get Rich in Mail Order*—read by over 350,000 people. Readers flooded my office with success stories. As a consultant to top cable television marketing companies, I applied my techniques to direct response TV. My clients made fortunes. As a direct response TV product marketer, I used my techniques to offer a course of instruction on an infomercial called "Mail Order Millionaire."

I'm Going to Let You in on a Little Secret

I have recently discovered what I believe to be the most outstanding entrepreneurial opportunity I have encountered in over 40 years of helping people to get into their own businesses.

How do I know it's great? Because I've been blessed with an instinct for winners. I get a certain indescribable rush when a product has enormous potential. I don't get this feeling often, but every time I have experienced it and acted on it, big, big money rolled in.

I had not experienced that surge of energy for some time—that unique, internal signal that says, "This is it!" Then I heard something that immediately brought on the familiar rush that has been largely responsible for making me a multi-millionaire. I knew positively that this product program would be remarkably successful, and already it appears that, once again, my instinct was right. I am so excited by my results so far and by the accolades pouring in from other people involved in the program that I can hardly wait to let you in on my incredible discovery.

The Discovery That Can Change Your Life

On March 13, 1991, a revolutionary formula called Cellular Nutrition burst forth from the research laboratory of a well-established and well-regarded company with an outstanding 12-year track record in the health, nutrition, and weight loss industries.

Cellular Nutrition is a unique nutritional formulation that blends centuries of Eastern and Western scientific knowledge and expertise in herbs and special botanical factors, vitamins, minerals, and micronutrients. It provides the body with all the tools it needs to heal itself and to establish and maintain optimal health. It's the most significant nutritional science breakthrough in the history of the nutrition industry.

People who want to lose weight can use the Cellular Nutrition weight control program to take off 10-29 pounds a month safely, without hunger or fatigue. The program takes off inches quickly, noticeably improves cellulite, and tightens and tones the skin. It blocks fat and cholesterol and controls and normalizes the appetite. It is unique in its health-building capabilities and unparalleled in its success rate. Individuals using it rave about how easy it is to stay on, how fabulous they feel, and how different it is from the other diet regimens they've tried. It's 100% natural, 100% safe, and 100% guaranteed.

This discovery has created a rare, ground floor opportunity to earn incredible amounts of money by bringing a message of hope, health, and well-being to a virtually unlimited marketplace that wants and needs exactly what you have to offer.

The Cellular Nutrition Weight Control Program
Has Every Element Necessary To Qualify It as a Virtual Gold Mine

The Market for It Is Gigantic

The continuous public desire to lose weight creates an endless supply of new customers. The weight reduction industry has more than doubled in the last ten years, and experts predict it will almost double again in the next five—generating more than $60 billion per year. The company that discovered Cellular Nutrition has sold 3½ billion dollars worth of diet products over the past 12 years. Their new and improved weight control program with Cellular Nutrition places them in a better position than ever to fill the increasing demand for diet products.

It Practically Sells Itself

Millions of people have lost weight using this program, while building up their bodies and feeling better than they ever felt in their entire lives. Customers become avid users of these consumable products. Even when they have achieved their weight loss goal, many remain on the basic nutritional products. That means on-going repeat business.

And . . . You Can Have Other People Sell It for You

Fortunately, the company that manufactures the weight control program is a multi-level marketing company. In addition to making a profit from selling product yourself, you can make money on other people's sales, if you wish.

You Can Change Your Life Forever

I'm looking for a limited number of special individuals to join the Melvin Powers Wealth-Building Team. You don't need a "higher" education, sales or marketing experience, or a background in health or nutrition. But you do need a strong desire to make more money and to take control of your life. You also need a good attitude, a willingness to take direction, and a dedication to consistency and perseverance. If you meet these qualifications, I have a personal interest in helping you achieve your financial goals.

You'll Be Given a Tested, Proven Blueprint to Follow

I will give you a plan that works. A plan that is responsible for selling a million dollars worth of products a day. A plan that has already made many people very wealthy. If you do what they did, you'll get what they got—and more—because I've committed my 40 years of successful mail order marketing experience to multiplying the earning potential of the plan. There is no question that the plan works. The only question is whether or not you will work the plan.

I'll give you step-by-step instructions on how to get your weight control mail order business up and running and bringing in money immediately. Included will be the exact copy used in classified ads and for flyers that are pulling in hundreds of thousands of dollars in sales every day. I'll tell you how your telephone answering machine can make money for you and how you can get dozens of people to help you build your business—without paying them a cent.

Once your business gets going, I'll show you how to build it as big as you want it to be—quickly, easily, and inexpensively. You can work as many or as few hours as you wish.

My marketing expertise will be at your service—not at my usual $250-an-hour consultation fee—but for free! Your success will be my success. My staff and I will be available to you at all times to help you every step of the way. We'll hold your hand and guide you as you build your business from the first day on.

Your Earning Potential Will Soar

Your value in the marketplace can be measured by what you are being paid. Corporation presidents are paid hundreds of thousands or millions of dollars a year. Why? Because they are valuable!

I'll teach you skills that will make you valuable. That means you will earn what valuable people earn. You will bring valuable products to the marketplace, and you'll have the option of offering other people a business opportunity that will make them valuable, too.

My Unusual Promise When You Join the Melvin Powers Wealth-Building Team

I'm inviting you to take a wealth-building journey with me that will change your life in ways you may never have imagined. Becoming more valuable, making a lot of money, and feeling satisfied with what you have chosen to do in life are only part of what the Melvin Powers Wealth-Building Team offers.

As a member, you will get a sense of belonging to a new family that is supportive of your goals and self-development. A family you will find psychologically uplifting. A family with an ongoing personal growth program that will empower you to reach both your personal and financial goals. The continuing personal contact with me and my staff will help you become a winner in this endeavor...and in life.

Don't Neglect Your Future
Cash In on the Midas Touch of Melvin Powers

If you want your life to change, you must change. If you want things to be different, you must do something different. Be good to yourself—allow yourself to be a winner. You have the chance to associate with winners and to be part of a winning team.

Where will you be one year from today if you don't join me? Two years from today? Think about it. Take 100% responsibility for where you are and where you want to go. Take charge of your future. Remember, you are not only what you are today, but also what you choose to become tomorrow.

You Are Teetering on the Precipice of Success

If wishing could make money for you, you'd already be rich. <u>Now is the time to do what it takes to get what you want. Create a miracle in your life by taking the steps that have made fortunes for others.</u>

Get ready to take loads of cash, checks, and money orders to the bank. And get ready to lead the life you've dreamed of, but never really thought possible to attain.

This Is the Moment of Truth

You now have access to a winning game plan and an experienced coach. Are you going to pick up the ball and run with it, or lose the game by default? <u>Don't be left out.</u> Don't lose one precious minute. Get the tools you need to get started right away. Order your tax deductible Herbalife Distributor Kit and Supplemental Training Package now.

I look forward to welcoming you to the Melvin Powers Wealth-Building Team.

Sincerely,

Melvin Powers

Melvin Powers

P.S. The secret of success in life is to be ready for opportunity when it comes. I hope you're ready . . . because it doesn't get any better than this!

———————————————— **ORDER FORM** ————————————————— ✂

YES, I want to join the Melvin Powers Wealth-Building Team.

Please send me the following:

☐   Herbalife Distributor Kit (☐ English ☐ Spanish)
     Career manual, video, and audio cassettes
     Includes the Cellular Nutrition Health Program—
               An $86.54 retail value—FREE $_____59.00_____

☐   Distributor Kit Weight Control Supplement Program
     For distributors who want to lose weight.
     Price includes distributor discount. $_____59.85_____

MAYBE, but I'm still not sure. I need more information.

☐   Please send me the Herbalife video tape and some brochures.
     (☐ English ☐ Spanish) $10.00 applicable to distributor kit. $_____10.00_____

                                              TOTAL $_____

Enclosed is my ☐ cashier's check ☐ money order ☐ personal check payable to Melvin Powers for $_____. (Allow four weeks for checks to clear.)

Charge to my ☐ Visa ☐ MasterCard (Or call 818 765-8529 to charge by phone.)

Number_____ Expiration date_____

Name_____
                          PLEASE PRINT

Address_____
                          STREET ADDRESS FOR UPS

City_____ State_____ Zip_____

Mail to: Melvin Powers, 12015 Sherman Road, North Hollywood, California 91605

HOTEL EXPRESS

April 22, 1991

Mr. Melvin Powers
Wilshire Book Company
12015 Sherman Road
North Hollywood, CA 91605

Dear Mr. Powers:

Mail Order Millionaire has changed my life! It is without doubt one of the most helpful mail order programs I have ever purchased--and I've purchased most of those available.

Several years ago, I answered an advertisement for your course. Using your innovative, proven techniques and formulas, I sold over 1,000,000 Hotel Express discount travel club memberships through the mail in only two years. My sales last month alone were $200,000.

Your mail order instruction has helped me to succeed beyond my wildest dreams. I am now CEO of my own multi-million dollar a year mail order company. I have earned enough money to purchase a 5,000 square foot, ocean view home with an indoor swimming pool and five automobiles--and I've taken some fabulous vacations around the world.

I am living proof that the "good life" you suggest as a possibility for mail order entrepreneurs is more than just advertising hype--it's an attainable goal. Thank you for sharing the knowledge that made it all possible for me.

Sincerely,

Keith C. Monen
CEO Hotel Express

P.S. Mr. Powers, you have done for the mail order industry what John Wayne did for westerns. You are truly my star in Hollywood!

3052 El Cajon Blvd. • San Diego, CA 92104 •

HERE'S HOW YOU CAN MAKE MORE MONEY
FASTER AND EASIER
THAN YOU EVER THOUGHT POSSIBLE!

Dear Friend:

Congratulations on your decision to become a mail order entrepreneur. You have taken an important step toward a lifetime of financial independence for you and your family.

Now for some great news that can get you into business and making money in one day! I am going to share with you one of the most exciting business opportunities I've encountered in over 40 years in mail order.

YOU CAN CASH IN ON
THE HOTTEST-SELLING PRODUCT OF THE CENTURY

The growing leisure market has created a travel boom that's making a lot of people very wealthy. Keith Monen is one of them, and he will do everything possible to make sure that you become one of them, too. Who is Keith Monen and what does he get from your success? Read on.

A SUCCESS STORY THAT CAN CHANGE YOUR LIFE

A few years ago, Keith Monen had a small travel agency and a big dream. He wanted his business to grow—a lot. He envisioned himself CEO of a large international travel club, and then he set about to make his dream come true. Keith researched what people want most when they travel, and he became determined to find a way to give it to them.

Keith immediately went to work convincing hotels, motels, resorts, condominiums, major airlines, cruise ships, and auto rental agencies that they could increase their business by filling their empty rooms or seats with his future travel club members. What would entice Keith's club members to fill those empty rooms and seats? A discount of up to 50% would undoubtedly do it! Hundreds of lodging establishments and carriers in over 400 cities clamored to sign up.

Next, using my mail order cassette program as a guide, Keith sold over 1-million memberships worldwide in his new travel club in only two years. He, personally, sold thousands of memberships. And he helped other people to sell tens of thousands more. His vision and diligence culminated in the launching of what is today, America's largest discount travel service— Hotel Express.

SO WHERE DO YOU COME IN?

Every day, more and more hotels, motels, resorts, and cruise lines sign up to become part of the Hotel Express family. That means more and more travelers will have the opportunity to take fabulous discount vacations—or travel for business—in more and more places for less and less money. Keith's new dream is to double or triple the number of Hotel Express members in the next year—and to realize this dream, he needs you.

HOTEL EXPRESS DISTRIBUTORS MAKE BIG MONEY

Keith is not the only person who's made a lot of money from the Hotel Express program. Many of his distributors have, too. Now you have the opportunity to duplicate their success, using the same ads, brochures, and techniques that have been working for them. Here's what two of Keith's distributors have to say about Hotel Express:

Sales Over $25,000 Weekly

"Thank you for such a great opportunity. In my first six months, I sold over 25,000 Hotel Express memberships. Our sales are over $25,000 a week."

James R. Rautio, Hawaii

Anticipate Making $1,000,000+ This Year

"I just wanted to thank you for the Hotel Express program. We are enjoying fantastic results through our various marketing endeavors, and we anticipate sales this year to exceed $1,000,000."

Richard Burnham, Maryland

THE TRAVEL BUSINESS IS BOOMING
HERE'S HOW TO GET YOUR SHARE OF IT!

Selling the Hotel Express program is easy and the return is immediate. The membership fee is so low that it pays for itself the first time it's used. That makes sales nearly effortless.

You can pyramid your membership fee earnings plus accumulate yearly renewal fees for all the people you sign up—just like your insurance agent does with his initial policy sales and renewals. One sale can generate hundreds...even thousands of dollars.

I have arranged with Keith Monen to make available to my associates three special Hotel Express plans. Choose the one you prefer and test the program on a trial basis to see how easily it works.

THREE FAST, EASY WAYS TO GET STARTED

Hotel Express Kit—Plan #1   Least Expensive

Take-one/direct mail 4-color brochures with space for you to stamp your name and address	$12.00 per hundred
Purchase memberships now or later—any amount	$24.95 each

Hotel Express Kit—Plan #2   Retail Plus

1000 Take-one/direct mail 4-color brochures	$120.00
10 Take-one stands	$ 20.00
TOTAL	$140.00
California residents	$151.55
Purchase memberships now or later—any amount	$24.95 each

Hotel Express Kit—Plan #3   Highest Profit

1000 Take-one/direct mail 4-color brochures	$120.00
10 Take-one stands	$ 20.00
20 Hotel Express memberships at $4.95 each	$ 99.00
FREE BONUS GIFT from Melvin Powers	
5 Hotel Express memberships—A $249.75 value	N/C
Official Hotel Express Distributor Instruction Manual	$ 34.95
Hotel Express 30-Minute TV Informercial	$ 19.95
TOTAL	$293.90
California residents	$318.14

GREAT TECHNIQUES FOR MAKING MONEY WITH HOTEL EXPRESS

You can sell Hotel Express memberships using a variety of mail order and person-to-person techniques. Here are a few ideas that have proven successful for other Hotel Express distributors:

Place take-one brochures under windshield wipers of parked cars at hotels and motels (especially those near airports), swap meets, shopping centers, race tracks—anywhere large numbers of cars are parked. Brochures can also be distributed to homes. You may want to have students do the foot work for you. Also include Hotel Express brochures in all of your mail order solicitations for other products.

Run classified or small display ads. They can really get the ball rolling! (Examples of ads that have made it are in the Hotel Express Instruction Manual.)

Sell memberships to businesses and organizations as premiums and fund raisers. (The instruction manual explains how.)

Distribute take-one stands (with 50 brochures in each) to a variety of businesses, such as luggage shops, airport shops, video stores, cleaners, coffee shops, beauty shops, hobby shops, grocery stores, fast food restaurants, instant printers, and car washes. Offer the store owner a free membership or percentage on each sale to allow you to place your stand and brochures next to his cash register. (Be sure to assign each outlet its own ID number on the circular so you can identify the source when the order comes in.)

Need help? Hotel Express maintains a toll free 800 number for your convenience.

WHEN YOUR ORDERS COME IN...

If you choose plan #1 or 2, you will send your Hotel Express membership orders to me as you receive them, with your payment of $24.95 for each. Your profit will be $25.00 per membership on the retail selling price of $49.95. I'll send you the membership packages, which you will forward to your customers. (You can at any time elect to increase your profit to $45.00 per membership, plus get an extra 5 memberships free, by ordering Hotel Express Kit—Plan #3. Unlimited additional memberships are $4.95.)

With all three plans you make $45.00 for each annual renewal. Those renewal fees can add up to big bucks, and what a thrill to be receiving them every month!

All brochures, supplies, manuals, books, postage, office supplies, telephone calls, and labor expenses pertaining to the Hotel Express business are tax deductible. In essence, Uncle Sam is helping you financially to get started.

ARE YOU READY FOR SUCCESS?

Keith Monen became a millionaire following my advice. He's offering you the same opportunity by sharing his proven advertising literature, ads, and concepts. You don't have to invent the wheel. His success plan will work for you as it has for him and for many others.

If you are motivated for success...here it is, being offered to you on a silver platter. Keith Monen and I have both made millions of dollars in business, and we are willing to be of assistance to those who seek success in this business. What could be better? If you are serious about wanting to supplement your income and achieve your financial goals—this opportunity is for you. It has created wealth for others. It can create wealth for you.

I invite you to join our winning team and to watch as your commission and renewal checks transform your desire for financial security and wealth into a reality beyond your wildest dreams.

Success starts with a winning attitude. It begins in one's mind. Think like a winner and you'll be one. Remember, you are not only what you are today, but also what you choose to become tomorrow.

Good luck! I look forward to welcoming you into our family of millionaire entrepreneurs. It can happen to you!

Sincerely,

Melvin Powers

Melvin Powers

P.S.   If wishing could make money for you, you'd already be rich. This is the moment of truth. Will you do what it takes to get what you want? Make the decision that could change your entire life. Order your Hotel Express Kit now.

—————————————— **ORDER FORM** ——————————————

YES, I want to join the Melvin Powers family of millionaire entrepreneurs!

Enclosed is my ☐ cashier's check ☐ money order ☐ personal check payable to Melvin Powers for $_____. (Allow three weeks for personal checks to clear.)

Charge to my ☐ Visa ☐ Mastercard (Or call (818) 765-8579 to charge by phone.)

Number _____ Expiration date _____

Please send me the following:

☐ Hotel Express Kit—Plan #1
  _____ 4-Color brochures at $12.00 per hundred $_____
  _____ Memberships—$24.95 each $_____

☐ Hotel Express Kit—Plan #2 $140.00 $_____
  California residents $151.55 $_____
  _____ Memberships—$24.95 each $_____

☐ Hotel Express Kit—Plan #3 $293.90 $_____
  California residents $318.14 $_____
  _____ Additional memberships—$4.95 each $_____

☐ Hotel Express 30-minute TV Infomercial $19.95 $_____

TOTAL $_____

BE SURE TO ORDER A MEMBERSHIP FOR YOURSELF!

Name _____
          (PLEASE PRINT)
Address _____
          (STREET ADDRESS FOR UPS DELIVERY)
City _____ State _____ Zip _____

Mail to: Melvin Powers, 12015 Sherman Road, North Hollywood, California 91605

HOW I MADE $1,000,000 IN MAIL ORDER

by E. JOSEPH COSSMAN

"The ideas in this book—and the practical, step-by-step system explained in detail—will give anyone who has an atom of persistence and creative imagination the key to financial independence in his own mail order business."

Elliott A. Meyer
President
NATIONAL DYNAMICS CORP.

"Joe Cossman is one of the two authentic geniuses I have met in 14 years in the business. Not only does he have an almost prophetic sense for picking winning items, even when they have been discarded as "worthless" by so-called experts, but he has an uncanny knack of squeezing the absolute maximum dollar profit out of each of them. If this book can convey even a fraction of 1% of his money-making ability, it will be worth 100 times its cost."

Eugene M. Schwartz
President
EXECUTIVE RESEARCH INSTITUTE, INC.

30-DAY TRIAL PERIOD

As Joe Cossman says: *"I know of no business in the world that requires such a small investment to start, and yet holds promise of such tremendous financial gains as mail order!"*

ABOUT THE AUTHOR

Mention E. Joseph Cossman in mail order circles, and you get a reaction similar to mentioning Thomas Alva Edison to an electrical engineer. Joe Cossman is rightfully regarded as one of the "miracle men" of the field because of his amazing record of resounding successes.

Starting in his spare time, with a kitchen table for an "office", Joe Cossman built an international mail order empire that has made him a millionaire. He learned the ins and outs of mail order the hard way . . . and you can benefit from his experience in these pages. Here Cossman tells you how he thought up—tested—marketed—produced—and sold his products. His mail order methods pulled an astounding total of *ten million sales* on six products alone—and that was just the beginning!

Today, Joe Cossman knows that anybody can find, advertise and sell a product in mail order. Capital—experience—even the product—all these are of secondary importance. The important thing is to know how to go about it—and that you will discover, spelled out in fascinating detail, in this book. Let this book be *your* first step towards starting your own company—in your spare time. In just a few years you may be wealthier than you ever dreamed!

The greatest business opportunities in the world today are in the booming field of mail order. That's the only field in which you can start small—with a minimum capital outlay—and build a fast-growing, money-making business right at home.

Joe Cossman, one of the biggest men in mail order, can tell you exactly how to do it. He shows you how to think up a product (with an infallible system responsible for his own list of successful products)—how to test the product—how to get lists—how to produce and sell the product . . . and all of this can be done right in your own home!

Here are the professional "trade secrets" of a mail order giant who started small and wound up with one of the biggest mail order companies in America. He shows you how to do it, every step of the way. From getting the original idea, and writing the advertising, to how and which lists to rent, and where to get them. He details for you other successful mail order campaigns—shows you how other men started small and founded a booming business.

Cossman gives you valuable tips and pointers on how to produce your product inexpensively—and how you can branch out and develop new products.

If you've ever wanted to start your own business—here's the chance for you. Opportunities are actually unlimited in mail order. Nobodies have become millionaires overnight—and if anybody can show you how, Joe Cossman can.

If you follow his tested, fool-proof rules, you can start with little cash—working even in your spare time—and build a good income out of mail order. In a short time you can achieve the financial independence you have dreamed of . . . and be your own boss, with your own business. This is your chance to break out of the old rut and hit the big time years earlier than you ever dreamed you would!

Contents

HOW I MADE $1,000,000 IN MAIL ORDER

tells how

YOU CAN MAKE $1,000,000 IN MAIL ORDER

WHAT THIS BOOK CAN DO FOR YOU

If you want to break out of the old rut—start your own business with little or no capital necessary—and be your own boss at last—mail order is the greatest business opportunity that can do this for you.

In this book I will show you how to think up a mail order product and test it inexpensively (following the advertising system given in these pages), produce it and market it. Starting with just one product, and working in your spare time or just on weekends, it is actually possible to bring in several thousand dollars a day in cash-in-advance orders!

That is what makes mail order the fastest-growing and most profit-making business in the world today. This book will show you how to go about it, from getting the first idea right on through to establishing an entire line of successful merchandise for your own mail order business.

I started out using the kitchen table as a desk and working on weekends while keeping my regular nine-to-five job. Today I own the office building in which I work and sit behind a $1,000 desk.

In these pages you'll discover how with common sense, imagination, and perseverance you can do the same, building a business with unlimited potential and adventure.

E. JOSEPH COSSMAN

"I have been in the mail order business for 40 years and during this time I have read every book I could find on the subject. In my opinion, Joe Cossman's book, **How I Made $1,000,000 In Mail Order,** is one of the best mail order books ever written."

Melvin Powers

Wilshire Book Company

12015 Sherman Road, North Hollywood, California 91605

(818) 765-8579
FAX (818) 765-2922

YOU CAN MAKE MONEY
WITH
900 & 976 TELEPHONE LINES

Dear Friend:

How would you like the telephone company to send you a check for thousands of dollars every month, month in and month out, year after year? <u>You can start that money rolling in by becoming your own boss</u> in a part-time business you've probably read about in magazines and seen on television. <u>It's the amazing new 900 and 976 "pay-per-call" telephone business.</u>

Here's the Secret

Working with major telephone companies, 900-lines bring in literally thousands of calls per month and make their owners up to $1.40 or more with every call. That means <u>large second incomes for many 900-line owners and whopping primary incomes for others.</u> And its all done with <u>no direct selling and no special skills</u>--just by offering information that's in demand by the public!

Anyone Can Do It

Nine-hundred phone lines have become one of the most promising ways for entrepreneurs to cash in on the exploding field of telecommunications. <u>Anyone with information to offer the public,</u> such as horoscopes, financial information, employment news, entertainment and nightlife events, or sports updates, <u>can sell it over the phone and make substantial profits.</u>
<u>People from all backgrounds and income levels are jumping into this lucrative field to launch their own 900 and 976 lines.</u> The industry is just beginning to pick up momentum, and experts predict it will at least double in size over the next two years.
How can you <u>make big money with your own 900 or 976 line</u>? By learning the secrets of starting and running a successful telephone business from those who are already doing it.

Your Key to 900 & 976 Wealth

<u>A new in-depth manual,</u> *How to Make a Fortune With Your Own 900 & 976 Telephone Business,* <u>reveals all the insiders tips to starting your own money-making line.</u> Written by two former researchers for *Entrepreneur Magazine,* <u>this comprehensive manual takes hard-to-get information from successful line owners and puts it all together,</u> showing you how to:

* Evaluate your program ideas by using the list of hottest current programming subjects.
* Find existing programs that can make money for you.
* Test your ideas.
* Determine what price to charge the caller.
* Deal with the phone company.
* Set up joint ventures with service bureaus.
* Use the three forms of advertising that have proven to make phones ring off the hook. (Including specific ads that are pulling in big profits.)
* Get people to keep calling again and again.
* Locate industry associations, trade publications, service bureaus, program suppliers, and more.

Opportunity Is Knocking

How to Make a Fortune With Your Own 900 & 976 Telephone Business comes with an UNCONDITIONAL GUARANTEE: If you're not satisfied that this manual reveals a wealth of insiders tips and knowledge, simply return it within 30 days for a complete refund. It's that simple.

The 900 and 976 telephone business is already making some people very rich. More are destined to follow. Will you be one of those who got in on the ground floor, or will you be one who's wondering why you didn't? Take control of your financial future now by filling out the coupon below.

Sincerely,

Melvin Powers

Melvin Powers

YES! Send me my copy of *How to Make a Fortune With Your Own 900 & 976 Telephone Business*. I have enclosed my check or money order for $22.00 (CA residents $23.75. Outside U.S. $25.00) made payable to Melvin Powers. For immediate delivery, call (818) 765-8579 and use your Visa or MasterCard.

NAME _____(PLEASE PRINT)_____

STREET _____

CITY _____ STATE _____ ZIP _____

Send to: Melvin Powers
            12015 Sherman Road
        North Hollywood, California 91605

The Knight in Rusty Armor
A Case Study in Marketing a Book

When I received *The Knight in Rusty Armor* manuscript in the mail, I was intrigued with the title. Why rusty armor instead of shining armor? I wondered. Naturally, I had to find out. On Fridays, I have the habit of taking home a few manuscripts of particular interest to me to read leisurely over the weekends. I find it very relaxing. I had planned to take home *The Knight in Rusty Armor*, but became caught up in the story while still at the office and couldn't wait to finish it. I loved it and I knew I had a winner.

I gave the manuscript to my receptionist, who enjoys psychological books. She loved it, too. I also gave the manuscript to one of my readers, and he loved it. Then I made a dozen copies, which I sent to several of our professional readers and to some family members and friends. They were unanimous in their praise of the manuscript and wanted to share the story with others. My sixth sense based on 40 years of publishing told me loud and clear, Here's another multi-million seller.

Publishing a book is the easy part. The hard part is selling it. I'm going to share with you some of the ways I'm selling *The Knight in Rusty Armor* so you can borrow whatever parts are suitable for your bookselling campaign. These techniques have repeatedly proven themselves to work for me. They will work for you as well.

Bookstore Sales

I sent sample copies of the book to my salesmen throughout the country and told them to give the book freely to book buyers and bookstore personnel. Because bookstore buyers often become oblivious to book promotions and/or hype, I often send free copies of my new books to selected customers. This puts the book into their hands. Some buyers place orders because they like the book, and many more order when they sell their sample copy.

I sent out thousands of copies of the book to bookstore buyers, particularly those specializing in psychology, metaphysics, recovery, and new age. You can rent a list of about 2,000 of these bookstores. Along with the book, I sent a one-page sales letter and wholesale order form. (See page 222.) The mailing was very successful.

See page 223 for a response typical of many bookstores. We sold the book to Medieval Times, a well-known dinner theater near Disneyland, and to the Excalibur Hotel gift shop in Las Vegas. We are looking for other places with a knight theme.

I realize your sending out sample books may not be practical because of the expense involved, but you might want to consider doing it on a limited scale to a targeted market. I have used this technique many times in my publishing career and it invariably works well.

The Knight in Rusty Armor has a profound impact on most readers, many of whom buy copies to give as gifts. The book gets a lot of word of mouth advertising—and that's the best kind. One couple bought copies for everyone at their wedding.

We have bookstores that order a case (72 copies) or two every month. When I asked how they were selling so many, the usual reply was that they loved the book so much that they had placed copies face out at the cash counter, and they were recommending it to customers. The customers, in turn, were recommending it to others. This snowball effect is what makes bestsellers.

Wholesalers

I am reproducing two wholesale orders that include *The Knight in Rusty Armor*. (See pages 224 and 225.) Note the amount of books ordered for *The Knight* compared to my other titles.

For a list of wholesalers, radio and television talk shows, syndicated columnists, magazine and newspaper addresses, and a host of other valuable publicity sources, see *Literary Market Place*, a reference book available at all libraries. It's referred to as the LMP.

Mail Order Sales

My first love is selling books by mail. I wanted to use a special mailing piece to sell *The Knight in Rusty Armor*. I didn't want to just extol the virtues of the book in a four-page mailing piece. I wanted to promote it differently. I thought about how the first chapter of a sequel or of a new book appear at the end of some paperback novels. It's a sure-fire way to get those who enjoyed the first book to purchase another. Condensations and excerpts of books appearing in newspapers and magazines get people to buy books. Television shows give glimpses of what is coming the following week to interest people in watching the next show, and movie trailers entice you to see forthcoming movies.

How long do you need to listen to a song to know if you like it? Would you believe no more than 15 seconds? In

Wilshire Book Company

12015 Sherman Road, North Hollywood, California 91605

(818) 765-8579
FAX (818) 765-2922

Dear Book Buyer:

Not since *Jonathan Livingston Seagull* first enthralled the reading public has there been a story that captivates the imagination so thoroughly as *The Knight in Rusty Armor*. It's a delightful, inspiring adult fantasy about each of us struggling up the mountain of life. The knight's journey reflects our own--filled with hope and despair, belief and disillusionment, laughter and tears. His psychological pilgrimage is depicted in graphic, physical terms. Powerful concepts, imparted with wit and humor, are woven into the story in such a manner that each additional reading offers new insights. *The Knight* is more than a book: It's an experience that expands the mind, touches the heart, and nourishes the soul.

The author, Robert Fisher, is a well-known comedy writer who has written for such comedy greats as Groucho Marx, Bob Hope, George Burns, Jack Benny, Red Skelton, Alan King, and Lucille Ball. He has 400 radio and 1,000 TV shows to his credit, including episodes of "Alice," "Good Times," "All in the Family," "The Jeffersons," and "Maude."

In *The Knight*, Mr. Fisher skillfully uses humor to break through defenses that often impair our ability to see ourselves and our lives as they really are. People easily identify with the knight as they, too, often hide behind their armor in an attempt to shield themselves from their beliefs about themselves, the judgments of others, and the vicissitudes of life.

An increasing number of bookstores have been repeatedly ordering *The Knight* in quantities three and four times the size of their usual individual book orders. Some bookstores are ordering a case a month--that's 72 books!

We asked their secret. It was simple. The owners, managers, and salespeople read *The Knight* and were so excited about it, they recommended it to customers. After reading it, many people shared their enthusiasm with others who soon began coming in to request the book. In addition, readers returned to purchase copies for friends and relatives. As we know, this is how best sellers are made. We saw the same thing happen with our internationally-known, multi-million bestsellers *Psycho-Cybernetics, Think and Grow Rich,* and *A New Guide to Rational Living.*

Give *The Knight* an opportunity to boost your profits as it has for so many others. We've enclosed a complimentary copy which we believe you will find entertaining and thought-provoking. Order some copies for your store, share your enthusiasm for the book with your customers, and watch your profits rise. The book is available at a 40% discount in both softcover at $5.00 and hardcover at $10.00.

Sincerely,

Melvin Powers

Melvin Powers, Publisher

MP/mg
Enc.

Dear Mr. Fisher,

We all love your book. The Bookstore received a sample copy the last week of July. By the first of August we had ordered 10 copies which were promptly sold and sent to Nashville and points north, south, east and west. Our ministers have read it and recommended it for others. Our mailman loves it (read it twice) our church treasurer called me at 9:30pm to say "Thanks for the book, Alice." Most of the Bookstore staff has read it and bought a copy for gift giving. Our favorite astrologer bought it. The church secretary bought 2 copies. (one to keep and one for her son) I bought 4 for my sons and daughters and grandchildren.

The second order in August was for 10 more copies — (we have 4 on the shelf as of today). How's that for a testamonial and request for a sequel to "A Knight in Rusty Armor?"

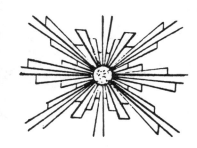

Temple of the Living God

1950 SECOND AVENUE NORTH

ST. PETERSBURG, FLORIDA 33713

PHONE: 822-3157 or 822-8628

MOVING BOOKS, INC.™

Mail:	P.O. Box 20037 Seattle, WA 98102
Office:	948 S. Doris St. Seattle, WA 98108
Phone:	(206) 762-1750
FAX:	(206) 762-1896

EASYLINK 8910916C001 20DEC91 19:33/19:33 EST
FROM: 62498010
      MOVING BOOKS INC (CRN: 13728)
TO: 8187652922

PURCHASE ORDER   13728
PO Date: Our Phone# is 206-762-1750
Printed: 12/20/91   ***OUR FAX # 206-762-1896***

Vendor: WILSHIRE BOOK COMPANY   Ship To: MOVING BOOKS
                                                 948 S DORIS ST
         12015 SHERMAN RD
         NORTH HOLL   CA 91605   SEATTLE   WA 98108

Account#:   Bill To: Moving Books Inc
FOB:CA   PO Box 20037
Discounts:
Ship Via:150+#'S=WOSCA   SEATTLE   WA 98102

200 21800 KNIGHT IN RUSTY ARMOR; FISHER, ROBERT   0879804211   5.00 50 500.00
  5 8619 3 MAGIC WORDS; ANDERSEN, U S   0879801654   7.00 50 17.50
  3   997 PALMISTRY MADE PRACTICAL; SQUIRE, ELIZAB 0879801158   7.00 50 10.50
 10 7478 NEW GUIDE RATIONAL LIVING; ELLIS, ALBERT 0879800429   7.00 50 35.00
  1 10531 REFLEXOLOGY FOR GOOD HEALTH; KAYE, ANNA   0879803835   7.00 50   3.50
  2 10278 SECRET OF SECRETS; ANDERSEN, U S   0879801344   7.00 50   7.00

Total: 573.50

INVOICE TO:

INGRAM DISTRIBUTION GROUP, INC.
ACCOUNTS PAYABLE DEPT. NO. 366
1125 HEIL QUAKER BLVD. – P.O. BOX 3006
LA VERGNE, TENNESSEE 37086-1986

PURCHASE ORDER

P.O. NUMBER	ORDER DATE	PAGE NO.	FORM NO.	
CQ31879R	11/14/91	1	020206	U

FROM

INGRAM BOOK COMPANY
20445 EAST BUSINESS PKWY
WALNUT CA 91789-2993

SHIPTO

INGRAM BOOK COMPANY
20445 EAST BUSINESS PKWY
WALNUT CA 91789-2993

VENDOR

WILSHIRE BOOK COMPANY
12015 SHERMAN ROAD
NO HOLLYWOOD CA 91605

SHIPPING INSTRUCTIONS
UPS TO 200 LBS/
200-10000 LBS-VIKING
OVER 10000 LBS CALL
INGRAM TRAFFIC
615-763-5000 EXT.7413

SHIPPING DATE	CANCEL DATE	TERMS
1/14/91	01/13/92	NET 85 DAYS

QUANTITY ORDERED	I.S.B.N.	TITLE	BIND	DISC. %	UNIT PRICE	EXTENDED PRICE	FOR INGRAM USE ONLY
10	0-87980-339-8	GREATEST POWER IN UNIVERSE	PA	50.0	7.00	35.00	084772
10	0-87980-395-9	GT PERSONAL HAPPINESS	PA	50.0	7.00	35.00	017191
15	0-87980-373-8	HT GET RICH IN MAIL ORDER	PA	50.0	20.00	150.00	046979
312	0-87980-421-1	KNIGHT IN RUSTY ARMOR	PA	50.0	5.00	780.00	194580
15	0-87980-345-2	WINNING AT CRAPS	PA	50.0	5.00	37.50	084263

362	TOTAL QUANTITY	LINE ITEMS 5		ORIGINAL (THIS IS NOT A COPY)	TOTAL EXTENDED PRICE	1,037.50

225

the same way, most people can get a sense of a book from the first chapter. I can usually get it by reading a few pages.

So guess what I decided to do . . . reproduce and send out the first chapter of *The Knight in Rusty Armor* accompanied by a one-page sales letter. (See pages 227 through 230.) I reasoned that the chapter would hook prospective buyers just as I had been hooked by it. And that's exactly what happened. Numerous delighted buyers wrote that they were fascinated by the story, liked the entertaining tone of it, and were curious to find out what happened to the knight in his quest to resolve his dilemma. The mailing piece worked like a charm.

Publicity
Irwin Zucker, a leading Hollywood publicist, handled our radio and television campaign, and the author, Robert Fisher, actively promotes the book. He is a popular lecturer in Los Angeles, where he lives, and he sells tons of books at his lectures and seminars. He has been invited to many schools and colleges to talk about the messages in his book. (See pages 231 and 232.) To my complete surprise, many teachers throughout the country are reading the book to their classes and discussing the lessons it contains. My daughter, Joy, was surprised and delighted when her 6th grade teacher unexpectedly read the book to her class.

Book reviews such as those on pages 233 and 234 help to sell lots of books. When you get a review, duplicate it and send out copies when doing mailings to bookstores and individuals. The reviews add impetus to your sales letter.

There is hardly a day that passes without people stopping by our offices and warehouse to buy copies of *The Knight*. We always ask where they first heard about the book. It's great research that helps us track the effectiveness of our sales promotion.

Psychologists keep ordering the book for their patients. The patients order it to give as gifts. I've had this happen other times in my publishing career; once with *Psycho-Cybernetics* by Maxwell Maltz, M.D. and again with *New Guide to Rational Living* by Drs. Albert Ellis and Robert Harper. The wonderful, exhilarating feeling of having a bestseller permeates everything you do. I hope you get to experience it. When you do, I would love to hear about your success.

Follow-Up Books and Products
There are natural follow-ups to some books and you should be mindful of them. When I first read *The Knight*, I knew immediately that it was a perfect first book for a trilogy. If you read the book, ask yourself what books two and three would logically be about. If you get it right, you are on your way to becoming a successful publisher.

Whenever I talk to people who have read *The Knight* and are enthusiastic about it, I always ask if they would have any interest in writing a fable that teaches principles of psychological growth, gives guidance in living, and/or explores the meaning of life. Why do I ask people whether they are interested in writing such a book? Because you never know who is capable of doing it, and it means big money and a lot of fun for everyone involved.

To those individuals who express interest in such a project, I suggest reading *The Little Prince* by Antoine de Saint Exupéry and *The Greatest Salesman in the World* by Og Mandino and analyzing the elements that make these two books and *The Knight* so successful. Then I ask them to send me a synopsis and three sample chapters, or to call me to discuss the proposed story line and psychological messages. I also advertise for writers.

Remember how important the bounce-back is to mail order? We want to create a built-in sales program that never ends. As part of accomplishing this with *The Knight*, we produced a musical production and then an audio cassette based on it. I advertise the cassette at the end of the book.

We are currently involved in talks with a major studio about doing the book as an animated movie or weekly television show. It's exciting to contemplate, but I've learned not to count on it until the papers are signed and the show produced. Can you imagine the sales from all the ancillary products and clothing?

The sales campaign never ends as long as there's life to the book. Have I had campaigns that didn't work? Yes, and after I've given it my best shot, I stop the campaign and move on to another project. It's been my experience that with enough publicity, the first edition of any book can be sold out if it is good enough for

Chapter 1

The Knight's Dilemma

O nce a long time ago, in a land far away, there lived a knight who thought of himself as good, kind, and loving. He did all the things that good, kind, and loving knights do. He fought foes who were bad, mean, and hateful. He slew dragons and rescued fair damsels in distress. When the knight business was slow, he had the annoying habit of rescuing damsels even if they did not want to be rescued, so, although many ladies were grateful to him, just as many were furious with him. This he accepted philosophically. After all, one can't please everybody.

This knight was famous for his armor. It reflected such bright rays of light that villagers would swear they had seen the sun rise in the north or set in the east when the knight rode off to battle. And he rode off to battle frequently. At the mere mention of a crusade, the knight would eagerly don his shining armor, mount his horse, and ride off in any direction. So eager was he, in fact, that sometimes he would ride off in several directions at once, which was no easy feat.

For years this knight strove to be the number one knight in all the kingdom. There was always another battle to be won, dragon to be slain, or damsel to be rescued.

The knight had a faithful and somewhat tolerant wife, Juliet, who wrote beautiful poetry, said clever things, and had a penchant for wine. He also had a young, golden-haired son, Christopher, who he hoped would grow up to be a courageous knight.

Juliet and Christopher saw little of the knight, because when not fighting battles, slaying dragons, and rescuing damsels, he was occupied with trying on his armor and admiring its brilliance. As time went on, the knight became so enamored of his armor that he began wearing it to dinner and often to bed. After a time, he didn't bother to take it off at all. Gradually his family forgot how he looked without it.

Occasionally, Christopher would ask his mother what his father looked like. When this happened, Juliet would lead the boy to the fireplace and point above it to a portrait of the knight. "There's your father," she would say.

One afternoon, while contemplating the portrait, Christopher said to his mother, "I wish I could see Father in person."

"You can't have everything!" snapped Juliet. She was growing impatient with having only a painting to remind her of her husband's face, and she was tired from having her sleep disturbed by the clanking of armor.

When he was at home and not completely preoccupied with his armor, the knight usually delivered monologues on his exploits. Juliet and Christopher were seldom able to get a word in edgewise. When they did, the knight shut it out either by closing his visor or by abruptly going to sleep.

One day, Juliet confronted her husband. "I think you love your armor more than you love me."

"That's not true," answered the knight. "Didn't I love you enough to rescue you from that dragon and set you up in this classy castle with wall-to-wall stones?"

"What you loved," said Juliet, peering through his visor so that she could see his eyes, "was the *idea* of rescuing me. You didn't really love me then, and you don't really love me now."

"I *do* love you," insisted the knight, hugging her clumsily in his cold, stiff armor and nearly breaking her ribs.

"Then take off that armor so that I can see who you really are!" she demanded.

"I *can't* take it off. I have to be ready to mount my horse and ride off in any direction," explained the knight.

"If you don't take off that armor, I'm taking Christopher, getting on *my* horse, and riding out of your life."

Well, this was a real blow to the knight. He didn't want Juliet to leave. He loved his wife and his son and his classy castle, but he also loved his armor because it showed everyone who he was—a good, kind, and loving knight. Why didn't Juliet realize that he was any of these things?

The knight was in turmoil. Finally he came to a decision. Continuing to wear the armor wasn't worth losing Juliet and Christopher.

Reluctantly, the knight reached up to remove his helmet, but it didn't budge! He pulled harder. It held fast. Dismayed, he tried lifting his visor but, alas, that was stuck, too. Though he tugged on the visor again and again, nothing happened.

The knight paced back and forth in great agitation. How could this have happened? Perhaps it was not so surprising to find the helmet stuck since he had not removed it for years, but the visor was another matter. He had opened it just that morning over a breakfast of scrambled eggs and suckling pig.

Suddenly the knight had an idea. Without saying where he was going, he hurried to the blacksmith's shop in the castle courtyard. When he arrived, the smith was shaping a horseshoe with his bare hands.

"Smith," said the knight, "I have a problem."

"You *are* a problem, sire," quipped the smith with his usual tact.

The knight, who normally enjoyed bantering, glowered. "I'm in no mood for your wisecracks right now. I'm stuck in this armor," he bellowed as he stamped his steel-clad foot, accidentally bringing it down on the smith's big toe.

The smith let out a howl and, momentarily forgetting the knight was his master, dealt him a smashing blow to the helmet. The knight felt only a twinge of discomfort. The helmet didn't budge.

"Try again," ordered the knight, unaware that the smith obliged him out of anger.

"With pleasure," the smith agreed, swinging a nearby hammer with vengeance and bringing it down squarely on the knight's helmet. The blow didn't even make a dent.

The knight was distraught. The smith was by far the strongest man in the kingdom. If he couldn't shuck the knight out of his armor, who could?

Being a kind man, except when his big toe was crushed, the smith sensed the knight's panic and grew sympathetic. "You have a tough plight, Knight, but don't give up. Come back tomorrow after I'm rested. You caught me at the end of a hard day."

Dinner time that evening was difficult. Juliet became increasingly annoyed as she pushed bits of food she had mashed through the holes in the knight's visor. Partway through the meal, the knight told Juliet that the blacksmith had tried to split open the armor but had failed.

"I don't believe you, you clanking clod!" she shouted, as she smashed her half-full plate of pigeon stew on his helmet.

The knight felt nothing. Only when gravy began dripping down past the eyeholes in his visor did he realize that he'd been hit on the head. He had barely felt the smith's hammer that afternoon either. In fact, when he thought about it, his armor kept him from feeling much of anything, and he had worn it for so long now that he'd forgotten how things felt without it.

The knight was upset that Juliet didn't believe he was trying to get his armor off. He and the smith *had* tried, and they kept at it for many more days without success. Each day the knight grew more despondent and Juliet grew colder.

Finally, the knight had to admit that the smith's efforts were useless. "Strongest man in the kingdom, indeed! You can't even break open this steel junkyard!" the knight yelled in frustration.

When the knight returned home, Juliet shrieked at him, "Your son has nothing but a portrait for a father, and I'm tired of talking to a closed visor. I'm never pushing food through the holes of that wretched thing again. I've mashed my very last mutton chop!"

"It's not *my* fault that I got stuck in this armor. I *had* to wear it so that I would always be ready for battle. How else could I get nice castles and horses for you and Christopher?"

"You didn't do it for *us*," argued Juliet. "You did it for *yourself!*"

The knight was sick at heart that his wife didn't seem to love him anymore. He also feared that if he didn't get his armor off

soon, Juliet and Christopher would really leave. He *had* to get the armor off, but he didn't know how to do it.

The knight dismissed one idea after another as being unlikely to work. Some of the plans were downright dangerous. He knew that any knight who would even think of melting his armor off with a castle torch, freezing it off by jumping into an icy moat, or blasting it off with a cannon was badly in need of help. Unable to find aid in his own kingdom, the knight decided to search in other lands. *Somewhere* there must be *someone* who can help me get this armor off, he thought.

Of course, he would miss Juliet, Christopher, and his classy castle. He also feared that in his absence Juliet might find love with another knight, one willing to remove his armor at bedtime and to be more of a father to Christopher. Nevertheless, the knight had to go, so, early one morning, he got onto his horse, and he rode away. He didn't dare look back for fear he might change his mind.

On his way out of the province, the knight stopped to say goodbye to the king, who had been very good to him. The king lived in a grand castle atop a hill in the high-rent district. As the knight rode across the drawbridge and into the courtyard, he saw the court jester sitting cross-legged, playing a reed flute.

The jester was called Gladbag because, over his shoulder, he carried a beautiful rainbow-colored bag filled with all sorts of things that made people laugh or smile. There were strange cards that he used to tell people's fortunes, brightly colored beads that he made appear and disappear, and funny little puppets that he used to amusingly insult his audiences.

"Hi, Gladbag," said the knight. "I came to say farewell to the king."

The jester looked up.

"The king has up and gone away.
To you there's nothing he can say."

"Where has he gone?" asked the knight.

"He's taken off on a new crusade.
If you wait for him, you'll be delayed."

The knight was disappointed that he had missed the king and perturbed that he couldn't join him on the crusade. "Oh," he sighed, "I could starve to death in this armor by the time the king returns. I might never see him again." The knight felt very much like slumping in his saddle, but, of course, his armor wouldn't let him.

"Well, aren't you a silly sight?
All your might can't solve your plight."

"I'm in no mood for your insulting rhymes," barked the knight, stiffening in his armor. "Can't you take someone's problem seriously for once?"

In a clear, lyrical voice, Gladbag sang:

"Problems never set me a-rockin'.
They're opportunities a-knockin'."

"You'd sing a different tune if *you* were the one stuck in here," growled the knight.

Gladbag retorted:

"We're all stuck in armor of a kind.
Yours is merely easier to find."

"I don't have time to stay and listen to your nonsense. I have to find a way to get out of this armor." With that, the knight kneed his mount forward to leave, but Gladbag called after him:

"There is one who can help you, Knight,

to bring the real you into sight."

The knight pulled his horse to a stop and, excitedly, he turned back to Gladbag. "You know someone who can get me out of this armor? Who is it?"

"Merlin the Magician you must see.
Then you'll discover how to be free."

"Merlin? The only Merlin I've ever heard of is the great and wise teacher of King Arthur."

"Yes, yes, that's his claim to fame.
This Merlin I know is one and the same."

"But it can't be!" exclaimed the knight. "Merlin and Arthur lived long ago."

Gladbag replied:

"It's true, yet he's alive and well.
In yonder woods the sage doth dwell."

"But those woods are so big," said the knight. "How will I find him in there?"

Gladbag smiled.

"One never knows be it days, weeks, or years,
when the pupil is ready, the teacher appears."

"I can't wait for Merlin to show up. I'm going to look for *him*," said the knight. He reached out and shook Gladbag's hand in gratitude, nearly crushing the jester's fingers with his gauntlet.

Gladbag yelped. The knight quickly released the jester's hand. "Sorry." Gladbag rubbed his bruised fingers.

"When the armor's gone from you,
you'll feel the pain of others, too."

"I'm off!" said the knight. He wheeled his horse around, and with new hope in his heart, galloped away to find Merlin.

Gardena Valley News

417 S. WESTERN AVE., GARDENA (213) 329-6351 25 CENTS

37th YEAR NO. 20 **FRIDAY** MARCH 8, 1991

able helps students ned armor, find self

by Gary Kohatsu
GVN Staff Writer

nce upon a time, in Classm 28 at Denker Avenue mentary School, a fair nsel named Maureen Hicks d to her class a fable itled, "The Knight in Rusty nor." Her students lised and soon became hralled by the story's ssages.

he damsel, however, ated to bring the story ser to her children, so she t out a distress call knowthat only one person in all land could come to her ue.

Please brave Knight," she ided, "I need you to come ak to my children."

a a short while she eived a note: "Yes, fair den, I will come visit your dren and I will bring them h a gift."

mighty banner was then ad across the auditorium ain Wednesday afternoon. ead in bold letters, "Welme Robert Fisher, the ght in Rusty Armor."

nd when the knight arrived, wore a dark jacket and k striped pants, a red ater and matching sneak-

But there was no armor to found anywhere, and this e reassurance to Teacher ureen Hicks and approxiely 60 school children.

or the knight has shed his or long ago and instead he armed instead with

"love." That is the message of Fisher's book, the removal of barriers that prevents people from knowing and loving themselves, so in turn they can give love to others and receive love back.

"On the count of three I want you to shout out your names," Fisher instructed his audience.

Then came a collective throng of names, "Nancy and Sydney and Abraham and Linda..."

"You just shouted different names, but what if I told you there's no difference between us," Fisher informed. "We're all one."

"The whole idea of the Knight in the story, is that he is separated by layers and layers of armor, which separated him from others and from himself. Then the knight cried and cried, and his tears rusted the armor..."

Fisher, a thin, bearded man in his late 60's told his audience that the knight he wrote about in the book was really himself 25 years ago. He was dying of cancer then, when an inner voice guided him to discover the meaning of his life. Soon after his spirit gained renewed strength and destroyed the cancer in his body, and he was inspired to write his one and only book.

He spoke Wednesday with frankness and feeling. He involved his audience by ask-

(Please turn to Page A-6)

WARM HUGS—Author Robert Fisher gives Nancy Torres a hug Wednesday afternoon, following an assembly where Fisher spoke to Denker Avenue Elementary School children about his book, "The Knight In Rusty Armor." Other students from left, are Cecilia Valdez, Zara Leon, Arlette Gonzalez and Deserea Chavez. —*Photo by Gary Kohatsu*

Fable

(Continued from Page One)

ing them questions and encouraged them to join him in singing a song he had written. The initial armor of intimidation in the children, was beginning to wear thin. Afterwards, he said he could read into his audience; sense when he was "connecting" with them.

As Fisher sat cross-legged on a pile of tumbling mats, he focused intently on the children that sat crosss-legged a few feet before him.

"Who is it we should learn to love first?" Fisher asked.

"Yourself," a small voice answered. "Right on," Fisher smiled. "Do you know why?"

"Because if you don't love yourself, you can't love others," another student answered.

"That's right," Fisher replied. "Otherwise you're a pretender." Fisher's lesson emphasized being honest with yourself and that we learn later through our mistakes. And that mistakes are okay to make, as long as we don't allow mistakes to make us defensive.

"(When you make) mistakes, you (often) put on armor to protect yourself," he explained. "Then you make a second mistake by putting on more armor and (you do it by

choice), which is wrong.

"Don't put blame on yourself, because if you do, how can you love yourself?"

Hicks had read "The Knight of Rusty Armor," to her class a little more than a month ago and the impact of the story messages were dramatic.

"(My class's) response to the book was so heartwarming and inspirational, that I immediately contacted the publisher and wanted to invite the author to visit our school," Hicks recalled. "The fable shared deep messages with the children. It's phenomenal in this day and age, that (kids) would be attentive enough to listen to a story."

She then instructed her class to write essays on their feelings.

"I learned to take my armor off and feel proud of who I am. I think that I won't be blaming my problems on others," wrote Stephanie Nakamura.

"Everybody has armor and don't be afraid to show your real self expression...do not try to live your life pleasing someone...love yourself as much as you love others," DeForest Burns said.

"Whatever you do is your problem, your fault, your happiness, because you are your own person...never mistake need for love...I will

remember that knowledge is the light by which you shall find your way," Gabriela Contreras wrote in her paper.

Fisher, a renown playwright and comedy writer (he has written for Bob Hope, Lucille Ball and for several television shows, including "Alice," "The Jeffersons," and "All in the Family") was touched by the children's response.

"I feel exhilirated. I'm drunk with joy," he commented.

The assembly ended with hugs. Fisher hugged Hicks, followed by several students who stopped forward to conquer their "dragons" (fears) and offer hugs. "Fear is the opposite of love," Fisher told everybody. "(The dragons) can't touch somebody filled wih love."

His words filled the auditorium. "When you hug you shed some of your armor," Fisher said. "Look at your neighbor. Are you willing to hug the person next to you?

Some children hugged. Others were a bit shy. Then many came to hug Fisher, and to have him sign copies of his book that he had given them.

"I believe this book will influence their lives." Hicks smiled.

Gardena class takes a shine to 'Armor' man

By Vivien Lou Chen
STAFF WRITER

For several weeks, teacher Maureen Hicks' sixth-graders at Denker Avenue Elementary School sat transfixed as she read them a tale of a mythical knight preoccupied with slaying dragons and rescuing damsels.

But the poor knight was so busy doing battle that his armor thickened to the point where his family couldn't see him.

So the knight stopped using his metallic skin to impress others and his armor began to break off and reveal the man underneath.

That knight walked into the Gardena school's assembly hall last week for a lesson in self-awareness.

'I started to die'

"I was 43 and had so much armor that the energy of love from other people wasn't reaching me and I started to die," said Robert Fisher, author of *The Knight in Rusty Armor.*

"The whole idea of this book is to let go of all this armor."

Fisher's self-modeled knight journeyed to the Castles of Silence, Knowledge and Will and Daring. The story, with its underlying words of advice to just be yourself, has grabbed the imagination and hearts of its readers, among them schoolchildren, psychologists and drug and alcohol abusers.

Fisher never intended to write the book. Now 68, he

spent a lifetime scripting punch lines for some of America's funniest comedians and nearly 1,000 television episodes.

He was diagnosed with cancer 25 years ago and wrote *The Knight in Rusty Armor* during rehabilitation, aiming for an audience "between the ages of 9 and 90."

Born in Long Beach and now living in West Hollywood, Fisher began his career as a comedy writer at the age of 20. In the years since, he wrote for Lucille Ball, Jack Benny, George Burns, Bob Hope, Groucho Marx and Red Skelton.

After he was diagnosed with cancer — and told he didn't have long to live — Fisher said he stopped going to doctors because "I never did anything to include in my belief system that I would die."

He said an inner voice named Sam told him how to write *The Knight in Rusty Armor,* which has sold 100,000 paperback copies and 10,000 hardcover issues since its publication in 1990.

In written summaries of the book, Hicks' students uncovered some story morals.

"One thing the book taught me is don't stay inside your armor, you might get stuck," wrote one student.

"Be happy with what you are," wrote another, "because no one expects you to be different. Also be grateful for your family and friends because without them you have nothing."

The whole idea of this book is to let go of all this (emotional) armor.

— **Robert Fisher**

The Knight in Rusty Armor

Robert Fisher is available for public speaking engagements to large and small groups. Join organizations, churches, schools, chiropractors, psychologists and more in hearing his joyful message about life.

Children from nine to ninety find Robert heartwarming and inspirational.

Slaying Dragons

Hiding beneath the protective armor there's a brave knight in each of us.

A FRIEND OF MINE RECENTLY recommended a book to me, called *The Knight in Rusty Armor* by Robert Fisher. The knight in the story considers it his sole and noble mission to be the best knight there is. When not saving damsels or slaying dragons, he is trying on his armor and admiring its brilliance.

As the story progresses, the knight grows to love his armor not only because it shows everyone who he is, but also—most importantly—because it keeps him from feeling anything. Furthermore, he wears the armor for so long he forgets how things feel without it. Then, when he tries to remove it, he can't—it won't come off. He asks the advice of Merlin, the magician, who helps him realize that the only way to rid himself of the armor is to *rust* it away. To do so he must feel something so deeply that he cries, thereby rusting the armor and causing it to fall away, part by part.

No matter how brave or strong we are, we all wear a type of invisible armor to protect us from some aspect of life. Fear is a significant, powerful force that we feel on many levels—physically, mentally and emotionally.

I admit, with apprehension, that fear is a significant part of my life. As a child with athletic tendencies, I learned to be strong physically, mentally and emo-

tionally. Being strong is comfortable for me. It is also my armor—it protects me from conflict, anger, pain and disappointment.

Learning to face and express these feelings is what I'm afraid of and what I deal with every day. However, I'm learning to move through this fear. I still have to remind myself every day that all feelings are OK, that I can feel safe if I recognize, acknowledge and deal with unpleasant feelings. I believe that fear is one of our greatest teachers. Whatever our fears, they are neither good nor bad—they just are. All we risk by uncovering them is becoming healthier, more fully human, and tasting another part of life.

I may climb mountains, strive to run a seven-and-a-half-minute mile and take care of the rest of my physical needs, but my daily training isn't complete until I've hiked a trail through my fears and tasted the waters at the summit, where my feelings continue to flow whether I recognize them or not.

It's scary to try something different, whether it's a walking program, in-line skating or expressing your feelings. Uncover your fears and what's behind them. Read "Overcoming Fear" on page 100, and learn to remove each small piece of your armor at a time, moving through your fears one by one, to a richer, fuller life.

Yours (and getting rustier),

Barbara Harris
Editor in Chief

RONI RAMOS

Parent Survival Training: A Complete Guide to Modern Parenting, *by Marvin Silverman and David A. Lustig, North Hollywood, Calif.: Wilshire Book Co., 1987, 315 pages, $10.*

One of the best books out for parents on the management of children, "Parent Survival Training" is mandatory reading for parents and parent educators. Drawing on Behavior Therapy and Rational Emotive Therapy principles, Silverman and Lustig provide a comprehensive and practical guide which deals with real problems and situations that come up with children, and techniques to handle them. While many parenting books offer general guidelines and theories, PST provides detailed examples of how to approach problems ranging from tantrums to sibling conflicts—and even more challenging situations such as the fearful child, or problems arising from poor school performance. In every case, they offer a clear explanation of a behavioral treatment approach that is geared towards teaching children responsibility and self-discipline, without sacrificing a loving relationship between parent and child.

The most informative and innovative approaches in this book are in the chapters on school problems and runaway emotions. Chapter Eight provides examples of progress reports which can be checked out by the teacher when assignments are completed and then brought home by the child. Privileges, such as watching T.V. are given for completed assignments, and privileges are taken away for missed assignments. According to the authors, "You must realize that it is better to have the child feel some misery now than for both of you to go through these school problems for the years to come."

Chapter Ten, on runaway emotions, will probably be the most helpful to parents who tend to lose control of their emotions and undermine their efforts by yelling, using idle threats, or name-calling. When conflicts arise at home, parents are advised to use the three R's—face reality, offer a rational response, and have positive and controlled results planned. Parents can learn to take charge of their emotions and gain more respect from their children by using these powerful techniques.

The PST model gives parents a practical and positive way of disciplining children without using authoritarian tactics or physical punishment. It is refreshing to see so many examples of techniques that are easy to understand. Family counselors and parent educators will find this a good source of information and a handy reference to keep on their bookshelf.

Reviewed by Terry Clifford, Women's Resource Center, Bustol Community College, Fall River, Mass.

readers to recommend it to others. If not, it's bound to fail—no matter how much publicity it gets. It's like movies that are hyped in major ad campaigns, yet still fall flat because people who see it don't recommend it to others.

I have lunch most Mondays with some members of my staff. Invariably, the conversation comes around to what movies people have seen over the weekend. When I get laudatory reports on a particular movie, I usually go see it. I've learned to trust the opinions of my associates, friends, and family more than superlative newspaper and magazine reviews. Too many times, I have been disappointed in movies highly praised by reviewers. Because many people have come to the same conclusion as I, your goal is to produce a book that readers will recommend.

I published some books that I knew immediately wouldn't be commercially profitable. Obviously, I didn't publish them to make money. I did it because I knew the information in the books was needed, even though the market for it was small. I get pleasure with every sale, knowing I'm touching people's lives in a constructive way. I hope you reach the point in your publishing career where you can afford to do as I'm doing. The satisfaction is indescribable.

Before You Print Your Book
Take the time to study the ads I have included in the new section of this book, as well as other successful ads and direct mailing pieces. Go to the library and research books on advertising. Become a student of advertising. It's an important key to your success.

Give careful thought to your sales strategy before printing your book. I've heard from many unhappy authors who have three-to five-thousand books stacked up in their garages. To prevent yourself from getting into such a predicament, I suggest that before printing your manuscript in standard book form, you print out an 8½" x 11" version on a computer and have your instant printer reproduce it. Hand out some copies to people you think would give you honest feedback. If you can also get a professional's critique, that would be very helpful. Pay attention to the suggestions you receive, and make changes accordingly.

Don't let your ego get in the way of your success. Accept constructive suggestions. I know amateur songwriters who have written hundreds of songs and have yet to sell one. When I was in the music business, many came to my office and played their songs for me. When I

suggested changes that would make the songs sale-able, they didn't listen. They also refused to enroll in any of the wonderful songwriting courses being offered by hit songwriters in the Los Angeles/Hollywood area. I finally decided to stop giving feedback to these aspiring songwriters. I asked them to send me tapes of their three best songs, rather than having them continue to come to my office.

An excellent way to test ad copy you've written for your book is to use it to sell a similar book—one that has already been published. Use the *Subject Guide to Books in Print.* It's a reference guide available in all public libraries, containing one-million books in thousands of categories. When you find a book similar to yours, write to the publisher telling him you want to mail order the book. You'll get a 46% to 50% discount. Order a few books to get started and gradually increase your orders. Some publishers will drop-ship your orders. This means you don't have to carry inventory, and they'll do the shipping for you. At Wilshire Book Company, we drop-ship for many types of customers. It's good for them and for us.

Since remainder books sell for a fraction of the original price, you can get a discount of more than 50% if you can find a book similar to yours at a remainder book company. For the most current list, look under Wholesale Remainder Dealers in the *Literary Market Place.* Write to all the companies inquiring about the book(s) you want.

As soon as your sales campaign is successful, print your book and substitute it for the one you have been selling. Do you remember I told you how I did this with *How to Get Rich in Mail Order?* Writing the book wasn't difficult. The challenge was to write ad copy that would sell it. It's been 12 years since my book was first published and although I've sold hundreds of thousands of copies, I still experiment with ad copy in an attempt to improve sales. I love the brainstorming and creativity involved in continuously making good ads even better. The lesson for you is, even when something is working, try to improve it.

If you need help, feel free to call or write me. I wish you much success and hope you will have the fun and excitement of being a bestselling author.

MELVIN POWERS SELF-IMPROVEMENT LIBRARY

ASTROLOGY

____ ASTROLOGY: HOW TO CHART YOUR HOROSCOPE *Max Heindel*	5.00
____ ASTROLOGY AND SEXUAL ANALYSIS *Morris C. Goodman*	5.00
____ ASTROLOGY AND YOU *Carroll Righter*	5.00
____ ASTROLOGY MADE EASY *Astarte*	5.00
____ ASTROLOGY, ROMANCE, YOU AND THE STARS *Anthony Norvell*	5.00
____ MY WORLD OF ASTROLOGY *Sydney Omarr*	7.00
____ THOUGHT DIAL *Sydney Omarr*	7.00
____ WHAT THE STARS REVEAL ABOUT THE MEN IN YOUR LIFE *Thelma White*	3.00

BRIDGE

____ BRIDGE BIDDING MADE EASY *Edwin B. Kantar*	10.00
____ BRIDGE CONVENTIONS *Edwin B. Kantar*	10.00
____ COMPETITIVE BIDDING IN MODERN BRIDGE *Edgar Kaplan*	7.00
____ DEFENSIVE BRIDGE PLAY COMPLETE *Edwin B. Kantar*	15.00
____ GAMESMAN BRIDGE—PLAY BETTER WITH KANTAR *Edwin B. Kantar*	5.00
____ HOW TO IMPROVE YOUR BRIDGE *Alfred Sheinwold*	7.00
____ IMPROVING YOUR BIDDING SKILLS *Edwin B. Kantar*	7.00
____ INTRODUCTION TO DECLARER'S PLAY *Edwin B. Kantar*	7.00
____ INTRODUCTION TO DEFENDER'S PLAY *Edwin B. Kantar*	7.00
____ KANTAR FOR THE DEFENSE *Edwin B. Kantar*	7.00
____ KANTAR FOR THE DEFENSE VOLUME 2 *Edwin B. Kantar*	7.00
____ TEST YOUR BRIDGE PLAY *Edwin B. Kantar*	7.00
____ VOLUME 2—TEST YOUR BRIDGE PLAY *Edwin B. Kantar*	7.00
____ WINNING DECLARER PLAY *Dorothy Hayden Truscott*	7.00

BUSINESS, STUDY & REFERENCE

____ BRAINSTORMING *Charles Clark*	7.00
____ CONVERSATION MADE EASY *Elliot Russell*	5.00
____ EXAM SECRET *Dennis B. Jackson*	5.00
____ FIX-IT BOOK *Arthur Symons*	2.00
____ HOW TO DEVELOP A BETTER SPEAKING VOICE *M. Hellier*	4.00
____ HOW TO SAVE 50% ON GAS & CAR EXPENSES *Ken Stansbie*	5.00
____ HOW TO SELF-PUBLISH YOUR BOOK & MAKE IT A BEST SELLER *Melvin Powers*	20.00
____ INCREASE YOUR LEARNING POWER *Geoffrey A. Dudley*	3.00
____ PRACTICAL GUIDE TO BETTER CONCENTRATION *Melvin Powers*	5.00
____ 7 DAYS TO FASTER READING *William S. Schaill*	5.00
____ SONGWRITERS' RHYMING DICTIONARY *Jane Shaw Whitfield*	10.00
____ SPELLING MADE EASY *Lester D. Basch & Dr. Milton Finkelstein*	3.00
____ STUDENT'S GUIDE TO BETTER GRADES *J. A. Rickard*	3.00
____ TEST YOURSELF—FIND YOUR HIDDEN TALENT *Jack Shafer*	3.00
____ YOUR WILL & WHAT TO DO ABOUT IT *Attorney Samuel G. Kling*	5.00

CALLIGRAPHY

____ ADVANCED CALLIGRAPHY *Katherine Jeffares*	7.00
____ CALLIGRAPHY—THE ART OF BEAUTIFUL WRITING *Katherine Jeffares*	7.00
____ CALLIGRAPHY FOR FUN & PROFIT *Anne Leptich & Jacque Evans*	7.00
____ CALLIGRAPHY MADE EASY *Tina Serafini*	7.00

CHESS & CHECKERS

____ BEGINNER'S GUIDE TO WINNING CHESS *Fred Reinfeld*	5.00
____ CHESS IN TEN EASY LESSONS *Larry Evans*	5.00
____ CHESS MADE EASY *Milton L. Hanauer*	5.00
____ CHESS PROBLEMS FOR BEGINNERS *Edited by Fred Reinfeld*	5.00
____ CHESS TACTICS FOR BEGINNERS *Edited by Fred Reinfeld*	5.00

___	HOW TO WIN AT CHECKERS *Fred Reinfeld*	5.00
___	1001 BRILLIANT WAYS TO CHECKMATE *Fred Reinfeld*	7.00
___	1001 WINNING CHESS SACRIFICES & COMBINATIONS *Fred Reinfeld*	7.00

COOKERY & HERBS

___	CULPEPER'S HERBAL REMEDIES *Dr. Nicholas Culpeper*	5.00
___	FAST GOURMET COOKBOOK *Poppy Cannon*	2.50
___	HEALING POWER OF HERBS *May Bethel*	5.00
___	HEALING POWER OF NATURAL FOODS *May Bethel*	5.00
___	HERBS FOR HEALTH—HOW TO GROW & USE THEM *Louise Evans Doole*	5.00
___	HOME GARDEN COOKBOOK—DELICIOUS NATURAL FOOD RECIPES *Ken Kraft*	3.00
___	MEATLESS MEAL GUIDE *Tomi Ryan & James H. Ryan, M.D.*	4.00
___	VEGETABLE GARDENING FOR BEGINNERS *Hugh Wiberg*	2.00
___	VEGETABLES FOR TODAY'S GARDENS *R. Milton Carleton*	2.00
___	VEGETARIAN COOKERY *Janet Walker*	7.00
___	VEGETARIAN COOKING MADE EASY & DELECTABLE *Veronica Vezza*	3.00
___	VEGETARIAN DELIGHTS—A HAPPY COOKBOOK FOR HEALTH *K. R. Mehta*	2.00
___	VEGETARIAN GOURMET COOKBOOK *Joyce McKinnel*	3.00

GAMBLING & POKER

___	HOW TO WIN AT DICE GAMES *Skip Frey*	3.00
___	HOW TO WIN AT POKER *Terence Reese & Anthony T. Watkins*	7.00
___	WINNING AT CRAPS *Dr. Lloyd T. Commins*	5.00
___	WINNING AT GIN *Chester Wander & Cy Rice*	3.00
___	WINNING AT POKER—AN EXPERT'S GUIDE *John Archer*	5.00
___	WINNING AT 21—AN EXPERT'S GUIDE *John Archer*	7.00
___	WINNING POKER SYSTEMS *Norman Zadeh*	3.00

HEALTH

___	BEE POLLEN *Lynda Lyngheim & Jack Scagnetti*	3.00
___	COPING WITH ALZHEIMER'S *Rose Oliver, Ph.D. & Francis Bock, Ph.D.*	10.00
___	DR. LINDNER'S POINT SYSTEM FOOD PROGRAM *Peter G. Lindner, M.D.*	2.00
___	HELP YOURSELF TO BETTER SIGHT *Margaret Darst Corbett*	7.00
___	HOW YOU CAN STOP SMOKING PERMANENTLY *Ernest Caldwell*	5.00
___	MIND OVER PLATTER *Peter G. Lindner, M.D.*	5.00
___	NATURE'S WAY TO NUTRITION & VIBRANT HEALTH *Robert J. Scrutton*	3.00
___	NEW CARBOHYDRATE DIET COUNTER *Patti Lopez-Pereira*	2.00
___	REFLEXOLOGY *Dr. Maybelle Segal*	5.00
___	REFLEXOLOGY FOR GOOD HEALTH *Anna Kaye & Don C. Matchan*	7.00
___	30 DAYS TO BEAUTIFUL LEGS *Dr. Marc Selner*	3.00
___	YOU CAN LEARN TO RELAX *Dr. Samuel Gutwirth*	3.00

HOBBIES

___	BEACHCOMBING FOR BEGINNERS *Norman Hickin*	2.00
___	BLACKSTONE'S MODERN CARD TRICKS *Harry Blackstone*	5.00
___	BLACKSTONE'S SECRETS OF MAGIC *Harry Blackstone*	5.00
___	COIN COLLECTING FOR BEGINNERS *Burton Hobson & Fred Reinfeld*	7.00
___	ENTERTAINING WITH ESP *Tony 'Doc' Shiels*	2.00
___	400 FASCINATING MAGIC TRICKS YOU CAN DO *Howard Thurston*	7.00
___	HOW I TURN JUNK INTO FUN AND PROFIT *Sari*	3.00
___	HOW TO WRITE A HIT SONG & SELL IT *Tommy Boyce*	7.00
___	JUGGLING MADE EASY *Rudolf Dittrich*	3.00
___	MAGIC FOR ALL AGES *Walter Gibson*	4.00
___	MAGIC MADE EASY *Byron Wels*	2.00
___	STAMP COLLECTING FOR BEGINNERS *Burton Hobson*	3.00

HORSE PLAYER'S WINNING GUIDES

___	BETTING HORSES TO WIN *Les Conklin*	7.00
___	ELIMINATE THE LOSERS *Bob McKnight*	5.00
___	HOW TO PICK WINNING HORSES *Bob McKnight*	5.00

____ HOW TO WIN AT THE RACES *Sam (The Genius) Lewin*	5.00
____ HOW YOU CAN BEAT THE RACES *Jack Kavanaqh*	5.00
____ MAKING MONEY AT THE RACES *David Barr*	5.00
____ PAYDAY AT THE RACES *Les Conklin*	5.00
____ SMART HANDICAPPING MADE EASY *William Bauman*	5.00
____ SUCCESS AT THE HARNESS RACES *Barry Meadow*	5.00

HUMOR

____ HOW TO FLATTEN YOUR TUSH *Coach Marge Reardon*	2.00
____ HOW TO MAKE LOVE TO YOURSELF *Ron Stevens & Joy Grdnic*	3.00
____ JOKE TELLER'S HANDBOOK *Bob Orben*	7.00
____ JOKES FOR ALL OCCASIONS *Al Schock*	5.00
____ 2,000 NEW LAUGHS FOR SPEAKERS *Bob Orben*	7.00
____ 2,400 JOKES TO BRIGHTEN YOUR SPEECHES *Robert Orben*	7.00
____ 2,500 JOKES TO START 'EM LAUGHING *Bob Orben*	7.00

HYPNOTISM

____ ADVANCED TECHNIQUES OF HYPNOSIS *Melvin Powers*	3.00
____ CHILDBIRTH WITH HYPNOSIS *William S. Kroger, M.D.*	5.00
____ HOW TO SOLVE YOUR SEX PROBLEMS WITH SELF-HYPNOSIS *Frank S. Caprio, M.D.*	5.00
____ HOW TO STOP SMOKING THRU SELF-HYPNOSIS *Leslie M. LeCron*	3.00
____ HOW YOU CAN BOWL BETTER USING SELF-HYPNOSIS *Jack Heise*	4.00
____ HOW YOU CAN PLAY BETTER GOLF USING SELF-HYPNOSIS *Jack Heise*	3.00
____ HYPNOSIS AND SELF-HYPNOSIS *Bernard Hollander, M.D.*	5.00
____ HYPNOTISM *(Originally published in 1893) Carl Sextus*	5.00
____ HYPNOTISM MADE EASY *Dr. Ralph Winn*	5.00
____ HYPNOTISM MADE PRACTICAL *Louis Orton*	5.00
____ HYPNOTISM REVEALED *Melvin Powers*	3.00
____ HYPNOTISM TODAY *Leslie LeCron and Jean Bordeaux, Ph.D.*	5.00
____ MODERN HYPNOSIS *Lesley Kuhn & Salvatore Russo, Ph.D.*	5.00
____ NEW CONCEPTS OF HYPNOSIS *Bernard C. Gindes, M.D.*	10.00
____ NEW SELF-HYPNOSIS *Paul Adams*	7.00
____ POST-HYPNOTIC INSTRUCTIONS—SUGGESTIONS FOR THERAPY *Arnold Furst*	5.00
____ PRACTICAL GUIDE TO SELF-HYPNOSIS *Melvin Powers*	3.00
____ PRACTICAL HYPNOTISM *Philip Magonet, M.D.*	3.00
____ SECRETS OF HYPNOTISM *S. J. Van Pelt, M.D.*	5.00
____ SELF-HYPNOSIS—A CONDITIONED-RESPONSE TECHNIQUE *Laurence Sparks*	7.00
____ SELF-HYPNOSIS—ITS THEORY, TECHNIQUE & APPLICATION *Melvin Powers*	3.00
____ THERAPY THROUGH HYPNOSIS *Edited by Raphael H. Rhodes*	5.00

JUDAICA

____ SERVICE OF THE HEART *Evelyn Garfiel, Ph.D.*	7.00
____ STORY OF ISRAEL IN COINS *Jean & Maurice Gould*	2.00
____ STORY OF ISRAEL IN STAMPS *Maxim & Gabriel Shamir*	1.00
____ TONGUE OF THE PROPHETS *Robert St. John*	7.00

JUST FOR WOMEN

____ COSMOPOLITAN'S GUIDE TO MARVELOUS MEN Foreword by *Helen Gurley Brown*	3.00
____ COSMOPOLITAN'S HANG-UP HANDBOOK Foreword by *Helen Gurley Brown*	4.00
____ COSMOPOLITAN'S LOVE BOOK—A GUIDE TO ECSTASY IN BED	7.00
____ COSMOPOLITAN'S NEW ETIQUETTE GUIDE Foreword by *Helen Gurley Brown*	4.00
____ I AM A COMPLEAT WOMAN *Doris Hagopian & Karen O'Connor Sweeney*	3.00
____ JUST FOR WOMEN—A GUIDE TO THE FEMALE BODY *Richard E. Sand, M.D.*	5.00
____ NEW APPROACHES TO SEX IN MARRIAGE *John E. Eichenlaub, M.D.*	3.00
____ SEXUALLY ADEQUATE FEMALE *Frank S. Caprio, M.D.*	3.00
____ SEXUALLY FULFILLED WOMAN *Dr. Rachel Copelan*	5.00

MARRIAGE, SEX & PARENTHOOD

___ ABILITY TO LOVE *Dr. Allan Fromme*	7.00
___ GUIDE TO SUCCESSFUL MARRIAGE *Drs. Albert Ellis & Robert Harper*	7.00
___ HOW TO RAISE AN EMOTIONALLY HEALTHY, HAPPY CHILD *Albert Ellis, Ph.D.*	7.00
___ PARENT SURVIVAL TRAINING *Marvin Silverman, Ed.D. & David Lustig, Ph.D.*	10.00
___ SEX WITHOUT GUILT *Albert Ellis, Ph.D.*	5.00
___ SEXUALLY ADEQUATE MALE *Frank S. Caprio, M.D.*	3.00
___ SEXUALLY FULFILLED MAN *Dr. Rachel Copelan*	5.00
___ STAYING IN LOVE *Dr. Norton F. Kristy*	7.00

MELVIN POWERS' MAIL ORDER LIBRARY

___ HOW TO GET RICH IN MAIL ORDER *Melvin Powers*	20.00
___ HOW TO WRITE A GOOD ADVERTISEMENT *Victor O. Schwab*	20.00
___ MAIL ORDER MADE EASY *J. Frank Brumbaugh*	20.00

METAPHYSICS & OCCULT

___ CONCENTRATION—A GUIDE TO MENTAL MASTERY *Mouni Sadhu*	7.00
___ EXTRA-TERRESTRIAL INTELLIGENCE—THE FIRST ENCOUNTER	6.00
___ FORTUNE TELLING WITH CARDS *P. Foli*	5.00
___ HOW TO INTERPRET DREAMS, OMENS & FORTUNE TELLING SIGNS *Gettings*	5.00
___ HOW TO UNDERSTAND YOUR DREAMS *Geoffrey A. Dudley*	5.00
___ IN DAYS OF GREAT PEACE *Mouni Sadhu*	3.00
___ MAGICIAN—HIS TRAINING AND WORK *W. E. Butler*	5.00
___ MEDITATION *Mouni Sadhu*	10.00
___ MODERN NUMEROLOGY *Morris C. Goodman*	5.00
___ NUMEROLOGY—ITS FACTS AND SECRETS *Ariel Yvon Taylor*	5.00
___ NUMEROLOGY MADE EASY *W. Mykian*	5.00
___ PALMISTRY MADE EASY *Fred Gettings*	5.00
___ PALMISTRY MADE PRACTICAL *Elizabeth Daniels Squire*	7.00
___ PALMISTRY SECRETS REVEALED *Henry Frith*	4.00
___ PROPHECY IN OUR TIME *Martin Ebon*	2.50
___ SUPERSTITION—ARE YOU SUPERSTITIOUS? *Eric Maple*	2.00
___ TAROT *Mouni Sadhu*	10.00
___ TAROT OF THE BOHEMIANS *Papus*	7.00
___ WAYS TO SELF-REALIZATION *Mouni Sadhu*	7.00
___ WITCHCRAFT, MAGIC & OCCULTISM—A FASCINATING HISTORY *W. B. Crow*	7.00
___ WITCHCRAFT—THE SIXTH SENSE *Justine Glass*	7.00

RECOVERY

___ KNIGHT IN RUSTY ARMOR *Robert Fisher*	5.00
___ KNIGHT IN RUSTY ARMOR *Robert Fisher (Hard cover edition)*	10.00

SELF-HELP & INSPIRATIONAL

___ CHARISMA—HOW TO GET "THAT SPECIAL MAGIC" *Marcia Grad*	7.00
___ DAILY POWER FOR JOYFUL LIVING *Dr. Donald Curtis*	7.00
___ DYNAMIC THINKING *Melvin Powers*	5.00
___ GREATEST POWER IN THE UNIVERSE *U. S. Andersen*	7.00
___ GROW RICH WHILE YOU SLEEP *Ben Sweetland*	7.00
___ GROW RICH WITH YOUR MILLION DOLLAR MIND *Brian Adams*	7.00
___ GROWTH THROUGH REASON *Albert Ellis, Ph.D.*	7.00
___ GUIDE TO PERSONAL HAPPINESS *Albert Ellis, Ph.D. & Irving Becker, Ed.D.*	7.00
___ HANDWRITING ANALYSIS MADE EASY *John Marley*	7.00
___ HANDWRITING TELLS *Nadya Olyanova*	7.00
___ HOW TO ATTRACT GOOD LUCK *A.H.Z. Carr*	7.00
___ HOW TO DEVELOP A WINNING PERSONALITY *Martin Panzer*	7.00
___ HOW TO DEVELOP AN EXCEPTIONAL MEMORY *Young & Gibson*	7.00
___ HOW TO LIVE WITH A NEUROTIC *Albert Ellis, Ph.D.*	7.00
___ HOW TO OVERCOME YOUR FEARS *M. P. Leahy, M.D.*	3.00
___ HOW TO SUCCEED *Brian Adams*	7.00
___ HUMAN PROBLEMS & HOW TO SOLVE THEM *Dr. Donald Curtis*	5.00
___ I CAN *Ben Sweetland*	7.00

____ I WILL *Ben Sweetland*	7.00
____ KNIGHT IN RUSTY ARMOR *Robert Fisher*	5.00
____ KNIGHT IN RUSTY ARMOR *Robert Fisher (Hard cover edition)*	10.00
____ LEFT-HANDED PEOPLE *Michael Barsley*	5.00
____ MAGIC IN YOUR MIND *U.S. Andersen*	10.00
____ MAGIC OF THINKING SUCCESS *Dr. David J. Schwartz*	7.00
____ MAGIC POWER OF YOUR MIND *Walter M. Germain*	7.00
____ MENTAL POWER THROUGH SLEEP SUGGESTION *Melvin Powers*	3.00
____ NEVER UNDERESTIMATE THE SELLING POWER OF A WOMAN *Dottie Walters*	7.00
____ NEW GUIDE TO RATIONAL LIVING *Albert Ellis, Ph.D. & R. Harper, Ph.D.*	7.00
____ PSYCHO-CYBERNETICS *Maxwell Maltz, M.D.*	7.00
____ PSYCHOLOGY OF HANDWRITING *Nadya Olyanova*	7.00
____ SALES CYBERNETICS *Brian Adams*	10.00
____ SCIENCE OF MIND IN DAILY LIVING *Dr. Donald Curtis*	7.00
____ SECRET OF SECRETS *U.S. Andersen*	7.00
____ SECRET POWER OF THE PYRAMIDS *U. S. Andersen*	7.00
____ SELF-THERAPY FOR THE STUTTERER *Malcolm Frazer*	3.00
____ SUCCESS-CYBERNETICS *U. S. Andersen*	7.00
____ 10 DAYS TO A GREAT NEW LIFE *William E. Edwards*	3.00
____ THINK AND GROW RICH *Napoleon Hill*	8.00
____ THREE MAGIC WORDS *U. S. Andersen*	7.00
____ TREASURY OF COMFORT *Edited by Rabbi Sidney Greenberg*	10.00
____ TREASURY OF THE ART OF LIVING *Sidney S. Greenberg*	7.00
____ WHAT YOUR HANDWRITING REVEALS *Albert E. Hughes*	4.00
____ YOUR SUBCONSCIOUS POWER *Charles M. Simmons*	7.00
____ YOUR THOUGHTS CAN CHANGE YOUR LIFE *Dr. Donald Curtis*	7.00

SPORTS

____ BICYCLING FOR FUN AND GOOD HEALTH *Kenneth E. Luther*	2.00
____ BILLIARDS—POCKET • CAROM • THREE CUSHION *Clive Cottingham, Jr.*	5.00
____ COMPLETE GUIDE TO FISHING *Vlad Evanoff*	2.00
____ HOW TO IMPROVE YOUR RACQUETBALL *Lubarsky, Kaufman & Scagnetti*	5.00
____ HOW TO WIN AT POCKET BILLIARDS *Edward D. Knuchell*	7.00
____ JOY OF WALKING *Jack Scagnetti*	3.00
____ LEARNING & TEACHING SOCCER SKILLS *Eric Worthington*	3.00
____ MOTORCYCLING FOR BEGINNERS *I.G. Edmonds*	3.00
____ RACQUETBALL FOR WOMEN *Toni Hudson, Jack Scagnetti & Vince Rondone*	3.00
____ RACQUETBALL MADE EASY *Steve Lubarsky, Rod Delson & Jack Scagnetti*	5.00
____ SECRET OF BOWLING STRIKES *Dawson Taylor*	5.00
____ SOCCER—THE GAME & HOW TO PLAY IT *Gary Rosenthal*	7.00
____ STARTING SOCCER *Edward F. Dolan, Jr.*	3.00

TENNIS LOVER'S LIBRARY

____ BEGINNER'S GUIDE TO WINNING TENNIS *Helen Hull Jacobs*	2.00
____ HOW TO BEAT BETTER TENNIS PLAYERS *Loring Fiske*	4.00
____ PSYCH YOURSELF TO BETTER TENNIS *Dr. Walter A. Luszki*	2.00
____ TENNIS FOR BEGINNERS *Dr. H. A. Murray*	2.00
____ TENNIS MADE EASY *Joel Brecheen*	5.00
____ WEEKEND TENNIS—HOW TO HAVE FUN & WIN AT THE SAME TIME *Bill Talbert*	3.00

WILSHIRE PET LIBRARY

____ DOG TRAINING MADE EASY & FUN *John W. Kellogg*	5.00
____ HOW TO BRING UP YOUR PET DOG *Kurt Unkelbach*	2.00
____ HOW TO RAISE & TRAIN YOUR PUPPY *Jeff Griffen*	5.00

The books listed above can be obtained from your book dealer or directly from Melvin Powers. When ordering, please remit $2.00 postage for the first book and 50¢ for each additional book.

Melvin Powers
12015 Sherman Road, No. Hollywood, California 91605